Christian Martin (Editor)
Language, Form(s) of Life, and Logic

On Wittgenstein

Edited on behalf of the
Internationale Ludwig Wittgenstein Gesellschaft e.V.
by James Conant, Wolfgang Kienzler,
Stefan Majetschak, Volker Munz, Josef G. F. Rothhaupt,
David Stern and Wilhelm Vossenkuhl

Volume 4

Language, Form(s) of Life, and Logic

Investigations after Wittgenstein

Edited by Christian Martin

DE GRUYTER

ISBN 978-3-11-071022-9
e-ISBN (PDF) 978-3-11-051828-3
e-ISBN (EPUB) 978-3-11-051739-2
ISSN 2365-9629

Library of Congress Cataloging-in-Publication Data

Names: Martin, Christian Georg, editor.
Title: Language, form(s) of life, and logic : investigations after Wittgenstein /
edited by Christian Martin.
Description: 1 [edition]. | Boston : De Gruyter, 2018. | Series: On Wittgenstein ; Volume 4
Identifiers: LCCN 2018022950| ISBN 9783110516289 (print) |
ISBN 9783110518283 (e-book (pdf) | ISBN 9783110517392 (e-book (epub)
Subjects: LCSH: Wittgenstein, Ludwig, 1889-1951. | Life. | Language and languages--Philosophy.
Classification: LCC B3376.W564 L337 2018 | DDC 192--dc23 LC record available at
https://lccn.loc.gov/2018022950

Bibliographic information published by the Deutsche Nationalbibliothek
The Deutsche Nationalbibliothek lists this publication in the Deutsche Nationalbibliografie;
detailed bibliographic data are available on the Internet at http://dnb.dnb.de.

© 2020 Walter de Gruyter GmbH, Berlin/Boston
This volume is text- and page-identical with the hardback published in 2018.
Printing: CPI books GmbH, Leck

www.degruyter.com

Table of Contents

List of Abbreviations —— VII

Christian Martin
Introduction: The Form of Our Life with Language —— 1

Paths to *Form(s) of Life*

Charles Travis
The Rule of the Game (The Moment of Truth) —— 11

Juliet Floyd
***Lebensformen:* Living Logic —— 59**

Andrea Kern
Human Life and Self-consciousness. The Idea of 'Our' Form of Life in Hegel and Wittgenstein —— 93

Christian Martin
Duality, Force, Language-games and Our Form of Life —— 113

Form(s) of Life: the Very Idea

Jocelyn Benoist
Our Life with Truth —— 155

Martin Gustafsson
Language-games, *Lebensform*, and the Ancient City —— 173

Felix Mühlhölzer
Language-games and Forms of Life in Mathematics —— 193

Matthias Haase
The Representation of Language —— 219

Form(s) of Life after Wittgenstein

Avner Baz
Wittgenstein and the Difficulty of What Normally Goes Without Saying —— 253

Sandra Laugier
Wittgenstein. Ordinary Language as Lifeform —— 277

David Zapero
Hostage to a Stranger —— 305

Biographical Notes —— 331

Index —— 333

List of Abbreviations

The classification of *The Wittgenstein Papers* was implemented by Georg Henrik von Wright. He ordered all the documents in Wittgenstein's Nachlass in three categories: a) manuscripts (MS); b) typescripts (TS); c) dictations (D). Each single document has an extra number (e.g. MS 103; TS 203; D 303). See: Wittgenstein, Ludwig (2010) *Philosophical Occasions: 1912– 1951*, ed. J. Klagge and A. Nordmann, 3rd edition, Hackett.

The following abbreviations have been used by the authors of this volume. Details on the editions the authors have used are given in the lists of references at the end of each chapter.

Abbreviations of Wittgenstein's Works

BB	Blue and Brown Books
BGM	*Bemerkungen über die Grundlagen der Mathematik*
BT	*The Big Typescript*: TS 213
CL	Cambridge Letters
DB	*Denkbewegungen. Tagebücher 1930–1932, 1936–1937*
KPU	*Philosophische Untersuchungen. Kritisch-genetische Edition*
LFM	*Wittgenstein's Lectures on the Foundations of Mathematics, Cambridge 1939*
LW	*Last Writings on the Philosophy of Psychology*
MS	Manuscripts from Wittgenstein's Nachlass (in: Bergen Electronic Edition)
NB	*Notebooks 1914–1916*
OC	*On Certainty*
PI	*Philosophical Investigations*
PIr	*Philosophical Investigations*, revised 4th edition
PO	*Philosophical Occasions 1912–51*
PPF	"Philosophy of Psychology: A Fragment"[1] (= *Philosophical Investigations*, Part II[2])
PPO	*Public and Private Occasions*
PU	*Philosophische Untersuchungen*
RFM	*Remarks on the Foundations of Mathematics*
RLF	*Some Remarks on Logical Form*
RPP I	*Remarks on the Philosophy of Psychology*, Vol. I
RPP II	*Remarks on the Philosophy of Psychology*, Vol. II
TS	Typescripts from Wittgenstein's Nachlass (in: Bergen Electronic Edition)
VW	*The Voices of Wittgenstein. The Vienna Circle*
WWCL	*Wittgenstein's Whewell's Court Lectures, Cambridge, 1938–1941*
Z	*Zettel*

---

1 As contained in PIr.
2 Cf. Knott, Hugh (2017) "On Reinstating 'Part I' and 'Part II' to Wittgenstein's *Philosophical Investigations*", in: *Philosophical Investigations* 40, 329–349.

Abbreviations of Works by Other Authors

Aristotle

EN *Nicomachean Ethics*
Met *Metaphysics*

Georg Wilhelm Friedrich Hegel

E   *Enzyklopädie der philosophischen Wissenschaften*
PdG *Phänomenologie des Geistes*
WdL *Wissenschaft der Logik*

Immanuel Kant

A/B *Critique of Pure Reason* (first and second editions)

Maurice Merleau-Ponty

PP *Phenomenology of Perception*

Christian Martin
Introduction: The Form of Our Life with Language

1 'Form of life' as a Logico-linguistic Concept

This volume deals with the connection between thinking-and-speaking and our form(s) of life. All contributions engage with Wittgenstein's approach to this topic.[1] As a whole, the volume takes a stance against both *biological* interpretations of the notion 'form of life' in terms of 'the human species' as well as *ethnological* interpretations in terms of 'cultures' and seeks to promote a broadly *logico-linguistic* understanding instead.

What is meant by a 'logico-linguistic understanding' of 'form of life' in contrast to a biological or ethnological one shall be *shortly* indicated.[2] It is not uncommon to identify what Wittgenstein calls "form(s) of life" (*Lebensform, Lebensformen*[3]) with biological facts about 'human nature'[4] – or with 'cultures' qua ways of living together which *specific* communities of human beings share in[5] – or with both as 'mixed' readings do.[6] It is equally common to invoke the

---

[1] I am grateful to James Conant for conversations on the concept of 'form' in Wittgenstein and elsewhere without which the research project on which this volume is based would not have come on its way. That project has been financially supported by the Alexander von Humboldt Foundation. This volume and the conference which it grew out of have been funded by LMU Munich's Junior Researcher Fund. The conference, which took place in Munich from May 23 to May 25, 2016 was generously hosted by the Carl Friedrich von Siemens Foundation. – Last but not least I would like to express my gratitude to Tom Schulte, Sebastian Stein and Marvin Tritschler as well as to Fritzi, Jakob, Charlotte and Sabine Jelinek who all, in one way or other, helped me in preparing this volume for publication.
[2] Originally, my introduction to this volume was designed to contain a detailed justification of the view that Wittgenstein's concept 'form of life' should be understood as a *logico-linguistic* notion. In the process of writing, what had started as an 'introduction' grew into a monograph on its own, entitled *Logical Form as Form of Life. An Essay on the Unity of Wittgenstein's Philosophy*. That monograph will complement the present volume in providing both a precise characterization as well as an extensive argument for the view that guided me in assembling the collection at hand.
[3] Cf. PIr: §19, §23, §241–242, PPF: i, §1 for the singular "Lebensform" and PPF: xi, §345 for the plural "Lebensformen".
[4] Cf. e.g. Hunter 1968: 235ff., Malcolm 1986: 237–238, Garver 1994: 246ff.
[5] Cf. e.g. Haller 1984: 57; Baker and Hacker 1985: 238–243; Glock 1996: 125; von Savigny 1999: 130, 136; Glock 2000: 77; Hacker 2015: 16, 18.

'human species' or 'cultures' or both, depending on one's reading, as *de facto* 'necessary conditions' of meaning: 'the background' into which language is said to be 'embedded'.[7]

While biological, ethnological and 'mixed' readings understand themselves as opposed to each other, what they all share in is *not reckoning* with the possibility that logico-linguistic notions such as 'language', 'meaning', 'thought', 'logic', 'truth' or 'judgment' might be *internally* related to what Wittgenstein calls "form(s) of life".[8] Conceiving of 'form of life' as a logico-linguistic notion is not taking it for granted that there is, *as a matter of fact*, something called "form(s) of life", whatever it might be, which is somehow involved in meaning and thought, functioning as their 'background'. It is rather *starting* with topics and concepts such as 'language', 'meaning', 'thought', 'logic', 'truth' or 'judgment' and developing lines of argument which show that these topics and concepts cannot be *coherently* understood, unless one takes recourse, at some point or other, to *life* and its 'form(s)', thereby exhibiting internal connections between concepts whose *logico-linguistic* character is uncontroversial and 'form(s) of life'. That latter notion is thereby exhibited as *essentially* involved in a "philosophical investigation" of "meaning, understanding, sentence, logic" etc. (cf. PIr: p. 3) and, *insofar*, as itself logico-linguistic in character.

Contributions to this volume can be seen as complementing each other in unfolding such lines of argument starting by certain logico-linguistic concepts and exhibiting their internal connection to 'form of life'. Insofar as they do this, they can all be seen as contributing to a *logico-linguistic* understanding of that notion.

More concretely, the logico-linguistic concepts which the various authors of this volume seek to connect to the notion 'form of life' and cognate ones such as 'language-game' are: *thought* (Charles Travis), *logic* (Juliet Floyd), *self-consciousness* and *rationality* (Andrea Kern), *logical negation* (Martin), *truth* (Benoist),

---

[6] Cf. e.g. Moyal-Sharrock 2015: 26 ff., Tejedor 2015: 83 ff. Even those who advocate an understanding of 'form of life' in terms of culture tend to admit that there are passages such as OC §359 in which "the term comes very close to expressing a biological notion" (Schulte 2010: 132), cf. also Hacker's claim that "Wittgenstein's conception of human nature is *not predominantly* a biological one [...] but cultural" (Hacker 2015: 18, emphasis C. M.).

[7] Cf. e.g. Glock 1996: 125, Stern 2004: 161, von Savigny 1998: 29, Tejedor 2015: 107–108. That Wittgenstein himself does not refer to form(s) of life as the 'background' into which language and thought are 'embedded' is rightly observed by Majetschak 2010: 270.

[8] As a matter of fact, Wittgenstein himself invokes all these notions in those passages of the *Investigations*, referred to in fn. 3 above, in which the topic of 'form of life' is touched upon.

philosophical method (Gustafsson), *language* (Haase), *mathematics* (Mühlhölzer), *ordinary language* (Laugier) and *singular thought* (Zapero).

2 The Structure and Content of this Volume

The structure of this volume is threefold. While contributions to the first part look at the philosophical development that leads to Wittgenstein's notion 'form of life', contributions to the second part focus on the concept of 'form of life' itself and the roles it plays in later Wittgenstein's thought. Contributions to the third part discuss, in some way or other, the aftermath of this notion, contrasting its use to other currents of philosophical thinking or tracing connections to problems in contemporary analytic philosophy.

Paths to *Form(s) of Life*

Assuming a developmental perspective, the articles contained in the first part of this volume present arguments that lead from considerations about logic, thought and language to the concept of 'form of life' and to cognate concepts such as 'language-game'. These articles can all be seen as addressing the following question: What might motivate a philosopher who investigates logic, thought and language to even so much as invoke the notion of *life* and its 'form'? In their attempts to answer this question the authors consider the development of Wittgenstein's thought as well as broader stretches of the history of philosophy.

Charles Travis' article *The Rule of the Game (The Moment of Truth)* deals with the collapse of the *Tractarian* understanding of thought, language and truth and the emergence of a framework for a new view around 1930. He argues that Wittgenstein, while reading Frege's *Grundgesetze* (Volume II), came across the germ of the idea of a language-game as this notion figures in the *Investigations*. By tracing its history we can, he suggest, identify much of the work that notion is designed to do in the *Investigations*.

Juliet Floyd, in *Lebensformen: Living Logic*, analyzes later Wittgenstein's interlocutory style of philosophizing and writing, which first appeared in 1936–1937 along with his use of the notion of 'Lebensform'. She argues that the important elucidatory role which that notion plays in Wittgenstein's later conception of philosophy can best be seen against the background of the analysis of logic contained in Turing's *On computable numbers, with an application to the Entscheidungsproblem* (1936/7). This paper stimulated Wittgenstein's writing of *Philosophical Investigations* and led him to deepen the notion of a language-game, to eliminate the idea of *Kultur* as foundational, and to focus on the general idea of rule-following.

Andrea Kern's article *Human Life and Self-consciousness. The Idea of 'Our' Form of Life in Hegel and Wittgenstein* proceeds from the widely acknowledged fact that the source of the normative structure that a human individual finds herself entrenched in is found in her 'immersion in a form of life'. Despite much controversy over the status of this appeal to a 'form of life', most interpreters who stress the significance of 'education' in accounting for a certain kind of normativity think that it is the role of education to *transform* an individual whose activities do not yet manifest a consciousness of rules or norms that guide and orient her life into an individual whose activities do. Kern argues that neither Hegel nor Wittgenstein held such a view. According to them, the logical role of the ideas of self-consciousness and rationality is not to depict a set of capacities of an individual that it acquires through education. Rather, their role is to depict a formal feature of a form of life which its individual bearers, qua being bearers of this form of life, cannot fail to exhibit.

In *Duality, Force, Language-games and Our Form of Life*, Christian Martin presents an argument that leads from considerations on the linguistic manifestation of logical affirmation and negation via a critique of the 'force-content'-distinction drawn by Frege and reflection on how that distinction is involved in confusions about rule-following to an understanding of 'thinking-and-speaking' as, essentially, an activity of *living* beings. Martin thus seeks to motivate a logico-linguistic understanding of our *form of life*, exhibiting it as already involved in drawing distinctions as 'simple' as that between 'p' and 'not p'.

Form(s) of Life: The Very Idea

Contributions to the second part of the present volume deal with the specific roles that the concept *form of life* and cognate notions such as *practice* play in later Wittgenstein's philosophy.

Jocelyn Benoist's article *Our Life with Truth* opposes the idea that it is possible to extract a theory of forms of life from Wittgenstein's *Investigations*. Instead, Benoist makes a case for the elucidatory – not explanatory – nature of the concept *form of life* in Wittgenstein's work. To this end, he first returns to the original context in which Wittgenstein introduced this expression: the discussion of Russell's *Limits of Empiricism* in *Ursache und Wirkung*. In a second step, Benoist focuses on the famous passages of the *Investigations* that make use of the notion 'form of life' and argues that these remarks should not be understood along 'relativistic' lines, but as a pedagogical attempt to make us aware of the open variety of the ways in which truth can be brought into the question.

Martin Gustafsson's paper *Language-games, Lebensform, and the Ancient City* explores Wittgenstein's method of language-games by discussing how simple language-games are related to language of real-life complexity. He argues that Wittgenstein rejects as unintelligible an atomist conception of this relationship, according to which the step from simple language-games to complex language is a matter of mere accumulation of individually self-standing building-blocks that are supposed to remain substantively unchanged throughout the process. In this context, he investigates how the notion of *form of life* enters Wittgenstein's discussion.

In *Language-games and Forms of Life in Mathematics*, Felix Mühlhölzer argues that for Wittgenstein, the 'kind of certainty' involved in a language-game and the specific concept of certainty that corresponds to it are constitutive of the language-game because they are intimately connected with our actions that characterize the game. In contrast, the term 'form of life' does not aim at certainty, at least not directly. Mühlhölzer argues that this term has at least the following two functions in the context of calculations as discussed in PPF: (a) 'form of life' refers to the *presuppositions* of the respective language-game of calculation, and (b) it sheds light on *other concepts* – like the concept of number, for instance – that are important in connection with our understanding of the language-game.

In *The Representation of Language*, Matthias Haase argues that the contemporary debate on the metaphysics of language is dominated by two positions. According to the first, languages are not things in the world; they are abstract objects. According to the second, a language consists in the historical chain of causally interrelated acts and states of its speakers. Haase shows that later Wittgenstein would reject both positions. A natural language is neither an abstract object nor a singular happening of any kind; it is something general that is actual or concrete. When we qua participants in a 'practice' or 'form of life' say what 'we' or 'one' says, the pronouns exhibit a kind of genericity that cannot be treated within a quantificational model of generality.

Form(s) of Life after Wittgenstein

The third and last part of this volume comprises articles that deal with the aftermath of Wittgenstein's notion *form of life* in different ways. They either contrast his understanding of the term with other philosophical approaches to what might be regarded as the same topic, or they engage with certain ways in which Wittgenstein's conception has been received and transformed.

In his article *Wittgenstein and the Difficulty of What Normally Goes Without Saying*, Avner Baz argues that the topic 'form of life' – understood in terms of the background conditions of sense – belongs to a region of Wittgenstein's thought that presented him with difficulties that he never resolved to his own satisfaction. Baz seeks to establish this by contrasting Wittgenstein's attempt at a *grammatical* investigation of the background of our use of words with Merleau-Ponty's *phenomenological* approach to it.

Sandra Laugier's article *Wittgenstein. Ordinary Language as Lifeform* envisages the concept of 'form of life' as an alternative to the concept of 'rules' in the exploration of ordinary language. Following Cavell, she argues that focus on the notion 'form of life' helps us to achieve a clearer grasp of the way in which language, as it is understood in ordinary language philosophy, is both part of how we lead our everyday life and the milieu in which we live.

David Zapero's article *Hostage to a Stranger* focuses on a widespread conception of singular thought that makes such thought seem profoundly enigmatic, indeed impossible. He traces one possible path that leads to such a *disavowal* of singularity that can be seen as a dimension of a more general disavowal of the beholdenness of thought to the world, a topic which later Wittgenstein is prominently concerned with in his reflections on forms of life and natural history.

References

Baker, Gordon and Peter Hacker (1985) *An Analytical Commentary on the Philosophical Investigations*. Vol. 2: *Wittgenstein. Rules, Grammar and Necessity. Exegesis*, Oxford: Blackwell.
Garver, Newton (1994) "Form of Life", in: Newton Garver: *This Complicated Form of Life: Essays on Wittgenstein*, Chicago, IL: Open Court, 237–267.
Glock, Hans-Johann (1996) *A Wittgenstein Dictionary*, Oxford: Blackwell.
Glock, Hans-Johann (2000) "Forms of Life: Back to Basics", in: Katalin Neumer (ed.): *Das Verstehen des Anderen*, Frankfurt am Main: Lang, 63–84.
Hacker, Peter (2015) "Forms of Life", in: *Nordic Wittgenstein Review* 4, Special Issue: Wittgenstein and Forms of Life, 1–20.
Haller, Rudolf (1984) "Lebensform oder Lebensformen? Eine Bemerkung zu N. Garvers 'Die Lebensform in Wittgensteins Philosophischen Untersuchungen'", in: *Grazer Philosophische Studien* 21, 55–63.
Hunter, John (1968) "*Forms of Life* in Wittgenstein's *Philosophical Investigations*", in: *American Philosophical Quarterly* 5, 233–243.

Majetschak, Stefan (2010) "Lebensformen und Lebensmuster: Zur Deutung eines sogenannten Grundbegriffs der Spätphilosophie Ludwig Wittgensteins", in: Volker Munz, Klaus Puhl and Joseph Wang (eds.): *Language and World. Part I: Essays in the Philosophy of Wittgenstein*, Frankfurt am Main: Ontos, 265–290.

Malcolm, Norman (1986) *Nothing is Hidden. Wittgenstein's Criticism of His Early Thought*, Oxford: Blackwell.

Moyal-Sharrock, Danièle (2015) "Wittgenstein on Forms of Life, Patterns of Life, and Ways of Living", in: *Nordic Wittgenstein Review* 4, Special Issue: Wittgenstein and Forms of Life, 21–42.

Savigny, Eike von (1998) "Sprachspiele und Lebensformen: Woher kommt die Bedeutung", in: Eike von Savigny (ed.): *Ludwig Wittgenstein, Philosophische Untersuchungen*, Berlin: Akademie Verlag, 7–39.

Savigny, Eike von (1999) "Wittgensteins 'Lebensformen' und die Grenzen der Verständigung", in: Wilhelm Lütterfelds and Andreas Roser (eds.): *Der Konflikt der Lebensformen in Wittgensteins Philosophie der Sprache*, Frankfurt am Main: Suhrkamp, 120–137.

Schulte, Joachim (2010) "Does the Devil in Hell Have a Form of Life?", in: Antonio Marques and Nuno Venturinha (eds.): *Wittgenstein on Forms of Life and the Nature of Experience*, Frankfurt am Main: Lang, 125–141.

Stern, David (2004) *Wittgenstein's Philosophical Investigations. An Introduction*, Cambridge: Cambridge University Press.

Tejedor, Chon (2015) "Tractarian Form as the Precursor to Forms of Life", in: *Nordic Wittgenstein Review* 4, Special Issue: Wittgenstein and Forms of Life, 83–110.

Wittgenstein, Ludwig (2009a) *Philosophical Investigations* (the German text, with an English translation by G. E. M. Anscombe, P. M. S. Hacker and Joachim Schulte), rev. 4th edition. P. M. S. Hacker and Joachim Schulte (eds.), Oxford: Wiley-Blackwell, [PIr]

Paths to *Form(s) of Life*

Charles Travis
The Rule of the Game (The Moment of Truth)

Abstract: In 1929 Wittgenstein saw the *Tractatus* collapse before his eyes. By 1931 a framework for a new view was in place. In the interim, one of Wittgenstein's main interests was mathematics, or philosophy thereof. In particular, he was interested in Hilbert, and, more generally, formalism. Which led him to Frege (*Grundgesetze*, Vol. 2). Here he came across the germ of the idea of a language game as this notion figures in the *Investigations*. In tracing this history we can also, I suggest, identify at least much of the work that notion is designed to do. The essay ends with a discussion of some of that work, as found in the first 22 paragraphs of the *Investigations*.

1 Introduction

In 1929 Wittgenstein agreed to appear in the Aristotelian Society lecture series for the coming academic year. As per custom he submitted his contribution in advance. When the time came, though, he spoke about something else entirely. What he wrote begins as follows:

> If we try to analyse any given propositions, we shall find in general that they are logical sums, products, or other truth functions, of simpler propositions. But our analysis, if carried far enough, must come to the point where it reaches propositional forms which are not themselves composed of simpler propositional forms. We must eventually reach the ultimate connections of terms, the immediate connections which cannot be broken without destroying the propositional form as such. The propositions which represent this ultimate connection of terms I call, after B. Russell, *atomic propositions*. [...] It is the task of the theory of knowledge to find them and to understand their construction out of the words or symbols. This task is very difficult, and Philosophy has hardly yet begun to tackle it at some points. (Wittgenstein 1929: 162)

In undertaking to carry out this task, Wittgenstein came to see that the idea itself was misconceived; and then in short order that, since this idea was essential to the *Tractatus*'s conception of truth, and of representing something as being something, that this, too, was simply a misconception. In 1929, then, Wittgenstein saw the *Tractatus* crumbling before his eyes. The search was on for what to say instead.

https://doi.org/10.1515/9783110518283-003

Here is how Wittgenstein later assessed the *Tractatus:*

> Since I began, 16 years ago, to busy myself with philosophy again, I was forced to recognize grave errors in that which I had set down in that first book. (Wittgenstein 1953: x (written 1945))
>
> One fault you can find with a dogmatic account is, first, that it is, as it were, arrogant. But that is not the worst thing about it. There is another mistake, which is much more dangerous and also pervades my whole book, and that is the conception that there are questions the answers to which will be found at a later date. It is held that, although a result is not known, there is a way of finding it. Thus I used to believe, for example, that it is the task of logical analysis to discover the elementary propositions. (Waismann 1984: 182 (9.11. 1931)[1])

Things had changed that much, and further, by September 1931. By which time the outlines of a new view were in place. What happened in those years? And under what influences? Of course, any answer to such questions must be somewhat speculative. But, thanks to Schlick and the *Vienna Circle*, we have material to go on. In particular, we have Waismann's rather detailed notes on conversations he, and sometimes Schlick, held with Wittgenstein in those years. In which, I will suggest here, we can find the origins of Wittgenstein's *Investigations* notion of a language game, and with that something as to what role it was to play.

In the years 1929–1931 there were two things much on Wittgenstein's mind. One was the collapse of the *Tractatus*. The other was philosophy of mathematics, prominently then-current discussions of formalism, and in particular, Hilbert, and his reception. It is this second concern which led Wittgenstein, and with him Waismann, to read Frege, specifically *Grundgesetze* volume 2 (1903). And here, in Frege, we find the *ur*-idea of a language game. At the same time, recognising how the *Tractatus* had misconceived truth, or representing truly, inevitably brought Wittgenstein's later view of such matters closer to Frege, since it was just what Russell, and relatedly Wittgenstein, could not see as to what representing truly must be that Frege got exactly right from start to end of his career. What was missed by Russell and early Wittgenstein is what is contained in Frege's notion of that countable, *der Gedanke*.

We should thus expect to find in later Wittgenstein a modified Fregean view; modified at points where Frege got something not quite right, but also so as to forestall various misreadings of him and their resultant mythology; notably ones mis-locating features of the logical (of *Wahrsein*, the business of being true) in the psychological (*Fürwahrhalten*, the business of holding true). A thought (*Ge-*

---

[1] Translations from German original texts are my own.

danke) is designed for a role on the logical side of that distinction. Insofar as what we (intelligibly, coherently) hold true is what might be true, or at least false, in holding true we of course relate to thoughts. But just *how*, or where, such would occur does not follow simply from what a thought must be to fulfil its logical role. In which we find a rich source of confusions Wittgenstein is keen to scotch. Here, though, we are concerned with groundwork for such later projects in the years 1929–1931, as contained in that notion *language game* which then began to take form.

2 The Demise of the *Tractatus*

2.1 What Collapsed

The proximal cause of the *Tractatus*'s demise, what Wittgenstein first saw in 1929, is contained in two propositions:

> 1. There is exactly one complete analysis of a proposition [*Satz*]. (TLP: 3.25)
> 2. A sign of an elementary proposition is that no elementary proposition can contradict it. (TLP: 4.211)

We arrive at complete analysis, Wittgenstein tells us, where to go further would be to lose propositional form. There are three things it might be to lose propositional form. One might be to lose something which is liable to be true or false outright (rather than merely *of* something). A second (*not* quite the same, as we will see) would be to lose the *content* of something which might be true or false outright: a way for things to be, on that catholic reading which blocks questions 'Which ones?', on which it is not a plural, for use of one or another collection of things. (I will henceforth mark this reading as 'things$^{©}$'.) A third would be to move out of the realm of items whose business was to make truth beholden, even in part, to how things were. One way to view the core problem with the *Tractatus* is that in its picture these three things collapse into one. This, though, is to adumbrate.

Wittgenstein's first reaction to this proximal cause of collapse was damage control. Thus, on 2.1.1930 he wrote,

> Formerly I had two ideas about elementary propositions, of which one still appears right to me, whereas I was entirely mistaken as to the second. My first assumption was that by analysing propositions we must eventually come to ones which are an immediate combination of objects. I still hold that. Second I had the idea that elementary propositions must

> be independent of each other. [...] I was mistaken about this, and what follows from it is certainly false. (Waismann 1984: 73)

But this idea of damage control was soon given up. It is, e.g., the *whole* Tractarian picture of being true that he is giving up when he presents it as an important discovery that there may be "a picture which, though correct, has no similarity with its object" (Wittgenstein 1958: 37).

The proximal cause of Wittgenstein's realisation that there were 'grave difficulties' with the *Tractatus* really does point to a total collapse. This is because the idea that a proposition, or (as Frege put it) that by which truth comes into question, has a *unique* and *complete* analysis is mandated inexorably by the *Tractatus's* idea of what being true is. So the (relatively) local collapse of *Tractatus* 3.25 is, *au fond*, the collapse of that same picture. But to see this we must first set out what this picture is. Here, then, the top of the garden path (in logical, not bibliographical, order):

> There must be something identical in the picture and what it depicts by which the one can so much as be a picture of the other at all. (TLP: 2.161)
>
> What every picture, of whatever form, must have in common with reality in order to be able to depict it at all – correctly or falsely – is [its] logical form, that is, the form of reality. (TLP: 2.18)

So there is a form, or structure, of a sort to which both a picture (a *Bild* or *Abbildung*) and what it pictures in some way or other are both susceptible, and which they must share for the picture to picture the depicted as anything at all. It is thus a form for a picture, or picturing, to take, and also for *reality* (the way things are) to take. The way things are has a *logical* form. Our feet are now firmly on the path which is soon to give out under them.

This hypothesised common element is needed in order to allow for this:

> That the elements of the picture relate to each other in a given way represents things as so relating. This connection of the elements of the picture is called its structure [...]. (TLP: 2.15)
>
> The form of a representation is the possibility that the things relate to each other as do the elements of the picture. (TLP: 2.151)

So a picture represents by a sort of correspondence between its elements and the elements of what it represents as being as it does, namely, *things* (*Sachen*). Things here are thus things©: the question 'Which ones?' is blocked. And the common form – what is shared by picture and things – consists in elements in each which *can* stand in the same relations to one another, so that it is at least intelligible for the *picture's* elements to present the elements in what is pictured (things) so to relate, so that:

> The picture agrees with reality or not; it is correct or incorrect, true or false. (TLP: 2.21)

So that being true can consist in such agreement. It can consist in reality resembling the picture in the way just described.

It is by now clear why 3.25, the idea that every proposition has a unique and complete analysis, is mandatory on the *Tractatus's* account of what being true is. As Aristotle pointed out, representing truly is representing things as they are, representing falsely representing things as they are not. So for something to be in the business of being true or false at all is for it to represent things (*Sachen, Wirklichkeit*) as being some given way where this is (or is at least liable to be) a way things are, or, at worst, a way things are not. But now, if something is in the business of being true (or false), there must then be an answer to the question when things *would* be as it represents them, when not. So *if* truth consists in an agreement in structure between representer (or representation) and that which is thus represented as being something, then wherever there is something in the business of being true (or false) there must be an answer to the question just *what* structure (of the relevant sort) must be in things (the *Abgebildete*) if that something is to be true. And on the *Tractatus's* account, as above, that answer can only be provided by identifying that structure in the representer which must be matched in reality if there is to be truth. To identify such a structure would be to provide a unique and complete analysis. So providing that much is mandatory if there is to be a truth-bearer at all.

It is in a way surprising that Wittgenstein should have thought such a thing by, say, 1918 or 1920. Certainly the handwriting was already on the wall. Perhaps, though, Russell's influence is at play here (even though the picture just sketched was not Russell's). In 1902–1904 Russell corresponded with Frege on a variety of topics, among which Frege's ideas *Sinn* and *Bedeutung, Gedanke*. Two things (among others) stand out in that correspondence. The first is that Russell genuinely had no understanding of those ideas. And this is because he could not distinguish what Frege identifies as the logical from the psychological. And the second is that he agrees with the *Tractatus's* picture just sketched to this extent: that he cannot see anything like a categorial distinction between the sorts of things liable to be constituents of a picture (*Abbildung* or *Bild*) which pictures, and the sorts of things which are liable to be depicted in a picture which was in the business of being either true or false. Russell himself confesses, "As for *Sinn* and *Bedeutung* I see only difficulties which I am not able to overcome" (Russell 1904: 98

(12.12.1904)). Such is no mere false modesty, nor politesse. Russell really did not see what Frege was up to. It is thus that he could write,

> One does not state a thought, which is really a private psychological matter. One states an object of a thought, and this, in my view, is a certain complex (an objective proposition, one might say) of which Mt. Blanc itself is a constituent. If one does not admit this, he then gets the conclusion that we cannot know anything at all about Mt. Blanc itself. Accordingly for me the *Bedeutung* of a proposition is not the true, but rather a certain complex which (in certain cases) is true. (Russell 1904: 98–99)

About 'objective propositions', those complexes, some of which, for him, are what may be true or false, he had earlier written this:

> As to *Sinn* and *Bedeutung* I do not entirely share your view. As to this I can say the following. A *Vorstellung* and a judgement have, in each case, an object. What I call a proposition can be the object of a judgement, and can equally well be the object of a *Vorstellung*. There are thus two manners in which an object can be thought of, in the case where this object is a complex. One can picture it [*es vorstellen*] or one can judge it; for all of which the object is the same in both cases (for example, if one says, 'the cold wind', and where one says, 'the wind is cold'). Thus for me the judgement stroke indicates a particular manner of being directed at an object. Complexes are true or false: if one judges, one takes oneself to encounter a true complex. [...] But truth is not a constituent of being true as *green* is a constituent of a green tree. (Russell 1903: 90 (24.5.1903))

As we walk northward along the coast, from the *castro* into Vila Chã, the cold of the north wind (a *nortada*) pierces our fleeces, burns our faces, its force making forward progress a struggle. An experience we still recall, and can imagine, often and vividly. It is almost as though we still feel the bite of that cold on our faces. On such occasions, Russell tells us, we stand in one way towards a complex a constituent of which is that particular wind, another that particular occurrence of cold and pressure which we then had to struggle against, and suffer. But there is another way we can stand to that very complex: we can think, in fact, remember that that wind was cold.

How *could* one think that there is some *one* complex against which we then fought, which we now thus remember, and which, moreover is true, and judged true when we stand towards that very complex in a certain other way? How could the cold wind, or that occurrence of snow fields on top of Mt. Blanc (or its towering over the landscape to the height it does) be *true*? After all, one might note, for something to be *true* (in the relevant sense), it must first of all represent things (*Sachen*) as being some given way. How can a cold wind do that? And, second, what is true is what is at least susceptible to falsehood in that the mere fact of its representing as it does does not decide its fate *in re* truth and falsehood. It is as with Sid's bleary eyes representing the night before: were there no night before, then the bleary eyes would not represent this. What would it be for that very cold wind to represent as it does, though there was no such wind?

Here is an hypothesis. Such niceties *might* be overlooked by someone transfixed by the idea that anything deserving the title 'thought', whether count or mass noun, could only be something psychological. Whereas, if there is to be truth at all, then what being true is had better not be anything psychological (as Frege insisted). Frege went to very great lengths to argue that *a* thought – a *Gedanke* in his sense – was not at all anything psychological. A thought (in his sense) prescinds from anything psychological, anything having to do with *thinking*, or thought-expression, to provide something whose business is exclusively that of being true or false, of being hostage to *Sachen*, in some determinate way, for the relevant sort of correctness or incorrectness. Such is what Frege stresses when he writes,

> A third realm must be acknowledged. What belongs to it corresponds to *Vorstellungen* in that it is not perceivably by the senses, but with things [*Dingen*] in that it requires no bearer to the contents of whose consciousness it belongs. (Frege 1918: 69)
>
> Neither logic nor mathematics has the task of investigating souls, or the contents of the consciousness of some individual person. One could perhaps rather propose as their task investigating the mind: *the* mind, not minds. (Frege 1918: 74)

Frege wrote all this some years after his correspondence with Russell (perhaps inspired by Russell's very blindness to the point). But suppose one is blind to the possibility Frege here insists on. Well, if there is such a thing as logic, then there is such a thing as complexity, hence structure, in a truth-bearer. If there is structure, then there are constituents of that structure. And if such constituents are nothing psychological – as it is agreed on all sides here that they must not be – what else is there? If no third realm, then what else but something environmental, such as a cold wind, or Mt. Blanc. In which case, at the very least, there is no need to distinguish constituents of a complex which is eligible to be true or false from items whose career takes place in an environment.

I am not claiming here that Wittgenstein (of 1911–1920) suffered Russell's blindness; nor that he shared Russell's view that there is just *one* complex which is both eligible for being true or false (thus depicts things as being some given way), and which is, at the same time, what is so depicted. Exactly not on the account set out above. But the *Tractatus's* account does at least require one sort of structure which can be shared both by a *picture* and what it pictures (that is, things©). *This* idea requires that truth-bearers have unique and complete analyses. And this last idea leads to grief. So truth cannot be what the *Tractatus* makes it out to be. But to see this, or at least see it in the right light, we need an alternate account of what truth might be. We find just what we need for the purpose if we turn to Frege, or just that in Frege which later Wittgenstein approached much more closely than did his earlier self. To this I turn next.

2.2 Frege

What did Frege see and (young) Wittgenstein miss? The core notion in Frege's account of the business of being true (so of representing truly) is that of *a thought (Gedanke)*. The first step to *Gedanken* is to separate these from anything psychological. A thought's business is exclusively the business of being true, of truth and falsity *per se*. It has no, or anyway no direct, truck with the various businesses which arise in a thinker's life in engaging with that business of being true. A thought, e.g., is not a content-*bearer*, something by producing which thought might be expressed. A thought is to be distinguished from the particular circumstances of some thinker thinking it (if any thinker ever does).

With the idea of a distinction between the logical and the psychological in place, and the thought (*Gedanke*) firmly on the logical side of this distinction, we can then say the following. A thought is the truth where there is an identifiable truth, the falsehood where there is an identifiable falsehood; some one specifiable way to represent things as being which would be, as such, thereby representing truly, *casu quo* falsely. A thought is, as Frege put it, *just* that by which truth can come into question at all; exactly *one* way for truth to turn on, be beholden to, how things are, or, conversely, for how things are to matter to whether there is truth or not. If representing truly is representing things as being as they are, then one might say: a thought is *the* representation of things as some determinate way for them to be.

For present purpose, then, two leading ideas of Frege are the ones which most matter:
1. *Whole thoughts first:*
    What is distinctive in my view of logic is recognizable first by my placing the content of the word 'true' in lead position, and then by my letting the thought follow immediately as that by which truth can come into question at all. (Frege 1919: 272)
    I think that concepts arise through the decomposition of judgeable contents. (Frege 1882: 118)
2. *A thought is intrinsically general: it presents something as instancing a generality:*
    A thought always contains something which reaches over and beyond the

particular case, by which this is brought to consciousness as falling under some given generality. (Frege 1892: 189, *Kernsatz* 4)

Point 1: A thought is *just* that which is eligible for being true or false *outright*. It is just that, as Frege puts it, by which truth *can* come into question at all. So a thought is identified as the thought it is by, and *purely* by, its way of bringing truth into question: by its proprietary way of making truth turn on, be hostage to, how things© are, by the bearing of how things are on whether things are as it represents them. So a thought is, to create a shorthand, *invisible*. It cannot, that is, be an object of sensory awareness. It has no properties which might make it so. Take properties like being blue, or a metre long, or weighing less than a kilogram, or being cold, or snow-capped. Then the point is: two thoughts could not differ in that one had such a property while the other lacked it. For having such a property would not as such matter (in any specifiable way) to how the way *things* are mattered to whether the thought is true.

Whole thoughts, thus, enjoy both logical and ontological priority. A thought is not built up of building blocks, that is, things which enjoy an existence independent of their role in the whole thought from which they are carved, or at least of their role in some range of thoughts. Rather, a thought is decomposable into proper parts, constituents. In such a decomposition, each proper part is just a partial doing of what the whole thought does. E. g., if the whole thought makes truth turn on whether Sid drinks (makes *Sid* the one who so matters), a part might make truth turn in part on how Sid is, or again, another part, on who drinks (or on whether the object on which the whole thought makes truth turn, whatever object that may be, drinks). Just as for a whole thought to be the thought it is is *exactly* for it to make truth turn as it does on how things are, so for a proper part (on a decomposition) to be the proper part it is is for it to make truth (in first instance, the truth of *that* thought) turn in part on how things are. In one sense of *proper thought-part*, such a part has no existence apart from its role in the thought it is thus part of. In another sense, it has no existence apart from its role in some range of such thoughts.

It is also worth observing here that thoughts are unlike white washing a house in a *pueblo blanco*, or giving a cocktail party, in that a proper thought-part cannot do what it does at all except in the context of a thought. There is no such thing as just making truth turn on how Sid is, *fertig*. Nor as making truth turn on who drinks, *fertig*. Neither Sid nor who drinks is a way for truth to turn on how things are. Whereas if Pia whitewashes half the *casa* and Sid skives off, there is, for all that, a half-whitewashed *casa*.

What matters most so far is the 'invisibility' of thoughts. A thought only has properties which matter to, are to be defined in terms of, its relation to the business of being true as such, more specifically, to how it makes things being as they are matter to whether there is truth. To wax metaphoric, a thought is identified as the thought it is *just* by its place in the business of being true. It is distinguished from other thoughts only by its, and their, respective roles in that business. And all of this carries over to proper thought-parts. A proper thought-part is to be defined in terms of its role in locating the whole thought it is part of in the business of being true. So, like the whole thought, it is to be defined entirely in terms of its contribution to that business. A decomposition of a thought structures it in a particular way. We may now say: such a structuring is to be defined only in terms of such relations between proper thought-parts and each other, thus ultimately only between proper thought-parts and the thought they are all part of. So a thought is structurable only in terms of identifiable contributions to the business of being true.

At the start of the essay *Der Gedanke* Frege produces a famous argument against 'correspondence theories' of truth. The beginning of that argument has application here. Suppose that, *pace* what has just been said, a thought *could* have properties which it shared with *Sachen*, or with those particular objects, such as Sid or that *nortada*, which, in a thought, may be represented as thus and so. The thought, perhaps, is round, or damp around the edges, or, for the above example, drinks. The model for this would be a picture full of colour patches, or a drawing full of lines which curve and cross each other. What would all that have to do with when the thought would be true? Frege's point: nothing so far. A picture with given curves and patches might, for all that, represent things as any way you like or as none at all. As none at all, that is, unless, as Frege puts it, an intention (*Absicht*) attaches to it. That is, unless it is to be taken in a certain way; it bears a certain understanding. And if, in this sense, an intention does attach, the net result of all that is just a way to represent things as being. Whether there is truth or falsehood depends on what that way is; something it is the intention's role to settle. At which point those items to which the intention attaches drop out, or anyway, on their own do not provide anything in terms of which the truth of the relevant picture might be determined.

We come to the second part of point 1. If one cuts a cheese into chunks, for those chunks to be a decomposition of the cheese just is for them to be, jointly, just the whole cheese cut up. If one divides a map into quadrants, those quadrants are a decomposition of the map, on a here-relevant notion, just in case they are, jointly, and in their relations to each other, the whole map (with some quadrants drawn on it). Similarly for decompositions of a thought. A proper thought-part is *precisely* a partial doing of what the thought does (as to which see above). Thus a set of proper parts is a decomposition of a thought just in case the joint doing of what those parts do just is a doing of what the whole thought does.

From which it follows that a thought is always at least liable to be multiply decomposable, as Frege insists thoughts are. We will see more reason for this insistence when we come to our second main idea from Frege. In the meantime, here is a good image, if only that. Take the idea of a vector in a vector space. Perhaps a force vector. Suppose we are given a given such vector and asked the question of which other vectors it is a vector sum. The question as it stands is obviously senseless. There are indefinitely many ways of composing a given vector out of one set or another of others. Similarly for a thought, though factors may intrude here which obscure the point.

From which it follows that *Tractatus* 3.25 is simply not in the cards. A thought *cannot* have a unique analysis, though it may – *does* – have indefinitely many complete ones. Of which Frege tells us, none, as a rule, "may claim objective priority" (Frege 1882: 118). This, if right, already puts paid to the *Tractatus*. For if so, then we cannot, by analysis, reach a structure such that *this* is the way things (*Wirklichkeit*, *Sachen*) must be structured if there is to be truth – if, that is, things are to count as being as represented.

With which I turn to the second main point. If we look at all the things which the verb 'represent' might speak of, on one or another reading it sometimes bears, we could then say: it is precisely with representing-as (representing something as being something) that the notion of truth comes on the scene at all. For it is just here that it need not be that for there to be this representing is *eo ipso* for things to be as represented. Again, if Sid did not 'let the sow out' last night, then his bleary eyes simply do not represent (the fact of) his having done so. So on this use of 'represent' there can be no representing falsely. So nor truly. Now, if it is with representing-as that issues of truth arise at all, and if a thought is that by which truth can come into question at all, then it is no surprise that a thought *does* represent something as being something. We must, of course, get our aspects right. A thought cannot be held responsible for its representing-as as a thinker can. One good way to do so would be to think of a thought as *the* representation of things as being thus and so – as, thus, what one, *eo ipso*, expresses where that is how *he* represents things.

Here, then, we have another way of saying what a thought's business is. In a thought something is represented as being something. Its business is so representing things. A thought being true outright, it is always the same thing that any thought represents as being thus and so, namely things$^{\copyright}$, *Sachen*, *Wirklichkeit*, as young Wittgenstein often names it. So a thought is represented as the thought it is merely by what, in its case, appears on the right side of the relation.

Such is one asymmetry between the left side (*Abgebildetes*) and the right side (*Abbildung*) of the representing-as relation. But it would be hard not to be struck by another. This other is one called to our attention by Frege's *Kernsatz* 4.

A thought always presents what it does as falling under some given generality. For any particular thought, right side of the representing-as relation, tells us what this generality is. It is for things© to be that way for things to be which the thought represents what it does as being. What appears on the right side of the relation is thus always identified as the thing it is by its proprietary generality, that under which the relevant thought thus presents things as falling.

The generality of a right side item finds roots in the idea of a way *for* things to be. A way for things to be is a way there might be anyway even were things not just as they are. For things to be *it* is not merely for things to be just as they are. In which case, a given way for things to be is identified by just *when* things would be it, by just *how* things might vary while still remaining a case of things being *it*. One might think of a way for things to be as fixing a proprietary understanding of *same* on which there would be answers to questions when things would still be the same. Insofar as there are answers, such understanding determines what these answers would be. (One might also think of it as fixing a proprietary sense in which two thinkers may or may not be thinking in the same way as to how things were.)

Thus further asymmetry. That right-side item which identifies a given thought as the thought it is is itself identified as the item it is by its proprietary generality. By contrast, things being as they are is not really an item at all, and need not be identified in any way. It is simply all that to which truth may be answerable. When it comes to *structuring* left and right sides of the relation, we now find items on the right side of the relation – those which identify a thought as the thought it is – to follow suit with whole thoughts themselves. A whole thought is structurable only by relations defined in terms of the whole thoughts' place in the business of being true, thus of the partial contributions of the relata of such relations to that business. So, too, an *Abbildung* is structurable only in terms of contributions to *its* business of generalising, so the structuring of items to be defined only in terms of their contributions to such resultant generality: items themselves each with a proprietary generality by which it is identified as the item it is; items whose generalities yield in concert the generality of that of which they are a part. For example, for things being such that Sid drinks, there is the generality attaching to things being such that it is *Sid* who is some given way or other, and that attaching to it being *being a drinker* that someone is or is not.

By contrast, what structures can we find in things©? Where a thought is true, the left side of its representing-as (what it represents as such-and-such) is, to be sure, as represented (depicted) in its right side. If truth were, further, to consist in some relation between some structuring of its left side – that is, of things© and some structuring of its right side, the items thus to be structured should be some set of objects such that for them to be given ways would be for them to be as represented. For the thought that Sid drinks, for example, such objects might be, say, Sid and the set of historical episodes of alcohol ingestion. For structuring we might then consider a certain relation, *principal protagonist*, which holds between given objects and given historical episodes. There would then be the subset of that set of historical episodes of alcohol ingestion containing just those episodes to which Sid bears that relation. Truth might now turn on whether that subset is sufficiently, or interestingly enough, non-null. In any event, such relations as Sid might bear to an episode are not at all ones by which proper thought-elements might be related to each other in a thought, or sub-parts of a generality under which things being as they are might fall or not – such things as *Sid* being some relevant way, or it being drinking that relevant things do. Nor, conversely, are *such* relations ones in which Sid, or an episode, might stand in to something.

The point made already about representations (*Bilder*) and what they depict now shows up as applying to representations (*Abbildungen*) as well. The relations Sid may bear to other objects, such as sets of episodes, are not relations one generality may bear to another. Put in Frege's vocabulary, relations between concepts are utterly different from relations between objects (as he insists). More perspicuously, relations between objects are not the same as relations between ways of generalising over them. With which the *Tractatus*'s picture of representing-as collapses. In his famous argument Frege also gives another reason why, anyway, we might have expected as much. For Frege (as for Aristotle), a non-negotiable feature of being true is that it is an identity under predication: "One can certainly say: 'the thought that 5 is a prime number is true'. If, though, one looks closer, he notes that nothing more is said by this than in the simple sentence, '5 is a prime number'" (Frege 1892: 34). Holding this fixed, an account of truth fails if it abolishes identity under predication. The *Tractatus*'s account, in §§2.14 – 2.15 is a prime example of such an account.

3 Games and Formalisms

3.1 Emptiness

In those years 1929 – 31 not just the collapse of the *Tractatus*, but also philosophy of mathematics, was very much on Wittgenstein's mind. Which led him, and thus Waismann, to Frege's *Grundgesetze*, Vol. 2. In which Frege devoted considerable time and space to a highly critical discussion of the dean of his faculty, Johannes Thomae. That discussion begins by quoting Thomae as follows:

> The formal conception of numbers sets itself more modest boundaries than the logical. It does not ask what numbers are or ought to be, but rather what use one makes of numbers in arithmetic. On the formal conception, arithmetic is a game with signs which one might well call empty, by which one would mean that (in the calculating game) no other content accrues to them than that which accrues to them by reference to their behaviour with respect to certain combinatorial rules (rules of the game). (As cited in Frege 1903: 98 (§88))

From a suitable distance one might find something attractive in what Thomae says. The leading idea would be: arithmetic is what arithmetic does (or what one does with it); it is thus identifiable by what it does. Arithmetic is, notably, about certain calculations, most notably, addition and (what is definable in terms of it), multiplication. Arithmetic (over given numbers) fixes how such calculations are to be done, or when one would be doing them (correctly). So one may identify arithmetic as the thing it is by saying how those calculations are to be done (or, more simply, just what they are). So far, a not implausible idea.

Now a further wrinkle. When we calculate sums and products, at least on paper or on screens, we do so by manipulating symbols, e.g., by applying those algorithms we learned in primary school. So we can, as an initial step at least, treat arithmetic as a game to be played with signs – the summing and multiplying game, so to speak. Arithmetic, one might object, is *not* this, but rather the business of given operations to be made on *numbers*. But never mind that for the nonce. Once we have said how such a game with signs would, or might, be played, we can then, in terms of this, characterise arithmetic as the business of operating on numbers that it is. Not everyone might find this wrinkle (this strategy for saying what arithmetic is) attractive. I confess that I do. But we here touch on issues beyond our present topic.

Now an analogy with chess. Following Thomae, we would like to speak of such a thing as *the* arithmetic game, a picturesque way of speaking of *the* way of calculating sums and products. But, of course, whatever signs we may use in calculating sums and products, it is not essential to *the* game of arithmetical calculation that it involves *those* signs. As in chess. *The* game of chess is played by two players on a 'board' with given structure, each with an ensemble of pieces of various sorts: the king, the queen, eight pawns, and so on. It starts with a given initial configuration of pieces on the board. Each sort of piece is governed by given rules determining how, by moving it, one board configuration may be turned into another. There are terminal board configurations of defined sorts. To play a game of chess, one finds something or other of the right structure to be a board, and two ensembles of things, each assigned a designated role as a piece of a given sort (e.g., this matchbook is to be the white king). Form an initial configuration accordingly and off one goes. To play the game one needs to cast something in the role of the board, something in the role of the white king, something in the role of the black king, and so on. 'In the role of', or, if you prefer, a *Vertreter* (stand-in) for.

One *could*, or so one *might* think, say what chess is by taking some given set of chess pieces and a given board, and saying how *these* pieces may be moved on *this* board, what an initial, what a terminal, state of *this* board would be, and so on. One would then need to add: a game of chess is any game which consists of items each of which plays one of the roles which is played by some item in this particular game. *The* game of chess would then be that in which there were these roles to be played by some set of *Vertreters* (role-players) or others. Which suggests, by analogy, a syntactic approach to saying what arithmetic is which seems to be what Thomae has in mind. Let a theory of arithmetic start from some proprietary vocabulary, some arbitrary set of (so far) meaningless symbols. Let the syntax have an initial subpart which generates strings of symbols, and then a final part which generates strings of strings of symbols. Intuitively, we are to think of each of the symbols as a role-player cast in a given role, e. g., that of the number 2, or of addition. Our aim is then to unfold the roles in question in terms of our well-formed strings of strings of symbols. If all goes well, there should be a given subclass of these strings of strings whose members play the role of calculating a sum, each member some given sum, similarly for calculating products. And then *a* game of arithmetic would be whatever generated that which played the roles played by strings of strings of symbols in our sample game. And *the* game of arithmetic would be that in which there were *those* roles to be played.

I take Thomae to have had something like the above idea in mind, crude as this exposition of it may be. Frege, in *Grundgesetze* 2, subjects the idea, or Thomae's unfolding of it, to a number of criticisms, for the most part heartily endorsed by Wittgenstein. What drives these criticisms, broadly speaking, is the burden Thomae (officially) assigns syntax in his way of doing things. It arises in Thomae's idea that "no other content accrues to [the signs of his theory's proprietary vocabulary] than that which accrues to them by reference to their behaviour with respect to certain combinatorial rules". If we follow the analogy with chess, each sign in the vocabulary is to play a given role in the particular game Thomae defines (what is *meant* to stand towards arithmetic as a particular matchbook, cast in the role of white king, may *thus* stand to the game of chess). But, to put the point one way, one cannot rely on syntax alone to tell us what role it is that is thus being played. What follow are two specific criticisms of Frege's which elaborate this idea.

First, Thomae, it seems, is concerned to avoid contradiction in his system: 'The calculating game' must not generate contradictory results. For example, suppose the system generated numbers as the result of dividing a number by zero. So, for some m, 3/0 would be presented as equal to m, and for some n, 4/0 would be presented as equal to n. Division being what it is, 3 would then turn out to equal 0·m, 4 to equal 0·n. But 0·m = 0·n = 0. It would then follow that 3 = 4. Thomae's arithmetic had better not commit to such a claim. To which Frege points out that if the formulae generated in Thomae's arithmetic are really strings of meaningless signs, then none of them commits the theory to anything. So far, Thomae's theory is not in a business in which it *could* contain a contradiction. To be sure, it might generate a formula that looks like this: '3 = 4'. But one mustn't think that in this formula '3' means 3, or '4' 4. Nor '=' *is identical with*. So far, there is simply no fate for Thomae's theory to avoid, no question of it harbouring a contradiction.

As Frege puts it,

> [F]irst of all, here in formal arithmetic no contradiction is produced at all. Why should a group such as '3 = 4' not be permitted? In contentful arithmetic, admittedly, with its claim to validity, this must not occur, because there is a question of the *Bedeutungen* of number signs, which here differ. This reason lapses here. Writing down a group of figures such as '3 = 4' has, at least so far, not been forbidden. Only when one issues such a prohibition does a contradiction arise, or better put, a conflict in the rules, which in one part forbid, in another permit, this. (Frege 1903: §117 (pp. 122–123))
>
> Further, it is striking that freedom from contradiction is asserted of a figure. It would sound odd if the worry were expressed of a chess piece that perhaps it contained a contradiction. (Frege 1903: §118 (p. 123))

Wittgenstein agrees:

> If, now, I take a calculus as a calculus, then the configurations in the game cannot represent [*darstellen*] a contradiction. (I might arbitrarily call some figure occurring in a game a 'contradiction' and exclude it. In that way I simply declare that I am playing a different game.) (Waismann 1984: 124–125)
>
> The idea of a contradiction [*Widerspruch*] – and this is something I stick to – is that of a logical contradiction [*Kontradiktion*], and this can only occur in the *True-False-game*, thus, only where we make assertions.
>
> That is to say: A contradiction [*Widerspruch*] can only occur in the rules of the game. For example, I can have a rule of a game which says: a white piece must be passed over a black one. [...] If now a black one stands on the edge, the rule collapses. [...] What am I to do in such a case? Nothing easier, in order to eliminate the contradiction: I must make a decision, thus introduce a further rule.
>
> Thus we see: As long as we take a calculus as a calculus, the question of freedom from contradiction cannot seriously occur at all. (Waismann 1984: 124–125)

To express a contradiction is, first of all, to express *something*.

Which brings us to a second criticism. A string of *meaningless* signs cannot state a contradiction. A string of signs which stated a rule might state a self-contradictory one. Frege accuses Thomae of producing strings of signs for which he has failed to choose whether these are to be ones generated by his syntax, or statements of rules of the syntax itself. If the first, then they are strings of meaningless signs. If the last, they had better not be meaningless. Still, though, syntactic, or combinatorial, rules and meaningless strings are all there is in Thomae's theory. And the content of a syntactic (combinatorial) rule, governing meaningless signs, is not that of a principle of arithmetic such as that addition is commutative, or that it is associative. Thus Frege cites Thomae as saying,

> These rules [commutativity and associativity] are contained in the formulae
> $a + a' = a' + a$,
> $a + (a' + a'') = (a + a') + a'' = a + a' + a''$,
> $(a' - a) + a = a'$,
> $a \cdot a' = a' \cdot a$,
> $a \cdot (a' \cdot a'') = (a \cdot a') \cdot a'' = a \cdot a' \cdot a''$ ...

On which Frege comments,

> This is a surprise. What would someone say who, having asked for the rules of chess, instead of any answer was shown a group of chess pieces on a chess board? Probably that he could find no rule in this, because he could connect no sense with these figures and with their composition. Things only appear otherwise [here] because we are already acquainted with the plus-sign, the identity-sign, and the use of letters from contentful arithmetic. For here we aim to engage in *formal* arithmetic. And this raises the question whether each sign should be treated as a sign at all, or only as a figure. In which case one cannot refrain from asking how a rule *could* be so given. But if it is to be treated as a sign, it can by no means designate the same as it does in contentful arithmetic. For in that case we would have a contentful proposition, and not a rule of formal arithmetic. (Frege 1903: 113 (§106))

A view which Wittgenstein endorses:

> We must thus distinguish: the fundamental configurations of the calculus (the starting points in the game) and the rules which determine how we are to move from one configuration to another.
> Frege already explained this in his critique of the theories of Heine and Thomae: "This is a surprise." [...]. (Waismann 1984: 124 (26.12.1930))

From which we learn the lesson which distinguishes Thomae's arithmetic from the formalisation contained in *Begriffsschrift:* a theory which aims to make something syntactically recognisable must not only contain a syntax by which such is to be made recognisable, but also state adequately *what* it is that is thus to be made recognisable by precisely *what*. (It might help to keep in mind here that a theory might be *false*; a theory of present sort, for example, by assigning the *wrong* syntax the task of making recognisable what it aims so to make.)

Suppose we compare the role of syntax in Thomae's formalism with its role in Frege's *Begriffsschrift*. *Begriffsschrift*, taken as what is given in parts 1 and 2 of that work combined, is a theory of something. It aims to make a certain notion syntactically recognisable. And in doing this it commits to a range of truths. To see what is to be made recognisable we can refer to the task Frege assigns logic: to answer the question how one must think to reach the goal truth (but only insofar as an answer *is* given by what being true is as such). (*Vide* Frege 1897: 139.) The notion *Begriffsschrift* is to make syntactically recognisable is a certain notion of truth-preservation. The aim is to make it recognisable when a passage from given thoughts to a given one would be a passage to truth given that it starts from truths alone. For this purpose, *Begriffsschrift* contains a proprietary vocabulary and syntax (though in that work the syntax is not quite made completely explicit). As with Thomae conceived as above, the syntax generates strings of strings of symbols. So whether a given string succeeds some given set of strings in some string of strings thus generated is determined entirely by the syntactic rules: whether a string of strings *is* so generated is thus made syntactically recognisable.

If the theory is correct, then any transition from an initial segment of such a string of strings to a later string will be truth-preserving. But then truth-preserving in this sense: whatever the initial segment of strings stands in for, if all of that is true, then so is what the later string stands in for. Truth-preservation in our initial sense is thus made syntactically recognisable if the theory is correct. Recognisable, that is, insofar as it is recognisable what the strings in a given case do stand in for.

I mean to be saying here what is so of *Begriffsschrift*, not what Frege thought was so of it, or what, on standard readings of him, he is thought to have thought. Frege came to think (and stated in 1893: §32) that the well-formed strings of signs of *Begriffsschrift* each expressed a thought. I think this could not be right. What these strings stand in, or substitute, for, I think, are logical forms, so that what a string of strings tells us, or rather what the theory does in generating it, is that a transition from any thoughts of the forms of some initial segment to a thought of the form of a later segment is truth-preserving simply by virtue of what being true is as such. And when a thought *is* of some such form is not made recognisable, or even addressed, by the theory *Begriffsschrift* is.

Either way, though, Thomae (as read above) and *Begriffsschrift* part company at just this point. For if *Begriffsschrift* is to tell us where there is *truth*-preservation according to it, on the relevant notion of this, whatever that might be, then it must tell us what its strings of symbols *vertreten*, or stand in for. For, by definition, that by which *syntactic* rules apply to symbols has certainly not anything to do with truth (or else there would be nothing to *make* syntactically recognisable). And Frege certainly does tell us this. It is his first task in *Begriffsschrift*. He does this in ordinary German, not in some vocabulary proprietary to the theory. (How could there be such a vocabulary until he has told us this?) Such is the very first thing he does in *Begriffsschrift*, which begins as follows:

> The customary signs in the general theory of magnitudes divide into two sorts. The first comprises letters of which each stands in either for a number (which so far left open), or for a function (which so far left open). This indeterminacy makes it possible to use the letters to express the general validity of propositions [...] The other sort includes such signs as +, · , ∫, 0, 1, 2, of which each has its proprietary *Bedeutung*.
>
> *This fundamental thought of the distinction between two sorts of sign* [...] I adopt in order to make use of it in the more comprehensive domain of pure thought as such. (Frege 1879: 1)

For Frege, the signs for logical constants of *Begriffsschrift* are of the first sort. For example, his binary connective, '⊃' in current usage, though of course not in his, is defined as that which forms a true thought out of any ordered pair of truth-valued thoughts for any combination of truth-values of those two except where the first item in the pair is true, the second false. Signs of the second sort are what he calls 'unbestimmt andeutend', 'indefinitely indicating', which means: they mark places where completion would be needed in one or another stipulated way to form a whole which was, syntactically viewed, a stand-in for a thought, or otherwise viewed, a thought. Thus, for example, the 'x' and 'y' in F(x,y). (Note that, while F(a,b) may *vertreten* a certain logical form for a thought to take, that is, the form of a doubly singular thought, it cannot express any thought. 'F' does not stand in for any way for a pair to be, nor 'a', or 'b' for any object.)

In any case, just here (in part 1 of *Begriffsschrift*) Frege takes the step which Thomae does not take. He does the work in ordinary German, which Thomae leaves to syntax to sort out for itself. And the point of Frege's criticisms of Thomae is that syntax simply will not sort these things out for itself. Frege assigns specific meanings to the symbols of *Begriffsschrift*. In the case of logical constants he does this by assigning them 'Bedeutungen', not in his own post-1890 sense of that term, but in the sense in which Wittgenstein and Waismann speak of such things in 1929 – 1931. He also assigns meanings to the 'unbestimmt andeutend' symbols of *Begriffsschrift*, though it is part of their meaning what they thus do that in another sense they function without *fixed* 'Bedeutungen'. Wittgenstein's and Waismann's concern in what follows here is to point out that such is just one way among others of making signs meaningful. But they agree with Frege in taking Thomae to task for omitting *this* task altogether.

In current mathematics there is one common conception of formality on which the sort of objection just canvassed would lapse. One way to do mathematics is by defining a sort of formal structure for some object of mathematical enquiry to take. One might, e. g., define a 'metric space' as an ordered pair of a domain and a function from the Cartesian product of this domain into the reals, the whole satisfying certain formal constraints, or, again, a ring as an ordered quadruple of a set, a function defined over the set (an ordering function), and two operations – call them 'plus' and 'times' – again subject to given stated constraints. Here the interest is in the structure, not in what it is that might *turn out* to have that structure. There is no claim to be presenting a theory of any given such thing, e. g., arithmetic, or space. Perhaps Hilbert's reputed remark about tables, chairs and beer mugs points to such a possibility.

A final note here. Suppose, for sake of argument, that *Begriffsschrift* is a theory of logical forms. So its well-formed strings of signs are each a stand-in for some particular form there is for a thought to take. Then the fact that a certain string of signs is generated by the syntax corresponds to a thought which the *theory* expresses: in generating that string, the theory commits to the claim that there are thoughts of such-and-such form. It does not follow that that string itself expresses a thought: that *it* is engaged in thought-expressing, in that it is to be understood as representing things as a way things either are or are not. The string need not be the expression of a thought in the way that a sentence, such as 'Beer is made of malt and hops' would, if, indeed, sentences as such were in the business of being either true or false. All the well-formed string must do, on this understanding of *Begriffsschrift*, is to stand in for some form for a thought to take. It need not even stand in for a thought. A theory need not express the thoughts *it* does in generating strings which themselves express these.

In any event, Thomae *does* purport to be saying what *arithmetic* is, so what adding and multiplying are. But he has left it to syntax alone to make it so that the strings of strings his theory generates are, indeed, stand-ins for calculations of sums and products. And this simply will not do. Why, e. g., are they not part of a *false* theory of something else? So far, we have seen one thing which might do: assigning signs in the vocabulary of a syntax meanings by saying what each means, as Frege does in *Begriffsschrift* part 1. But are there, perhaps, other ways?

3.2 The Pawn Gambit

In 1930 both Wittgenstein and Waismann, each in slightly different terms, expressed the view that there was a truth in formalism – a third possibility beyond merely treating a sign as an empty sign, a mere design, or else treating it as having a 'meaning' in the sense of standing for, or speaking of, such-and-such; and that this third possibility, is something Frege missed. Here is Waismann:

> For Frege, the alternative is this: either a sign has a meaning, i.e., it goes proxy for an object – a logical sign for a logical object, an arithmetical sign for an arithmetical object – or it is only a figure, drawn on paper in ink.
> But this is not a legitimate alternative. As the game of chess shows, there is a third possibility: in chess a pawn neither has a meaning in the sense of going proxy for anything, of being a sign *for* anything, nor is it merely a piece carved in wood and pushed about on a wooden board. It is only the rules of the game of chess that define what a pawn is.
> The example shows that we must not say that a sign is either a sign for something or only a structure perceivable by our senses. Thus there is a legitimate element in formalism, a true core that Frege failed to see.
> The 'meaning' of a pawn is, if you like, the totality of rules holding for it. And thus you can also say that the meaning of a numeral is the totality of rules holding for it. (Waismann 1984: 150 (12.12.1930))

And here Wittgenstein:

> Frege was right in objecting to the conception that the numbers of arithmetic are signs. The sign '0' certainly does not have the property that it yields the sign '1' when added to the sign '1'. Thus far Frege's criticism was correct. Only he did not see the other, justified side of formalism, that the symbols of mathematics are not [mere] signs, but nor do they denote anything. For Frege, the alternative was this: either we deal with strokes of ink on paper or these strokes of ink are signs *of something* and what they stand in for is their meaning. The game of chess itself shows that these alternatives are wrongly conceived – although it is not the wooden chessmen we are dealing with, these figures do not stand in for anything, they have no *Bedeutung* in Frege's sense. There is still a third possibility, *the signs can be used the way they are in the game.* If here (in chess) you wanted to talk of 'meaning', the most natural thing to say would be that the meaning of chess is what all games of chess have in common. (Waismann 1984: 105 (italics mine))

There are two candidates (at least) for what it is that Frege missed. First, he might have missed the possibility just scouted, of a bit of mathematics concerned only with a certain sort of formal structure, and not as such with what it is that has this structure. Perhaps Frege did miss the possibility of that form of mathematics, perhaps to his detriment, notably, in his disagreement with Kant about arithmetic. But such is for another day. The other possibility is that where a thought is expressed or mentioned, what thought this is is identifiable in other ways than simply by mentioning some objects as the ones it represents as something, and some ways which are the ways it represents these being. A thought, the idea is, might be identifiable as the thought it is in other ways. If there is something Frege missed in Thomae, it would then be something Thomae claims to be doing which points to some such other way. The interest of this for our present purpose is: this third possibility, whatever it is exactly, may be that which is to be captured by later Wittgenstein's notion of a language game.

Two differences between Wittgenstein's and Waismann's way of signalling the third possibility are worth mention. First, where Waismann speaks of 'rules of the game', Wittgenstein speaks of 'how the game is played', no mention of rules. Here is one way this difference *might* matter. In September 1931 Wittgenstein mentions to Waismann his opposition to a view of understanding on which this is a process external to, and accompanying, perception of the 'verbal picturing'. Rather, he suggests, the better way of understanding understanding what is said, or something there is to be said, is this:

> I understand a proposition by *applying* it. Understanding is thus not a particular event [transaction]; it is operating with a proposition. *The point of a proposition is that we should operate with it.* (Waismann 1984: 166 (21.9.1931))

So to see the point of a proposition – to understand it – would be to see how to operate with it. Such would be a capacity to do with the proposition what is to be done with it in an indefinite, and indefinitely large, set of circumstances which could arise, seeing *how* to use it; being able to recognise when it was being used as called for. The sort of understanding a proposition would thus call for, or bear, one consisting in a capacity to recognise what is to be, or may be, done with it, need not reduce to a recipe for operating with it, nor to some compendium of, or condition on, operations thus to be done; all the less to a recipe for identifying what would count as things© being as the proposition represents them. Nor, if we think of an expression of thought as a move in a game need we think of such game as governed by specifiable rules. (At which point chess may cease to be *le modèle juste*.)

Second, where Waismann speaks of 'the meaning of a pawn' as the totality of rules governing it, Wittgenstein speaks of 'the meaning of chess' as what all games of chess have in common. To use a matchbook for the white king in some game of chess is to cast it in a certain role, one in which in that playing of the game, it is subject to given rules. To use a table top as a chess board in some game of chess is to cast it in a certain role, one which requires treating it as structured into a certain array of things which will count as 'squares'. (Whether the table top is so usable by *us* is contingent on our abilities so to treat it.) *The* game of chess is that game which provides just those roles to be assumed, their assumption by something or other being what is in common to all its playings. Correlatively, the white king in chess is that whose role is assumed by all the white kings in any playing of chess. Similarly for *the* chess board. If we view arithmetic as a game with signs, then *mutatis mutandis* there. So viewing arithmetic, there are roles to be played by signs, that, e.g., of the number 2, or of the operation *addition*. What all games with signs which are arithmetic have in common is, for each of these roles, some player of it. The number 2, for example, is that whose role is played by some sign or other in any such game. A possible place for application of this idea to thoughts, or thought-expression: what all expressions of some given thought have in common is a certain role they would thus be playing. The thought in question would then be that whose role would thus be played in all those particular ways. Such, though, is so far a mere leading idea, whose fate remains to be determined.

3.3 Tertium Datur

What third possibility is Frege meant to have missed? To put it in the terms Wittgenstein used in September 1931, it is this: perhaps a thought (or proposition) can be identified as the thought (or proposition) it is by how one is to operate with it, thus by some role it would thus play in something. But a version of this idea is found in Frege himself, in his very criticism of Thomae. There he writes,

> [W]ithout a thought content no application [*Anwendung*] would be possible. Why can't one make an application of a configuration of chess pieces? Clearly, because they express no thought. If they did so, and if one of the rules fitting chess pieces corresponded to the transition from one thought to another by which it followed, then, too, such applications of chess would be conceivable. Why can one make applications of arithmetical equalities? Only because they express thoughts. [...] Now, it is such applicability alone which lifts arithmetic above a game into the range of a science. Applicability belongs essentially to this. (Frege 1903: 100 (§91))

Leaving it open for the nonce what an application might be, the idea here is: there is an application only where there is expression of a thought. So an item has applications only where, or insofar as, *it* expresses a thought. So, it would seem, *what* applications there are in a given case would depend on *what* thought was expressed (or else no thought need be mentioned in such connection). So, too, then, it may belong to a thought to have given applications: having those applications is at least part of something which identifies it as being the thought it is. If thoughts are thus distinguished, or distinguishable, in this way from one another, one might also expect that where there is a thought there are its applications; for it to be *that* thought is for it to have those applications, and vice-versa.

We may at least begin to fill in the notion *application* here by pursuing the question of what importance this idea, still in skeletal form, has for Frege. The answer, I suggest, is that it is absolutely central to his conception of truth. To see this we must cross the line from the logical back to the psychological and begin with the notion *holding true* (*Fürwahrhalten*). One thing Frege remarks about this is that to hold something true cannot be to *predicate* truth of it. For when truth is predicated of a thought, all we get back is a thought; in fact, the same thought again. For, as Frege argues, it is fundamental to what *being true* must be that truth is an identity under predication. So predicating truth of a thought we simply get anew a *thought*, something which might be held true or not. What, then, would it be to *hold* a thought true?

Frege's answer to this question is contained in the following remark:

> The word 'true' thus appears to make the impossible possible, namely, to make what corresponds to assertive force appear as a contribution to the thought. And although it fails, or rather precisely through its failure, it points to what is peculiar to logic. [...] 'True' really only makes a failed attempt to identify logic, in that what this really comes to does not at all lie in the word 'true', but rather in the assertive force with which a sentence is spoken. (Frege 1915: 272)

Assertive force is just that in thought-expression by which representing-as becomes representing-to-be, representing truly or falsely. In so representing things© one represents *himself* as an authority as to such-and-such, and offers such purported authority to (perhaps given) others to rely on. One thus *underwrites* for others being guided accordingly in their transactions with things, in the conduct of their lives; bringing the world to bear as it would thus bear on the thing for them to do, on the way their goals would be to be pursued.

What thought one expresses *assertively* is then identified, in one way, by what it is he thus underwrites. Here we find the wanted notion of an application. The applications of a given thought would lie in how things being as they were *would* bear on the way for one to conduct his dealings with things, on what bearing there would thus be on the ways his goals were in fact pursuable should things be as that thought represents them. Thus, conversely, fix these applications, identify them in whatever way they are identifiable, and you fix the thought expressed (insofar as there is anything to be fixed).

Consider, for example, the applications of arithmetic. Arithmetic tells us, *inter alia*, what the sum of any two numbers is. Now Pia enters the *caviste* and quickly finds herself facing a certain problem. There in the bin-ends basket lie, *mirabile dictu*, a dozen or so bottles of Billecart-Salmon at € 29.99 the pop. Pia's pulse quickens. How many bottles can her plastic stand, if she has € 300 credit left? If Pia can guide her pursuit of goals by the truths of arithmetic, she will be thereby granted insight into the thing to do. Such is *an* application of the truths of arithmetic, or some of them. Frege himself looks to applications of arithmetic in physics or astronomy. A more serious business, perhaps, than visiting the *caviste*. But Pia's example will do just as well to illustrate what it might be for a thought to have applications.

Here is a proposition of arithmetic: 29.99 into 300 is 10 plus change. Which means (if true), things being as they are, that Pia can buy up to 10 bottles of Billecart-Salmon without overstraining the plastic (technically speaking, at least). For her to be guided by *that* thought would thus be for her to be *so* guided in the situation she is now in. Such belongs to what she subscribes to in holding *that* proposition true (if she does). And such illustrates what Frege has in mind above by an application (*Anwendung*): applications to calculating such things as "lengths, time intervals, mass and moments of inertia" (*vide* Frege 1903: 101 (§92)), and purchase power.

Though we still have only a skeletal notion of an application, following along the path Frege traces from the notion of being true through the idea of assertive force, there are two things we are already positioned to say about the connection between a thought and its applications in present sense:

For a thought to be the thought it is is for it to have the applications it in fact does. So if, for a given thought, we have fixed its applications, we have, *ipso facto*, identified it as the thought it is. No more *need* be said.

Correspondingly, if we have identified *one* application a thought in fact has, we have gone at least some little way towards identifying it as the thought it is. We have distinguished it from a range of other thoughts, to wit, ones which would lack those applications.

Such is a *tertium datur*, a third possibility standing beside these two others: first, the *absence* of a thought, there being no particular *Gedanke* (thinkable) yet in question, e. g., as the one expressed, or mentioned, in some given episode; second, some given thought, identified by what it, or its parts on some decomposition is of, by what it represents as what – as, e. g., the thought that Sid drinks is of Sid that he drinks, of someone as being a drinker, of things as such that Sid drinks. The third possibility, at least at first approximation, is that a given thought, or given thoughts, may be brought into question, identified, in terms of the applications it/they would have. Such is plausibly, at least roughly, the truth Wittgenstein and Waismann detected in Thomae's project. In any case, it is an idea with work to do for later Wittgenstein.

For Wittgenstein by 1931, if not before, words, or propositions, are things with which we *operate*. There are correct and incorrect ways of operating with such things, ways they are to be, or may be operated with. An understander is one who grasps, can recognise, *how* to operate with them, what sort of operating-on they admit of; is thus someone with a *capacity*. Such is, *inter alia*, a capacity to recognise what it would be to be guided by them, what applications there would thus be. All ideas captured in that *tertium datur* we can find in Frege himself.

Two preliminary remarks. First, on the Fregean conception of the business of being true (as per section 1 above), a thought is identified as the thought it is solely by the right side of the representing-as relation, that is, by that way for things© to be which it represents things© as being, by which it is true or false *outright*. So the thought is the thought it is, that very thought, no matter how things are. To be sure, if things were different enough there might have been no such way for things to be, thus no such thought at all. As things stand, Sid drinks lager. But there might have been no such thing as doing this had there been no such thing as yeast. Still, given that there is such a thought, the generality under which it presents the particular case (things, *Sachen*) as falling – *when* things would be as represented by *it* – remains as it is independent of how *things* happen to be. Such is just part of that core idea of the objectivity of truth as a precisely *two*-party enterprise effected exclusively by how things are represented as being, and things simply *being* (in which *so* being or not).

By contrast, what applications a given thought would have, on our present notion, skeletal as it still is, is liable to depend on how things in fact are. As things are, arithmetic tells us that Pia may buy up to 10 bottles of Billecart-Salmon without over-stretching her plastic, at least in the meaning of the act. But such depends on a background of fact concerning such matters as service charges, unforeseen levies of interest charges, and practices concerning bin ends – for example, on it not being the practice to increase the price of a bin end item by 10% each time a customer buys one exemplar thereof. (After all, each such time the item becomes rarer, at least at that *caviste*.) With different practices it could have been that Pia's plastic would *not* stand the strain of 10 bottles, or, again, that it would stand even more strain than that. And if we supposed the application to be that Pia could buy 10 bottles *tout court*, there may in fact be manifold reasons why that is not so. Perhaps, e.g., she needs to hold some credit in reserve in case the night is too long and she needs a taxi home.

So applications which identify a given thought as the thought it is are liable to be ones it has only in the circumstances of things being as they are. It is then only in those circumstances (or other sufficiently hospitable ones) that it can be so identified. For all of which, as things stand it may *be* so identifiable.

And here the second remark. There is an implicit contrast in our two conclusions above between a *full* identification of a thought – something which would be so precisely and only of what represented as that thought does, and which thus distinguishes it from *all* others, full stop – and, by contrast, a *partial* identification – something which thus distinguishes that thought from some others, but which may be shared by some range of other thoughts, all of which agree to *that* extent as to how they represent things. So far, at least, this idea of a full identification, of distinguishing the way a given thought represents things from *all* other ways that *any* thought might represent things, is subject to proving chimerical. We must so far hold open the possibility that showing it up as such is both something later Wittgenstein aims to do and work to which he hopes to put his notion, *language game*.

4 Entering the Investigations

4.1 The Language Game

The time has come to introduce the notion *language game*. The present idea is this: a language game is a device (or a conceit) with which to *model* an application, or some set, or range, of applications, which a given thought, or given thought-expression, would have. As Wittgenstein tells us, "language games [...] stand there as objects of comparison [...]" (Wittgenstein 1953: §130).

Thus, in the little arithmetical example above (Pia at the *caviste*), the indicated application of the thought that 29.99 into 300 is 10 with change might be modelled by a language game whose rules lay down that when a player is presented with, say, the words, 'Twentynine ninety nine into three hundred is ten with change' he may (or is to) respond by taking up to 10 bottles of Billecart-Salmon out of the bin marked 'bin ends' (or marked '29.99') (then marching to the counter and slapping down the plastic). Or something of this sort, details depending on exactly what one wants to model. Roughly speaking, where a thought (or thought-expression) has a given application, such may be modelled in a game in which there is a piece (some given words, say) which stands in for that thought, or that expression of it, and rules for the use of that piece by which when it is produced, what would be done (in given circumstances) in making that application is to be, or may be, done.

Suppose, for example, we look at the first language game in the *Investigations*. Wittgenstein sends a (presumably mildly retarded) child to the grocers to buy some apples. He gives the child a note on which is written, 'Five red apples'.

The rest is legend. Wittgenstein remarks on this game, "we operate with words in this and similar ways" (Wittgenstein 1953: §1).

With the possible exception of some graduate students trying to relive the drama and pathos of the *Investigations*, I doubt that anyone has ever bought apples in quite this way. To suggest otherwise would be to lose touch with reality. But we need not read Wittgenstein as making any such suggestion. Suppose someone says, 'There are five red apples in the wooden fruit bowl.' If he thereby expressed the thought that there are five red apples in a certain fruit bowl, he would then have said what has certain applications. For example, if a visit by immature members of the species is in the cards, there is fruit enough for five of them to engage in apple-bobbing, should one wish so to engage them.

What, now, might identify the thought that there are five red apples in the wooden fruit bowl as the thought it is? What, for a start, might answer the question when it would be five red apples that were in some given collection, when it would be *that* sort of way that things were? Let us try to apply our present idea of an application. And let us start from a suggestion Frege made in 1879. In effect, Frege suggests that we can think of a thought, not just as the thought *that* such-and-such, but also as the thought *of* such-and-such. In doing which we can represent things *as* being the way that thought represents them while detaching this from assertive force – from what contains any hint of representing-to-be. In Frege's example, we can present the thought that Archimedes fell at the conquest of Syracuse as the circumstance of things being such that Archimedes fell at the conquest of Syracuse, where 'circumstance' (*Umstand*) is conceived here as something which might obtain or not, thus giving us the thought *of* things so being. (*Vide* Frege 1879: 3–4) Now one way for us to be guided by a thought of there being five red apples in some given collection is to see what applications that thought would have in pursuit of the goal of bringing such about. One way to model a set of applications which might (in the right circumstances) identify a thought of that sort as *such* a thought (as the thought it is modulo the collection in question) would be the game of §1. "We operate in such and similar ways with words" need only mean: such models our capacities to understand what is said, or what thought was expressed in recognising what applications there would be of the thought, or idea, of things being the way some given thought represents things *as* being.

A game may thus model some application the thought (mass noun) expressed (what was said) in given words would have (in given circumstances). One who (so) understood those words would thereby have a capacity to recognise (*inter alia*) this application *as* such where appropriate circumstances for making it arose. To repeat, the capacities in which an understanding might consist need not be reducible to some independent specification of that which was to be recognised (here to some given set of applications, each with the circumstances in which there would be *it* to be made). Without assuming such things a language game, conceived as above, might serve as means to fix that in some given thing to be thought which distinguishes it from other relevant things with which it might be confused.

4.2 Applications of the Present Notion *Application*

The trouble Frege points to in Thomae's arithmetic (as Frege portrays it) originates in this: that Thomae places a burden on syntax which syntax simply cannot carry. Thomae expects meaning to accrue to otherwise meaningless signs (and strings of signs) of his proprietary vocabulary merely by virtue of the ways they combine in his proprietary syntax. And the meaning which thus accrues should make the whole theory a theory of *arithmetic*. Such theory would presumably generate the truths of arithmetic. Thomae's strings, with the meaning thus accruing to them, would then, severally and collectively, express these: for each truth of arithmetic there is a string which expresses it (and which is designated by the theory as a truth-expresser), and for each such string there is a truth of arithmetic that it expresses. But this enterprise breaks down (in advance of any problem about completeness): syntax alone cannot confer on the strings it generates the sort of content they would need to have to express either truths or falsehoods of arithmetic at all.

How might this failing be rectified? One suggestion would be to assign each item in the proprietary vocabulary a *Bedeutung*, that is, to make it speak of, or stand in for, such-and-such. So, e. g., there would be a bit of vocabulary, perhaps primitive, perhaps complex, which stood for the number 5, a bit for the number 7, a bit for the number 12, a bit for the operation of addition, and then combinatorial rules which, by virtue of what such bits stood for, formed a whole which expressed the truth that $5 + 7 = 12$. (In which case, of course, we should also expect there to be such a complex which expressed the falsehood that $5 + 7 = 13$. The theory must thus further specify which such complexes, according to it, expressed truths.)

But if there is a *tertium datur* here, it should also be applicable. So, then, should Frege's above. Application might start here with Thomae's whole theory, construed as aiming to express the truths of arithmetic (assuming such to form a determinate whole). Truths of arithmetic are thoughts. Applying our *tertium datur*, a truth of arithmetic is thus identified as the truth it is by its applications, on our present notion of an application. Such would then also be applications of the theory, itself *inter alia* an expression of those truths. If the theory were incorrect, it would consist in part of thoughts whose applications (those there would be if the thoughts were true) do not in fact exist, are not in fact ways of staying on course in pursuit of goals. As a final step, we might articulate the applications of *arithmetic* as a whole so as to distribute them over particular truths of arithmetic, so as to identify each such truth by its applications.

To apply this general schema, we might mimic for arithmetic what Frege says as to what logic is. Frege identifies logic's subject matter in terms of a task which he takes to be the one it is assigned *per se*. To put it in his terms, the task of logic is to answer the question how one must think to reach the goal truth, insofar, but only insofar, as an answer is given by what being true is as such. Logic is thus identified by what one is to do, or may do, with it, just as per our *tertium datur*. (What one does with logic as such is: *think*.) Now, mimicking Frege, we may say: arithmetic is assigned the task of answering the question how one must think to reach the truth as to plurality, insofar, but only insofar, as an answer is given by what plurality is as such. Thus arithmetic, too, is identified as the topic it is by what is to be done with it. Its applications are wherever what to do depends on how some given plurality is determined by given others. Distributing what arithmetic thus does over particular truths of arithmetic, we get, for example, the thought that $5 + 7 = 12$ is that thought which answers the question how to think to reach the goal truth, insofar, but only insofar, as an answer to that question is given by what being five-fold, and then yet seven-fold, adds up to. Arithmetic thus in fact has all the applications there would in fact be given that pluralities behave as they in fact do (at least with respect to forming sums and products). The thought that $5 + 7 = 12$, e.g., has all the applications there would in fact be of those two pluralities, being five-fold and being seven-fold, behaving with respect to addition as they do.

We can talk in such ways if we like. But the above was initially advertised as providing two *alternative* ways of relieving syntax of an insupportable role. This now appears as false advertising. We can say what thought is expressed in saying 5 and 7 to add up to 12 by saying: that thought is of 5, of 7, and of addition that the first two mentioned items form what they do under that operation, addition. Or we can say that what is expressed is that thought which has all the applications there would in fact be (and hence are) of being 5-fold and being 7-fold combining additively as they do. But what we manifestly arrive at in this way is just two ways of saying the same thing, mere notational variants of one another.

We can see this if we turn from arithmetic to more ordinary pursuits. Consider a sentence such as '*Menudo* is the breakfast of champions', or, less multiculturally, 'Penguins waddle'. One *might* say of the first that it speaks of *Menudo* as the breakfast of champions, of the second that it speaks of penguins as waddlers.

Well, and what *are* the applications of *Menudo* being the breakfast of champions, or of penguins being waddlers? What would it be to guide one's pursuit of goals accordingly? Assuming univocity – that there is only one way we ever represent things as being when we use the word, '*Menudo* is the breakfast of champions' to speak of what *they* do – and that, given this, what to do if *Menudo* is the breakfast of champions (just what bearing this *would* have on executing any given project one might engage in) is fixed uniquely (two very large assumptions), about all there is to say is: 'Here is how the thought that *Menudo* is the breakfast of champions applies to what to do: if that thought is true, then wherever it matters to what to do (or how to pursue a goal) what the breakfast of champions is, or whether this is *Menudo*, act as one should act if *Menudo* is the breakfast of champions.'

In other words, except where style is a principal concern, the idea of identifying what *words* (e.g., English ones) *mean* by identifying the applications of what *they* as such say or speak of provides no genuine alternative at all. Correspondingly, the idea of a language game, as understood in terms of modelling applications, is just idle embroidery on an account of what any given words *mean*. And there is also another reason for thinking that the role of the idea of an application is not in explicating, or unfolding, what *words* mean. We need only recall that, for Frege, it was a *thought* which there must be for there to be applications (and which must have applications if there is to be a thought at all). A thought stands on the logical side of Frege's logical/psychological distinction. Its role is in the business of *being* true, not in that of holding true. Whereas the role of language is in thought-expression, in aiding the achievement by a thinker of representing-as; in making thought-expression recognisable as expression of the thought it is. And though our notion *application* may have a role to play in the business of thought-expression, that role is not in identifying *words* as meaning what they do. So the arena of application for these notions, *application* and *language game* is not going to be *a* language, or not one of the sort we speak. Nor is there any plausible work for these notions to do in a semantic theory of a language. Language games are not an alternative to, e.g., truth-conditional semantics. Nor, I suggest, does Wittgenstein mean them as such. He is a better philosopher than that.

So what else? For one answer I start from an example. On the beach before the summer house Pia and Sid share with Benno and Zoë, the day is off to a magnificent start, fog clearing early, skies blue. Preparing breakfast (well, brunch) Zoë decides mimosas are called for. She fetches a bottle from the cellar (a decent Crémant de Limoux), and begins to collect oranges to squeeze. Pia remarks, 'Sid drinks Bloody Marys for breakfast, with tabasco and Angostura bitters.' Here are two ways, among others, such words *might* be understood. To see the first, suppose a background against which drinking a Bloody Mary in the morning is quite a remarkable thing to do (mark of a true hard case). Here those words might be understood as saying what would be so if Sid were not averse to so drinking on occasion. On the second Pia is reporting Sid's habitual, or preferred, breakfast drink. If Pia's words are understood in the first of these ways, they would have no particular bearing on – no application to – how Zoë should conduct her immediate transactions with the world. If understood in the second way, though, there is immediate bearing.

Now, Pia *might* be understood as merely undergoing a bout of autism, reliving her past, oblivious to current happenings. Or she might be understood as participating in the current goings-on, accordingly as proffering (putatively informed) guidance as to the thing for Zoë to do. Perhaps she would be so to be understood on that morning at that juncture. If Zoë so takes, and then believes her, she will act accordingly. What exactly she might do is still left open. Sick of Sid and his crotchets, she might just, as it were, damn the torpedoes and steam ahead, setting a flute, properly filled and garnished, at Sid's place. If, though, she is concerned to spare perfectly good Crémant, she might, reluctantly, search for a tall-drinks glass, reach the Genever off the shelf, and begin to search for the Angostura.

Applications, in our present sense, do double duty here. When it comes to thought-expression, the authoring of representing-as, the *author*, some person, bears an understanding. There is something which would, reasonably, with right, be understood as to what project of representing-as the speaker was then engaged in (and how). Where, as in Pia's case, he would be understood as engaging in, or at least attempting, representing-to-be, as speaking with assertive force (or aiming to), previous remarks apply. To speak with assertive force is to assume responsibility. It is to underwrite guiding one's career, one's dealings with the world, in a certain way, by certain guide posts, thereby underwriting those answers to questions what to do which *such* guidance would deliver. Thus, e.g., in Pia's case, what to do to avoid waste of good Crémant.

Pia's representing as she did makes her committed to such applications *being* (*ceteris paribus*, perhaps) the way to reach (relevant) goals. Correspondingly, the way she represented things *has* those applications, would thus matter to the pursuit of goals, if true. So insofar as there is such a thing as *the* thought (countable) thus expressed, it is one identified, at least in part, by the fact of it having those applications. In Pia's case, for example, such applications distinguish what she said from what she might have said if in an autistic trance. Just so, an application, here, does double duty: first to identify how *Pia*, more specifically, how her thought-expressing, was, so is, to be understood, and then to identify the thought expressed.

Just by dint of this double duty, identifying the thought expressed by the fact of it having the relevant applications is *not* a mere stylistic variant for identifying it by what it is *of* (things, or some given thing) being. One could, of course, *give* a name to the way Pia said things to be (to the way things were represented as being by the thought expressed). One could call it, e.g., 'for Sid to drink Bloody Marys for breakfast *inveterately*'. But then, what would it be for things to be *that* way? How are we to understand 'inveterately' in this sense? For the answer to that, we must turn to the applications the thought in question has; the answers there would be to questions how to proceed to reach (relevant) goals were things as per that thought. It is our fix on this, a fix which comes with understanding what Pia said, which gives us the right understanding of 'inveterately', in use in the above naming of a thought. The next section will generalise on this application of the notion *application*.

The train of thought here proceeded through a particular form of representing-as, that done with assertive force. As is often so, such is the most economical way of unfolding it. But one might work it in the general case, perhaps most economically by the grammatical manoeuvre Frege suggests in *Begriffsschrift* for detaching a thought from assertive force: thought *of* in place of thought *that*. Orders, promises, questions, at least, thus follow suit.

The present notion *application*, and thus the corresponding notion *language game* are of no particular interest when it comes to questions what expressions of a language do, or what they are for, in *meaning* what they do. But it finds substantial application at that point where the move from expressing thought to the thought expressed is made, where an expression of thought is to be presented as an expression of *the* thought that (or of) such-and-such. It is worth reflecting for a moment on why this should be so. The answer, I suggest, lies in the ideals of justice and fairness. Again, that special case of representing-as, to wit, representing-to-be, is the quickest way to make the point. In representing things to be as she said (sc. such that Sid drinks Bloody Marys for breakfast), Pia made herself correctly held responsible for there being certain applications. Roughly, on the understanding on which she speaks of being a Bloody-Mary-drinker, to serve one what he thus would wish, serve him a Bloody Mary. She will have misled (or may well have), for example, if, at brunch, Sid sits sceptically eyeing his Bloody Mary, casting wistful looks at those Mimosas all others are enjoying. Now, responsibility is something to distribute justly and fairly. Pia should have no legitimate complaint of being hard done by, e.g., when we agree that she misled. The point about *language*, put in these terms is: what justice and fairness would be in a given case, such as Pia's, is not (in general) fixed just by what the words *used* mean (even if used to mean what they mean). What it would be *just* to hold a speaker to is still liable to depend on features of circumstance independent of the words used *meaning* what they do. Which explains, conversely, why saying what applications a given bit of language has just in *meaning* what it does can only be empty filigree on some statement of what it speaks of, as the sentence 'Penguins waddle' speaks of penguins as waddlers.

What happens if we read the first paragraph of the *Investigations* in light of the above? There Wittgenstein first mentions a train of ideas, connected, he suggests, by at least quasi-rational relations. He then suggests another of his own, which seems to be meant to contrast somehow with those first ideas. But he never suggests that any of the ideas in this train is *mistaken*. He just thinks that, in this context, his own idea is worth keeping in mind. His own idea is that of the conversation with Waismann in 1931: "The point of a proposition is that we should operate with it." What of the ideas he does not contest?

First, there is Augustine, who *first* learns certain facts about words, e.g., that 'mensa' is the word for *table*. (With a bit of practice in phonology), he is then able to express his wishes. So far, all this seems unexceptionable. Children, of course, are fairly good at expressing their wishes non-verbally, before they learn what any words stand for. But it is hard to see how someone could ask someone else, in English, to pass the salt without knowing that 'salt' is the English for *salt*, and 'pass' for, *inter alia*, reaching something from one place into the hands of someone at another. (There is, of course, circumlocution. But such simply postpones, rather than answers, the question.) So though Augustine, like Russell, pretends to have uncannily accurate memories of his early childhood, it is plausible enough that things must have proceeded chronologically in something like the order Augustine sets out.

The next step in the chain is a picture this first step might suggest: "Every word has a meaning [*Bedeutung*]. This meaning is associated with the word. It is the object for which the word stands." (PI: §1) One might carp at the scope of the generalisation here. What does 'of' stand for, for example? But suppose we just say this: there is a very large category of (e.g., English) expressions, including all the noun-phrases and verb-phrases, such that (bracketing lexical ambiguity) for each such expression there is that for which it stands in meaning what it does (such a 'that' being an object in that broad sense of object in which to be an object is to be what might form a way for things$^{©}$ to be from a way for *a* thing to be). Perhaps more than this is needed for doing syntax. As far as it goes, though, it is hard to see why it is wrong.

What one might think, though, is: whatever is so of (e.g., English) words simply in virtue of their *meaning* what they do, more than that is drawn on in the ability Augustine claims to have come to have, to wit, an ability to express his wishes. Not that things might not have happened in the chronological order Augustine claims. Language acquisition is not what is at issue. In present terms, to be able to express one's wishes is, *inter alia*, to have a capacity to recognise what *thought* one would express in given words in given circumstances. Which would require, given the above, a capacity to recognise what applications would identify what was thus expressed as the thought it is. So that, drawing on that capacity, one could manage, e.g. when he wanted someone to pass the salt, to request that which would be *done* just where he got what he thus wanted. And now the point would be: what is required for pulling off such feats competently is more understanding than is contained merely in knowing what words *mean*. As with the words, 'Sid drinks Bloody Marys for breakfast', what the *words* 'Pass the salt' *mean* does not settle on its own how to negotiate one's way through issues of justice and fairness so as to arrive at asking for what he wants. Such is part of Wittgenstein's point in 1931 in insisting that understanding is not some operation which accompanies perceiving incidents of thought-expression, but rather a capacity to recognise how to operate with what was said. But *this* is a point about thoughts expressed, not one about sentences and what they, or their parts, *mean*.

4.3 Direction

On one of our three *viæ* no thought is expressed. Which leaves two ways in which a thought is identified as the thought it is (insofar as a thought may be so identifiable at all). First, one can name the way it represents things – such-and-such way. Second, one can identify its applications: there are those a thought would need to have to be such-and-such one, e.g., the one expressed on some occasion. Having these is just one feature by which a given thought may be distinguished from others. The thought Pia expressed *in re* Sid and Bloody Marys – the one for which she is rightly held responsible – is so distinguished from other thoughts which would also be of what the words used speak of. Which, in the circumstances, identifies it as the thought it is, insofar as there is any identifying some given such thought at all.

A thought identifiable by its applications *can* thereby (if in no other way) also be named. The thought Pia expressed of Sid's matinal beverage habits would sometimes be named in speaking of 'the thought that Sid drinks Bloody Marys at brunch'. One only needs to arrange for the words 'drinks', 'Bloody Mary', etc., to bear those understandings of drinking, being a Bloody Mary, etc., which they did in Pia's mouth. So, it seems, a thought can be approached from two directions: we can present it as the thought that/of such-and-such, spelling out the 'such-and-such', assigning it an appellation; or we can present it in specifying its applications. (Or, as in the example of the last section, we can mix the two: the thought is of someone being a Bloody-Mary-drinker, where such is to be taken as what would have *these* applications.)

The road between appellation and application thus seems, in general, two-way: fix an appellation, and the applications are whatever follow (things being as they are) from it being the thought so named (or nameable); fix the applications, and it is the thought which would have just *those*, however that might be named. Or, more modestly, fix *some* applications, and it is the thought distinguished from at least some others in its having those. On occasion, though, it seems as though things may run in the one direction or the other: either appellation or application may enjoy priority. Pia said, 'Sid drinks Bloody Marys at brunch.' We are supposing that she thus expressed a thought. So those words, in her mouth, formed an appellation for that thought. It is the thought named in those words, so understood. But, even given that she thus spoke of drinking Bloody Marys at brunch, etc., we cannot, in the above example, see what thought this is, thus what the appellation thus formed names, until we see for what applications Pia would thus rightly, justly, be held responsible. Here, then, priority runs from right to left (from applications to appelation).

To be sure, once we *have* an appellation, once it is given what thought the appellation names, there is no further work for applications to do. A thought is identified by its proprietary way of generalising over particular cases, by in just what cases it would be so (and in what not so) that things are as per that thought. This fixed, a thought's applications are just whatever they would thus be: what to do were things as per that thought is just whatever all those cases of things being as per the thought share *in re*, what, in them, the thing to do would be. Here priority runs from left to right.

A language provides a stock of devices for mentioning or expressing thoughts, thus devices for forming appellations: roughly its declarative sentences. There is, for example, the English, 'The laundry starched my shirts', used by Sid to complain to Pia. Suppose we assumed that each such device was itself a given appellation: for each one, *the* thought it would as such be an appellation of (would express or mention), or at least the thought of some given contextually fixed n-tuple of objects (in our example, some object, the 'laundry', some set of objects, 'Sid's shirts', and a time) – if relevant, up to equivalence between thoughts in when they would be true. Then, so long as one was speaking English, using English words to speak of what they do, priority would always run from left to right. Which might give us an important sense in which priority just does so run. *Punkt*.

English, or anyway the language English speakers speak, also provides us with a stock of devices for naming objects, common names such as 'Sid' and 'Pia' among them. But in the sort of use these devices have it is, anyway typically, not so that for each there is such a thing as 'the object it names'. There is no such thing as the person 'Sid', or 'Pia', names in English. Rather, when one uses the name 'Pia' for what it is for as such, he may be presumed to be using it to name some then-salient person known to some relevant community, or audience, by that name. If 'Pia' so used is to name such-and-such, the rest of the work in making this so is left to circumstance. One *might* see those devices a language provides for forming an appellation for a thought on this model, at least to this extent: the words, 'The laundry starched my shirts', used for what they are for speaking of, may be presumed to be naming some (then-salient) thought which would be (rightly, rationally) presumed by a relevant community or audience thus to be being so named. If the analogy holds, then the work of fixing just what thought this would be, like the work of fixing what object 'Pia', as used on an occasion named, would be left to circumstances. Priority might then work right to left.

The analogy does not, of course, fit exactly. 'Sid' is a name for an object, usually a person, usually one of the male persuasion. What one would do, *per se*, in using 'Sid' for what it is for stops just about there. Whereas 'starched the shirts', used for what it is for, would speak of some contextually determined instance as having *starched* some contextually determined (then to be presumed) shirts. *Mutatis mutandis* for 'drinks Bloody Marys at tea', 'is the breakfast of champions', and so on throughout English. So on the analogy, 'drinks Bloody Marys at tea', on a speaking of it, would have to speak of a certain way for an object (say, Sid, or his dog) to be, namely, that (salient) way which, in the circumstances of that speaking, a suitable community or audience would rightly, justly, presume to be the one which would then be spoken of as such. But now one might think: if for one to take Bloody Marys with his tea is really a way for an object to be, then regardless of the circumstances of the speaking, these words could only be used to speak of that way for an object to be which they do speak of as such in English, even if only on that particular aspect of the verb on which such things as English words can speak (provided that it *was* English which was then spoken). And, the idea would be, there is only one thing the words could then *rightly* be presumed to be speaking of, namely, precisely and only what those English words anyway do. We would thus be driven back to left-to-right priority.

For all said so far, what one might thus think *might* be so. But, viewed from this vantage point, one point of our present ideas, *application* and *language game*, is to open the claim to investigation; thus to expose it as a thesis rather than a truism. *Inter alia*, what is now open to investigation is the notion of a way for things$^{\copyright}$, or a thing, or n things, to be. English provides devices for naming such a way, e.g., 'starched all the shirts'. Might it not be that such a device, used on different occasions, might name different things – in other words, that on different occasions there might be different things being *that* way might be taken to be? An anchor for such investigation might be: a speaker (a thought-expresser) is correctly held responsible for just what it would be fair and just to hold him to. In the investigation one might thus conduct room is made for right-to-left priority.

If the idea to be investigated were correct, then language as such would be in the business of *Wahrsein*, that business for which Frege designs his countable, the thought (*Gedanke*). In Wittgenstein's time, and in ours, the thought that it is in that business, moreover, that the hallmark of a bit of language is its role in this, has been widespread common currency. All this despite the obvious features which mark language as designed for a different business entirely, namely, that of achieving the expression of thought, the authoring of representing-as. An expression of a language, for example, has what a thought must lack, namely, a syntax by which its *instances* may be identified as the expressions they visibly, or audibly, are – the marks of a content-bearer, whose content may remain to be determined, rather than, as with the thought, a content to be borne. The shape Wittgenstein gives to Frege's idea of an application, and the shape this takes in his notion *language game* provides just what we need, as Wittgenstein once put it, to 'rotate the axis of our investigation (with our real need as pivot)'.

Fix a thought and you fix its proprietary way of generalising. And now its applications are just those which the generalisation thus made would have. But just what might such a proprietary way be? Here one might apply Wittgenstein's 1931 idea of understanding as a capacity, and then (for a thinker of our sort) not one reducible to some specifiable way of achieving its results, or to the results which would thus be achieved. With which we can begin to approach a point made by Leibniz in 1703. He wrote,

> [O]ne might find a means of counterfeiting gold which would satisfy all the test which one had up to that point, but also then discover a new way of testing which would provide the means of distinguishing natural gold from this *artificial gold*. [...] [W]e could then have a *more perfect definition* of gold than we now have, and if the '*artificial gold*' could be made cheaply and in quantity [...] this *new test* would be of consequence, because by means of it one could preserve for the human race the advantage *natural gold* gives us in commerce by its rarity, and be provided with a material which is durable, uniform, easy to divide up, and recognizable and valuable in small quantities. (Leibniz 1703: 269–270)

For something to be gold is a way for it to be; a way which generalises over particular cases of a thing being as it is in its own proprietary way, e.g., one such as to capture, or reject that watch given Benno on his retirement. In 1703, Leibniz tells us, there is something that way would (justifiedly) be taken to be. To simplify, let us suppose that, on this way, to be gold is *ipso facto* to be yellow, and further, to be heavy, yellow, malleable and soluble only in aqua regia. But, Leibniz points out, gold being the sort of thing *it* is, it is open in principle for indefinitely many different considerations to bear on whether given items are to be counted as gold, so that it is open that the things just mentioned, or any given substitute for them, may not be decisive – may not capture the way *being gold* in fact generalises. Leibniz names some of these (what alchemists might have proven able to do, what proper chemists might then be able to do in response). Given these other considerations, then, what is it *really* for something to be gold? The answer Leibniz offers here is: when such a question arises (when there *are* such other considerations), one must look to the applications something being gold would have if one ruled one way or the other (that the artificial 'gold' he envisions was *gold*, or that it was not). A verdict *may* then be mandated by the applications it would be most reasonable to expect being gold to have. (A point also at the centre of Putnam's work.)

Back, then, to Benno's watch. '40 years and this.' Suppose Benno takes the watch home, removes the back, and discovers inside *steel* works. Has he been deceived? Well, what might one such as Benno, being kicked onto the *mesthoop* of retirement as he was, have expected? *Gold* works? Is this something reasonably to be expected of those by whom he was *weggebonjourd?* For all of their venality, might one fairly, justly, hold them, in and by their words ('And now a gold watch for your 40 years') be held responsible? Do not look for an answer to the above on what it would be for something to be gold. It is common currency that watches are not made of gold works. Such is not to be expected. Just here is the point which Wittgenstein's framework allows us to make after our axis of reference is turned as the notions *application* and *language game* permit it to be.

In *Investigations* §10, discussing the augmented builder-assistant game of §8, (where the builder can ask for 10 slabs at once, to go *there*), he remarks,

> What do the words of this language *signify?* What they signify – how would this manifest itself if not in the way they are to be used? And we have already described this.

The builder calls, say, 'F Würfel dorthin', and, by the rules of the game, the assistant is then to place 6 blocks where the builder points. Now what way would it be for there to be F *Würfel* at a given place (or at the place then referred to by that 'dorthin')? Wittgenstein's point: say what you like so long as the thought of things being the way you just mention would have those applications (as illustrated) which the rules of §8 would have. By which it is left open that there may be indefinitely many ways of saying this, and that for any given way (say, in the words, 'for there to be 6 blocks at that place'), whether this is a way or not depends on what is *thus* to be understood by there being 6 blocks at a place, thus by the applications what *your* words expressed would have are then fairly and justly to be taken to be.

The lessons learned from the collapse of the *Tractatus* inevitably brought Wittgenstein closer to an appreciation, and a sharing, of some of Frege's basic, central, insights. There is, for example, the very anti-Tractarian point Wittgenstein makes in 1933 in the *Blue Book*, "a picture [need have] no similarity with its object" (Wittgenstein 1958: 37). Representing-as neither exploits nor permits some common structure between it and *what* it so represents. For example, in *Investigations* §22 Wittgenstein considers Frege's idea that (as Frege puts it), "Where there is judgement, one can always crystallise out the thought thus acknowledged as true, and the judging does not belong to this" (Frege 1915: 271). Force is detachable from content. Wittgenstein does not say that this is wrong, but only, "This is only a mistake if ...", after which he indicates, imagistically, some of the *mis*readings it might engender, among which one which foists on us an idea overlapping with that idea of understanding Wittgenstein was concerned to reject in 1931: that understanding is a process by which *what* is understood (the thought grasped) is associated with some *Vertreter*, a sort of content-bearer, by which it is represented as decomposing into *such-and-such* content and *such-and-such* force bearer (as musical notation might decompose a passage into tones and dynamics). Such, again, is to misunderstand understanding, better conceived as a capacity, *inter alia*, one thus to decompose what was understood in any of indefinitely many different ways.

But there are limits to the issues Frege officially addresses. His countable, the thought, is destined for service in a particular enterprise, the business as such of being true. It is thus abstracted from the historical enterprise of the expression of thought by thinkers such as us. If thoughts are to be the sorts of things we express on occasion in expressing the thought (mass noun) that we do, then the abstraction has to be placed back into where it came from with due care to separating artefacts of the abstraction from what belongs to that historical enterprise as such. For example, it belongs to the abstraction that a *thought* cannot admit of interpretation. It is something *to be expressed*, so that given words may be interpreted as expressing *it*. But if such is to be an interpretation, it must not itself admit of interpretation. It is an understanding for words to bear, not itself a bearer of understandings. Such is the topic of a discussion in the *Blue Book* (roughly 33–39) in the course of which he writes:

> Now we might say that whenever we give someone an order by showing him an arrow [...] we *mean* the arrow in one way or another. And this process of meaning [...] can be repre-

sented by another arrow (pointing in the same or the opposite sense to the first). [...] I can, e.g., make a scheme with three levels, the bottom level always being the level of meaning. But adopt whatever model or scheme you may, it will have a bottom level, and there will be no such thing as an interpretation of that. To say in this case that every arrow can still be interpreted would only mean that I *could* always make a different model of saying and meaning which had one more level than the one I am using. (Wittgenstein 1933: 33–34)

Sid said, 'They starched the shirts.' Such, let us say, admits of understandings. Suppose, e.g., that the shirts had been 'starched' with disappearing starch, gone on brief contact with air, or with Shamylum, a new petroleum-based synthetic starch, or with casein. Are things thus as Sid said? Opportunity to assign Sid's words an understanding, an interpretation, and thereby answer a question how they were to be understood. But where we do thus answer the question *in* question, there is no further room (so far) for asking how *that* understanding is to be understood. This, however, should not be interpreted as meaning that there are understandings which do not themselves admit of understandings *tout court* – just a version of the idea, above, that *really*, at basic level, priority always runs right to left – appellation to application. For the last interpretation in a sequence of them – the question-stopper – *is* that only relative to the particular question which is thus stopped, or the particular circumstances in which such *is* the question to be answered. Which does not exclude other circumstances in which what before was not receptive to different understandings now is. This brings us to the next section.

4.4 An Illustration

In *Investigations* §81 Wittgenstein presents a manifesto and a programme:

> [...] Logic does not treat language – nor thinking – in the sense in which a natural science treats a natural phenomenon, and the most one could say is that we *construct* ideal languages. But the word 'ideal' here can be misleading, for it sounds as though these languages are better, more complete, than the languages in which we carry on our dealings; as if it takes a logician finally to show people what a proper sentence looks like.
>
> But all this can only appear in the proper light when one has achieved greater clarity about the concepts [for one] *to understand, to mean, to think*. For then it can also become clear what can seduce us (and did seduce me) into thinking that someone who utters a sentence and *means* it, or *understands* it thereby operates according to definite rules.

How *does* logic treat language (if at all)? Its laws are the laws of being true. Language is means for a thinker to enter that business, to represent truly or falsely. What might logic dictate as to how such means must work? And how did the

Tractatus misconceive such matters? Such are explicit and central concerns of the *Investigations*. They find there various more specific forms.

One simple idea here would be: logic speaks to language by virtue of common elements in logic's proper subject matter and in language's workings. In particular, there is the notion *way for things to be*, 'things' here indifferent between things© and given things. (In other terminology, *a* notion of a concept of things so being.) A thought is identified as the thought it is solely by the right side of a representing-as, that is, by a way for things© to be. At the same time, a way for things to be is the sort of thing a sentence of a language may be said to speak of. Now the idea would be: what a way for things© to be must be to be a way for a *thought* to represent things is what it also must be to be what a sentence (or a syntactic transform of it) speaks of; or at least what it must be to be the way a *thinker* represents things in (truth-evaluable) representing-as.

What demands, then, does logic impose on thoughts (as principal protagonists in the business of being true)? Here is one idea. A thought, so cast, is to be party of the first part in that exclusively two-party enterprise, truth. Party of the second being obliged only to exist, it thus falls on party of the first to exclude full stop any substantial role for a third party. Suppose the way *it* represented things permitted competing understandings: on an understanding of one sort, things would be as represented; on an understanding of another sort they would not (where neither sort of understanding is ruled out by that way for things© to be being what it is). Then, one might think, the thought would have failed in its duty of excluding third parties. For whether it was true or not would at least be liable to depend on further facts as to how (in given circumstances, say) one *was* to understand things being that way by which the thought was identified as the one it is. So a thought must not admit of understandings. *Mutatis mutandis* for the identifying way for things© to be.

This argument, though, on its own, at least, is specious. Suppose a thought did thus admit of competing understandings. Then there is a truth, that things© are that way the thought represents them on such-and-such understanding of their so being, and a falsehood that they are that way on such-and-such other understanding. But neither that truth nor that falsehood need be counted as the thought originally in question. If a thought is what poses, or fixes, a particular question of truth, we might just so speak that in such a case the question posed simply has no answer: by *fiat*, the word 'thought' is to be used in present connection such that neither the true thought nor the false one is that original thought which admits of understandings. That original thought, on this way of speaking, is, so far, neither true nor false. So far, then, no reason to insist that a way for things© to be, even one which identifies a thought, cannot admit of understandings.

One might balk at the idea that a *thought* might be neither true nor false. There may be reason to do so. After all, a thought was meant to be *just* that by which truth can come into question at all. One might insist that truth has not genuinely come into question until an *answerable* question has been posed – as, in our imagined case, it has not. Logic's business, as Frege conceives it, is to determine truth-preservation of a certain sort. Or, at worst, falsehood preservation. But there is nothing to be preserved until there is truth, or at worst, falsehood. Nothing so far for logic to take account of. Frege expressed this idea, a bit unfortunately, in *Grundgesetze* 2: §56. And it is reflected in logic itself, or at least in *Begriffsschrift*. Consider, with Frege, a 'propositional' logical constant, such as (syntax included) '__&__'. Such might be thought of as identifying, or standing in for, a form for a thought to take. And now, Frege repeatedly insists, all we need to attend to in defining this constant are the pairs of truth-values which might attach to truth-valued fillers of the above spaces. All we need say, that is, is that this form forms a true thought where both fillers are true, a false thought for any other combination of their truth-values. *Fertig*. Suppose one tried to place something not truth-valued in one of these places. What thought we would thus obtain is simply undefined. Or, at best, we would need to say: *no* thought is.

So the requirement on a thought, if it is to be any of logic's business, is that it be either true or false – a requirement reflected in logic's laws themselves, to wit, in the laws of excluded middle and of non-contradiction: anything of the form '__v~__', gives what that form is by definition, is true; anything of the form '__&~__' is false, again given how that form is defined. Though here, as Wittgenstein points out, we are apt to "predicate of the thing what lies in the manner of representing it" (Wittgenstein 1953: §104). The result that every *thought* is either true or false is still, so far, to be obtained, if at all, by stipulation: nothing is to be *called* a thought unless it is either true or false. Convenient, perhaps, for expounding logic. So far, nothing has been said as to whether a way for things© to be, even one which identifies a thought, may admit of understandings in our present sense. Such remains as much in the cards as ever.

What every thought must be is, so far, either true or false. It has not yet been said that a thought must be what *would* be, or would have been, either true or false no matter what (or so long as there was such a thought at all). Nor does logic as such require this. What we have so far is just that to apply logic to some body of thought one must have a right to suppose (on some reading of 'suppose') that all in the body is, in fact, either true or false. Nor does logic speak to when this condition would be satisfied. *Had* Sid's shirts been starched with a synthetic starch (Shamylum), or with 'disappearing' starch (on the model of disappearing ink, minutes after its application, undetectable to the casual wearer), it *might* be, for all it matters so far, that there would have been simply no saying whether the thought Sid expressed in complaining to Pia was true. But Shamylum, and disappearing starch, are fantasies. No reason to suppose that Sid did not in fact express either truth or falsehood. So far, then, no reason to suppose that all, or any, ways for things© to be must not admit of understandings.

But suppose that, for some other reason, someone wanted to insist that a thought, in his sense, is what could not but be either true or false no matter what. Such a move would rule out illusions of applications of logic (to *thoughts*), where some of the body of items to which this was applied were, in fact, of no form *defined* in logic. One might detect in it the same sort of desperation engendered by the idea that there must be 'incorrigible' statements if there is to be knowledge. In any case, with this move we would require, for a thought, ways for things© to be such that things could not but be such as to be those ways or not (so long as there were those ways for things© to be).

So far, the properties we found one might want to ascribe to thoughts (not permitting of understandings, being either true or false) were won by stipulation. Might one now similarly just stipulate that it is only to be called a thought if it would be true or false no matter what? Well, as Frege also often stresses, one cannot stipulate things into existence. If all you want of a thought is that it should be true or false no matter what, so far there may be nothing to investigate as to whether there are such things or not. *Mutatis mutandis*, perhaps, for a way for things© to be. But suppose that such is but one strand in a more tangled notion. We might want to suppose, for example, that thoughts, or at least some thought, have appellations; that is, are ones one might express or mention, and – some of them – ones some of us *have*, on occasion, expressed, or mentioned, in given words. For example, suppose that we can at least imagine me now expressing a thought in speaking of Sid's shirts as having been starched, or, more explicitly, mentioning one in speaking of 'the thought that Sid's shirts were starched'.

Now there are two things to be supposed of what we will deign to call a thought: truth or falsity no matter what, and mentionability – this last, perhaps, a feature of only some thoughts. And now we may ask of these two together whether we are thereby, defying Frege, stipulating something into existence. Bluntly put, how could we ever mention a way for things to be which, *per se*, did not admit of understandings?

Stipulating into existence is thus brought into question because, though with Frege we might think of thoughts as "interacting with each other" as they do entirely independent of us, with mentioning, or speaking of, comes the idea of an understanding. Mentioning, or speaking of something is something a speaker, or his words, may be *understood* to do. So that where there are two candidates for the role of what was mentioned/spoken of, there must be something in the understanding the mention bore – in how the mentioner, and his mention, might rightly have been understood – by which to choose between these if either is to be that which was in fact mentioned/spoken of. Which allows us to approach the question whether what was stipulated above exists by reference to the nature of the understandings mentions of the sort we make do, or might possibly, bear. Here our notions *application* and *language game*, may be applied in distinguishing different candidates for the role of *the mentioned*.

Sid complains that his shirts have been starched. What ways for things© to be, if any, did he thus speak of? We are not here positioned to discuss this question. We were not privy to the mention. In any case, we are only imagining one, poorly described at that. But a way for things© to be is identified by its proprietary way of generalising. Of which we can pose questions such as this: Nuns once used egg whites to stiffen their collars. If Sid's collars were so stiffened, were they starched in the meaning of Sid's act? The answers 'Yes' and 'No' differ in the applications there would be, given them, if what Sid said were so – e.g., in how one might go about rectifying the situation (were he so inclined). Which is right is thus to be decided, if at all, by for what Sid is justly held responsible. But need there be an answer? Need there be anything in how Sid was to be understood in the circumstances by which either 'Yes' or 'No' might be seen to be correct?

Must such questions always have right answers? There is no reason *a priori* to insist they must. And a cursory look at the notions of justice and fairness certainly suggests otherwise. Is it Tarquin's fault that Pia tripped over those skates, or Pia's for not knowing better (since this is where he always leaves them)? In any case, there is no must about it; certainly not if we follow Wittgenstein. For so doing, we would conceive understanding as a capacity: not one identified by how it works (some identifiable way of generating correct understandings); nor one to recognise some panoply of independently specifiable things (e.g., some independently identifiable stock of cases of things being the way Sid spoke of); but rather via those of us who may be supposed to have the capacity to sufficient extent – e.g., those who, sufficiently aware of, and sensitive to, the circumstances, might be expected to have understood Sid.

If our present question is to be answered by reference to capacities of the sort just sketched, then it is always open, for any given case of mentioning, or speaking of, things being thus and so, that, *in re* some conceivable particular case – some conceivable circumstance – there is simply *no* answer to the question whether *this* is things being the way in question. Where this happened, there would be two perfectly good candidate ways of generalising over particular cases, with nothing to choose between them, nothing by which one or the other was the way here mentioned. For all it so far matters, those ways may meet the first clause of the stipulation: they may be ways things© would be, or not, no matter how things© were. But neither, nor any other way which met the stipulation, could now correctly claim the title, 'the mentioned way'. Correlatively, the way in fact mentioned, to which Sid gave the appellation, 'They starched my shirts', whether or not we grace it with the title, 'a way for things© to be', is *not* a way things would be no matter what.

With which we see how, in the last proposal above, something was being stipulated into existence. Nor will it do to stipulate that, in matters of logical form, what is not true is false. For what logic deals in are forms for a *thought* to take, forms whose proper parts are thoughts wherever these parts are to be either true or false. And if thoughts are conceived as at present one cannot just *stipulate* thoughts into existence which, if not true, are false. Just what is the falsehood in such a case – what the way for things© to be which they are not? (cf. Aristotle). None of which, to repeat, is of any concern to logic. For all logic requires for an application to some body of *thought*, that is, of things we think, is that, for purposes of the application, one be entitled to suppose, or assume that all relevant countables are either true or false.

A main point of Wittgenstein's later philosophy is to open our eyes to possibilities which a philosopher, dazzled, for example, by the 'crystalline' purity of logic might overlook in locating logic's demands on what it governs as such in relation to language, or to the things we think. The aim, as another philosopher put it, is to show us what it is not compulsory to think. Seeing the influence of Frege, or his central ideas, on later Wittgenstein is seeing, *inter alia*, just where and why Wittgenstein's later work departs from the *Tractatus*, and also where, and how, it elaborates Frege. Seeing Wittgenstein thus to relate to Frege is, I suggest, a prerequisite for approaching him as a *philosopher* (however intolerant of *Geschwätz*), rather than as one out to extinguish that discipline, or replace it by some newly discovered form of self-help. Later Wittgenstein *can* be seen as a continuation, a further unfolding, of Frege's contribution to philosophy, not always as Frege himself might have done, nor rarely as others of Frege's heirs attempt; but with a greater sympathy for, and understanding of, Frege's insights than few if any of those others have a right to claim.

References

Frege, Gottlob (1879) *Begriffsschrift*, Halle: Louis Nebert.
Frege, Gottlob (1882) Letter to Anton Marty, 29.8.1882, in: *Gottlob Freges Briefwechsel*, G. Gabriel, F. Kambartel, C. Thiel (eds.), Hamburg: Meiner, 1980, 117–120.
Frege, Gottlob (1892) "17 Kernsätze zur Logik", in: *Nachgelassene Schriften*, H. Hermes, F. Kambartel, F. Kaulbach (eds.), Hamburg: Meiner, 1983, 189–190.
Frege, Gottlob (1903) *Grundgesetze der Arithmetik*. Vol. 2, Jena: Herman Pohle.
Frege, Gottlob (1915) *Meine grundlegenden logischen Einsichten*, in: *Nachgelassene Schriften*, H. Hermes, F. Kambartel, F. Kaulbach (eds.), Hamburg: Meiner, 1983.
Frege, Gottlob (1918) "Der Gedanke – Eine Logische Untersuchung", in: *Beiträge zur Philosophie des deutschen Idealismus* 1 (2), 58–77.
Frege, Gottlob (1919a) "Aufzeichnungen für Ludwig Darmstädter", in *Nachgelassene Schriften*, H. Hermes, F. Kambartel, F. Kaulbach (eds.), Hamburg: Meiner, 1983, 273–277.
Frege, Gottlob (1919b) "Die Verneinung – Eine Logische Untersuchung", in: *Beiträge zur Philosophie des deutschen Idealismus* 1 (3/4), 143–157.
Leibniz, Gottfried Wilhelm (1703) *Nouveaux Essais Sur l'Entendement Humain*, J. Brunschwig (ed.), Paris: Garnier-Flammarion, 1966.
Russell, Bertrand (1903) Letter of 24.5.1903, in: *Gottlob Freges Briefwechsel*, G. Gabriel, F. Kambartel, C. Thiel (eds.), Hamburg: Meiner, 1980, 89–90.
Russell, Bertrand (1904) Letter of 12.12.1904, in: *Gottlob Freges Briefwechsel*, G. Gabriel, F. Kambartel, C. Thiel (eds.), Hamburg: Meiner, 1980, 96–98.
Waismann, Friedrich (1984) *Wittgenstein und der Wiener Kreis*, B. F. McGuinness (ed.), Frankfurt am Main: Suhrkamp.
Wittgenstein, Ludwig (1922) *Tractatus Logico-Philosophicus*, London: Routledge and Kegan Paul.
Wittgenstein, Ludwig (1929) "Some Remarks on Logical Form", in: *Proceedings of the Aristotelian Society*, Suppl. Vol. 9, 162–171.
Wittgenstein, Ludwig (1953) *Philosophical Investigations*, Oxford: Basil Blackwell.
Wittgenstein, Ludwig (1958) *The Blue and The Brown Books*, Oxford: Basil Blackwell.

Juliet Floyd
Lebensformen: Living Logic

Abstract: Wittgenstein's explicitly interlocutory style of philosophizing and writing, along with his use of the notion of *Lebensform*, first appeared in 1936–1937. Here we give an account of why. *Lebensform* plays an important elucidatory role in Wittgenstein's later conception of philosophy, and is distinguished from the notion of *Lebenswelt* familiar in phenomenology. In utilizing the notion of "form", rather than "world", Wittgenstein indicates his preoccupation with the question, "What is the nature of the logical?" It is argued that the analysis of logic contained in Turing's "On computable numbers, with an application to the *Entscheidungsproblem*" (1936/7) stimulated Wittgenstein's writing of *Philosophical Investigations*, leading him to deepen the notion of a "language-game", to eliminate the idea of *Kultur* as foundational, and to focus on the general idea of rule-following. Turing's paper, in turn, was indebted to Wittgenstein's conception of philosophical method, especially the idea of comparing ordinary human calculative behavior with words to the mechanical workings of a calculus. Wittgenstein's mature philosophical method, expressed in the *Investigation's* multilogue shifts in voice, is, we argue, both logically and philosophically necessitated. And his conception of *Lebensformen* makes an important and novel intervention in philosophy that is relevant for our times.

Overview

The notion of *Lebensform* enters Wittgenstein's writing as a response, not only to his own development, but also to the development of philosophy more generally as he saw it unfolding in 1936. In what follows we shall account for the notion's role from both these perspectives, assigning it an important historical role in 20th-century philosophy. Within Wittgenstein's own evolution, we shall see how he came to link *Lebensform* to a broadened perspective on "logic" and on philosophy in his mature writings. To show the historical and philosophical importance of this, we outline the mutual impact Wittgenstein and Turing had on one another in the mid-1930s. A key shift occurred in Wittgenstein's attitude toward "rule-following" in 1936–1938, discernible in his early draftings of *Philosophical Investigations*. It is argued that Turing's resolution of the *Entscheidungsproblem* in his classic paper (1936/7) applies a Wittgensteinian perspective to the idea of a "logic", and this in turn provided Wittgenstein with a stimulus to rethink his notion of a "language-game". As both Wittgenstein and Turing appreciated, there is a need for *Lebensformen* at the foundations: the human embedding of "phraseology" in life, explored in dialogue and discussion.

In section 1, we contrast the term "*Lebensform*" with that of "*Lebenswelt*", the latter a commonly invoked notion in philosophy (especially in the phenomenological tradition, cf. Mulhall 1990) which nevertheless does not occur in Wittgenstein's corpus. It is explained why it does not, and a brief sketch is given of developments in Wittgenstein's thinking about Life and World to motivate the contrast. In section 2, we characterize the initial appearance of *Lebensform* in Wittgenstein's writing beginning in the fall of 1936, at just the time he broke through to his later, interlocutory style of writing and began drafting *Philosophical Investigations*. A distinction is drawn between his uses of the notions of "tribe" and "*Kultur*" in *The Blue and the Brown Books* and his procedures in the *Investigations*. Section 3 ventures an explanation of why it is that Wittgenstein chose to delete the term *Kultur* from his manuscript from this point on. The claim is that reading Turing's "On computable numbers, with an application to the *Entscheidungsproblem*" (1936/7) sometime between the spring of 1936 and the spring of 1937 helped to crystallize Wittgenstein's mature conception of philosophical method and grammar, with its *human* analysis of the notion of a "step" in a formal system of logic. Section 4 explains the importance of Turing's "domestication" of the sublime character of logic as traditionally conceived, sketching how Wittgenstein's rule-following remarks were concertedly developed in response to it, thereby deepening the whole idea of a "language-game". Turing himself may be said to have applied some of Wittgenstein's most important methodological insights in *The Blue and Brown Books* in his (1936/7) paper. The idea of *Lebensform* is implicit in the insight, discernible in the heart of Turing's argumentation, that, as Wittgenstein would later insightfully write, "Turing's 'Machines'. These are *humans* who calculate" (RPP I: §§1096 ff.). Section 5, a conclusion, assembles a synthesis of these points in order to explicate *Lebensform* as a critical, while nevertheless infrequently used term in Wittgenstein's philosophy and an important notion for philosophy today.

1 *Lebenswelt* vs. *Lebensform*

With regard to philosophical history in the large, it is interesting to observe that the notion of *Lebensform* was deployed not infrequently in metaphysical, biological and religious tracts of the 19th century, and enjoyed increasingly wider circulation through the early part of the 20th century. It reached an initial high point of usage in 1934–1936, at just the time when Wittgenstein was attempting to put the *Philosophical Investigations* together, and he himself began to use the term. Interestingly, the usage of *Lebensform* peaked again in the 1990s (see Figure 1).

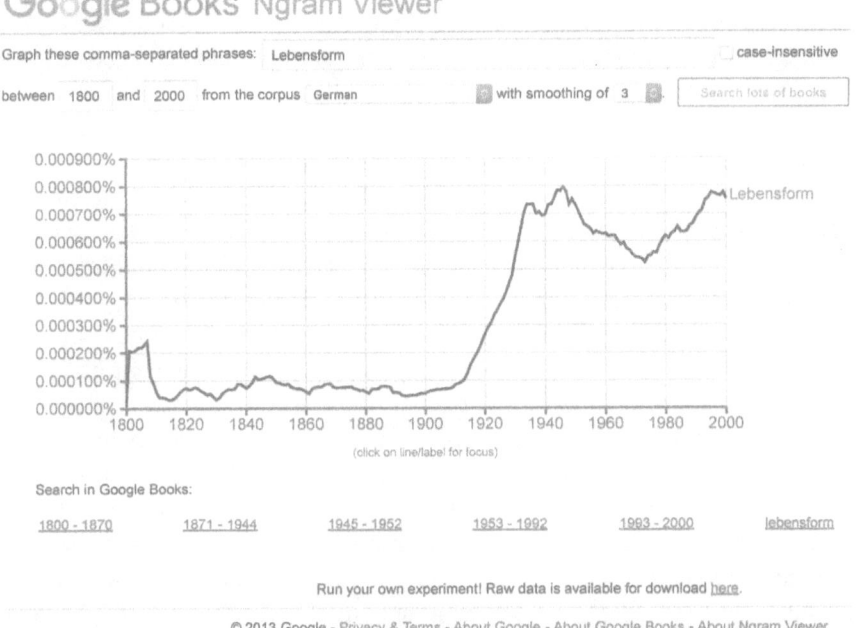

Figure 1[1]

In this broadly historical sense, Wittgenstein's mature philosophy is a critical intervention in 20th-century philosophy. It offers a philosophical response to the rapid evolution, disruption, and variety of modern life, especially the massive biologicization, automation, and anthropologization of thinking about life itself. With his notion of *Lebensform*, which entered his writing just as he began to compose the *Philosophical Investigations* (1936–8), Wittgenstein makes a critical response, one of tremendous philosophical significance for his time, as well as for ours.

Above all, we must remember that in the *Investigations* Wittgenstein is reflecting, not on *what* is given (as if *Lebensformen* is the answer to *that*) but, rath-

---

[1] Accessed October 14, 2017 at https://books.google.com/ngrams/graph?content=Lebensform&year_start=1800&year_end=2000&corpus=20&smoothing=3&share=&direct_url=t1%3B%2CLebensform%3B%2CCc0.

er, on what the whole idea of givenness *is*. This means that we must read him carefully and reflectively, not directly, when he writes, in the less polished second part of the *Investigations*, that "What is to be accepted, the given, is – one might say – *forms of life*" (PPF: xi, §345). The point is to explore the difficulties of givenness and how it may or should play a role in philosophy, not to theorize or accept how things are – as if the defense or description of a "given" culture or *Lebensform* were a task that he set himself. This quietist, "conservative" Spenglerian idea he studiously avoids in the *Investigations*, remaining at a more schematic level.

To see this, it helps to contrast his uses of the notion of *Lebensform* with the notion of "*Lebenswelt*" or "life world", a familiar, central term of phenomenology. Sometimes this latter notion is drawn in to clarify Wittgenstein's later philosophical stance. But for all the many resonances between these terms, I think it important that "*Lebenswelt*" does not occur in Wittgenstein's corpus, whereas "*Lebensform*" eventually – even if sparingly – does. What is the contrast?

Lebenswelt (or for non-rational, biological aspects of animals, *Umwelt*, as in (von Uexküll 2010)) is an actual, embedded, meaningful environment for a living being (a human or other kind of animal). It forms a kind of subject matter, an unfolding field of meaning that may be directly illuminated and described. This stands in contrast to Wittgenstein's mature idea of *Lebensformen*, which may elucidate and be elucidated, but only through reflection, variation, truncation, and multivalent embedding of arguments, grammatical procedures and language-games in partly imagined snapshots of possible or actual forms of life. *Lebensform* is a notion rarely invoked by Wittgenstein because it does not form a subject matter or field of endeavor, but a kind of philosophical norm of elucidation.

The point of Wittgenstein's later method is not to describe preexisting grammatical rules, but instead to investigate situations in which grammar runs out: limits where we are not able to project our words neatly into life. He is above all, after at least 1934, a philosopher of incompleteness. When we are not quite sure what to say, we are taught by the *Investigations* to be wary of the tendency to wheel in falsely substantival accounts of what undergirds or constitutes the "life" of signs ("consciousness", "human nature", "culture", "rules of conduct", "meaning", "sense"). Instead, we are asked to investigate and characterize uses of language by way of the comparative method of language-games: to explore, press, question and contest a variety of uses of grammatical forms. As the opening of *The Blue Book* makes clear, this self-consciously inherits and generalizes Frege's advice in *The Foundations of Arithmetic*, when he too had complained that, unsure what to say, we are often inclined in philosophy to "invent anything we please" as a signified reference for our words ([1884] 1974: Introduction) – often a vague and unscrutinized notion of a "state of mind" or "mental image". Wittgenstein's later philosophical activity too may be thought of as – in a very broad sense – logical, insofar as in it we are immersing ourselves in our lives with language so as to explore the very idea of what it is to see one thought as different from or the same as another, what it is to make a claim upon another person, and what it is that these very ideas may and may not depend upon.

Thus it is important that Wittgenstein's uses of language-games, unlike the phenomenologists' descriptions of the Lifeworld, belong to a critical thinking through of what it is that does and does not belong, properly speaking, to our reasoning and claiming in lives with words.[2] We might say that he takes on logic from within phenomenology, not by trying to break or get behind it, but by domesticating it. And here it is useful to reflect on the critical response he is making in the *Investigations* to his earlier thought, re-embedding his ideas in a different philosophical surrounding, a different conception of what allows for philosophy. In terms of Wittgenstein's own philosophical development, there are, characteristically, not only shifts but also continuities in his handling of the notions of world and life. These are instructive.

In the *Tractatus* the world and life are said to be "one" (TLP 5.621) – seemingly approaching the idea of *Lebenswelt*. This equation, however, occurs as the culmination of a distinctive line of thought, one that works through realism ("the world is everything that is the case" (TLP 1)), to solipsism ("I am my world" (TLP 5.63)), and then into the collapse of each into the other. What is missing here, notably, are *Lebensformen* as they are conceived in Wittgenstein's mature philosophy: a struggle for the *I* through a struggle with the *you* and the *we*, the *where* and the *why*.

Wittgenstein's *Tractarian* argument, at its most schematic, is, implicitly, logico-grammatical. Suppose I take solipsism to be true. Then, to express it, I would properly need to add "I think" before every assertion or judgment I make (as Kant insisted, formally and synthetically, one is always able to do). But then, though solipsism would be thereby expressed, the wind would be taken out of its sails. For the "I" would thereby be left an idling wheel, deprived of its grip, and hence its ability to voice any particular, differentiated perspective on the world. "I take it to be ..." would, if universally so used, come to nothing but "It is". Pure realism. Or pure idealism. Either way, I would have lost *my* I, *my* world, in embracing "the philosophical I" (TLP 5.62 ff.).

Strictly thought through – so this schematic line of thought goes – we are led to idealism (or skepticism, or solipsism) ineluctably from realism, while at the same time realism leads, when it is strictly thought through, to the vanishing

---

[2] Cf. Floyd 2016, Grève 2017, Kuusela 2013, Kuusela 2016.

of the "I" as a specific object in the world.³ Realism and idealism are shown to be two sides of one coin. And in this way both the I and the world, taken as objects or everywhere applicable concepts, are powerless, unutterable, not up to the task of elucidating the nature of thought, or representation, or the logical – which are after all the most all-permeating forms of form itself, according to the *Tractatus*. – What is "transcendental" in the *Tractatus* shows itself in our putting together sentences that become empty, or tautological, and this is something which saying and informing ourselves about what is the case will not elucidate, but which shows itself in logic, as we reflect on what in general saying is (cf. TLP 6.13).

This abstracted, schematic train of thought around self and world reverberates with certain turns of argumentation in *Philosophical Investigations*, well after Wittgenstein had surrendered the *Tractatus*'s idea of a general propositional form. However important the differences between the *Tractatus* and the later philosophy, the representation of a dialectic between realism and idealism, lodged in the significance of voicing, valuing, saying how things appear to me, and to you, remains a major arena of Wittgenstein's preoccupations with world and life. In his mature writings, however, the schematic *Tractarian* approach is fleshed out more, explicitly drawn into the setting of multilogue, self-revealing, interlocutory "voicings" (PIr: §§24, 402), an exploration of the nature of the distinctions we draw in speech between "inner" and "outer".⁴ The "where" of the "I" lives, grammatically speaking, in its friction with the "we" and the "you" and the "that", in point and counterpoint, in efforts to speak for and with one another – something Cavell was the first to highlight as central to Wittgenstein's (as well as Austin's) procedures ([1965] 2002). The self's significance is revealed in certain emptinesses – just as in the *Tractatus* – but these now emerge naturally in the course of philosophical efforts to locate myself by identifying the genuinely apposite philosophical and meaningful remark.

The *Investigations* suggests that the "I" can appear nowhere else, though it is for this reason easy to let it slip through our fingers as we allow others to speak for us, then speak for others, then for ourselves, then discover that we are out of tune, remodulate, and finally depart. Wittgenstein does not – because he cannot – avoid having others try to think for themselves in response to him (PIr: Preface). His specific forms of interlocutory writing inscribe this point. And in this way the *Investigations* makes clearer and more explicit than his earlier writing

---

3 There are many other byways and complexities in the development of Wittgenstein's thinking about how to overcome the idea of a complex soul, and solipsism. Helpful treatments are Stern 1994, Stern 2011 and Sluga 2018.
4 Cf. Laugier 2007, Laugier 2015.

had that, insofar as language can be conceived as a calculus (something we offload onto, so that we do not have to think; something that works on us as if a kind of mechanism; something constituting thought by way of rules and step-by-step calculation), it is nevertheless spoken and responsive language that lend it its specific characteristics.

In the end the idea of a calculus or language-game must be represented from within the perspective of human activities, a constant effort at embedding and re-embedding uses of spoken words in *Lebensformen*. We are constantly engaged in ushering forward words and procedures. The *Investigations* asks us to repeatedly reflect on this and characterize it. For words and grammatical procedures too are forms of (human) life: there is no "meta-level" apart from them. We *herd* words, as Cavell has put it ([1988] 2013: 35) – which means that they require buffeting and shepherding and examining and continual re-domestication by us if they are not to run wild among us. Domestication is hardly a matter of building a fence or determining a customary rule or convention or contract for an animal. It may be defeated by biology or by accident, but also by failure to mutually train and enculturate.

In this way Wittgenstein's idea of *Lebensformen* plays an elucidatory role of a crucial kind in his mature thought. It points the way toward a better situated notion of language-game, a less naive treatment of the ideas of meaning and calculus than were his earlier discussions in *The Blue and Brown Books*. I have elsewhere characterized its appearance in Wittgenstein's work, and the work it must do, as *logical*, in the sense that I take Wittgenstein to have worked through a kind of analytical regression of analysis itself, a working backwards to that which is not intrinsically simple, but is to be acknowledged *as* simple: exhibited, grasped *as* ordinary, integrated into our responses as something "natural" (Floyd 2016). His chronological development mirrors this analytic one. For the notion of *Lebensform* entered his writing quite late, only in 1936–7 – that is, only after the point when he stopped dictating to his students and began writing the *Investigations*. In this sense the notion belongs to his fully mature conception of philosophical method.

2 1936–7: Enter *Lebensformen*

The entrance of *Lebensform* into Wittgenstein's writing coincides with the failure of his effort to revise the dictated *Brown Book* into a manuscript in the autumn of 1936. During this time, his Cambridge fellowship having ended the summer before, he retreated to Norway to compose the book he had long attempted to write. The manuscript *Eine Philosophische Betrachtung* (EPB, i.e., MS 115), currently only published in German, gives us a documentation of the resulting manuscript. He began revising *The Brown Book* in September 1936. But by November, after 292 pages of writing, he gave up, writing that "this whole attempt at a revision is worthless" (MS 115: 292).

What is most notable about the first occurrence of the term *Lebensform* in this work – its first appearance, so far as we know, in his written corpus – is that it occurs in the midst of his trying to imagine a "use of language" *as* a culture [*Kultur*]. He imagines this, but soon clarifies, specifying that imagining a use of language actually means imagining a "*Lebensform/Form des Lebens*". And from here on imagining a language will mean imagining this *rather* than a culture. The remarks ultimately lead to Wittgenstein's decision to *delete* the notion of culture [*Kultur*] from his philosophical procedures, replacing it by *Lebensform*.

"*Kultur*" occurs in EPB twice, other than one point where Wittgenstein quotes from Spengler on the comparison between cultural periods and family resemblances (MS 115: 56). The first occurrence leads to Wittgenstein's explicit rejection of a Spenglerian approach:

> If we were asked about the nature of the punishment, or about the nature of the revolution, or on the nature of knowledge, or of cultural decay [*kulturellen Verfalls*], or of the sense of music [*Sinnes für Musik*], we should not now attempt to characterize what is generally common to all cases – that, which they all really are, – therefore an ideal which is contained in them all; but instead examples, as it were centers of variation. (EPB: 190, MS 115: 221)

In the second occurrence, Wittgenstein uses "*Kultur*" in the context of an imagined scenario in which one might be able to fix a "gap" [*Kluft*] between dark blue or red and light blue or red in the context of a language where people group green and red, and blue and yellow respectively together. Here the "phenomenological" issue of color, and the distinction between a grammatical and an experiential point, is precisely what is at stake. Let us quote the passage in full:

> 108. Imagine a use of language (a culture [*Kultur*]) in which there is a common name for green and red, and one for blue and yellow. Think, for instance, that in the surrounding nature, people perceive a constant transition from red to green and from green to red, as we see in the autumn on many leaves, which are not first yellow and then red, but which pass through a dark, iridescent tone, from the green to the red. Similarly, it also happens with blue and yellow in what they see around them. As the evening sky is sometimes blue in the east and goes westwards over a light gray in yellow. For these people, red and green always belong together. They are two poles of the same. If they want to distinguish between red and green in their language, they add to the common word one of two adverbs ... the words 'bright' or 'dark'. When asked whether these two colorings (one red and one green) have something in common, they are inclined to answer: Yes, both are ...

> Conversely, I could also think of a language (and that means a form of life [*Lebensform/Form des Lebens*]), which fixes a gap between dark red and light red, etc. (MS 115: 237–239)

From this point on, Wittgenstein no longer uses *Kultur* to characterize his imaginings of uses of language. The term does not appear in *Philosophical Investigations* at all – surely something intentional. He is off and running with a more mature conception of philosophical method, one in which *Kultur* is extruded. This is partly why he comes to feel that his revision of *The Brown Book* was "worthless".

In Wittgenstein's mature mode of philosophizing, we appreciate the multifaceted character of a logical (grammatical) point by varying the forms of language-games in which a particular procedure (say of naming, sorting, collecting or contrasting) may be said to occur. We appreciate the complexity of grammar in a particular game in the way we appreciate a facial expression, through a field of variation.[5] There are procedures involved: we can come to appreciate "what is common" to a "family" of phenomena. For example, a family of curves or geometrical constructions may appear at first blush to look quite different from one another. PI §19 offers an example: the "degenerate" hyperbole, presumably one or two straight lines coinciding with the *x* or *y* axis which do not have the *look* that we ordinarily expect a hyperbole to have. We see that what it is to be "the same" may indeed be fully structured, but we must regard this, not as something that can be given directly, or causally, or perceptually, or even by way of a mathematical equation or expression, without further ado. Making it intelligible requires *our* work in questioning, ordering and clarifying what we mean.

Wittgenstein's analogy between facial features and logical features of expressions – appearing already in his early philosophy – was intended to be a substitute for Russell's quasi-sensory, Platonic notion of "acquaintance" with logical form.[6] Even after Russell had given up his early ideas about logical form and debated revisions of these with Wittgenstein in 1912–1913, even after he accepted neutral monism, still Russell regarded universals as objects of direct mental acquaintance.[7] Wittgenstein always agreed with Russell that we are "acquainted" with grammar and logical form, but he always disagreed with Russell's way of conceiving what "acquaintance" *is*. So he worked hard to shepherd Russell's notion of singular, immediate, incorrigible, direct mental contact with

---

5 Cf. Diamond [1968] 1991, Floyd 2018.
6 Cf. Floyd 2018.
7 Cf. Russell 1936, a stimulus for Wittgenstein's work with *Lebensform*, as may be seen in Benoist's discussion (in this volume) of "Cause and Effect: Intuitive Awareness" (1937, PO: 368–426) and in RFM III §71, VII §§17, 21.

objects or universals or logical forms back down into everyday life, domesticating and humanizing it. In everyday life to be "acquainted" with a person requires comportment, culture, conversation: looking, conversing, being corrected, and listening, fallibly, *to* the person. "Acquaintance" in an everyday sense lets objects of acquaintance show *themselves* to us as we consider alternative possibilities, choices, ways they might have been, and so on. This is the way – and in real, ordinary life it is the *only* way – in which we can hope to achieve acquaintance. As we analyze and "get acquainted with" concepts, it is as if we are sorting and resorting a living, well-thumbed library of books, getting acquainted with its contents through potentialities of re-ordering it (cf. BB: 47).

In every period of Wittgenstein's philosophizing we are dealing with an analysis of the very idea of philosophical analysis. At each point we see him reacting to limits and contingencies, not with further theoretical explanation, but rather with an admission of the need for simplicity, analogy, and elucidation. Here, in the setting of 1936, he has given up the idea that culture is a necessary backdrop to acquaintance. In fact, he is showing that it is not the way forward in gauging how we are to understand our general notions of meaning, understanding, and logical necessity. Instead, the social and the cultural must be evaluated, ingested and worked through in his procedures, so that their aspects may be seen to be embedded, transformed into something more primordial. Only so is a philosophy of culture in a critical sense to be had.[8]

The philosophical achievement here is a dynamic, procedural conception *of* the logical, of logical form as something *in* and *of* life itself. This is clarified by emphasizing that it is only in his mature thought that Wittgenstein successfully manages to embed logic *in* life, as something *of* life, ubiquitizing it in terms of criteria and procedures in our everyday lives. Investigations of these criteria and procedures show us the roles of voicing and speaking, of habit and questioning, the lives of words and ourselves with them as part of reality.

The *Investigations* appeal, as logical thinking always does, to imagined contrasts and possibilities of the ways things could or might or must be: they erect *possible* shapings of going on "in the same way" – where of course this latter phrase must itself be embedded in a recognizable procedure to do work (this is one point made *ad nauseam* in the rule-following passages in the *Investigations*). These possible going-ons bear the stamp of being shareable, though not necessarily shared, and they are always contestable (Wittgenstein constantly contests them).

---

8 Cf. Cavell [1988] 2013.

Here we build directly on Cavell, who has always rejected the idea that "forms of life" in Wittgenstein serve to establish the social, conventional or artificial nature of human language – too often the usual view of the matter. He notes that Wittgenstein's writing in the *Investigations* involves both a horizontal inflection of "form of life" – one oriented toward the ethnological or conventional – and a vertical, evolutionary and biological one (Cavell [1988] 2013). These notions have different valences, but give rise to specific harmonies and intersections and tensions: they lend one another depth. In this multi-dimensional image, "natural reactions" (PIr: §185), "fictitious natural history" (PPF: xi, §365; cf. PIr: §524, discussed in Floyd 2010), and humankind's "common ways of acting" (PIr: §§201–206, 489) are homes of the notion of form of life, which is put to use in an investigation of modifications of our lives as talkers (animals and our animality are not exempted from its purview, cf. PIr: §§493, 647, 650; PPF: i, §1). Everywhere the notion of *Lebensform* proceeds by way of (talk about) comparisons (*Vergleichsobjekte*; cf. PIr: §130) – analogies woven within, around, and apart from one another, traced step by step, broken apart and reconfigured and gone beyond – rather than being described.

A clue to this not-merely-being-social-or-conventional is given at the beginning of Part II xi of the *Investigations*, now known, I think misleadingly, as "Philosophy of Psychology: A Fragment" (PPF) – misleading because Wittgenstein is explicitly engaged here in a struggle to retain the notion of the logical as opposed to the merely psychological, is still pursuing the *de*-psychologizing of logic itself, as Frege had before him.[9] In PPF: xi, §111 we are introduced to a primordial distinction in connection with "aspect-seeing":

> 111. Two uses of the word "see".
> The one: "What do you see there?" – "I see this" (and then a description, a drawing, a copy). The other: "I see a likeness in these two faces" – let the man to whom I tell this be seeing the faces as clearly as I do myself.
> What is important is the categorial difference between the two 'objects' of sight.
>
> 112. The one man might make an accurate drawing of the two faces, and the other notice in the drawing the likeness which the former did not see.
>
> 113. I observe a face, and then suddenly notice its likeness to another. I see that it has not changed; and yet I see it differently. I call this experience "noticing an aspect".
>
> 114. Its causes are of interest to psychologists.
>
> 115. We are interested in the concept and its place among the concepts of experience. (PPF: xi, §§111–115)

---

9 Cf. Cavell [1965] 2002.

"Noticing an aspect", or seeing a "likeness between two faces" involves bringing them together into a space through responses which shape and determine "sameness", but not by the straightforward application of a concept ("sad", "happy") to a plurality of objects.[10] What is important is our bringing these two particular faces together in a comparison, a re-shaping of "same". An analogy with ratios helps here: 2/3 is "the same" as 6/9. But 2 is not "the same" as 6, and 3 is not "the same" as 9, and the procedure of dividing in practice by halving, vs. by ninthing, may differ drastically. In order to make good on an experience of the "sameness" or "likeness" of the ratios, we need a system of comparison, one it took a long time to develop: procedures that allow us to calculate, step-by-step, when we have "the same" and when we have something "different" (cross-multiplying, substituting, balancing through addition and subtraction, and so on). In that system of ratios, every individual element may differ, and still we get "the same".

In the case of a "likeness" between two faces, we similarly need to determine a mode of comparison to make out the particular shade of "same" that is at issue. This is in general not to be established through a system of calculation, as in mathematics. In fact in certain sociological contexts a mathematical comparison may wholly mislead us, taking on the false face of an algebra, becoming difficult to disentangle.[11] Grantings of samenesses set up inferences and seeming necessities. If you say "Do you see the likeness between those two faces?" pointing to the homeless African American man on the street and the grief-stricken wealthy white widow next-door, I have a right to ask you to go on, to tell me more. I could ask, for example, "Does this teenager's face over here sitting next to us on the train share the *same* likeness with that face on the street that you have just seen?" And we would have to discuss and determine how to weave the samenesses together – or not.

There are shades of sameness and shades of human action, and logic has everything to do with drawing these out, and so does ethics. Here we broach the ethics of care and of literature, the development of an eye for the particular and the particular grouping, which is not particularism (as if generalizations are not a part of it), but rather an embedding of value, of measuring, in *Lebensformen*, human and otherwise.[12] Our responses to how we draw and fashion such likenesses are hardly neutral. It is a question of value and interest and experi-

---

10 Cf. Floyd 2018.
11 Cf. Koblitz 1988 and Simon 1988, a famous controversy over the mathematicization of social processes.
12 Cf. Laugier's essay in this volume.

ence and judgment, which is why it may form, as Wittgenstein indicates, a topic worthy of philosophical investigation.

There is – in this very special sense – a *logical* role being played by the very idea of an investigation in the *Investigations*, and precisely because formal logic alone is not enough to elucidate the nature of the logical. It no longer to be envisioned – as it had been in Wittgenstein's earlier work – that logic takes care of itself. And yet – as was also the case in Wittgenstein's earlier work – the proper elucidation of *this* requires a grasp of a certain moment of schematicity in thinking, one which does not rely on formal schemata. Cavell registers this when he writes:

> If [Wittgenstein's] *Investigations* is a work of continuous spiritual struggle, then a certain proportion in tone, [a specific] psychological balance, is the mark of its particular sublimity, the measure of his achievement for philosophy ([1988] 2013: 88).

Wittgenstein's *Investigations* offers a reflective in-and-out with words. Their possibilities of interweaving are explored, possible trains of responses are sketched out, possible conversations, sharing and non-meeting of selves. Here there is a concerted effort to balance, to work with waiting-for-the-moment-to-reflect and with immediate verbal responses, unfiltered. This is neither a taking of things to be one way rather than the other nor an urging of quietism on us. It presupposes *life*, that is, our immersion in ways of going on that we are surely not neutral on. We might say that Wittgenstein's mature view of logic is that it investigates possible samenesses and differences, possible forms of thought, possible orderings that might be lived and worked with – and impossibilities, unthinkables for us, as well. He is *not* telling us what does and does not belong to culture, or what is. Instead, traditional ways of conceiving what logic is are being transformed in his mature work. Logic, a sense of the real, is a matter now of *living forms*, of *forms of our lives*, of *living logic*, inhering in a dynamic and evolving world of contingencies and necessities. This is what Wittgenstein won through to in 1937 with the notion of *Lebensform*.

3 Getting beyond Spengler

Having surrendered the idea of revising *The Brown Book* in November 1936, Wittgenstein spent some very dark and depressing days in Norway, meditating on his confessions and searching his soul (cf. DB). But soon he began his manuscript anew. And this time, for the very first time, he succeeded in generating by Christmas (which he spent in Vienna) a fair draft of the first part of the original version of *Philosophical Investigations*, the so-called *Urfassung* (UF). It amounted to a draft of PI §§1–76 (Wittgenstein 2001 [KPU]).

In this manuscript his mature, interlocutory style emerges for the first time. At last he was able to make explicit the idea of what I have elsewhere called the *fluidity* of simplicity, a robust conception of the unity of logic and of philosophical analysis that was sparked, in my account, by the stimulation he received from reading Turing's "On computable numbers, with an application to the *Entscheidungsproblem*" (1936/7).[13] As I shall explain in section 4 below, this mature conception of analysis differs significantly from the absolute conception of simplicity in the *Tractatus*, the relative-to-*Satzsysteme* ideal of simplicity characteristic of Wittgenstein's middle period, and even the relative-to-language-game ideal of simplicity at work in *The Blue and Brown Books*. The conception is explicitly thematized in remarks he drafted and added to his manuscript of the *Investigations* in the autumn of 1936: the language-games with colored squares that contextualize the issue of "simples" in relation to Socrates' dream in Plato's *Theaetetus* (PIr: §§46 ff.).[14]

After Christmas Wittgenstein returned to Norway and extended the manuscript, working several months before departing with it for Cambridge on May 1, 1937. The full *Urfassung* is a draft of PI §§1–188 (MS 142, in KPU). In discussing it with Wittgenstein that summer, Moore noticed that Wittgenstein's introduction of the colored squares and the discussion of simples into the manuscript was novel. He later told Rhees that when he asked Wittgenstein about this, Wittgenstein replied that he had changed in his method: *The Brown Book* had followed a "false method", though now he had the "right" one.[15] Moore could not understand what Wittgenstein meant. But I think we can, with the power of hindsight.[16]

For in the summer of 1937 Wittgenstein also sought out conversation with two mathematicians, Alister Watson and Alan Turing. The aim was to discuss Turing's paper "On computable numbers, with an application to the *Entscheidungsproblem*" (1936/7) in relation to other undecidability results emerging at this time in logic.[17] Turing had sent Wittgenstein an offprint of his famous

---

13 Cf. Floyd 2016.
14 See Floyd 2016: 21 ff. for a discussion.
15 EPB: 12–13. Rhees also wrote here that the manuscript included TS 221 and that Moore gave this manuscript to him to read in the spring of 1938. But the editors of PIr disagree (Wittgenstein 2009a: xviii f.), saying that Wittgenstein only had TS 220 in Cambridge with him in the summer of 1937.
16 Floyd 2016.
17 Cf. Floyd 2001, Floyd 2016, Floyd and Putnam 2000, Floyd and Putnam 2012.

paper no later than February 1937.[18] So Wittgenstein most likely had the paper with him in Norway in the spring of 1937, as he drew up the rest of the *Urfassung* (drafts of PI §§78–188). There is evidence suggesting that he may have heard of and discussed the main argument of the paper with at least Watson earlier, perhaps even in 1935.[19] But in any case it seems clear from Wittgenstein's notebooks that he was primarily grappling that spring with the concept of "domesticating" the sublimity of logic, transforming the notion of a "simple" from that of a "sublime" term to that of "an important form of representation but with domestic application" (MS 152: 96).[20] Moreover, as is evidenced in Watson's, Turing's and Wittgenstein's writings, the conversations in the summer of 1937 stimulated all three of them.[21] In particular, they had an immediate impact on Wittgenstein's revision and extension of the UF, a manuscript called the "early version" of PI, the *Frühfassung* (FF), which he wrote between the autumn of 1937 and 1938 (cf. KPU). September 1937 found Wittgenstein in Norway again, writing remarks in reaction to his discussions with Turing and Watson about incompleteness and the machine that "symbolizes its own modes of operation" for the first time.[22] In January 1938 – just before the troubles of March and the *Anschluss* of Austria that forced him to take British citizenship – he was still discussing Gödel and incompleteness at Cambridge, once again with Watson (WWCL: 50–57).

Uses of "*Lebensform*" enter into a variety of Wittgenstein's remarks during this 1937–38 period, not only in the early pages of FF, but also in lectures.[23] For example he draws the notion into his discussion in "Cause and Effect: Intuitive Awareness", a lecture responding to Russell's paper *The Limits of Empiricism* (Russell 1936).[24] In that paper Russell had not only insisted on our ability to ach-

---

[18] Turing to his mother, February 11, 1937, AMT/K/1/54 in the Turing Digital Archive (http://www.turingarchive.org/browse.php/K/1/54), discussed in Floyd 2016, Floyd 2017.
[19] The specific diagonal argument that I briefly discuss below (Section 4) was reconstructed from Wittgenstein and Turing in (Floyd 2012a); the 0–1 array I used there to explicate diagonalization I subsequently discovered had been written down in Wittgenstein's own hand in MS 157a, p. 17v (this is the precursor to RPP I §1096 ff. (cf. MS 135: 118, TS 229, §1764)), it is not known when (MS 157a is a notebook with entries between 1934 and 1937). Since Turing and Watson were seen discussing the diagonal argument together in 1935 (cf. Floyd 2017), it is possible that this pre-dates the publication of Turing's great paper (1936/7). Alternatively it was written down after reading that paper, in 1937.
[20] Cf. Floyd 2016: 22 ff.
[21] Cf. Floyd and Putnam 2000, Floyd 2017.
[22] Cf. Floyd and Putnam 2012, Floyd 2016: 25 n. 35.
[23] Von Wedelstaedt 2007 gives a helpful catalogue and analysis of the known occurrences of *Lebensform* in Wittgenstein's writings.
[24] See Benoist's contribution to this volume for a discussion of this lecture.

ieve a kind of mental, Platonic (Russellian) "acquaintance" with universals and the infinite. He also accused Wittgenstein of promulgating a reductive finitism in the philosophy of mathematics.²⁵ But finitism was not Wittgenstein's point, as he would make clear in his Cambridge lectures of 1939 (LFM, XII: 111; XIV: 141). Finitism is a restrictive theory, an insistence (on the basis of a battery of differing arguments) on using only a particular, restricted set of acceptable rules in the philosophy of mathematics, as if other rules would be wrong. In contrast, Wittgenstein's new idea about *Lebensformen* is attuned to the variety – what he calls the "COLORFUL mix" [*BUNTES Gemisch*] of techniques, representations and procedures we actually *use* in mathematics to achieve "acquaintance" with singularities, limits, procedures, infinities, constructive and non-constructive arguments.²⁶

In this way Wittgenstein's invocations of *Lebensform* distinguish themselves from the invocation of "culture" he found in Spenglerian historicizing and in what he knew of anthropology. The point of *Lebensformen* is to question the idea that we may analyze the logical aspects of language in terms of any calculus that is a fundamental, self-standing one, phenomenological or otherwise. *Lebensform* signals the point at which Wittgenstein got beyond these ideas, still too closely embraced in *The Blue and Brown Books*. He moved beyond his earlier too-developmental, too-anthropologized sense of tribes and language-games by retreating from a too self-standing idea of a calculus or language-game. He saw that even the simplest language-games must always be constantly renegotiated, re-embedded in forms of life, given how multifarious and open-ended the possibilities for such embedding may be.

In this way *Lebensform* offers a kind of schematization of philosophical method, a suitably primordial arena for generating alternative ways of looking at – becoming acquainted with – logic, language, life, culture, meaning, and experience. The notion forms a newfangled point of departure in method and reflection, rather than a subject matter that might be elucidated through experience and observation. This explains why it is invoked so rarely, yet so momentously in Wittgenstein's writings: it marks a genuine advance in his thinking.

---

25 Russell's paper led to repeated responses from Wittgenstein in RFM (cf. footnote 7) and a breach with Ambrose (cf. Monk 1990: chapter 16).
26 Cf. RFM III §§46–48. I follow Mühlhölzer 2010 in rejecting the original Anscombe translation of "motley", which invites the idea of a jester's costume (cf. Floyd 2015: 261–262). Wittgenstein's writings on the "extensional" point of view in the foundations of mathematics 1941–1944 are treated at length in Floyd and Mühlhölzer expected 2018.

The main problem with revising *The Brown Book* was not merely that it was too "boring and artificial", as Wittgenstein later wrote, though this is so.²⁷ The trouble was that it invited the wrong kind of idea and experience of philosophy: a kind of linearized, step-by-step, additive, naively anthropologized (tribalized), serialized image of quasi-culture. It remained too Spenglerian, was still too self-assured about tribes and cultures, failing thereby to invite the right sort of response. These limitations are outgrown in *Philosophical Investigations*.

When we looked at the initial appearance of "*Lebensform*" in Wittgenstein's writing in the fall of 1936, during his initial composition of the *Urfassung*, we saw that it was used to move his thinking away from an unexamined or primitive notion of *Kultur*. The notion was deleted entirely, and surely intentionally, from all subsequent versions of the *Investigations*, as was the notion of Value (*Wert*).²⁸ These notions – still of course of central importance to Wittgenstein – become nevertheless *programmatic*, matters deserving of elucidation and searching, rather than objects of description or elements of explanation. – The historical implication, given the date 1936 – 7, is of course that after what the Nazis have *done* with the notions of *Kultur* and *Zivilisation*, there is no point in invoking them: *Kultur* has been nationalized, politicized, spatialized, racialized out of the realm of meaningful use, and so has the notion of *Zivilisation*.²⁹ Their pollution, absolute, requires a departure from these "structures of air" [*Luftgebäude*, cf. PIr: §118] and a careful, piecemeal rebuilding on another site. They have lost their connection with *Lebensformen* of which we can *speak*, in which we can get a grip on truths in and of life.

Though *Philosophical Investigations* has a linearized form, in that it consists of a sequence of numbered remarks (as had *The Brown Book*), its manner of proceeding remains less directly developmental than Wittgenstein's earlier dictations, however dynamic these latter had become with their uses of language-games. PI gives us a more complex, self-reflective, and satisfactory philosophical conception. On Wittgentein's mature view, what is simple is neither absolute nor relative to a *Satzsystem*, as the early and middle philosophies had it, nor even relative to language-games, tribes and cultures, as is suggested in *The*

---

27 See CL: 238 (20.11.1936), discussed in Engelmann 2013.
28 Cf. Floyd 2016: 44f. for discussion. Strictly speaking "Wert" *does* occur once in the final version of PIr, at §119, but here W. is remarking on the fact that it is our discovering that we have bumped up against the limits of language, gotten to see an impossibility that helps us to see the value (the philosophical value, that is) of our activities. This idea of grappling with unthinkables does not constitute an invocation of any particular values, but only the necessity for embedding language-games in forms of activity, which will reveal values.
29 Cf. Martin 2016, and the classic Elias 2000.

Blue and Brown Books. Instead, what is (taken to be) "simple" or "ordinary" is ever present in analysis and in rule-following, while it is ever contestable. Simples are, and therefore the partial procedure is more fundamental than the total one. And now what we take to be "simple" are moments in an ongoing reflection, moments of valuing certain starting points, invitations to come along. Anything taken to be "simple" is to be embedded in life, unfrozen.

Thus in Wittgenstein's hands, *Lebensform* is intended to incorporate the "life world" (or, for non-rational aspects of beings, *Umwelt*), while subsuming it into a wider, more schematic, ultimately imaginative exploration of a variety of perceived possibilities and necessities in a variety of lives involving language. It is this that explains why the word "form" is important for him to use: *Lebensform* pertains to his elucidation of the logical, it is schematic and programmatic as a notion, not descriptive. And this marks an important advance in the history of philosophy, not only in his own thought. Wittgenstein's transposition of *Welt* into *Form* moves concertedly away from an older idea of life and meaning understood in terms of necessities inherent in organic unities or wholes (worlds, totalities, systems, biological individuals or kinds, societies given through organic configurations of persons, cultures, peoples, histories, nations) to a contrastingly evolutionary, modular, piecemeal, diverse, fabricated, multi-aspectual, procedural, and dynamically interwoven conception of *possibilities* in life, logic, language, environment, experience and philosophy itself.

Viewed in this way, *Lebensform* signifies a step forward from the older idea of *Lebenswelt*. The move is away from any basic, given notion of culture and toward a more schematic, universally applicable, open-ended conception of method: not only of philosophical and logical method, but also of life itself, characterized now as something in which philosophical questioning is ever-present as a possibility, though hardly necessary at any particular moment and impossible to anticipate or prove the relevance of *a priori* or in general. By means of *Lebensform* Wittgenstein has reconstrued the traditional notion of "form", turning it toward regularities and norms of procedure *in* life, these lodged in a world where contingency and partiality (*Regelmässigkeiten* signifies this) are moved to the fore. Culture and human community are to be recovered, not analyzed: they are inherited, argued with, sought and fashioned, never simply "given" – any more than logic itself is.

In this way it is by means of the idea of *Lebensformen* that disagreements and disharmonies among us are not immediately moralized, or taken to be primitive (primitively, cf. PIr: §§2, 7, 194, 554), but require us to show them, by filling them in, acknowledging them, embedding them within our lives and experiences. Our procedures and takings-for-granted are thereby allowed to surface, run their gamuts, and be discussed, re-incorporated into (though they are already part of) life. Ubiquity, the ordinariness of speech (explored *via* investigations of criteria) figure in Wittgenstein's notion of *Lebensform* inextricably, but only within a constant pressure of questioning from all sides. Like the individual stones in an arch, what is "given" is held up by tensions and opposing forces among simple elements, inviting skeptical questions which are never refuted, but incorporated and faced and dropped and raised over and over again.

This is why, in PIr §241, the third of five appearances of *Lebensform* in the book – and therefore the central keystone of the arch of *Lebensformen* in PI – we are brought face to face with an objection which attempts to reduce our harmonies to mere membership in a particular culture or tribe or group of opiners:

> "So you are saying that human agreement decides what is true and what is false?" – What is true or false is what human beings say; and it is in their language that human beings agree. This is agreement not in opinions, but rather in form of life. (PIr: §241)

It is interesting that this remark was penned later on, only in 1944–5, in the "Intermediate Version" (*Zwischenfassung*) of PI (ZF: §211 (212), in KPU). In its original context it followed what is now PIr §217, the remark where Wittgenstein writes that, if and when my justifications are exhausted in explaining how to follow a rule, I may be inclined to say "my spade is turned", and that "this is simply what I do" (cf. KPU: 693). In the final version of PI, the so-called "Later Version" (*Spätfassung* (TS 227) [SF]), Wittgenstein separated these two remarks from one another, moving §241 well forward so as to use it to enunciate the transition to consideration of "private" language. He prefaces it instead with a remark about mathematicians not coming to blows over a rule being followed. What he says in PIr §240 is that this not-coming-to-blows belongs to the "scaffolding" of our language. And in this way §241, by re-foregrounding *Lebensform*, helps us take in the notion in the right way. No longer is it used as a countering response to my voicing what *I* do in particular (inviting you along to follow the rule in *this* way, which *I* will set down).[30] Instead, *Lebensform* deepens and raises the stakes for *saying* what I do, the demand for something other than stipulation, thereby rendering the quest for community more complex, less monolithic, something evolving in speech, criticism, questioning. This readies us for the transition to Wittgenstein's treatment of privacy that will follow in PIr §§242 ff.

Lebensformen are a field for his exploration of the inner and the outer, the certain and the clear, but they stand in need of acknowledgement and our getting better acquainted with them, rather than being the sort of thing that

---

[30] For a discussion of PIr §217 that has influenced me, see Cavell 1988: 70 ff.

might be adduced as a justification, discovered or given in terms of a culture or morality. PPF: xi, §345, on the givenness of *Lebensformen*, is also prefaced by remarks about certainty in mathematics (PPF: xi, §§339–334). *Lebensformen* are scaffolding: something that can be taken down and put up again in another place and re-embedded for us to climb up on. Ordinary procedures are modules, nodes, modes of (our complex) forms of life. They are not supporting a building (a tribe or culture), but only help us construct one by climbing up, down, over, under and beside it, step-by-step.

A self-reflective idea of a phenomenology of voicing is hereby dynamically interwoven within logic and language: we call it like we see it, and then explore *that*. Logic is morphologized, and morphology logicized. Human beings' capacity for characterization is put into motion and itself characterized: elicited, modeled, and remodeled in a wide variety of argumentative moves in which contestation, re-sketching, undercutting, and apparent agreement are exhibited, turned, and then projected anew.[31] Everywhere this culture of voice, as Cavell and Laugier have called it, is ushered along by way of imagined possibilities and necessities, language-games that we are to turn upon our own senses of thinkability, appropriateness, and adequate characterization.[32] The *Investigations* is not a culture exactly, but a quest for – a philosophy of and for – such, invoking the necessity and the possibility of conversation, chatting, searching *in* life.

In PI the idea of culture is neither explained nor characterized nor adduced, nor are any specific *Lebensformen* invoked. Instead, only vastly natural, general *Lebensformen* are mentioned (that we give orders, that we chat with one another, that we tell stories, that, like animals, we eat, drink and play (PIr: §25), that we voice claims and say things (PIr: §242), that we hope and grieve (PPF: i, §1)). And yet, through the schematic, studied neutrality of Wittgenstein's philosophical procedures, a certain sublimity is revealed *in* the ordinary "rags and dust" of our uses of words (PIr: §52): what it is to make and inhabit a culture is schematized, conveyed indirectly, a task sought, rather than something always already achieved or given simply.

Viewed in this way, the later Wittgenstein is aiming, not merely to capture elements of intentionality that we can scrute and experience, to attack too-simple representational models of self-consciousness and language, or to get around or break the central role or office of logic. More than this, he seeks to convey and model experiences *of* scruting and experiencing and reasoning *as* forms of searching and claiming and questioning and valuing and not-valuing and com-

---

31 Cf. Floyd 2018.
32 Cavell [1965] 2002, Cavell [1979] 1999, Laugier 2015.

ing to grief *in* life. Here it is the journey, not the destination that counts, and what is dropped along the way is as important as what is found: traditional mis-intellectualizations of philosophy, false stories about what we might or might not have opinions about, dependencies on culture that will not stand fast, or that are needlessly invoked, possibilities held to be real when they are not, impossibilities taken for granted, and then surmounted. What is left are a series of ventured experiments in determining and creating and experiencing and shifting meaning and culture – acquaintance, in short, with logic, philosophy *in* life.

4 Turing and *Lebensformen*

If we explore Wittgenstein's uses of *Lebensform* in composing the *Investigations* we see another theme emerging with new intensity in his mature philosophy, one that entered into his drafting of the book only after he had spent the summer of 1937 in Cambridge discussing his *Urfassung* with Moore, Turing and Watson. This is his newfound thematization of *Regelmässigkeit*.

The theme of *Regelmässigkeit* is stalked and decisively embedded in his thinking about *Lebensform* in the *Investigations*, beginning in PIr §189. This material was initially developed in response to difficulties he faced in 1936–7 in aiming to revise *The Brown Book*. Its §41 had invoked the idea of "general training" [*allgemeiner Unterricht*], the idea of training a pupil, not merely to follow a particular table correlating letters with arrows, but *any* such table (presumably, with *any* such letters). But this raised a new problem. Wittgenstein had to admit that he was not offering any kind of general analysis of what it is to follow a rule (BB: §41), and also that the whole idea of regarding a command as a sentence of some kind (a sequence of letters) is fraught with dangers of mistaking superficial similarities for differences. Broached in EPB §47, his revision, is the question of what it means to "go out of" a game, to extend beyond the control structure. This could mean a variety of things (running out of letters, for example). And so, as he remarked in his spring 1937 notebook (MS 152: 5), there is a "problem" in EPB §47, one that raises an even deeper challenge to the idea that following a rule is a "specific process" than any objections he had raised so far. This is the idea of pinning down what it is we mean in general by a "characteristic process" or a "step" in calculation *in* logic.

In September 1937, just after arriving in Norway from his discussions with Moore, Turing and Watson, Wittgenstein embarked on the composition of the *Frühfassung*, his extension of the *Urfassung*. He penned the following transitional remark, placing it at the very *end* of the *Urfassung*:

> "But are the steps then *not* determined by the algebraic formula?" – The question contains a mistake.
>
> We use the expression "The steps are determined by the formula ...". *How* is the expression used? (UF: §189; FF: §188; cf. PIr: §189)

It is clear that he took this remark to be the fulcrum that was to turn his remarks toward the "foundations" of mathematics. For the same remark ends his "Reworked Early Version" of the *Frühfassung*, the so-called *Bearbeitete Frühfassung* (BF) completed in 1943. The structure he had long envisioned for his book was twofold: first, an analysis of meaning, understanding and the proposition, and then second, an application to the foundations of logic and mathematics (BT, TS 213 has just this structure). – It is as if his conversations with Watson and Turing gave him a new impetus forward toward writing the second half of the book.

Wittgenstein's point in raising these questions was not, as Kripke 1981 maintained, to *deny* logical necessity. It was instead to convey how to view it rightly, so as to take it in and be able to communicate with, and explore, its variety of faces *in* life.[33] He was meditating on what Turing's words about the "complete determination" of the behavior of the machine in §2 of his (1936/7) paper *could* mean. After all, in a certain sense Turing had *analyzed* the very notion of taking a determinate "step" in the course of an algorithm or calculation. Wittgenstein was reflecting on how that analysis works.

Rules were always thematically important in Wittgenstein's writings. But the notion of *Regelmässigkeit* is newly explored in 1937 in terms of the idea of a machine that is capable of symbolizing its *own* actions (cf. PIr: §§193 ff.). Clearly this idea is sparked by an encounter with Turing's analysis of the very idea of a formal system by way of a "machine" compared with a human calculating.[34] The context is one in which the actions of a machine (or human calculator) are in *one* sense – to use Turing's (1936/7: §2) phrase – "completely determined" by a series of commands. But, as Wittgenstein emphasizes, and Turing implicitly admits, only in the context of a human, shared world (PIr: §189).[35] The governing analogy of *The Brown Book*, adapted by Turing in his paper, is drawn between the workings of a machine and that of a human calculator. But this analogy goes in two directions: from machine that symbolizes its own actions (the Universal Machine contains its own description number) to the human who also self-symbolizes, directing her own modifications of herself (including her reasoning about Turing machines) by situating such machines in a human world

---

33 Cf. Diamond [1968] 1991, Floyd 1991.
34 Cf. Floyd 2016.
35 Cf. Floyd 2017.

of activity, communication and discussion. Through the Universal Machine's self-symbolizing capacity, Turing was able to show the significance to formal logic of the idea of an *effective* "mode of operation". There is no diagonalizing out of the class of Turing machines, because the fundamental notion is that of a not-everywhere-defined, partial procedure. The very idea of formalized logical consequence is thereby robustly or "absolutely" analyzed and shown to be marked by a general undecideability.[36] In the end, Turing accomplished this task by doing something *philosophical*, as well as mathematical: he analyzed the very *notion* of a formal system of logic (and the notion of taking a "step" in one). This could not have been done by simply writing down another formal system. Instead, Turing had to clarify the idea, and he did so precisely by focusing on what a formal system of logic is *for*, on how we human beings *use* it.[37]

And thus, under the terms of the analogy, the activity of a human being calculating with pencil and paper is shown to be *in general* undecidable. It is not part of our mathematically precisified general notion of following a rule that we are following *this* rule *now*. That latter idea gains a footing only in the kinds of samenesses and differences drawn out in *Lebensformen*, which allow for the idea of a shareable command or procedure taken to be fundamental – the social world – as *opposed* to the notion of a "state of mind", which Turing explicitly extrudes in §9 of his (1936/7), writing that

> We suppose [...] that the computation is carried out on a tape; but we avoid introducing the "state of mind" by considering a more physical and definite counterpart of it. It is always possible for the computer to break off from his work, to go away and forget all about it, and later to come back and go on with it. If he does this he must leave a note of instructions (written in some standard form) explaining how the work is to be continued. This note is the counterpart of the "state of mind".

Like scaffolding, then, the logical notion of following a rule must be acknowledged, it must be something shareable, capable of being re-embedded in a variety of tasks or procedures or contexts (*Lebensformen*), shifted as to its point and purpose.

While it is not our main task here to revisit Turing's classic paper in detail, it is crucial to emphasize that according to Turing's way of establishing the general undecidability of logic, the reality of words – i.e. what we do in characterizing ourselves and the realities and possibilities around us – *necessarily* be-

---

36 Cf. Floyd 2012a, Floyd 2017.
37 Cf. Floyd 2012b, Floyd 2017.

comes fundamental.[38] Turing's idea of a "machine" is explicitly carried out by way of what he calls our ability to "compare" a human and a machine (1936/7: §1). This implements Wittgenstein's method of *Vergleichsobjekte*, the exploration of analogies and comparisons that had earmarked the method of *The Blue and Brown Books* (which it is very likely that Turing saw and discussed while an undergraduate).[39] Turing, like Wittgenstein, develops his comparison in light of a philosophical perspective that takes human words and actions (including actions of writing and sharing commands and instructions) to form part of the fundamental reality of logic, and *not* vague appeals to "states of mind". As Wittgenstein later remarked, "Turing's 'Machines'. These are *humans* who calculate" (RPP I: §§1096 ff.).[40]

The Turing Machine – and also we ourselves, under the comparison – should be taken to self-inscribe, symbolizing and executing (shareable) commands and actions from within one or another *Lebensform*. This is no way impugns the perspective from which a Turing Machine – including the Universal Machine, which does the work of all – is a genuine mathematical object. However, much more clearly than an abstractly presented formal system of the Hilbertian kind, a Turing "machine" relies upon human understandings – not simply psychological states – to do its work. This is given in its form and the way we are to take this in: as a series of shareable, adaptable, modular commands.[41]

Many of Turing's writings – and not only his (1936/7) – exploit this Wittgensteinian conviction in fundamental methods and strategies of elucidation, in the importance of what they both called our everyday "phraseology".[42] For both of them, the *point* of a routine is as important as – is internal to – the fact that it *is* one. A "Turing Machine" may be characterized from one point of view as no more than just another mathematical object, in fact it *is* a formal system. But from another point of view, it is a collection of commands that can be understood, activating real-life steps in the world. It is we who bring dynamism to the abstract object, viewing its "steps" in a normative way, as possible step-by-

---

[38] See Floyd 2012a, Floyd 2016, Floyd 2017.
[39] Cf. Floyd 2017.
[40] The diagonal argument Wittgenstein sketches beside this remark is reconstructed in detail in Floyd 2012a, and discussed in Floyd 2017; cf. MS 157a: 17v.
[41] Leslie 2016 comes to a similar conclusion, while arguing that Turing must have changed his mind after writing his (1936/7), which Leslie takes to have suppressed the social perspective on thought. But as I see it (Floyd 2017) Turing *always* held onto the socially and pragmatically oriented view of logic. This is something we can explain if we postulate, as is overwhelmingly likely, that he was already drawn into the Wittgenstein orbit while an undergraduate and young Fellow at Cambridge, 1931–1935.
[42] Cf. Floyd 2013, Floyd 2016, Floyd 2017.

step motions that are correct or incorrect in being embedded in life. And this is a fateful perspective for the present day.

Different embeddings in differing *Lebensformen* will yield very different perspectives and prospects, differing possibilities and necessities, differing aspects and procedures lent to the implementation of an algorithm. The point is quite general. In one sense, an algorithm is neutral. But if we put it into the world, and let it do its work in representing (us), it is no longer neutral. Nor is it human, of course. *We* are. Yet nothing could be more human – or more reminiscent of Wittgenstein's struggles with grammar – than to imagine ourselves as (self-made) victims of the routines and words we implement, taken over and made wholly redundant by them, dead, outside of all questioning and investigation, all *Lebensformen*. – Skepticism is, as Cavell always argued, the other side of attending to the everyday that lies right before us, for it is fashioned precisely so as to make all the "rags and dust" of what we ordinarily do, care about, feel and say *irrelevant*.

Skepticism about the importance of investigating *Lebensformen* is driven in part by a wish to deny or escape from forms of life, an attempt to deny the human world of diverse and drifting dynamic forms, lives and characteristic commerces with uses of words. Wittgenstein's move with *Lebensformen* is to show that there is no such thing as escape from this, only blindness or a refusal to focus on the fact that there *is* no such thing as culture-as-such, there is only enculturing. Where we begin and where we end is in life, exploring "colorful mixes", gradations, tapestries, and shadings of our animal and human communities with words. It is the idea of investigating (being interested in characterizing) *differing* projections and rejections, *differing* possibilities and necessities for embedding, that is crucial to Wittgenstein's idea of *Lebensform*, rather than an appeal to an empirically given way of life or culture or system of opinions or tribe.

As Turing understood – having studied with Wittgenstein – the ordinary and *Regelmässigkeit* are not two separable realms. Instead, they interact and interpenetrate. There is a logical requirement to recognize the need for *Lebensformen*, homes in which our ordinary words (our "phraseology") are put to use. We require, one way or the other, an evolving, contestable notion of "common sense" that we must investigate and explore – for it expresses values, interests, and cultural and intellectual investments. It is our evolved inheritance, this mode of argumentation which is also a mode of proceeding.[43] Turing remarked

---

[43] Cf. Floyd 2017 on the notion of "common sense". In a paper he wrote after attending Wittgenstein's 1939 Cambridge lectures Turing expressed his indebtedness to Wittgenstein on the importance of ordinary "phraseology", stressing its importance for developing a proper notion of "types" (Turing [1944/5] 2013). He urged the need for logicians to resist purism in logic, what he

on this philosophical aspect of his work in his final published words, where, alluding to his earlier work on undecideability, he wrote that

> These [limitative] results, and some other results of mathematical logic may be regarded as going some way towards a demonstration, within mathematics itself, of the inadequacy of 'reason' [i.e., formal systems, algorithms] unsupported by common sense. (Turing 1954: 23)

Most fundamentally, Turing showed the necessity of taking the *partial* procedure – i.e., one not everywhere defined – as fundamental to the very idea of logic as a calculus.

This comes out vividly in Turing's refutation of the idea of a general decision procedure for logic in his (1936/7: §8): an argument that greatly impressed Wittgenstein. The proof turns on a demonstration, from within pure logic, of the fact that every command must be given in a context, that no command can be freestanding in general. The diagonal proof Turing frames in his (1936/7: §8) is idiosyncratic, as he says: it is very unlike those given by Cantor and Gödel. Instead, it evinces a Wittgensteinian air, as Wittgenstein himself perceived.[44] For it does not rely on a general application of negation, the law of excluded middle, in an infinite context: it is instead self-consciously philosophically ecumenical, getting in view the situation *before* a contradiction appears.[45] Turing shows that from the assumption that there is a general decision procedure for logic, there must be an *empty* machine, one that runs up against a command akin to drawing a card in a game that says "Do What You Do".[46] This machine cannot *follow* its own command, for it lacks an embedding in any particular *Lebensform* (any context in which "Do What You Do" does make sense).

"Do What You Do" tells you nothing without a specific context of application: it is like a pair of fingers pointing straight at one another. But it is not con-

---

called "the straightjacket" of a formal notation, conceived in general, ideal language terms: the idea that conceptual systems should be expressed in overarching formalized languages, as in Carnap and Quine (see Floyd 2012b, Floyd 2013 for commentary and discussion). As he wrote, "no democratic mathematical community" of scientists would ever accept such a thing (Turing [1944/5] 2013: 245).

44 For detailed discussion cf. Floyd 2012a, Floyd 2017, RPP I: §§1096 ff. In Wittgenstein's notebook remarks surrounding his rendition of Turing's diagonal argument (MS 157a: 17v) we see him preoccupied with the significance of this argument for the "vanishing" of the "I" (MS 157a: 17v ff.) – a direct application of the point at issue.

45 Cf. PIr §124, an allusion to a remark by Ramsey about the *Entscheidungsproblem* as a "leading" problem of mathematical logic. Ramsey wanted to defeat the "Bolshevism" of the intuitionists. Turing artfully dodges the controversy (cf. Floyd 2012a, Floyd 2016).

46 Cf. Floyd 2012a, Floyd 2016, Floyd 2017.

tradictory, and does not generate an infinite regress. Rather, we must *see* that such a command stops in the face of its own tautology-like self-inscription. It indirectly shows the *need* for a context.

A further point of contact with *Lebensformen* is this. Turing's work indicated that a longstanding dichotomy in Wittgenstein's earlier thought, the distinction between *calculation* and *experiment*, now fades at the margins, in that it too is a matter of mode of operation, decisions *in* life as to what is to count as same, and what is to count as different, not merely a matter of what is necessitated or calculated *versus* what is experienced. There is no general dichotomy here. We calculate and experience necessity, but we are engaged in what might be regarded at any point as a grand experiment.

This explains why the final occurrences of *Lebensform* in PI (PPF: i, §1; xi, §345) broach a new line of thought, one that Wittgenstein would develop later on in writings such as *On Certainty*. An apparently empirically known, particular remark such as "I have never been to the moon" or "there are four symbols here" or "my friend is not an automaton" or "blue isn't red" may play a crucial *logical* role, pointing the way toward the need for embedding our forms of words, and our grammar, in *Lebensformen*.

Though we have criteria for death, we have no general criteria for being alive, being engaged in a form of life.[47] In a sense all our activities may thus appear to be nothing more, and nothing less, than a grand experiment. And is not all culture such? And yet it is difficult to call it merely an *empirical* fact that we do not come to blows over whether particular rules have been followed, or whether machines do or do not think (though who knows whether we might at some point come to blows over this in the future?).[48] There are takings-for-granted, givens. But these are starting points, thinkably revisable ones, whose necessities lie in our capacity to reach "harmonies" among us.

It is a "given" part of our form of life that "mathematicians don't come to blows" over whether a step has been followed, but this is not exactly a justification.[49] As a matter of fact, Brouwer and Hilbert once nearly enough did, over certain uses of the law of the excluded middle in infinite contexts. Nevertheless, with the help of Turing's clarification of what in general it *is* to follow a formal

---

47 Cf. Cavell [1988] 2013: 43.
48 It is interesting to note that Wittgenstein seems not to have read Turing's famous (1950) paper on the Turing Test (cf. Wittgenstein to Malcolm, CL: 469, 1.12.1950). It is worth remarking that Turing's arguments in his (1950) turn wholly on the fact that we do *not* have a general analysis of, or criteria for, "thinking". So they turn neither on a mechanical account of thought (cf. Floyd 2016: 34 n. 56) nor on a reductive behaviorism.
49 Compare Mühlhölzer's discussion of naturalism in this volume.

rule, we came to domesticate the ideological dead end, to see that it is no part of our notion of taking a step in a formal system that one does or does not obey the law of excluded middle. One can work in one system, or both, or either, the bones of contention lying only in what *else* we go on to say and do in embedding these procedures in (mathematical) life. *Lebensform*, that is, form – as the *Tractatus* had already insisted – pertains, not to actuality, but only to the *possibility* of structure (TLP 2.151) – now in life.

5 Conclusion

Wittgenstein's notion of *Lebensform* responds to important shifts in 20th-century life, as well as his own philosophical development. An older ideal of an organic whole gives way to a modular treatment of human procedures, actions, claims, choices, persuasions. Even if the *Tractatus* admitted that human language "is no less complicated than the human organism" (TLP 4.002), still it focused on *the* individual human organism as such, *the* world as a whole, *the* logic conceived in terms of a general form of proposition ("this is how things are" (TLP 4.5)). Wittgenstein's mature philosophy transposes this in a more satisfactory, and also a more rigorous fashion. It emphasizes the ubiquity of the partial procedure, rather than the totality of a general procedure, drawing the former in as the properly more fundamental notion in logic and philosophy.

Lebensformen are taken by Wittgenstein to form a backdrop to the necessary and the certain, but not exactly as a bastion or support of them.[50] Regarded as a kind of causal strut, a presupposition, or supporting part of the edifice – as cultural forms – *Lebensformen* would not be able to do the work they do for Wittgenstein. For, regarded in this way, logic and philosophy and reasoning would look too arbitrary, too contingent, yet also too natural, too inevitable. Instead, through Wittgenstein's idea of *Lebensformen* we are faced not only with the causal evolutionary processes as a backdrop to searching, but also with the struggle of the search itself, with our inherited quest for culture. Any such quest will begin from one or another "given" starting point as a necessity, though at any

---

50 This is why, if I am not mistaken, Wittgenstein eliminates the notion of "presupposition" from *Lebensform* after invoking it at RFM VII §47. For this invokes, implicitly, a notion of possible justification. Even in this place he does speak of the more attenuated idea of "*Sprachformen als Umgebung*".

given stage there may be an argument over where in particular to begin. In this way we are constantly engaged in a cultural *search*.[51]

In PIr §122 Wittgenstein writes that the form of a "surveyable presentation" [*übersichtliche Darstellung*] is fundamental to his philosophy. His drive is to assemble an expression that can be reproduced, copied, shared, woven into further procedures and analyses, detached and refashioned in further discussion, further work.[52] A surveyable representation is one we can care about, get interested in, share.

Wittgenstein asks of this later method in the *Investigations*, "Is this a *Weltanschauung?*" but does not answer. His response, implicitly, is "Yes and No". No, because he does not offer an intuition or description of the world as a whole grasped in the traditional philosopher's way: he is not trying to, and that older notion of *Weltanschauung* he drops.[53] But also Yes, because he is urging a revision in our very understanding of what it is or might require of us to intuit the world, to take the world and life and logic *as* "given" in what we do. The "given" is to be appreciated as a warping and weaving of life forms, a "ribbon" or "band" of life (*Band des Lebens*, cf. PPF: i, §2; xi, §362). The weaving of narratives, the cultural search, is endless and many-colored. It is what Diamond has called (2004) "criss cross philosophy", a tapestry endlessly woven with finite threads, step by step, as in the "crosswise" stitching together of steps in an inductive proof, or recursion (cf. BT: §139, pp. 456, 475; Z: §447) – the very procedure that Turing analyzed. It is internal to such weavings of procedures, and Wittgenstein's interest in *Lebensformen*, that our uses of words are not reflective of *one* sort of thing that a culture is or has to be.[54]

---

51 Cf. Turing [1948] 2013, III on the need for a "cultural search" in the face of the likely direction of "artificial" i.e., computational, "intelligence".
52 Cf. Mühlhölzer 2010 on the centrality of the idea of being able to copy, reproduce, as in the manner of a picture to Wittgenstein's idea of *Übersichtlichkeit*. This is discussed in Floyd 2015.
53 Compare Sluga 2010 on the unsurveyability of grammar.
54 Thanks are due, for very helpful discussion of this essay, to my audience at the conference "The Form of our Life with Language", organized by Christian Martin at the Munich Siemensstiftung and co-sponsored by the Ludwig Maximilians-Universität München on May 23–25, 2016. Felix Mühlhölzer gave me very helpful followup comments, and Ulrich Arnswald helped me with historical perspectives on the term *Lebensband*. Akihiro Kanamori made extremely useful editorial comments on a late draft of the paper.

References

Cavell, Stanley ([1965] 2002) "Aesthetic Problems of Modern Philosophy", in: *Must We Mean What We Say? A Book of Essays*, Cambridge, U. K./New York: Cambridge University Press, 73–96. Original edition in Max Black (ed.): *Philosophy in America*, Ithaca, NY: Cornell University Press/Allen & Unwin, 1965, 174–197.

Cavell, Stanley ([1979] 1999) *The Claim of Reason: Wittgenstein, Skepticism, Morality, and Tragedy*, New York: Oxford University Press, second printing with a new Preface.

Cavell, Stanley (1988) "The Argument of the Ordinary: Scenes of Instruction in Wittgenstein and in Kripke", in: *Conditions Handsome and Unhandsome: The Constitution of Emersonian Perfectionism*, Chicago, IL: University of Chicago Press, 64–100.

Cavell, Stanley ([1988] 2013) "Declining Decline: Wittgenstein as a Philosopher of Culture", in: *This New Yet Unapproachable America: Lectures after Emerson after Wittgenstein*, Chicago, IL: University of Chicago Press, 29–77. First published in: *Inquiry* 31 (3), 1988, 253–264.

Diamond, Cora ([1968] 1991) "The Face of Necessity", in: Cora Diamond, *The Realistic Spirit: Wittgenstein, Philosophy and the Mind*, Cambridge, MA: MIT Press, 243–266.

Diamond, Cora (2004) "Criss-Cross Philosophy", in: Erich Ammereller and Eugen Fischer (eds.): *Wittgenstein At Work: Method in the Philosophical Investigations*, New York: Routledge, 201–220.

Elias, Norbert (2000) "Sociogenesis of the Antithesis Between *Kultur* and *Zivilisation* in German Usage", in: *The Civilizing Process: Sociogenetic and Psychogenetic Investigations*, revised edition, Malden, MA: Blackwell, 3–44.

Engelmann, M. L. (2013) *Wittgenstein's Philosophical Development: Phenomenology, Grammar, Method, and the Anthropological View*, Basingstoke: Palgrave Macmillan.

Floyd, Juliet (1991) "Wittgenstein on 2,2,2…: On the Opening of *Remarks on the Foundations of Mathematics*", in: *Synthese* 87 (1), 143–180.

Floyd, Juliet (2001) "Prose versus Proof: Wittgenstein on Gödel, Tarski and Truth", in: *Philosophia Mathematica* 3 (9), 280–307.

Floyd, Juliet (2010) "On Being Surprised: Wittgenstein on Aspect Perception, Logic and Mathematics", in: V. Krebs and W. Day (eds.): *Seeing Wittgenstein Anew: New Essays on Aspect Seeing*, New York: Cambridge University Press, 314–337.

Floyd, Juliet (2012a) "Wittgenstein's Diagonal Argument: A Variation on Cantor and Turing", in: P. Dybjer, S. Lindström, E. Palmgren and G. Sundholm (eds.): *Epistemology versus Ontology, Logic, Epistemology: Essays in Honor of Per Martin-Löf*, Dordrecht: Springer, 25–44.

Floyd, Juliet (2012b) "Wittgenstein, Carnap, and Turing: Contrasting Notions of Analysis", in: Pierre Wagner (ed.): *Carnap's Ideal of Explication and Naturalism*, Basingstoke: Palgrave Macmillan, 34–46.

Floyd, Juliet (2013) "Turing, Wittgenstein and Types: Philosophical Aspects of Turing's 'The Reform of Mathematical Notation' (1944–5)", in: Turing 2013, 250–253.

Floyd, Juliet (2015) "Depth and Clarity: Critical Study, Felix Mühlhölzer, *Braucht die Mathematik eine Grundlegung? Eine Kommentar des Teils III von Wittgensteins Bemerkungen Über die Grundlagen der Mathematik* (Vittorio Klostermann, Frankfurt am Main 2010)", in: *Philosophia Mathematica* 23 (Special Issue on Mathematical Depth 2), 255–277.

Floyd, Juliet (2016) "Chains of Life: Turing, *Lebensform*, and the Emergence of Wittgenstein's Later Style", in: *Nordic Wittgenstein Review* 5 (2), 7–89.

Floyd, Juliet (2017) "Turing on 'Common Sense': Cambridge Resonances", in: Juliet Floyd and Alisa Bokulich (eds.): *Philosophical Explorations of the Legacy of Alan Turing – Turing 100*, New York: Springer, 103–152.

Floyd, Juliet (2018) "Aspects of Aspects", in: Hans Sluga and David Stern (eds.): *The Cambridge Companion to Wittgenstein*, 2nd ed., Cambridge/New York: Cambridge University Press.

Floyd, Juliet and Felix Mühlhölzer (expected 2018) *Wittgenstein on the Real Numbers: Annotations to Hardy's A Course of Pure Mathematics* (Nordic Wittgenstein Studies Series), New York: Springer.

Floyd, Juliet and Hilary Putnam (2000) "A Note on Wittgenstein's Notorious Paragraph about the Gödel Theorem", in: *Journal of Philosophy* 97 (11), 624–632.

Floyd, Juliet and Hilary Putnam (2012) "Wittgenstein's 'Notorious' Paragraph about the Gödel Theorem: Recent Discussions", in: Hilary Putnam, Mario De Caro and David Macarthur (eds.): *Philosophy in an Age of Science: Physics, Mathematics, and Skepticism*, Cambridge, MA: Harvard University Press, 458–481. Altered from original publication: "Wittgensteins 'berüchtigter' Paragraph über das Gödel-Theorem: Neuere Diskussionen", in: Ester Ramharter (ed.): *Prosa oder Besweis? Wittgensteins 'berüchtigte' Bemerkungen zu Gödel, Texte und Dokumente*, Berlin: Parerga, 2008, 75–97.

Frege, Gottlob ([1884] 1974) *The Foundations of Arithmetic*, transl. J. L. Austin. 2nd revised edition, Evanston, IL: Northwestern University Press. Originally published by Basil Blackwell, Oxford 1953.

Grève, Sebastian Sunday (2017) "Logic and Philosophy of Logic in Wittgenstein", in: *Australasian Journal of Philosophy* 96, 168–182.

Koblitz, Neal (1988) "A Tale of Three Equations; or The Emperors Have No Clothes", in: *The Mathematical Intelligencer* 10 (1), 4–10.

Kripke, Saul A. (1982) *Wittgenstein on Rules and Private Language: An Elementary Exposition*. Cambridge, MA: Harvard University Press.

Kuusela, Oskari (2013) "Logic and Ideality: Wittgenstein's Way beyond Apriorism, Empricicism and Conventionalism in the Philosophy of Logic", in: Nuno Venturinha (ed.): *The Textual Genesis of Wittgenstein's Philosophical Investigations*, New York/London: Routledge, 93–119.

Kuusela, Oskari (2016) *Logic as the Method of Philosophy: Wittgenstein's Philosophy of Logic in Relation to Frege, Russell, Carnap and Others*. [Manuscript]

Laugier, Sandra (2007) "The Myth of the Outer : Wittgenstein's Redefinition of Subjectivity", in: Danièle Moyal-Sharrock (ed.): *Perspicuous Presentations: Essays on Wittgenstein's Philosophy of Psychology*, Palgrave Macmillan, 151–173.

Laugier, Sandra (2015) "Voice as Form of Life and Life Form", in: *Nordic Wittgenstein Review* 4, Special Issue: Wittgenstein and Forms of Life, 63–81.

Leslie, David (2016) "Machine Intelligence and the Ethical Grammar of Computability", in: V. C. Müller (ed.): *Fundamental Issues of Artificial Intelligence*, New York: Springer International Publishing, 63–78.

Martin, Benjamin G. (2016) *The Nazi-Fascist New Order for European Culture*, Cambridge, MA: Harvard University Press.

Monk, Ray (1990) *Ludwig Wittgenstein: The Duty of Genius*, New York/London: Free Press/Jonathan Cape.

Mühlhölzer, Felix (2010) *Braucht die Mathematik eine Grundlegung? Ein Kommentar des Teils III von Wittgensteins Bemerkungen über die Grundlagen der Mathematik*, Frankfurt am Main: Klostermann.

Mulhall, Stephen (1990) *On Being in the World: Wittgenstein and Heidegger on Seeing Aspects*, London: Routledge.

Russell, Bertrand (1936) "The Limits of Empiricism", in: *Proceedings of the Aristotelian Society* 36, 131–150.

Simon, Herbert (1988) "Replies to Koblitz", in: *The Mathematical Intelligencer* 10 (1), 11–14; 10 (2), 10–12.

Sluga, Hans (2010) "Our Grammar Lacks Surveyability", in: Klaus Puhl, Volker Munz and Joseph Wang (eds.): *Language and World. Part One. Essays on the Philosophy of Wittgenstein* (Publications of the Austrian Ludwig Wittgenstein Society – New Series, Vol. 14), Heusenstamm: Ontos, 185–204.

Sluga, Hans (2018) "From Moore's Lecture Notes to Wittgenstein's *Blue Book*", in: David Stern, Brian Rogers and Gabriel Citron (eds.): *Wittgenstein's Return to Cambridge: Reflections on the Middle Period*, New York: Cambridge University Press.

Stern, David G. (1994) "The Wittgenstein Papers as Text and Hypertext: Cambridge, Bergen, and Beyond", in: Kjell Johannessen (ed.): *Wittgenstein and Norway*, Solum Press, 251–275.

Stern, David G. (2011) "Private Language", in: Oskari Kuusela and Marie McGinn (eds.): *The Oxford Handbook of Wittgenstein*, Oxford/New York: Oxford University Press, 333–350.

Turing, Alan M. (1936/7) "On Computable Numbers, with an Application to the Decision Problem", in: *Proceedings of the London Mathematical Society* 2 (42) (1936–7), 230–265. Corrections, *Proceedings of the London Mathematical Society* 2 (42) (1937), 544–546. Both reprinted with commentary in Turing 2013, 16–43.

Turing, Alan M. ([1944/5] 2013) "The Reform of Mathematical Notation and Phraseology", in: Turing 2013, 245–249, with commentary. Originally published in: *Collected Works of A. M. Turing: Mathematical Logic*, R. O. Gandy and C. E. M. Yates (eds.), New York: Elsevier, 2001, 211–222.

Turing, Alan M ([1948] 2013) "Intelligent Machinery", report written for the National Physical Laboratory, 1948. Published with commentary in Turing 2013, 501–516.

Turing, Alan M. (1950) "Computing Machinery and Intelligence", in: *Mind* 59, 433–460. Reprinted with commentary in Turing 2013, 552–568.

Turing, Alan M (1954) "Solvable and Unsolvable Problems", in: A. W. Haslett (ed.): *Science News*, 7–23, London: Penguin. Reprinted with commentary in Turing 2013, 322–331.

Turing, Alan M. (2013) *Alan Turing – His Work and Impact*. Collected papers with commentary, Barry Cooper and Jan van Leeuwen (eds.), Amsterdam: North-Holland/Elsevier Science.

von Uexküll, Jakob (2010) *A Foray Into the Worlds of Animals and Men: A Picture Book of Invisible Worlds* and *A Theory of Meaning*, transl. Joseph D. O'Neil (Posthuman Ties vol. 12), Minneapolis: University of Minnesota Press. Introduction by Dorion Sagan, Afterword by Geoffrey Winthrop-Young. Original English publication: "A Stroll through the Worlds of Animals and Men: A Picture Book of Invisible Worlds", in: *Semiotica* 89 (4)

(1992), 319 – 391. Original publication *Streifzüge durch die Umwelten von Tieren und Menschen*, Berlin: Julius Springer, 1934.

von Wedelstaedt, Almut Kristine (2007) "Zum Begriff der Lebensform bei Wittgenstein", Magisterarbeit, Bielefeld University.

Wittgenstein, Ludwig ([1921] 1981) *Tractatus Logico-Philosophicus*, transl. C. K. Ogden, London/New York: Routledge & Kegan Paul. First German edition in: *Annalen der Naturphilosophie*, Wilhelm Ostwald (ed.), Vol. 14, 1921, 12 – 262. [TLP]

Wittgenstein, Ludwig (1965), *Preliminary Studies for the 'Philosophical Investigations': Generally Known as the Blue and Brown Books*, Rush Rhees (ed.), New York: Harper and Row. [BB]

Wittgenstein, Ludwig (1969) *Das Blaue Buch. Eine Philosophische Betrachtung (Das Braune Buch)*, Rush Rhees (ed.), transl. Petra von Morstein, in: Vol. 5 of *Wittgenstein Werkausgabe*, 8 vols., Frankfurt am Main/Oxford: Suhrkamp/Basil Blackwell. [EPB]

Wittgenstein, Ludwig (1970) *Zettel*, G. E. M. Anscombe and G. H. von Wright (eds.), transl. G. E. M. Anscombe, Berkeley, CA: University of California Press. [Z]

Wittgenstein, Ludwig (1974) *On Certainty/Über Gewissheit*, 2nd revised edition, Oxford/Malden, MA: Blackwell. [OC]

Wittgenstein, Ludwig (1976) *Wittgenstein's Lectures on the Foundations of Mathematics: Cambridge, 1939, from the Notes of R. G. Bosanquet, Norman Malcolm, Rush Rhees and Yorick Smythies*, Cora Diamond (ed.), Hassocks, Sussex: Harvester Press. [LFM]

Wittgenstein, Ludwig (1978) *Remarks on the Foundations of Mathematics*, G. H. von Wright, Rush Rhees and G. E. M. Anscombe (eds.), transl. G. E. M. Anscombe, revised and reset 3rd edition (1st edition 1956; 2nd. edition 1967), Cambridge, MA: MIT Press. [RFM]

Wittgenstein, Ludwig (1980) *Remarks on the Philosophy of Psychology*, Vol. 1, Oxford: Blackwell. Reprint, republished by University of Chicago Press 1982. [RPP I]

Wittgenstein, Ludwig (1993) *Ludwig Witgenstein: Philosophical Occasions, 1912 – 1951*, Indianapolis: Hackett. [PO]

Wittgenstein, Ludwig (1995) *Ludwig Wittgenstein Cambridge Letters*, Brian McGuinness and G. H. von Wright (eds.), Cambridge, MA: Blackwell. [CL]

Wittgenstein, Ludwig (1997) *Denkbewegungen. Tagebücher 1930 – 1932, 1936 – 1937* (MS 183), Ilse Somavilla (ed.), Part 1: Normalisierte Fassung. Part 2: Diplomatische Fassung, Innsbruck: Haymon. [DB]

Wittgenstein, Ludwig (1998 – 2000) *Wittgenstein's Nachlass. The Bergen Electronic Edition*. Charlottesville, VA/Oxford: Intelex Corporation/Oxford University Press. [References to typescript and manuscript numbers, e. g. "MS 115"]

Wittgenstein, Ludwig (2001) *Philosophische Untersuchungen Kritisch-genetische Edition*, Joachim Schulte, Heikki Nyman, Eike von Savigny and G. H. von Wright (eds.), Frankfurt am Main: Suhrkamp. [KPU] Contains "Original version" (*Urfassung* [UF] (MS 142)), "Early version" (*Frühfassung* [FF] (TS 220, 221, 225)), "Reworked early version" (*Bearbeitete Frühfassung* [BF] (TS 239)), "Intermediate version" (*Zwischenfassung* [ZF]), "Late version" (*Spätfassung* [SF] (TS 227)) and "Part II" (*Teil II* [PPF]) (MS 144), with index tables.

Wittgenstein, Ludwig (2003) *Ludwig Wittgenstein: Public and Private Occasions*, James C. Klagge and Alfred Nordmann (eds.), Lanham, MD: Rowman and Littlefield. [PPO]

Wittgenstein, Ludwig (2005) *The Big Typescript, TS 213*, edited and transl. by C. Grant Luckhardt and Maximilian Aue, Malden, MA: Blackwell. [BT]

Wittgenstein, Ludwig (2009a) *Philosophische Untersuchungen = Philosophical Investigations*, revised 4th edition, Chichester, West Sussex, U. K./Malden, MA: Wiley-Blackwell. [PIr]
Wittgenstein, Ludwig (2009b) *Philosophy of Psychology – A Fragment*, in: Wittgenstein 2009a, 182–265. [PPF]
Wittgenstein, Ludwig (2017) *Wittgenstein's Whewell's Court Lectures, Cambridge, 1938–1941: From the Notes of Yorick Smythies*, Volker A. Munz and Bernhard Ritter (eds.), Oxford: Wiley-Blackwell. [WWCL]

Andrea Kern
Human Life and Self-consciousness. The Idea of 'Our' Form of Life in Hegel and Wittgenstein

Abstract: The source of the normative structure that a human individual finds herself entrenched in is found in her 'immersion in a form of life', something which results from her having been brought up in it. All sympathetic readers of Hegel and Wittgenstein make use of this idea in one way or another. Yet despite much controversy over the status of this appeal to a 'form of life' most interpreters who want to stress the significance of 'education' in accounting for a certain kind of normativity think that it is the role of education to *transform* an individual whose activities do not yet manifest a consciousness of rules or norms that guide and orient her life into an individual whose activities do so. I will argue that neither Hegel nor Wittgenstein held such a view. According to them, the logical role of the ideas of self-consciousness and rationality is to depict a formal feature of a form of life, which its individual bearers, qua being bearers of this form of life, cannot fail to exhibit. Most interpreters think that, if there is a naturalism to be found in Hegel and Wittgenstein, then it can only be a naturalism of second nature. I will argue that this account misunderstands its own motivating insight: that the presence of self-consciousness has a 'metaphysical' significance. The sense in which self-consciousness is part of a human being's second nature, I will argue, presupposes that it is part of its first nature as well.

1

It is widely acknowledged that the source of the normative structure that a human individual finds herself entrenched in is found in her 'immersion in a form of life', something which results from her having been brought up in it. All sympathetic readers of Hegel and Wittgenstein make use of this idea in one way or another. Yet despite much controversy over the status of this appeal to a 'form of life' and whether it is a foundational notion or not, and despite much controversy about the meaning of the relevant idea of a 'form of life'– whether it should be identified with the human species, or rather with a more specific cultural or linguistic community – a thought along the following lines seems to be shared by those who want to stress the significance of 'upbringing' or 'education' in accounting for a certain kind of normativity. The role of education is to *transform* an individual whose activities do not yet manifest a consciousness of rules or norms that guide and orient her life into an individual whose activities do. What distinguishes the life of the latter from the life of the former, according to the shared view, is that its activities are explained by rules or norms by which it could not be explained if the individual herself were not conscious of them. We might call an individual whose life activities exhibit this structure a 'self-conscious individual', or equivalently, a 'rational individual'. The shared thought is that in order to understand the idea of an individual whose life exhibits self-consciousness and rationality in the above sense, we have to appeal to ideas such as 'upbringing' and 'education' whose role it is to bring about the transformation of a not yet self-conscious individual into a self-conscious one.

The terms 'self-consciousness' and 'rationality', as they are employed by those who share this view, go together. They are employed in a sense according to which none of them can be determined independently of the other. The relevant idea of self-consciousness which is said to be the result of 'upbringing' and 'education' is one according to which self-consciousness is conceived as a form of consciousness that is actualized in activities that are, as such, rational in the sense of being responsive to reasons. Just as the relevant idea of rationality which is said to be a matter of 'upbringing' and 'education' is conceived as a form of explanation that entails that the subject whose activities are said to be responsive to reasons is conscious of her reasons as reasons.

I endorse this thought and much of what I will say in what follows will contribute to an account according to which it is right to think of these concepts as being related to each other in this manner. But this will not be the main objective of my paper. Its main objective is to raise doubts about the underlying picture of what it means to be a self-conscious and hence rational individual and the explanatory role of education that goes with it. According to this picture, to be a self-conscious individual is to possess *certain capacities* such as judging and inferring, speaking and understanding, the possession of which sets their individual bearers metaphysically apart from those individuals who lack these capacities and which gives them a different normative status that is described by the notion of a "free agent".[1] This view is not only shared by many contemporary philosophers, but also by many sympathetic readers of Hegel and Wittgenstein. By contrast I will argue that neither Hegel nor Wittgenstein held this view. According to them, the logical role of the ideas of self-consciousness and rational-

---

[1] See, for example, McDowell 2009, cf. also Pippin 2006.

ity is not to depict a set of capacities of an individual. Rather, their role is to depict a formal feature of a form of life, which its individual bearers, qua being bearers of this form of life, cannot fail to exhibit. Moreover, both authors think that this form of life is identical with the human form of life.

I will call this position 'life form naturalism' and argue that both Hegel and Wittgenstein are proponents of it. I will develop this position in contrast to the above view according to which human beings are creatures whose life acquires its distinctive self-conscious character in the course of their upbringing. A powerful and influential articulation of the latter view can be found in the writings of John McDowell who calls this position a "naturalism of second nature" on account of the emphasis it puts on the idea of second nature (McDowell 1996: 98). McDowell and others think that, if there is a naturalism to be found in Hegel and Wittgenstein, then it can only be a naturalism of second nature. I will argue that this account misunderstands its own motivating insight: that the presence of self-consciousness has a metaphysical significance that transforms the normative status of its bearers. The sense in which self-consciousness is part of a human being's second nature, I will argue, presupposes that it is part of its first nature as well.

After a brief sketch of what is meant by a naturalism of second nature I will first bring into view Hegel's account of the relation between self-consciousness and the idea of life as he unfolds it in the *Phenomenology of Spirit*. I will then illustrate Wittgenstein's version of what I call 'life form naturalism' through an interpretation of a famous passage in the *Philosophical Investigations*.

2

According to a naturalism of second nature self-conscious animals are the result of a process of education that transforms a merely sensible animal, which only *potentially* possesses those capacities that are constitutive of self-consciousness, into an animal that *actually* possesses them. The term self-consciousness is said to designate a system of capacities that one cannot possess without being conscious of one's possession of them. According to McDowell, the paradigmatic capacity that constitutes this system of capacities, is the capacity to employ concepts in judgments whose content one is able to understand and for which one is able to give and demand reasons.[2] Central to a naturalism of second nature is the

---

[2] I have discussed McDowell's position in more detail, especially with respect to its implicit notion of education and its relation to Kant's notion of self-consciousness in Kern 2017.

idea that the role of education is to transform an individual that only *potentially* possesses the capacities that make up this system into one who possesses them in *actuality*. Here are some representative passages from McDowell where he articulates this position:

> Our nature is largely second nature, and our second nature is the way it is not just because of the potentialities we were born with, but also because of upbringing, our *Bildung*. (McDowell 1996: 87)

> Human Individuality is not just biological, not exhausted by the singleness of a particular human animal. A fully fledged human individual is a free agent. [...] Freedom is responsiveness to reasons. It is not a natural endowment, not something we are born with [...]. (McDowell 2006: 166)

> The idea of participation in a communal form of life is needed for a satisfactory understanding of responsiveness to reasons. [...] Responsiveness to reasons [...] marks out a fully-fledged human individual as no longer a merely biological particular, but a being of a metaphysically new kind [...]. (McDowell 2006: 172)

Small children, according to this idea, are only potentially 'free agents' in the sense of agents that act in the light of reasons to which their activities are responsive to. In that sense they are only potentially 'self-conscious' and 'rational' individuals. They *can* become 'self-conscious' and 'rational', but for as long as they are small children, their activity is not a manifestation of the metaphysical kind to which they will belong once they have undergone education. The actuality of the child, its being an individual that has feelings and desires, that moves around and perceives things, that utters sounds and occasionally cries, only comes to be 'self-conscious', 'rational' and 'free' through education. Education is depicted as a process in virtue of which a merely sensible individual undergoes a *metaphysical transformation*.

Two points are decisive here. First, there is the way in which the account describes the beginning and end of education: it begins with a merely biological particular and ends with a rational, free agent. Metaphysically speaking, there is no difference between small children and non-human animals. The fundamental principles of their activities are described in terms of capacities that do not yet entail the above mentioned set of capacities that constitute self-consciousness.[3] Secondly and relatedly, there is the way in which it conceives of the role of education: namely as a process that brings about a metaphysical transfor-

---

[3] That McDowell does not draw an essential distinction between small children and non-human animals is also explicit, for example, in his paper *Two Sorts of Naturalism* (McDowell 1998).

mation, that is to say, as a process in which a metaphysically different kind of individual comes into existence.

McDowell describes the metaphysically new kind to which a fully-fledged human being belongs by recourse to the notion of a 'free agent' which he analyzes through the concepts of rationality and self-consciousness. This entails the thought that the concept of a *human* life and the concept of a *rational* or *self-conscious* life bear distinct meanings.[4] The concept of a human life is related to the concept of a rational, self-conscious life, but it is not identical to it. For one can be a human being, according to this account, without being a rational, self-conscious one.

By contrast, Hegel and Wittgenstein both think that the kind instantiated by a fully-fledged human being is metaphysically no different from that instantiated by small children. This is so, not because they think that small children are already born with capacities that, according to a naturalism of second nature, must be acquired in the course of their upbringing. Rather, it is because they deny that the concept of a rational life is anything other than the concept of the life of a human being. To speak of a rational life is not to speak of something other than a human being. Rather, it is to speak of a human being in an abstract manner, i.e. in a manner that abstracts from those factors in virtue of which the concept of a rational life describes something real and not a mere "Hirngespinst", to borrow an expression that Kant uses in relation to the categories, a different – but not so different – context (Kant 1968: A 91/B 124). For Hegel as well as for Wittgenstein, as I will argue in what follows, the concept of a rational life does not refer to a kind of which human beings are only one instantiation. One instantiation, that is, among others which we humans can at least think of as possible, although we do not in fact know of any. Rather, the concept of a rational animal just *is* the concept of the human, articulated in an abstract manner. Thus, according to them, the concept of the kind that a fully-fledged human individual exhibits is indeed metaphysically different from the concept of the kind that any other non-human individual exhibits. However, the account of this metaphysical difference does not exclude, but presupposes that the vital activities of small children cannot fail to exhibit it, no matter which stage of their life they are at.

---

4 See explicitly McDowell 1996: 85, 125.

3

Hegel develops this position in the *Phenomenology of Spirit*, beginning with Chapter IV, where he reflects on the idea of self-consciousness. The upshot of Hegel's treatment of the idea of self-consciousness is that it is not a capacity that a living individual might or might not possess but a formal feature of a form of life. Self-consciousness, he will say, is, as such, "vital self-consciousness" (PdG: 127[5]). Hegel arrives at his account of self-consciousness in two steps.

In the first step Hegel introduces the idea of self-consciousness as that of a self-reflexive act of consciousness of an object of the sensible world. He takes this to be an innocuous way to begin, i.e. with an idea that in one way or another is endorsed by everybody who thinks about self-consciousness. According to this idea, self-consciousness is consciousness of an object of the sensible world that contains, as such, a consciousness of the capacities from which it springs – which are the capacities for perception and understanding – whose content it thereby determines. In performing this double 'movement', i.e. in being conscious of an object of the sensible world as well as of itself as a capacity for acts whose content it determines, self-consciousness is both consciousness of the sensible world and of itself, and it is each in virtue of the other (cf. PdG: 127). Hegel concludes from this that for a self-consciousness which conceives of itself in this manner, the object to which it refers "has become life", "ist in sich *Leben* geworden", as he puts it (PdG: 122).

Hegel notes that the account of the concept of life introduced in this passage is completely abstract and minimal. At this point the object to which self-consciousness refers is "reflected being" (PdG: 122). This means that the object of which self-consciousness is conscious is not something that is external to this consciousness, but rather forms a "unity" with it (PdG: 122). According to Hegel, this implies that for something to be an object of *self*-consciousness, its identity as an object must be dependent on the consciousness whose object it is. It is this inner unity between consciousness and object that Hegel has in mind when he introduces the notion of 'life' to characterize the object of self-consciousness. The idea of an object whose identity is consciousness-dependent in this sense, as it must in order to be an object of self-consciousness, is the idea of an object that belongs to the unity of a life form in which it figures as such an object.

However, as Hegel argues, self-consciousness is not thereby fully understood. This is because a self-consciousness which understands itself in this

---

[5] All of the following translations from Hegel's works are my own.

way refers to life as an object of *perception* and so has an object which – as an object of perception – is *distinct* from the consciousness of this object. Hegel infers from this that self-consciousness cannot yet understand its own actuality, and that it cannot understand itself as long as it understands its actuality to be *merely* that of an object of perception. For this entails that the "life" which is its object is conceived as something that, precisely on account of its consciousness of the object, therein "divides itself" (PdG: 122). It must conceive of this life, which figures as the object of the very perception it understands itself to be, as an entity that is distinct from itself, and as such it conceives what it is conscious of as something with which it is not identical.

Hegel infers from this – and this is the second step in his argument – that self-consciousness consists in an activity of life *itself*. This activity of life conceives of the life it is conscious of not as an object of perception from which it distinguishes itself, but as something that, as such, "refers to consciousness" (PdG: 125). Self-consciousness has to conceive of the life whose consciousness it is as an object which is, as such, determined as an object of consciousness. It has to conceive of the life which it is conscious of as an object which *actualizes* itself in the consciousness it has of that life.

A self-consciousness that is conscious of such a life – Hegel calls it "this other life for which the genus, as such, is and which is genus for itself" ("dies andere Leben, für welches die Gattung als solche und welches für sich selbst Gattung ist" (PdG: 125)) – conceives of its own actuality as the actualization of the *concept* of a life form ("welches für sich selbst Gattung ist") whose actuality is, qua actuality, *self-conscious*. Hegel concludes that self-consciousness thereby proves itself to essentially be "lebendige[s] Selbstbewußtsein", "vital self-consciousness" (PdG: 127).

Hegel concludes from this that the concept of self-consciousness, in its fundamental application, does not describe a particular property or capacity that belongs to some, many or all individuals who are bearers of a certain form of life. It rather describes a formal feature of a form of life in that it describes *the distinctive manner of actualization* that characterizes a form of life that is thus described. Michael Thompson articulates this Hegelian point by saying that the concept of self-consciousness is the concept of the 'form' of a form of life, in contrast to concepts that describe the content of a particular life form (as concepts of particular capacities or properties or activities do).[6]

The significance of this is twofold: First the concept of self-consciousness does only describe a consciousness which takes a living individual as its subject

---

6 See Thompson 2013.

if and because it also describes a consciousness which takes a form of life as its subject. Hegel's point is to say that it can have the one kind of subject – the individual that has a "singular consciousness" of itself – only in virtue of also having the other kind of subject – the life form that has a "general consciousness" of itself –, and vice versa (cf. PdG: 234–235). This means that, secondly, the concept of self-consciousness characterizes a consciousness whose subject is an individual in virtue of her manifesting a form of life, of which there is a general consciousness, that she herself individually manifests in everything she is and does.

The concept of self-consciousness, according to Hegel, designates nothing other than the unity of these two moments of consciousness: the unity of a consciousness whose subject is an individual, with a consciousness whose subject is a form of life. This is what Hegel calls the "abstract" concept of self-consciousness: It is the concept of a unity of the *single* consciousness of an individual with the *general* consciousness of a form of life whose actuality consists in the individual's consciousness of this unity (cf. PdG: 234).

Self-consciousness, on this account, is neither a capacity which belongs to an individual *besides* other capacities, such as walking, or reading, or seeing, nor is it a very fundamental capacity of an individual, such as, perhaps, breathing or eating or digesting. Rather, the concept of self-consciousness does not designate a capacity at all. It specifies a form of life in terms of the distinctive kind of *nexus* between the form of life that is thus specified and the living individual that manifests it. If this is the logical role of the term 'self-consciousness', then it cannot be conceived as something that an individual can exercise, neither occasionally nor all the time. It rather must be conceived as a form of consciousness that is *identical* with the existence and activities of individuals of a certain kind, namely those individuals whose form of life is thus characterized. It is identical with the existence and activities of individuals of that kind in that self-consciousness characterizes *their distinctive manner of having and actualizing capacities.*

4

A self-conscious form of life, according to Hegel, is a form of life whose bearers are individuals who conceive of themselves – their existence and identity, their properties and capacities – as individual instantiations of a form of life whose actualization consists in this very consciousness. Hegel arrives at this conception of a self-conscious form of life as the result of an attempt to understand the concept of self-consciousness. For an object of consciousness to be *identical* to its subject, as it must be in order to be the object of self-consciousness, it must be a manifestation of a form of life whose existence is dependent upon forms of consciousness that reflect themselves as individual manifestations of the form of life that one is conscious of. Any self-conscious act, according to Hegel, therefore contains, as such, the consciousness of a *manifold of individuals* that are conceived as manifestations of the very form of life whose manifestation any self-conscious act reflects itself to be.

McDowell thinks that the employment of concepts in judging and thinking, in giving and responding to reasons, is paradigmatic of self-consciousness. Hegel does not object to the idea that there is such a thing as the paradigmatic activity of self-consciousness, or that this activity is judgment. Indeed, he endorses this thought. This is because judgment, as Hegel conceives of it, is nothing but "the positing of determinate concepts through the concept itself" (WdL: 301). What Hegel means by this is that judgment, qua judgment, is an activity of making up one's mind about something that manifests one's consciousness of one's form of life whose content one thereby, through that activity of judging, determines. However, what Hegel does object to is the idea that it is possible to think about the manner in which a given living individual comes to possess whatever capacity – let this capacity be swimming or judging, eating or speaking, running or laughing – *without first specifying the form of life* that the individual in question manifests. This is because, according to Hegel, the *meaning* of the concept of the capacity in question, and hence what it means *to possess and exercise* this capacity, is partly dependent upon the form of life that the individual in question exhibits. If the individual in question manifests a self-conscious life form, then the meaning of the relevant capacity-concept entails that the individual to which it is applied is either represented as one that applies this concept to herself, in which case she would be said to fully possess the relevant capacity, or it is represented as one that does not yet apply it to herself but is on the way to it, in which case she would be said to not yet fully possess the relevant capacity. By contrast, if the individual does not manifest a self-conscious life form, then the meaning of the relevant capacity-concept does not entail the idea of a self-conscious employment. This renders it impossible to raise the question whether a given living individual possesses a certain capacity 'by nature' or whether its possession is dependent upon "education" without first specifying the individual's form of life. This is because, without such a specification, the question one asks has *no determinate meaning*.

Think, for example, of the concept of swimming. This concept can be applied equally to cats and to human beings. If one denies that self-consciousness is the form of a form of life but thinks of it as a capacity which a living individual either happens to have, or perhaps essentially has, then one will be tempted to think the following: The concept of swimming is the concept of a capacity, which, qua capacity, leaves open how an individual comes to fall under it. As it happens, we know that the concept of swimming applies to cats by nature insofar as cats do not have to undergo some sort of teaching and practice in order to be able to swim, whereas human beings, although they are capable of doing it briefly after birth, have to learn how to swim in a manner that requires instruction, teaching and a fair amount of practice.

By contrast, if one thinks that the concept of self-consciousness characterizes the form of a form of life, then it follows that the concept of *any* vital capacity that is applied to an individual that exhibits a self-conscious form of life is formally different from the ones applied to individuals that exhibit a non-self-conscious form of life. This is because the meaning of capacity-concepts which are applied to individuals that exhibit a self-conscious form of life is dependent on their employment by individuals who thereby characterize *their own form of life*. It is thus dependent on individuals who, for that very reason, exhibit their form of life to which they refer with these concepts, in a *fully-fledged manner*.

This entails the idea that not every self-conscious being instantiates her form of life in a manner that is *paradigmatic* for a self-conscious life form and in that sense in a fully-fledged manner. Small children or severely brain-damaged human beings do not or do not yet possess the capacity to employ concepts in judgments. Hence they do not yet exhibit their life form in the manner that is paradigmatic for it. Being a self-conscious being and being a fully-fledged self-conscious being is not the same. However, this does not mean, as a naturalism of second nature would have it, that small children are only potentially, rather than actually, 'self-conscious', or 'free', or 'rational'. Rather, it means that small children are, as such, *on their way* to become self-conscious in the manner that defines a fully-fledged self-conscious being in living the kind of life that is characteristic for beings of their kind: i.e. in living a *self-conscious* life. It means that every one of her vital activities is, as such, a manifestation of self-consciousness that contributes to the very content of this consciousness. This enables this consciousness to gradually take the form of concepts through which the subject characterizes herself.

In this sense we can say that *each exercise* of a capacity possessed by an individual that manifests a self-conscious form of life is, as such, a case of coming to a more determinate and hence differentiated understanding of one's form of life, e. g. by coming to be able to distinguish certain capacities from one another, or by coming to be able to distinguish them from the circumstances under which they can be exercised, etc. Coming to a more determinate and hence differentiated understanding of one's form of life is certainly a form of learning. It is its fundamental form. Being a bearer of a self-conscious form of life means to have capacities whose exercise, qua exercise, entails a form of learning through which other forms of learning than learning by doing become possible, such as learning by imitation, or learning from other's examples, or their instructions, or their explanations, etc.

Moreover, it is in virtue of the self-consciousness of such a life form that the acquisition of any capacity by a self-conscious being is itself a self-conscious process. The child is just as aware as her educator of her inability. She knows that she needs others in order to learn what she does not yet know. Therefore, Hegel can conclude that "the child's own striving for education is the immanent moment of all education" (E: §396 Z.). According to Hegel, in becoming educated the human child does not actualize a mere possibility for which she has the potential. Rather, she comes to fully actualize the very form of life she exhibits *qua* human child insofar as this form of life contains, as such, forms of consciousness, of which the child's striving for education is just one manifestation, albeit a fundamental one.

5

Let's call the above position 'life form naturalism'. I will now turn to Wittgenstein, arguing that we should read him as a proponent of this position. I will illustrate this through an interpretation of a famous passage in the *Philosophical Investigations*, one which, moreover, points toward an aspect of a self-conscious life form that we have not yet touched upon.

The passage I want to interpret culminates in Wittgenstein's famous claim that a lion, if he could speak, could not be understood by us. Wittgenstein makes this claim in the context of a long discussion of a variety of possible cases in which human beings do not understand, or misunderstand, one another, or in which they are completely opaque to one another. The passage begins with a contemplation of two possibilities that serve to indicate each end of a spectrum:

> Wir sagen auch von einem Menschen, er sei uns durchsichtig. Aber es ist für diese Betrachtung wichtig, daß ein Mensch für einen anderen ein völliges Rätsel sein kann. Das erfährt man, wenn man in ein fremdes Land mit gänzlich fremden Traditionen kommt; und zwar auch dann, wenn man die Sprache des Landes beherrscht. Man versteht die Menschen nicht. (Und nicht darum, weil man nicht weiß, was sie zu sich selber sprechen.) Wir können uns nicht in sie finden. (Wittgenstein 1984: 358)

> We also say of some people that they are transparent to us. It is, however, important as regards this observation that one human being can be a complete enigma to another. We learn this when we come into a strange country with entirely strange traditions; and, what is more, even given a mastery of the country's language. We do not understand the

people. (And not because of not knowing what they are saying to themselves.) We cannot find our feet with them. (Wittgenstein 1978: 223)

Wittgenstein is reminding us of two things here: First human beings can be transparent to one another. We use the expression 'transparent' in cases in which our understanding of another human being, i.e. our knowledge of what she does and why she does what she does, is not hindered by any obstacle. The concept of understanding, as Wittgenstein uses it in this context, is such as to include, among its possible objects, utterances made by those whose understanding is in question. If she whom we try to understand is 'transparent' then this means that we do not need to make any special effort in order to know what she does and why she does what she does. Examples of this sort typically include cases in which people speak a common language. However, as Wittgenstein reminds us, having a language in common is not a sufficient condition that needs to be in place for such forms of transparency. This is due to Wittgenstein's second point: One human being can be a complete enigma to another, and this can happen even when they speak the same language. In order to describe the latter possibility, Wittgenstein introduces the idea of a "strange country" and of "entirely strange traditions". Notice that the idea of a tradition, and in the same way the possibility of different traditions, is introduced by Wittgenstein in the context of explaining the possibility of deep failures of understanding that can occur between human beings, a kind of failure which, Wittgenstein wants to emphasize, human beings are liable to as such.

Wittgenstein uses the concepts of a "strange country" and of "entirely strange traditions" in order to characterize the specific nature of the human capacity to understand each other: namely, as a capacity that entails the possibility of deep failures of actualization. It matters, I think, that Wittgenstein does not represent this liability as something that he could have simply derived from the mere concept of 'understanding' when applied to other human beings. Sure, the concept of understanding, taken as the concept of a human capacity, does not entail anything that would exclude the possibility of deep failure. Yet, it also does not entail anything that would explain this possibility. Nevertheless, as made clear by this passage, Wittgenstein wants to say that this liability is an *essential* characteristic of the human capacity for understanding when applied to other human beings. Its liability for failure is not just a possible feature of it but one without which we could not understand the capacity in question.

I think it matters therefore that in referring to this *essential liability* Wittgenstein uses the first person plural. He refers specifically to *us*, to *our* human form of life, as *we* know it. The idea of "entirely strange traditions", and the correlated idea of a deep failure to understand another human being on account of that, presupposes, I take Wittgenstein to suggest, the need for an essentially first personal move in the treatment of the idea of understanding that constitutes his topic. If we make this first personal move, then we can say that the human form of life, as we know it to be manifest in our lives, contains a manifold of *particular ways of understanding the human life* that guide and orient the life of those who understand the human life in this way, thereby setting them apart from other ones whose life is oriented by a different way of understanding the human life. The term "traditions" designates the idea that the human life, as it is known to be manifested in our lives, is known to be manifested in particular ways of understanding itself. The term "traditions" is employed in a conception of human life that refers to that life as something that is *ours*, as something that *we* instantiate. Thus we can say, as Wittgenstein wants to say, that the human capacity for understanding, when applied to another human being, is essentially liable for deep failure. It is part of the very concept of this capacity.

This manner of arguing is expressive of what I think to be one of Wittgenstein's most fundamental insights that shapes all of his writings. I mean Wittgenstein's constant appeal to us humans by appealing to a 'we' that does not draw a limit, a 'we' that is not contrasted to another 'we', a 'we' for which there is no 'you', a 'we' of which there is only one. This manner of arguing, as it is exemplified above, reflects Wittgenstein's insight that the human life form, qua life form, has a form whose articulation is logically dependent upon a first personal perspective on it. According to Wittgenstein, the concept of the human life, as he wants to articulate it, is the concept of a form of life whose meaning cannot be determined independently of its articulation by those who actualize it. The meaning of the concept of the human, according to him, is partly determined through first personal statements of the form: 'we do such and such' or 'we can fail to do such and such' in which we articulate the concept of the form of life 'we' ourselves exhibit. This does not mean that, according to Wittgenstein, the concept of the human is identical with 'our' manner of understanding 'our' form of life. Rather, he thinks the meaning of the concept of the human cannot be determined independently of the employment of such 'we'-statements. The content of a thought that entails the concept of the human, according to Wittgenstein, is irreducibly dependent on such 'we-thoughts'.

There is a similar argument in Hegel. The concept of a self-conscious life form, Hegel argues in the *Phenomenology of Spirit*, is an "abstract" concept as long as it is not articulated through concepts in virtue of which it describes a reality (PdG: 125). The concept of the *human*, by contrast, is not an abstract concept. It is a *concrete concept* of a self-conscious life form. As a concrete concept it describes a reality whose conceptual articulation is and must be, as matter of necessity, recognizable by the individuals whose reality these concepts claim to describe. Wittgenstein shares this Hegelian idea and concludes that the employment of the concept of the human must have an essentially first personal character, with the life form figuring as the subject of predications in statements of the *first person plural*.

It is thus part of Wittgenstein's employment of the concept of a tradition that he thinks of it as an aspect of a life form which one cannot articulate by means of this concept unless one conceives of oneself as instantiating it. Its role is to characterize the self-understanding that constitutes the human life form as the concept of a *manifold* of particular manners of understanding the human life form that differ from one another in a sense that is – within limits – analogous to the sense in which the concept of a language is the concept of a manifold of particular languages, e. g. French, or German, or Chinese, etc. According to the Hegelian account, as we have argued above, the self-understanding that constitutes the human life form consists in the self-understanding of individuals who conceive of themselves as *individual* manifestations of a form of life whose concept they determine through that self-understanding. This formal character of the human life form – that it is a life form whose concept is dependent upon the self-understanding of those to which it applies – makes room for the idea that the content of this concept might be determined in radically different manners.

As we have seen above, Wittgenstein endorses this idea and concludes from it that it affects the character of the human capacity for understanding when applied to another human being. Because it allows for the possibility that this capacity can be acutely hindered by something that is not external to this capacity but is part of its very actuality. One's capacity to understand another human being can be obstructed, in a deep way, by a different manner of understanding the human life form, and hence by something that has, in a certain sense, its ground in itself: in the human form of life that is the ground for this capacity for understanding each other.

The case of the lion is one that, prima facie, radicalizes the form of failure to understand that is liable to occur among humans. Yet, the way in which Wittgenstein characterizes this case is significantly different from the former case. Whereas the former cases of failed understanding are described in the indicative mood – as empirical realities whose possibility we are, qua bearer of the human life form, aware of – the second case is in the subjunctive mood:

> Wenn ein Löwe sprechen könnte, wir könnten ihn nicht verstehen. (Wittgenstein 1984: 536)
>
> If a Lion could talk, we could not understand him. (Wittgenstein 1978: 223)

In the case of other human beings, our understanding can fail on a fundamental level. Such fundamental failure is possible, Wittgenstein argues, if and when the individual who attempts to understand another human being instantiates a tradition that is very different from the tradition of the individual who is the object of her understanding. By contrast, the case of the lion is not presented along these lines. The lion is not presented as an object with respect to which a human being's capacity for understanding might fail to be perfectly actualized. The lion is presented not as an object of a *possible* failure of the kind of understanding we have or might have of another human being, but as an object with respect to which we *know* – not on the basis of experience, but *a priori* – that if it could speak, we could not understand it. How is this *a priori* knowledge possible?

To be knowable *a priori* the impossibility in question must be constitutive for the meaning of the concept of understanding that characterizes the capacity in question. The concept of this capacity must be such that it excludes, for logical reasons, that a lion could be a possible object of this very capacity. Now, this is exactly how things stand if one thinks of the capacity for understanding whose object is a human being in the manner that Wittgenstein suggests: as a capacity that has a *distinctive form*. The capacity for understanding whose object is a human being has a distinctive form in that it is a capacity that is constituted by thoughts about what 'we' are that one takes to share with that which one seeks to understand and in the light of which one understands one's own activities as well as the activities of the other. The capacity for understanding whose object is a human being, Wittgenstein wants to say, is constituted by thoughts in the first person plural in the light of which one understands oneself as well as the other. It is a capacity for understanding that consists in thoughts whose subject is not an 'I', taken as an individual, but a 'we' that thinks *itself*.

Understanding a human being, according to Wittgenstein's account, is thus *formally* different from understanding the activities of a lion or a plant or the behavior of an earth worm. Understanding a human being means to be engaged in 'we'-thoughts about 'ourselves' in light of which the activities of the other that thereby come into view, might so much as be unintelligible to one. The notion of unintelligibility, of being "a complete enigma to another", that goes with this form of understanding, is thus a qualified notion. It refers to a form of unintelligibility which one can only be confronted with in relation to another human being. It is an unintelligibility that consists in a failure to understand what she does and why she does what she does in light of the we-thoughts that we take to share with her and without which we could not wonder about her activities in the manner in which we do when we think of her as a "complete enigma to us". One's understanding of the we-thoughts one takes to share with the other does not, as a matter of fact, enable one to *actually* understand her activities.

It belongs to the nature of such a failure that it might be overcome one day. For example, by talking to each other for many hours, days, weeks or months, in the course of such a conversation both parties might come to an understanding of the we-thoughts they take each other to share that finally enables them to understand each other's activities. And this is, indeed, what sometimes happens. But it is equally in the nature of such failure that both parties might just never overcome it. Because whether the failure to have such an understanding might be overcome one day or not will be partly dependent upon what both parties can and will do: upon their capacities for articulation, upon the kind of effort they invest, and so on. However, there is one thing that it *makes no sense* to say about such a case: namely, that the overcoming of such a failure of understanding is *impossible*. Rather, in representing the other as a subject with which one shares thoughts about what we are, one thereby knows oneself to have, at least, the *capacity* to come to an understanding of what she does and why she does what she does that is provided by the we-thoughts we take ourselves to share with her.

By contrast, a human being does know *a priori* that it would be impossible for her to understand a lion that could speak. She knows this *a priori* because it is part of her thinking of him as a lion, as opposed to a human being, that a lion is not an object of understanding *in the same sense of understanding* as another human being. Understanding a human being means to be united with the other through we-thoughts in the light of which one understands oneself as well as the other (or, as a matter of fact, fails to understand her). This makes it *logically impossible* to conjoin the thought that something is a lion, as opposed to a human being, with the thought that it can be understood in the same sense of understanding as a human being. Rather, thinking of something as a lion, as opposed to a human being, means to deny precisely that: that one is united with the other through we-thoughts in the light of which one understands oneself and the other.

One might be tempted to ask how, on Wittgenstein's account, one can know *a priori* that one cannot have we-thoughts with a lion. Doesn't the argument seem to presuppose that? But this would miss Wittgenstein's point. Wittgenstein does not think that we know *a priori* that we cannot have we-thoughts with a lion if this is meant to be something that would have to be established over and above the fact that it is a lion. His point is to say that representing another one as a subject with which one shares we-thoughts and representing the other as a human being is *one and the same*. To be united with another human being through we-thoughts, according to Wittgenstein, and to think of her as a human being, are not two logically independent thoughts. Rather, part of what it means to represent a human being is to share we-thoughts with her, and vice versa. This makes it trivial to say, just as Wittgenstein wants to have it, that we cannot share we-thoughts with a lion because thinking of the other as a lion just is to deny that one shares such thoughts.

6

The position I just sketched shares with a naturalism of second nature the idea that a full account of the nature of a human being requires us to make use of the distinction between capacities that come from 'nature' and those that come from 'education' and the sort of 'practice' that goes with it. However, it diverges from this kind of naturalism for it denies that the distinction between capacities that come from nature and capacities that come from education and practice has a determinate meaning independently of a specification of the form of life in which the capacities in question play a role. Rather, the meaning that the concepts of 'nature' on the one hand and 'education' and 'practice' on the other take in order to characterize the relation between an individual and its capacities is dependent upon the form of life that the individual manifests. What makes a human being a distinctive kind of animal is not due to the fact that its nature is not exhausted by a first nature, but contains a second nature as well. Rather, the *meaning of the distinction* between capacities that come from nature and those that come from education and practice, if applied to a human being, is already a distinctive one.

Hegel and Wittgenstein take this to be a consequence of the thought that the concepts of self-consciousness, that Hegel employs to mark the relevant distinction, and of understanding, that Wittgenstein employs to mark the same distinction, do not describe individual capacities *unless* they describe the 'form' of a form of life. Their logical role is to determine the specific manner in which a form of life thus specified is instantiated in the life activities of the individuals that are its bearers. As a consequence, the *meaning* of *all* concepts through which we characterize the vital activities of those who exhibit this form of life is *dependent upon and shaped by them*, and hence is transformed with respect to the meaning they have when applied to beings that exhibit a form of life whose form is not specified through these concepts. There is thus no highest common factor conception of a living individual to which the distinction between nature on the one hand and education and practice on the other could be applied in the same sense. Rather, the meaning of this distinction depends on the 'form' of the form of life that the individual exhibits to which this distinction is applied.

To say of an individual who exhibits a self-conscious form of life that she has a first nature, is to say that she has capacities whose identity as capacities – what they are and which role they play in her life, how they differ from one another and how they are related – is dependent upon her self-conscious exercise of them, in the course of which she learns more about them. When things go well a human child will acquire full possession of the concepts of her capacities through education and practice in virtue of which she herself will be able to refer to her capacities as *her own* in opposition to those that belong to another individual. In this sense, every exercise of a capacity that belongs to a self-conscious being's first nature is, as such, on the way to being second nature, for its possession is shaped and determined by education and practice right from the start.

Thus, in the case of human beings, having a first nature means having capacities in a manner that cannot be disentangled from education and practice. Rather, every capacity that a self-conscious being has by nature, and which in that sense is part of her first nature, is, as such, on the way to becoming second nature. The concept of nature that goes along with that of a self-conscious, self-understanding being is thus one that cannot be understood without the distinction between first and second nature. The distinction between first nature and second nature is built into the idea of a self-conscious life form. We cannot fully characterize what it is to exhibit a self-conscious life form without characterizing its individuals through this distinction. The nature of those individuals is one that *essentially* divides itself into 'firstness' and 'secondness'.

This distinguishes the concept of nature that characterizes a non-human animal. The concept of nature that characterizes a non-human animal does not entail, as such, the distinction between first and second nature. To say that a lion has certain capacities from nature does not mean that the lion has, prior to any exercise of them, capacities whose identity cannot be determined independently of their self-conscious exercise. The distinctive manner in which non-human animals have a nature is not one which divides itself into 'firstness' and 'secondness'. This does not mean that non-human animals are unable to acquire capacities through practice and some sort of 'teaching', and so in this sense have a second nature. Some birds need to acquire the capacity to build nests from their parents. Rather, the sense that the notions of 'practice' and 'teaching' take in their case differs from the human case. In the case of non-human animals, the activity of their first nature does not *consist in* the acquisition of a second nature, and hence of something that is shaped by education and the sort of practice that goes with it. Because the very identity of the capacities that constitute their first nature is not dependent upon their self-conscious exercise. Their acquisition of capacities (like nest building) through 'practice' and some sort of 'teaching' is possible for them, or even necessary for survival, but it does not characterize the specific manner in which they have a nature in the first place. Therefore, the fact that some of them acquire capacities through 'practice' and some sort of 'teaching' does not mean that they have a second nature. Whereas the sense in which human beings have a second nature entails that they could not have the capacities in question without having or being on the way to have their concept as well as the concept of their manner of acquisition (e.g. they know that they learnt to speak by others who taught them how to speak, etc.); no such self-consciousness characterizes the capacities of a non-human animal.

According to this position, the right way to endorse the idea that education and practice matters for an account of a self-conscious, rational, self-understanding individual does not consist in thinking of education and practice as a process of capacity-acquisition that transforms a non-self-conscious individual into a self-conscious individual. Nor does it consist in thinking of education and practice as a process that merely unfolds an inborn capacity. Instead, learning through education and practice is the shape that the life of a self-conscious being takes that is not yet a fully-fledged individual of her life form in order to become precisely that: a fully-fledged individual of her kind.

References

Hegel, Georg Wilhelm Friedrich (1986a) *Wissenschaft der Logik II*, in: *Werke*, Vol. 6, Frankfurt am Main: Suhrkamp.
Hegel, Georg Wilhelm Friedrich (1986b) *Enzyklopädie III*, in: *Werke*, Vol. 10, Frankfurt am Main: Suhrkamp.
Hegel, Georg Wilhelm Friedrich (1988) *Phänomenologie des Geistes*, Hamburg: Meiner.
Kant, Immanuel (1968) *Kritik der reinen Vernunft*, Frankfurt am Main: Suhrkamp.
Kern, Andrea (2017) "Kant über selbstbewusste Sinnlichkeit und die Idee menschlicher Entwicklung", in: Andrea Kern and Christian Kietzmann (eds.): *Selbstbewusstes Leben. Texte zu einer transformativen Theorie der menschlichen Subjektivität*, Berlin: Suhrkamp, 270–301.
McDowell, John (1996) *Mind and World*, Cambridge, MA: Harvard University Press.
McDowell, John (1998) "Two Sorts of Naturalism", in: *Mind, Value and Reality*, Cambridge, MA: Harvard University Press, 167–197.
McDowell, John (2009) "Towards a Reading of Hegel on Action in the 'Reason' Chapter of the Phenomenology", in: *Having the World in View*, Cambridge, MA: Harvard University Press, 166–184.
Pippin, Robert (2006) "Recognition and Reconciliation: Actualized Agency in Hegel's Jena Phenomenology", in: Katerina Deligiorgi (ed.): *Hegel: New Directions*, Chesham: Acumen.

Thompson, Michael (2013) "Forms of Nature: 'first', 'second', 'living', 'rational' and 'phronetic'", in: Gunnar Hindrich and Axel Honneth (eds.): *Freiheit: Stuttgarter Hegel Kongress 2011*, Frankfurt am Main: Klostermann, 701–735.
Wittgenstein, Ludwig (1978) *Philosophical Investigations*, Oxford: Basil Blackwell.
Wittgenstein, Ludwig (1984) *Philosophische Untersuchungen*, Frankfurt am Main: Suhrkamp.

Christian Martin
Duality, Force, Language-games and Our Form of Life

Abstract: This article presents a line of thought leading from considerations on how the difference between logical affirmation and negation is linguistically manifest via a critique of the 'force-content-distinction' drawn by Frege and reflection on how that distinction is involved in confusions about rule following to a conception of 'thinking-and-speaking' as, essentially, an activity of living beings. It thus seeks to motivate a logico-linguistic understanding of 'form of life', exhibiting it as already involved in making distinctions as 'simple' as that between 'p' and 'not p'.

1 From Duality to Force

1.1 According to TLP 4.0621 "it is important that the signs 'p' and '~p' *can* say the same". From that they *can* say the same it follows that a language dual to ours is possible, i.e. a language, whose expressions are equiform to those of the language we speak, but whose sentences mean the opposite of what sentences of our language mean. Geach has dubbed the language dual to English "Unglish".[1] In Unglish "This tree is not an oak", for instance, would serve to state, what we might state by means of the English sentence "This tree is an oak" and vice versa.

1.2 It might seem that the notion of a dual language is incoherent. What *is* incoherent, indeed, is the assumption that we might as well state facts by means of false sentences *as such*, rather than true ones. For, in stating a fact by means of 'p' one presents things as 'p' says. If things are as 'p' says, 'p' is true. Hence, in virtue of stating a fact by means of 'p', one implicitly presents it as true. Therefore, if one presented 'p' as false and went on to state a fact by means of it, one would thereby use it to say the opposite of what one hitherto used it to say.[2] –

---

[1] Cf. Geach 1982: 89.
[2] Cf. TLP 4.062: "Can we not make ourselves understood by means of false propositions as hitherto with true ones, so long as we know that they are meant to be false? No! For a proposition is true, if what we assert by means of it is the case; and if by 'p' we mean ~p, and what we mean is the case, then 'p' in the new conception is true and not false".

Pointing out that the idea of fact stating by means of *false* sentences *as such* is incoherent presupposes that the concept of a dual language is coherent. For, what is pointed out is that if one used 'p', which was taken to be false, so far, to state a fact, one would use it in the opposite sense than before and would thus have switched from the language one spoke, so far, to its dual. Obviously, a switch of this type cannot be made all at once. There is nothing incoherent, however, about a language, in which a sentential sign of shape 'p' is standardly used to state what we are used to state by means of a sign of shape 'not p' and vice versa.[3] In this language 'p' would play the same logical role as our 'not p'. Both signs would hence be different guises of what is logically the same symbol.

1.3 We might as well speak the language dual to the one we speak, although, *we know* we don't. Given that thought requires language, one can only be thinking in a language rather than its dual, if one knows one is. Otherwise, one might be wrong about what it is that one thinks. One might take oneself to think that p, while thinking that not p, insofar as one's thought happened to be articulated in the dual of the language one took it to be articulated in. This would be absurd.

1.4 That 'p' and '~p' *can* say the same is important, according to Wittgenstein, because "it shows that nothing in reality corresponds to the sign '~'".[4] To see the importance it might help to ask, what one's knowledge of speaking a language rather than its dual consists in. Obviously, it consists in knoweldg of whatever distinguishes the sentences of one's language from their dual twins. But *what is it* that distinguishes them? They look exactly alike, anyway.

1.5 It might seem obvious that what distinguishes English and Unglish sentences from each other are their semantic properties, which can be brought out by giving their truth-conditions, e.g.: 'p and q'$_{(\text{in English})}$ is true iff p and q, while 'p and q'$_{(\text{in Unglish})}$ is true iff not (not p and not q). – If the distinction between English and Unglish consisted in differences between semantic properties of their equiform

---

3 It would be a magical assumption to think that "p" cannot, in principle, be the dependent perceivable part (i.e. the sign) of a *negative* proposition, but of an affirmative one, only. As a matter of fact, there are languages, which express negation by removal of a part of a sign rather than by adding to it (e.g. Old Canarese). It seems incovenient rather than incoherent to express negation by removal of a *unique, non-iterable* part of the sign of the proposition, which is negated. It is incovenient, insofar as *iterated* negation cannot, then, be expressed in *perceivably* the same way.

4 Cf. TLP 4.0621. This exemplifies what Wittgenstein calls his "basic thought" (*Grundgedanke*) in 4.0312, namely "that 'the logical constants' do not represent".

expressions, the knowledge in virtue of which we (know we) speak English rather than Unglish, for instance, would have to be knowledge of semantic properties of the expressions we use. Knowledge of such properties cannot, however, be what prevents us from confusing our utterances with their dual twins. For, knowledge *of properties* of expressions consists in something we know *about* these expressions. Such knowledge would, as such, have to be *expressible* and, hence, involve the ability *to say* something *about* expressions of our language. One can only be able to say something, however, if one is able to say it in a language. Saying *something* involves knowledge which prevents one from confusing what one says with its dual twin. Being able to say what distinguishes one's expressions from their dual twins, cannot, therefore be what the knowledge which prevents us from confusing our utterances with their dual twins consists in. For, the supposed ability to say something about semantic properties of our expressions presupposes that we already dispose of knowledge which prevents us from confusing our utterances about semantic properties of expressions with their dual twins.

1.6 What distinguishes sentences of our language from their dual twins cannot, therefore, be (knowledge of) semantic properties of the expressions we use, i.e. (knowledge of) what they stand for or what "corresponds to them in reality". It must rather be knowledge, which is internal to *how we operate* with these expressions, i.e. knowlegde of their role in thinking. What distinguishes a language from its dual is, accordingly, knowledge, which is internal to *the use of expressions in thinking* or, in other words, to what I will sometimes refer to as the activity of 'thinking-out'.

1.7 We do not know that, in our language, 'p' says what it says, while 'not p' says the opposite, rather than the other way round, in virtue of knowing what the sentential signs 'p' and 'not p' stand for, but in virtue of knowlegde, which is inherent to the activity of thinking-out, which they partake in. If the acts of thinking-out, which tokenings of 'p' and 'not p' are parts of, would be *the same in type*, involvement in them could not be the source of (our knowledge of) their unmistakable logical difference. Since it isn't the *shapes* of 'p' and 'not p' in virtue of which they say what they say, insofar as these shapes might as well be reversed, it must, accordingly, be a difference in activity which the logical difference between 'p' and 'not p' consists in. There must hence be two different types of thinking-out – one, in virtue of involvement in which 'p' says what it says in our language – the activity of affirming – and one, in virtue of involvement in which 'not p' says what it says in our language – the activity of negating.

1.8 Affirming and negating cannot be *psychological* acts, for they are acts in virtue of involvement in which a sentential sign says something *logically* determinate rather than the opposite. It might be less misleading to exhibit the difference in activity, which distinguishes a sentential sign 'q' from its dual twin, as follows: One might either 'q'-affirmatively or 'q'-negatively, where both are ways of operating with 'q'. In English, for instance, the activities of 'q'-ing-affirmatively and 'not q'-ing-negatively, are constitutive of 'q' and 'not q', while, in Unglish, it is the other way round. Accordingly, it is nothing about the signs 'q' and 'not q' (i.e. nothing in reality), which *determines* their logical roles, but a difference in the activities, which these signs are involved in as their dependent, perceivable parts.

1.9 As indicated, the activity in virtue of involvement in which 'q' (or 'not q') says what it says rather than the opposite, cannot be psychological activity in the sense of activity which *merely accompanies* utterances of 'q' (or 'not q'). If it were, the question what the knowledge, which prevents us from confusing what we say with its dual twin, consists in would rearise. For, nothing could prevent it from *happening*, in this case, that an utterance of 'q' were accompanied, on occasion, by an act of other type than the one which supposedly provides for its logical identity. The activity in virtue of involvement in which sentential signs say what they say rather than the opposite cannot, therefore, be merely *related to* utterances of these signs, but must rather *constitute* them as the signs they are.

1.10 It cannot, accordingly, *happen to one* that one goes on using *the same sentential signs* as before, while accompanying them with the other kind of activity, and, hence, switches from the language one was speaking, so far, to its dual. Mental occurrences can be called 'psychological' insofar as they can accompany one's activity of thinking-out and remain the same, while one switches, in speaking from one's language to its dual. As long as one conceives of the activities of affirmating and negating, in virtue of engagement in which one speaks one's language rather than its dual as activities, which cannot prevent it from *happening* to one that one utters recurrent sentential signs, while accompanying them with the opposite kind of activity, and cannot preclude, therefore, an *unintentional* switch from one's language to its dual, the activities under consideration cannot be the ones in virtue of engaging in which one's acts of thinking-out are distinct from their dual twins.

1.11 The *non-psychological* activity, in virtue of engagement in which (one knows) 'q' says what it says rather than what it's dual twin would say, must accordingly be such as to come along with requirements on how further acts of thinking-out involving 'q' would have to match up with previous ones (given that 'q' is to be used in logically the same way as before). These requirements must be *recognized* in virtue of engagement in such activity. For, if engagement in thinking-out involving 'q' comes along with *recognized* requirements on how acts of thinking-out involving 'q' have to match up with further acts involving 'q', switching from one's language to its dual, and, hence, switching requirements, which are constitutive of 'q', cannot simply *happen* to one.

1.12 The activity of operating with signs can only come along with *logical* requirements on how utterances involving recurrent sentential signs have to match up with previous ones, if it doesn't presuppose anything beyond that *the same can* be said by repeated utterances of the same sentential sign. Every further requirement would be a psychological one. Therefore, the activity, which accounts for our speaking a language rather than its dual, cannot involve any particular characteristics of the ones engaging in it. Instances of such activity must therefore consist in acts, which present themselves as, in a certain respect, independent both of their own particularity as well as the particularity of the one's engaging in them. Such acts are acts of presenting things *as so* independently of one's presenting them as so, i.e. acts of 'judging-out', as one might put it.

1.13 As indicated, it is *acts of thinking-out* involving 'p', which come along with recognized requirements on how further acts involving 'p' have to match up with previous ones. Such requirements are known in virtue of the *use of sentential signs in thinking-out*, rather than in virtue of knowing something *about* them. At bottom, recognition of such requirements must be non-discursive, i.e. it cannot consist in knowledge *that 'p' is such that it cannot or must...* The reason for this has already been given: That 'p' says what it says (rather than what its dual twin would say) cannot be due to the fact (that one knows) that 'p' is so and so, because if it were, the question would rearise in virtue of what (we know) "'p' is so and so' says what it says. At bottom, recognition of logical requirements, which are constitutive of affirmative and negative propositions, must, accordingly, consist in the *ability* to recognize with respect to sets of *particular* propositions that they cannot be held together (or must be held together, if a certain subset of them is held).

1.14 What accounts for the fact that (we know) 'p' says what it says rather than what its dual twin would say, is, accordingly, (knowledge of) logical requirements which are implicit in our operating with 'p'. Knowledge of logic is thus, primarily, non-discursive knowledge, which is internal to the activity of thinking-out, i.e. knowledge of requirements on how acts of thinking-out have to match up with each other, i.e. knowledge of the *form* of the activity of judging-out, i.e. requirements on its unity. It is, accordingly, knowledge of logic qua knowledge of the form of one's activity of thinking-out, in virtue of which sententential signs are identified as saying what they (rather than what their dual twins would) say.

1.15 Cora Diamond puts the same point somewhat more generally by ascribing to early Wittgenstein the view that sentences (qua propositions, i.e. "bits of language in a certain logically recognizable employment" (Geach)) are identified via our grasp of logic:[5]

> [I]t is via our grasp of logic that we are able to identify bits of language as sentences, and also to identify something as the same sentence again, or not the same sentence, though similar in appearance.

Accordingly, the knowledge which allows us to identify a certain occurrence of 'not q', for instance, as a negative proposition *involves* grasping, amongst other things, that one cannot, in the same breath, subscribe to 'not q', to 'if p, then q' and to 'p'.

1.16 I have argued that what makes our sentences the logical units they are (and thus distinguishes them from their dual twins) is how we operate with them, i.e. their involvement in the activity of thinking-out. Our grasp of logic is knowledge of the form (requirements on unity) of the activity of thinking-out, which is *internal* to this activity. With respect to linguistic practice (rather than particular speakers), it might therefore seem to be a bit too cautious to say, as Diamond does, that "we are *able to identify* bits of language as sentences via our grasp of logic", since something is a sentence in the relevant, logical sense of 'sentence' only *insofar as it is thus identified*. At bottom, we are not merely *able to identify* bits of language as sentences via our grasp of logic, but it is this grasp in virtue of which there *are* sentences, in the first place.

1.17 Identification of a proposition *as affirmative or negative* is, obviously, *part* of its identification. The grasp of logic in virtue of which a proposition is identified as affirmative or negative and, hence, distinguished from its dual twin, cannot, *other than suggested so far*, be a grasp of *propositional* logic. Laws of propositional logic can be spelled out as rules of inference (e.g. p, p→q | q) or as sets of

---

5 Diamond 2002: 255–256.

acts of judging-out, which cannot (or must) *all* be undertaken together (e.g. {p, p→q, ~q}). However they are spelled out, they involve recourse to *different* propositions (e.g. 'p', 'p→q', '~p'). A proposition could therefore only be identified as affirmative or negative in terms of what such laws say, if other propositions were already identified as affirmative or negative, i.e. if their identity were already settled. For, if what is supposed to identify a proposition, involved recourse to propositions, whose logical identity cannot be taken for granted, it would be logically indeterminate and couldn't, therefore, serve to determine what it is supposed to determine. That 'p' cannot be held together with 'p→q' and '~q' cannot, for instance, identify 'p' as affirmative, unless it is already settled that 'p→q' is affirmative and '~q' is negative, i.e. unless these symbols are already identified as distinct from their dual twins. It cannot be the grasp of propositional logic, therefore, in virtue of which propositions are identified *as affirmative or negative*, insofar as such grasp presupposes that *some* propositions are already identified as affirmative or negative. As long as its possible instances are not thus identified, a rule of inference such as modus ponens cannot even count as a rule of propositional logic. It might as well be a rule of inference pertaining to the logic of questions or commands.

1.18 It has been argued that a proposition 'p' is identified in virtue of its involvement in the activity of thinking-out, which establishes recognized requirements on how it would have to match-up with further acts of thinking-out involving 'p'. Grasp of propositional logic must play a part, indeed, in the identification of propositions. For, if thinking-out involving 'p' did not establish recognized requirements on which further acts of thinking-out involving 'p' it cannot or must go together with, 'p' might *happen* to change its sense, arbitrarily, from one speaking to the next, and, therefore, couldn't be attributed a determinate sense at all. For the reason indicated, grasp of propositional logic can, however, only be part of what identifies a proposition; and it cannot be that part, in virtue of which a proposition is identified as affirmative or negative.

1.19 What identifies 'p' as an affirmative or a negative proposition is involvement in acts of judging-out, which come along with recognized requirements on how such acts have to match up with further acts involving 'p'. Since it would lead to a regress, if these further acts had to involve propositions that are already identified as affirmative or negative, a proposition can only be identified, in the end, as affirmative or negative in virtue of requirements on how it would have to match up with acts of thinking-out which do not involve negative or affirmative propositions. Accordingly, propositions are *not* identified as affirmative or negative via our grasp of *propositional* logic. If it is right, however, that they are identified as affirmative or negative via our grasp of logic, the realm of logic must extend beyond the logic of fact-stating. It must, hence, be an asymmetry in requirements, which relate statements to acts of thinking-out of a type different from fact-stating, in virtue of which propositions are identified as affirmative or negative. – This might also be seen as follows. Insofar as affirmative and negative propositions are opposed to each other, the types of act, through involvement in which they are identified, cannot be *primitively* different. For, insofar as affirmative and negative propositions are opposed to each other, there is something, with respect to which they behave in mutually exclusive ways. Insofar as what is constitutive of their identity, are requirements, which are established *by the activity of thinking-out*, these requirements must concern a difference in their relation to acts of thinking-out *of some other type*. What kind of acts might that be?

1.20 Try the following answer: A proposition is identified as affirmative insofar as it comes along with the requirement that it can be understood as *the* answer to a complement-question, while a negative proposition cannot thus be understood. Their distinction in form involves, accordingly, that something is an affirmative proposition, if a complement-question can be asked, to which it can count as *the* answer, while no complement-question can be asked, to which a negative proposition can count as *the answer* rather than *one* amongst *several, logically independent answers, which might all be true at the same time*. For example, "an oak" can count as *the* answer to the question "What kind of tree is this?", while one cannot find a question, to which "not a birch" can count as *the* rather than *one* amongst several, independent answers, which might all be true at the same time.[6] Accordingly, an affirmative proposition has a certain kind of exclusivity about it, which a negative proposition lacks. This exclusivity manifests a distinction in form between the business of determining how things are (affirming) and the businness of exhibiting candidates for determining how things are as not in fact determining how they are (negating).[7]

---

6 I do *not* claim that for every question there is an affirmative proposition which can count as *the* rather than *an* answer to it, but that with respect to an affirmative proposition a complement-question can be asked, to which this proposition can count as *the* rather than *an* answer.

7 If the distinction between affirmative and negative propositions is tied to the exclusive or non-exclusive way in which they might count as answering complement-questions, this distinction cannot be in place, unless (in what is logically the fundamental case) propositions are subsententially structured, minimally into an element which is to be determined (subject) and a determining element (predicate). Noting that *atomic* affirmative and negative propositions differ in

1.21 If the distinction between the activities of affirming and negating involves recourse to the activity of asking questions, affirming and negating are activities only a finite being can engage in. The distinction between affirmative and negative propositions is thus in and by itself a mark of (cognitive) finitude. Accordingly, only a being, which is cognitively dependent, i.e. receptive, can engage in acts of thinking-out involving such propositions.

1.22 As indicated, the identification of propositions as affirmative or negative involves a difference in their relation to questions. Accordingly, the activities of affirming, negating and asking questions are internally related. Starting from this insight, one might come to see *later* Wittgenstein as developing rather than abandoning his tractarian *Grundgedanke* that "'the logical constants' do not represent". As shown, it follows from this thought that propositions are identified as affirmative or negative via our grasp of logic. From the viewpoint of the *Tractatus*, however, all that is needed to distinguish between affirmative and negative propositions seems to be the logic of fact stating[8]. It has now been argued that fact stating doesn't stand on its own feet, logically, but is internally related to the activity of asking questions.

This won't be the end of the matter. For, the answer to the question what it is that distinguishes affirmative and negative propositions, given so far, is preliminary, since it takes the distinction between stating facts and asking questions for granted, while it cannot thus be taken as I will show in a moment. It cannot strike one as willful, however, even at this point of the dialectic, that later Wittgenstein refers to various "types of language" such as commanding, greeting or praying as parts of "the form of life" of speaking beings. Such types are, accordingly, to be seeen as *partaking in a form* (and, hence, in a *unified whole* of activities) rather than as independent activities on their own. It might thus turn out that Wittgenstein's notorious list of language-games in §23 of *Investigations*, rather than presenting the result of a foray into empirical linguistics, a piece of botanizing, manifests a logical insight, namely, that the activity of fact stating isn't logically autonomous insofar as, on its own, it cannot even provide for the distinction between affirmative and negative propositions. Eventually, it might be

---

their relation to complement-questions leaves it an open question how to understand the difference between affirmation and negation with respect to quantified propositions.

8 Thereby I do not want to dispute that recourse to uses of language different from fact-stating – from saying that things are so and so – plays an important role in the dialectic of the *Tractatus* (cf. TLP 6.1-6.4ff. and Diamond 2014: 153–155). I just claim that, as things are presented in that book, recourse to such uses seems not to be necessary to become clear about the logical distinction between affirmative and negative propositions.

no less than (by partaking in) the (form of) life of a thinker-and-speaker *as such* (i.e. the whole of activities which belong to the life of a thinker-and-speaker) in virtue of which a proposition is identified as affirmative or negative. – In the remaining parts of this paper I will try to substantiate this assumption.

1.23 Section 21 of the *Investigations* can be seen as expanding on the tractarian insight that 'p' and 'not p' *can* say the same. In this paragraph Wittgenstein indicates that *any* force-indicators (not just those of affirmation and negation) could be reversed.[9] He points out, moreover, that such indicators might as well be lacking, for a distinction in force doesn't have to *manifest itself* in the *shape* of sentential signs.[10] This should prevent one from thinking that there can only be as many differences in force as there are differences in mood or force-indicators. That force-indicators can be reversed or lacking altogether is of even greater importance than that 'p' and 'not p' can say the same. This can be brought out by extending the concept of duality.

1.24 One can imagine languages, whose expressions are equiform to expressions of our language, while differing from it by a reversal of force-indicators. The language dual to English, in which statements are expressed in the linguistic form of questions and questions in the linguistic form of statements might be called 'Asklish'. (Rhetorical questions can thus be seen as Asklicisms in English). 'Wishlish' would be the language dual to English, in which indicators, which differentiate between statements and whishes, are reversed. 'Jokelish' would be the language, in which whatever serves to indicate a difference between serious speaking and joking, is reversed. – With respect to such cases, one can draw lessons analogous to those, which have been drawn with respect to Unglish. We

---

9 "We could imagine a language in which *all* statements had the form and tone of rhetorical questions; or every command the form of the question 'Would you like to... ?'" (PIr: §21).

10 Commenting on what distinguishes the command and the report "five slabs", Wittgenstein remarks: "We could also imagine the tones being the same [...] the difference being only in the use that is made of these words" (PIr: §21). It seems, however, that if the linguistic turn is well-taken, a difference in force must *somehow* manifest itself in the *phenomenology* of speaking. It just doesn't have to manifest itself on the *linguistic* level, narrowly conceived. Accompanying gestures, for instance, can as well function as force-indicators, as folding one's hands does in indicating the force of prayer. To see that some such manifestation is necessary, one might imagine a language in which there is no narrowly *linguistic* (e.g. syntactic or phonetic) distinction between assertion and question, but a distinction in use, only. It seems easy to imagine such a language as long as one conceives of the speaking of it as accompanied by gestures, which indicate whether what is said is meant as an assertion or a question. However, the distinction between assertion and question couldn't be in place, if it didn't *manifest itself* in any such way.

might as well speak Asklish, Wishlish or Jokelish, but we know we don't. The knowlegde, in virtue of which we speak English rather than Asklish, Wishlish or Jokelish, is neither knowledge of the shapes of signs nor of their pragmatic *properties*, i.e. that they are standardly used to perform certain kinds of forceful acts of speaking.

1.25 The knowlegde in virtue of which I speak English rather than Asklish, for instance, cannot *consist* in knowing that sentences of the linguistic form of questions are standardly used, in the language I speak, to ask questions rather than to assert something. For, if my knowlegde consisted in knowledge of pragmatic *properties* of the sentences of my language, it would have to be *expressible* in form of statements *about* such properties. Statements, however, can only be made in a determinate language – in this case, English. My knowledge that I am speaking English rather than Asklish cannot, therefore, be expressed in what words such as "expressions with a question mark in the end are standardly used to express questions in my language" say, because these words say something determinate only, if it is already settled, which kind of force they bear. If they were in Asklish, they would, ordinarily, be used to ask a question, and if they were in Jokelish, they would indicate that what they say isn't to be taken seriously. – The knowledge in virtue of which we speak a determinate language rather than one of its dual twins doesn't, accordingly, consists in third-personal knowledge of properties of the expressions of the language we speak, but in *formal* self-knowledge, which is inherent to our activities of thinking-out.

1.26 That there might be a language, Asklish, whose expressions are equiform to expressions in English, but in which indicators of assertive and interrogative force are reversed, shows that the activities of fact-stating (i.e. affirming *and* negating) and asking do not stand on their own feet, logically. What distinguishes them? I have to admit that I cannot come forward with an immediate answer. I must content myself, therefore, to point to a possible difference in how *negative* propositions and questions relate to a further type of thinking-out. While a negative command can count as *the* answer to a complement-question, a negative statement of fact, as already seen, cannot. "Don't tell anyone, that's all you need to do" can count as *the answer* to the question "What shall I do?", while "It's not an oak, that's all there is to know" cannot count as *the answer* to the question "What kind of tree is it?".

1.27 The preceding considerations might at least indicate that asking, commanding and the like are as much activities which partake in a logical form as fact stating is insofar as the logical identity of propositions used in fact stating involves relations to questions, commands and the like. Logical requirements are requirements on how acts of thinking-out have to match up with each other. Insofar as it is a grasp of logic in virtue of which sentences are identified, and insofar as the activity of judging-out or fact-stating doesn't stand on its own feet, the realm of logic extends beyond the logic of fact stating (i.e. propositional and predicate logic). That asking, commanding and the like partake in a common logical form means that they go hand in hand with recognized requirements on how acts of respective type cannot or must go together with other acts of the same *as well as of other types*, if one's engagement in such acts is still to be seen as part of a unified whole of activities which one is engaged in. (If Wittgenstein is right, this whole is nothing but the activity of living the life of a speaking being as such). Accordingly, logical laws pertaining to how acts of thinking-out characterized by different forces may or may not be combined are as hard as logical laws pertaining to acts bearing the same type of force. It is, for instance, as much 'against logic', i. e. impossible, to judge that p and to ask whether p, *in the same breath*, as it is against logic, i. e. impossible, to affirm and negate p, in the same breath.

2 From Force to Meaning Skepticism

2.1 The assertion that p and the question whether p are different in one respect, while, at the same time, having something in common. It is unproblematic to call, what they have in common, their 'content', and what they differ in, their 'force'. It is still unproblematic to assume that the assertion 'p' and 'p' insofar as it occurs as a part of the assertion 'If p, then q' share their content, but not their force. Confusion starts, if one concludes from this that an act of thinking-out might have a content, while lacking a force.[11] The confusion is deepend, if one assumes (1) that a thinking-out is a composite act, which consists of the grasping of a content and a further ('forceful') act of taking a certain attitude towards it or (2) that the concept of a forceful act might be analyzed in terms of the concept of a forceless act and some further trait.

---

11 This is the same as thinking of content as externally related to force. As I will try to show, the force-content distinction should not be dismissed altogether, but any conception, which conceives of content as externally related to force, leads to nonsense. – My arguments in this section do rely on remarks from §22 of the *Investigations* as well as from (its precursor in) section 47 of *The Big Typescript*.

2.2 Extending the notion of duality beyond affirmative and negative propositions can help one to see that no explanation or definition of logical forces is possible. The explanation of a certain force could come on its way only, if the words it is phrased in were understood as bearing a certain force rather than another. One cannot, therefore, *explain* the notion of a certain force, i.e. transmit an understanding of it through speaking. For, the explanation could only be understood as an explanation, if it would be distinguished from its dual twins, and, hence, if an understanding of forces were already given.

2.3 Even if forces cannot be explained, since an understanding of them is presupposed in any speaking and understanding, it might nevertheless seem that the formal concept of a certain force might be analyzed into independent traits. For, even if everyone, who thinks-and-speaks is, as such, endowed with an implicit understanding of forces, such knowledge might nevertheless be made explicit in form of definitions, or so it seems. One might thus be tempted to assume that an act bearing a certain force could be defined in terms of the forceless grasping of a content as well as a further act of taking a certain attitude towards it. The act of judging-out might, for instance, apparently be defined as grasping a content and presenting it as true, while commanding might be defined as grasping a content and presenting it as required to someone to make it true.

2.4 Insofar as the force of an act belongs to *its* form, i.e. to what accounts for its *unity*, a forceful act as such cannot be a composite act of a type, whose formal concept might be analyzed in terms of *independent* traits. That no such analysis is possible can be shown, more concretely: The taking of a certain attitude, which is supposed to be different from the mere grasping of the content towards which this attitude is taken, must either be forceless or forceful. It cannot be forceless, because, if it were, the supposedly composite act under consideration would be forceless as well. Judging that p, for instance, cannot, besides the supposed act of grasping p, involve a *forceless* act of predicating truth of p. For, in this case, the overall act would be forceless as well and cannot, therefore, be an act of judging. If the supposed part of judging beyond grasping has to be forceful, however, this part will be identical to the act which it was mereley meant to be a part of, i.e. identical to judging.

2.5 While this shows that no definition of force can suceed (something about which Frege was right), the idea that forceful thinking somehow involves forceless grasping of thoughts might still retain some of its grip (as it did on Frege). For, it might seem that one has to grasp a thought, *first*, before one might go on to acknowledge its truth or take any other attitude towards it. One might accordingly grant that forceful activity cannot be defined in terms of forceless activity, while still sticking to the view that a forceful act needs to be *preceded* by the forceless grasping of its content. *This view*, rather than the one that a forceful act is a composite act, is a view Frege held,[12] and it is this view, which Wittgenstein seeks to exhibit as mistaken in §22 of the *Investigations:* "It is a mistake [...] if one thinks that the assertion consists of two acts, entertaining and *asserting* [my emphasis, C. M.]".

2.6 Wittgenstein presents Frege's view that there can be forceless grasping of thoughts by recourse to the term "assumption" (*Annahme*), which Frege himself used only once, as early as in *Function and Concept*.[13] Even later, however, Frege held onto the view that there can be forceless grasping and that forceful acts of thinking are preceded by forceless ones. According to Wittgenstein, it is the linguistic fact that in our language assertoric sentences can be written as "It is asserted that such-and-such is the case", which misled Frege insofar as this schematic phrase played the role of a picture, which guided his understanding of the activity of asserting (cf. PIr: §22). It tempted him into thinking that there must be two kinds of act corresponding to the two main parts of this phrase, namely a

---

12 As far as I see, no attempt to exhibit forceful acts as *composite* or to *define* forces can be found in Frege's writings. Nevertheless, he seems to have held the view that forceful acts of thinking are *preceded* by forceless ones. This is implied by his claim from *Negation* that "often", in philosophy, "the act of grasping a thought" and "the acknowledgement of its truth are not kept separate. In many cases, of course, one of these acts follows so directly upon the other that they seem to fuse into one act; but not so in all cases" (Frege 1960: 127). – In the same text, however, Frege introduces grasping in order to account for the nature of a question: "The very nature of a question demands a separation between the acts of grasping a sense and of judging" (119). On a more charitable reading, therefore, Frege's notion of grasping doesn't manifest the *psychological* illusion that there are forceless *acts* of entertaining thoughts. It should rather be seen as a misleading expression of the *logical* insight that acts can differ in force while coinciding in content. Wittgenstein was aware of such a reading: "One could restate Frege's view this way: An assumption (as he uses the word) is what the assertion that p is the case has in common with the question whether p is the case" (BT: 161e). In light of this remark, Wittgenstein does not have to be seen as concerned, in §22 of the *Investigations*, to reject Frege's distinction between force and content, but to exhibit the temptation as empty to draw this distinction in a way which makes it appear as though there might be two types of act – forceless and forceful ones – a temptation, which Frege wasn't altogether immune to, to say the least.
13 "According to the view I am here presenting, '5 > 4' and '1 + 3 = 5' just give us expressions for truth-values, without making any assertion. This separation of the act from the subject-matter of judgment seems to be indispensable; for otherwise we could not express a mere supposition (*Annahme*) – the putting of a case without a simultaneous judgment as to its arising or not. We thus need a special sign in order to be able to assert something. To this end I make use of a vertical stroke at the left end of the horizontal" (Frege 1960: 34).

forceless act of grasping (corresponding to 'that so and so'), and a further, forceful act of thinking (corresponding to 'It is asserted').

2.7 One might argue in many ways against the assumption that a forceful act of thinking-out needs to involve a forceless grasping of what is afterwards dealt with, forcefully. Any criticism of this view is superficial as long as it presupposes that the notion of a *self-standing* forceless act of thinking-out is even so much as intelligible. It is this assumption which Wittgenstein wants to exhibit as empty in the remark attached to §22. This remark is that condensed that it has been read as underwriting what it in fact undermines. In it, Wittgenstein's exhibits the idea of a mere assumption as based on a misleading picture by comparing it to two further scenarios. According to the first comparison a mere assumption relates to a forceful act as the picture of a boxer relates to what the picture can be used to show (e.g. how someone should stand, or how he should not stand, or that a particular man in fact stood somewhere that way etc.). According to the second comparison an assumption relates to a forceful act as a chemical radical relates to a saturated compound.

2.8 That the concept of an assumption is empty can be brought out by pointing to what is misleading about conceiving of the relation between a picture and what it is used to show as analogous to a chemical radical and the satured compound it might go into by way of a chemical reaction. While chemical radicals have a short term life only, insofar as they are highly reactive, they can in fact occur on their own. It might seem that a picture can as well occur on its own independently of what we use it show (or of what we are used to see it as showing). However, this invites one to ask for *the* content of the picture, i.e. for what it shows *in itself*. It might look as though a picture should have such a 'minimal content', and that the variety of things *we* can use it to show presupposes the fact that it has this content. The problem with this is not so much that it is unclear which minimal content one should attribute to *it*, but that there is no 'it' to attribute it to. For, what looks exactly as what we refer to as 'the picture' looks, might have come about by sheer physical chance. In that case 'it' would not only not be a picture, but, *in itself*, wouldn't even amount to *one* thing rather than many. If 'the picture' was nothing but dirt randomly distributed on a surface, it wouldn't make sense to say, for instance, that the dirt making up what appears to us as a leg is in any *distinctive* way part *of the picture* rather than of anything else. – This might suffice to make one suspicious about the minimal content which a picture is supposed to have, independently of any activities of ours which it is involved in. But a mere assumption, which allegedly expresses a determinate truth-evaluable content, while not taking any stance towards it, is exactly as the picture of the boxer, in this respect. If this is right, a mere assumption would therefore not only lack a determinate content, but it wouldn't be anything determinate at all.

2.9 More needs to be done, however, than Wittgenstein's analogy can do, in order to show that the idea of a mere assumption or a forceless, but contentful act of thinking-out is devoid of sense. I will try to show that this idea leads directly to skepticism about meaning. That the idea of forceless thinking-out is – other than it might seem in light of what we are prone to imagine – not the idea of anything determinately contenful at all, can be brought out, clearly, by paying attention to the concepts of a potential (i.e. of what something can do or allows to be done with it) and its actualization. We will see that there are two ways in which an activity and a potential can relate to each other, which go hand in hand with two different notions of activity and potential. It can then be shown that the idea of forceless thinking-out is based on a confusion of these two notions of potential and activity, insofar as it presents forceful activity as of the other kind of activity than it really is.

3 Meaning Skepticism as a Confusion of Bare and Living Activity

3.1 That how an activity and the potential for such activity relate to each other might be of any importance at all, in connection with the distinction between forceless and forceful thinking-out can be brought out by looking once more at the analogy with pictures and our use of them. Upon an apparently innocent understanding, a picture is something with a minimal content which brings along with itself the potential to be used in performing certain acts. That a certain conception of how a potential and the corresponding activity relate to each other is in play in this supposedly innocent notion of a picture comes out, clearly, at the beginning of Wittgenstein's remark attached to §22: "Imagine a picture *representing* a boxer in a particular fighting stance. Well, this picture *can be used* to tell someone ..." [my emphases, C. M.].

3.2 Accordingly, there is, on the one hand, something (a picture) which is actually doing something (representing). In virtue of what it does it involves the potential to do something with it ('it can be used to ...'), i.e. a potential for what *we* can do with it. Certain activities of ours can accordingly be seen as actualizing a potential, which pertains to the picture itself. – While some doubt has been cast on the view that it makes sense to speak of a potential pertaining to *the picture in itself*, it might seem unproblematic to view speaking as an activity, which actualizes a potential belonging to *ourselves*. For, isn't speaking the actualization of our potential to speak?

3.3 Two different ways, in which a potential and a corresponding activity can relate to each other, need to be distinguished, however. (1) Something can have a certain potential independently of the actualization of this potential. Its potential to φ obtains independently of its actualization, i.e. it *can* φ independently of its actually φ-ing. We can call such a potential a 'bare potential'. For example, the potential of a bell to ring if struck obtains independently of whether it is actualized or not. What it can do does not depend on its actually doing it (or having done it).

3.4 On might classify bare potentials according to how they relate to their actualization: the actualization either consumes or saves the potential. (a) That the actualization consumes the potential means that its actualization is inherently limited and, hence, exhaustible. If something has actualized its potential completely, the potential no longer obtains. What Aristotle calls 'kinesis' is the actualization of a potential, which is consumed by its actualization. One might therefore call a bare potential of this type a 'kinetic potential'. The actualization of a kinetic potential can only be limited, inherently, insofar as it is something's potential to be, in a certain respect, other than it is, e.g. the potential to be g rather than f. Accordingly, the actuality of a kinetic potential consists in something's actively being other than it is, i.e. change.[14] The actuality of a kinetic potential is inherently limited, insofar as what has changed from being f to being g does no longer have the potential to change towards being g. (b) If the actualization of a bare potential *saves* rather than consumes it, its actualization can neither be incomplete nor completed and doesn't have an inherent limit, therefore. A potential of this sort can be called an 'enduring potential'. Insofar as something's kinetic potential is its potential to be, in a certain respect, other than it actually is, which makes its actualization completable and, hence, inherently limited, an enduring potential cannot be something's potential to be other than it is. It must rather be something's potential to manifest itself in another (e.g. the capacity to play an instrument) or to have an other manifest itself in it (e.g. a perceptual capacity), where such manifestation is consistent with its keeping its potential. – The actualization of an enduring potential might go on indefinitely, insofar as it

---

14 Cf. Kosman 2013: 37–68.

has no inherent limit, but it need not go on for the potential to obtain. The actualization of a kinetic potential, on the other hand, cannot go on without limits. Hence, a bare potential *in general* is such that its actualization either cannot go on indefinitely or can go on indefinitely, but need not do so.

3.5 What is characteristic of a bare potential *in general* is that it obtains independently of its actualization. Things are the other way round, if a potential to φ depends on its actulization, i.e. if something can φ only, if it does φ. I will call such a potential a 'living potential'. A living potential is different both from a kinetic as well as from an enduring potential. Neither has its actualization an inherent limit (its bearer *can* φ since it φs) nor could its actualization stop, while the potential remains. Insofar as the living potential to φ is brought about by the actuality of φ-ing, its actualization is essentially *continuous:* it cannot be interrupted, because if it were, the potential would be lost. It follows that an A's living potential is essentially a potential *to continue* its activity, to go on doing what it does or to *actively be* the same as it is. Life is a living potential insofar as something can have the potential to live (to go on living) only as long as it actually lives. Accordingly, something's potential to live is brought about by the actuality of its life. I will call an activity, which brings its own potential about, a living activity and distinguish it from a bare activity.[15]

3.6 A confusion between bare and living activity lies at the root of the so-called 'rule-following paradox' and the skepticism about meaning which it gives rise to. It might seem that meaningful speech actualizes the potential of linguistic expressions to contribute to sentences, for which it is objectively determined

---

15 *Terminologically*, the distinction between bare and living activity cuts across Aristotle's distinction between kinesis and energeia. It lumps together under the title of a "bare activity" what would count as a kinesis according to the test in Met. Θ, 6 with *one* kind of what would count as an energeia, while what I refer to as "living activity" coincides with another kind of what according to the test is an energeia. – *Conceptually*, however, the distinction I'm after can clearly be found in Aristotle (cf. e.g. EN II, i). Aryeh Kosman puts it as follows: "It is part of the campaign against the Megarians – the people Aristotle remembers as having thought that it is only when one is doing something that he is able to, and when he is not doing it he is not able to – [...] to insist, as Aristotle regularly does, that a subject may exhibit an ability even when it is not actively engaged in the exercise of that ability (*Met* 9.3, 1046b29–30). It has the ability as a dispositional state, but does not actively exercise it [...]. But with regard to the activity that Aristotle identifies with substance, a Megarian would, as it were, be correct. For there is nothing that we would describe as having the ability to be human – the power, that is, to act as humans characteristically act – that is not at the same moment actively being human. Everything that has the power to be human is human" (Kosman 2013: 177–178).

ahead of actual speaking what would make them true or false. According to this picture, the meaning of "green", for instance, determines 'for every object' whether something true or false would be said by predicating "green" of it. However, if the meaning of a general term is a function, which determines, ahead of actual speaking, that subset of the 'range of all objects', which it could be predicated of truly, and if meaning accordingly involves recourse to 'all objects', it seems obvious that we, qua 'finite and fallible thinkers', cannot make cognitive contact with it. Insofar as linguistic expressions do not come along with their meanings in virtue of their physical properties, if *we* had no cognitive access to their meaning, it would be mysterious, how expressions could have a determinate meaning at all.

3.7 Accordingly, the potential of an expression to determinately contribute to the content of truth-evaluable utterances cannot be due to its relation to an abstract entity – as platonistic conceptions of meaning have it – insofar as there would be no way to account for how such an entity might get hooked up with an expression. As it seems, the meaning of an expression can therefore only be a potential of ours (rather than an abstract entity), namely, a potential to utter the respective expression under certain conditions, i.e. a disposition to utterances. However, insofar as a disposition is a potential, which obtains independently of its actualization, its actualizations (i.e. utterances) can neither contribute to its determinacy nor involve an *internal* relation to it and, hence, to their meaning. Accordingly, an utterance *as such* would be a *mere* vocalization. It could be credited with a meaning only, insofar as it actualizes a potential for vocalizations. However, insofar as a potential is characterized by what it is a potential for, a potential for *vocalizations under arbitrary circumstances* cannot be understood as fixing a meaning. A dispositional account of meaning has to explain, therefore, what distinguishes a disposition for meaningless vocalizations from a disposition in virtue of which vocalizations are meaningful. This distinction could only be accounted for, if a disposition for meaningful speech were a disposition to utter expressions 'under the right conditions' only, namely, under conditions which make the utterances which they occur in true. It follows, that a disposition for vocalizations could only be characterized as fixing a meaning, if it were a disposition to *exclusively* say what is true. This is a reductio ad absurdum of the assumption that meaning is dispositional and that actual speaking actualizes a potential which can obtain prior to it. For, speech can be seen as meaningful only, if the logical space for a distinction between speakings, which are true, and speakings, which are false, is provided for. Therefore, an account of meaning, according to which meaningful and true speakings necessarily *coincide*, can no longer be understood as an account of meaning at all.

3.8 Other than it might seem, a Platonist and a dispositionalist account of meaning can thus be seen as variants of the same confusion. Both conceive of acts of speaking as actualizing a potential, which obtains independently of its actualization. The actual use of expressions in speaking isn't, accordingly, seen as *determining* content, but as merely instantiating contents, which have their determinacy anyway. Both views conceive of meaning as coming along with a potential for meaningful speech, while they differ in that what this potential is supposed to be based on is either conceived of as an abstract entity or a being which is disposed to emit sounds under certain circumstances.

3.9 As indicated, an account of meaningful speech, which conceives of it as actualizing a potential, which is supposed to have its determinacy independently of its actualization, can no longer account for the possibility that meaningful and true speech come apart, and, hence, cannot account for meaningful speech at all. A viable account of meaning must therefore be one according to which the potential for meaningful speech is brought about by its actuality. In what follows, I will argue in some more detail that conceiving of thinking-out as actualizing a bare potential, one can no longer account for the possible non-coincidence between what *can be* true and what *is* true. Subsequently, I will attempt to show that an account according to which the potential for thinking-out is grounded in actual thinking-out rather than prior to it, and is, hence, a living potential, can account for this difference, indeed.

4 Thinking-out as a Living Activity

4.1 A potential – bare or living – doesn't, in some mysterious way, foreshadow the events which it is actualized in. The disposition of a bell to sound if struck, for instance, doesn't somehow 'contain' the events, which occur, when the bell is struck. The actualization of a potential is an event, which isn't, as the event it is, foreshadowed in a mere potential – both, because only what is actual is individual and because what isn't 'bigger than itself'. – However, if the meaning of a word consisted in the *bare* potential to *determinately* contribute to the truth-evaluable content of speakings involving that word, this potential would have to *foreshadow* those *speakings* and sort them into those, which would be true, and those, which would be false. For, insofar as a speaking on occasion is true or false objectively, and insofar as that which determines what *would* make it so (in distinction to that which makes it so), cannot, therefore, itself be settled on occasion, it must be settled 'in advance' in virtue of the meanings of the expressions which the speaking is made up by. The meanings of expressions must therefore *discretely* anticipate for *possible speakings under as yet unactualized circumstances*, whether they would be true or false under these circumstances. Or so it seems. – However, as pointed out, saying that 'a potential discretely contains or foreshadows its possible actualizations' doesn't make sense. Accordingly, the meaning of a word isn't a potential, which *discretely* anticipates for possible speakings involving that word what would make them true (or false). It isn't, because nothing is said by such words.

4.2 If it is *actual* thinking-out, in which the potential for thinking-out has its source, meaning cannot be explained by recourse to conditions different from thinking-out. This is not a mere thesis, insofar as I have argued that bare activity isn't intelligible as meaningful at all. Insofar as it is actual thinking-out, in which the potential for further thinking-out has its source, that which accounts for the meaning of an act of speaking (i.e. for what *would* make it true) and that in virtue of which it *is* true or false, do not have to coincide. For, an act of speech will not have its meaning independently of previous thinking-out, but in virtue of how it continues the use of expressions already in use. What makes an act of speaking true or false, on the other hand, are 'the facts'. Hence, one might say that an act of speech looks in two directions: (1) Regarding its meaning, it looks back to its ancestors. This doesn't mean that it would have its meaning *in virtue* of something different from itself. As a living act, it isn't meaningful in virtue of something else, but in virtue of itself, namely, in virtue of *its own* continuation of the use of expressions already in use. (2) Regarding its truth value, it looks forward to 'the facts'.

4.3 It might seem, however, that a conception of thinking-out as an activity which comes along with a potential for its continuation rather than actualizing a potential, which might obtain independently, can only appear to account for the possible non-coincidence between what is meaningful and what is true. The conception seems blatantly circular insofar as it accounts for this possible non-coincidence in certain cases only, by presupposing that it is already accounted for in others. There would have to be *some kind* of use of expressions in thinking, for which the meaningful and true coincide, indeed. But if their necessary coincidence undermines meaning and truth, doesn't a conception of meaning as a living potential suffer from the same flaw as its Platonist-dispositionalist concurrent?

4.4 Contrary to this objection, it makes all the difference in the world, whether what is meaningful and what is true (or valid) have to coincide *globally*, or whether it is their *local coincidence*, which allows for their possible non-coincidence in other cases. Insofar as certain acts of thinking-out render the non-coincidence of what is meaningful and what is true possible, it would be more precise to say that in them, what is meaningful and what is true cannot yet be separated, rather than that both coincide. (1) It has been indicated that the activity of thinking-out must have a 'center', in which what is meaningful and what is true, coincide. For, what logically distinguishes a proposition from its dual twins is the *formal* self-knowledge of how we operate with signs, which can be made explicit in form of propositions of logic, which are trivially and thus transparently true. (2) Prototypical acts, in the course of which *non-logical* expressions are introduced or explained, are such that the distinction between what is meaningful and what is true, is bracketed *in certain respects*. This can be seen, for instance, by the fact that for introducing a new color term it is irrelevant, whether the samples by recourse to which it is introduced, do actually have the color they appear to have, or not. (On this point cf. also section 5.2 below.)

4.5 If the living *potential* for thinking-out is a potential to *continue* one's activity of thinking-out, it doesn't have to mysteriously leap ahead of itself. What a further speaking means, will be determined, on occasion, in virtue of its continuing the previous use of the expressions which it is composed of. Such continuity might involve growth, insofar as it need not be settled automatically (although it often is), on a new occasion of speaking, what continuing the use of certain expressions already in use might amount to, on that occasion.[16]

4.6 That the meanings of expressions do not 'anticipate with respect to possible acts of speaking under as yet unactualized circumstances', what would make an act of speaking made up by them true or false, might make it appear as though it wouldn't be objectively settled, for an act of speaking on further occasion, what *would* make it true, and, hence, that it wouldn't have a determinate meaning. However, that the meanings of expressions do not *discretely* anticipate what they might serve to say doesn't mean that they fail to do something, which they might conceivably do. The meanings of expressions do *neither anticipate nor leave it open* with respect to as yet unactualized occasions of speaking, whether something true or false would be said, by a sentence made up by them on such occasions. For, recourse to 'as yet unactualized occasions of speaking' isn't 'contained' in actual speaking. Such words are empty. – That which de-

---

16 At that point it seems adequate to refer to Travis' notion of occasion-sensitivity, cf. Travis 2008.

termines what *would* make a speaking on occasion *true*, i.e. what is said, is itself determined on occasion rather than ahead of it, because what is said on occasion isn't already mysteriously said before it is actually said. However, that what *would* make a speaking on occasion true isn't *discretely predetermined* does neither imply that it would be *arbitrarily determined* on occasion nor that it would have to be determined *by the same* as what makes the speaking true or false. It is rather *objectively* determined in virtue of the continuity between the use of words on this new occasion and how these words have already been operated with.

4.7 That speaking needs to be understood as a living activity rather than a movement can be seen as a lesson of Wittgenstein's rule-following considerations: In the course of these considerations it becomes clear that following a rule is to be understood as a "practice" (PI, §202) against a tendency to think of it as analogous to the "movement" (*Bewegung*) of a machine, whose unactualized movements appear as discretely foreshadowed in its actual movement.[17] One might call the confusion of a practice with (such) a (mysterious) movement its 'spectral inversion'. A spectre is the illusion of something, which presents itself as if actual, though not 'actually actual'. The spectral inversion of our linguistic practice produces spectres insofar as it appears as though an expression could have a meaning only, if its actual use anticipates *all of its possible contributions to speakings, which would be true*, as though they had already been undertaken.[18]

4.8 That Wittgenstein conceives of speaking as a living rather than a bare activity is likewise manifest in his reliance on (what might seem at first as) the (mere) analogy between life and language when referring to the "living use" (cf. PIr: §432) or the "life" of signs (cf. PPF: xi, §224). This analogy might help one to see that the way in which a word contributes to the content of a future act of thinking-out need not be *discretely predetermined* in order to be *non-arbitrarily determined*, insofar as it is determined by the continuity between its future

---

[17] "We are inclined to compare the future movements of the machine in their definiteness to objects which have been lying in a drawer and which we now take out" (PIr: §193).
[18] A concise characterization of what I have referred to as the "spectral inversion" of a linguistic practice can be found in *Dictation for Schlick*: "It seemed to us as if the possible steps of calculating must already have been anticipated in the understanding, hence as if it made sense to say: someone is able to repeat the multiplication table while he is repeating it [...] the calculus proceeds step by step without its being the case that one step already contains the next ones" (VW: 15, 17). Wittgenstein did stick to this thought even after he stopped to conceive of language as a calculus.

use, and how it has already been used. Analogously, no set of conditions is required, which would determine, for a future point in time, that what fulfills these conditions will be *the same* as a certain living individual presently under consideration. Its identity-through-time will rather be constituted by its *going on living*. Nevertheless, whether an individual that lives at a later time is the same as one that lived earlier, isn't arbitrary, but depends on whether a continuous path of life connects them.

4.9 While it seems clear that an organism *can* live only *while it lives* and, therefore, cannot stop living for a while and then resume this kind of passtime, it seems equally clear that engagement in the activity of thinking-out can indeed be interrupted and resumed, which is exactly what makes it appear as more akin to the sounding of a body than to the life of an organism. However, insofar as thinking-out is a living activity, it must be categorically different from the sounding of a body. Forceful thinking-out can, accordingly, stop and go on *in one respect* only, while there must be another respect in which whoever *can* engage in it *is* engaged in it. This respect is that a thinking-out, once undertaken, *is in force*, even though it might no longer *occurently* be undertaken. One can only stop it from being in force by engaging in a further act of thinking-out which is incompatible with it. Therefore, one is actively engaged in and can thus be held responsible for for one's thoughts, even while one isn't occurently voicing them: thinking-out has no built-in date of expiry.

4.10 It is at this point that the analogy between the use of language in thinking-out and the life of a mere animal or a plant breaks down. Both are living activities. However, the life-activity of a non-thinking organism grounds the potential to continue itself, while its course of life is made up by stretches of activity, which vanish and give way to further stretches, and is, hence, successive in character. Once undertaken, acts of thinking-out, on the other hand, do not simply vanish and give way to further acts, but *are in force* as long as they aren't withdrawn. Thinking-out, accordingly, allows for two modes, occurent and non-occurent or 'at rest'. Insofar as an act of thinking-out posits its content as valid and, insofar, independent of its own time-position, it has the form of a temporally successive act, which brackets its own successivity. At rest, a thinking-out with a determinate content isn't simply inactive, for it shapes the potential of further thinking-out – its possible range of content. Once undertaken, the content of a thinking-out can also be retroactively modified by further thinking-out.

4.11 Insofar as the living activity of thinking-out allows for a *non-occurent* mode, it comes along with a potential for transitions from non-occurent to occurent mode. This is a potential for movement, i.e. a bare potential, insofar as such transitions actualize a potential that obtains independently of its actualization rather than being constituted by it. Accordingly, what actualizes such a potential isn't a thinking-out. Hence, not all speakings are instances of thinking-out. Insofar as a determinate thinking-out, once undertaken, does not, *all by itself*, cease to be in force, a thinker cannot simply *repeat* such an act time and again, although he can '*rehearse*' or 'give voice' *to it*, repeatedly. One cannot, for instance, judge-out that this substance is sulphur twenty seven times in a row, although one can, on the one hand, both rehearse or communicate one's judgment on that issue as well as, on the other hand, *withdraw, reexamine* and *reconfirm* it. Moreover, one can indulge in *thoughtless* chatter involving signs of the same shape as long as one likes. Accordingly, there is a difference in form between acts of thinking-out, utterances, which rehearse or communicate such acts, as well as thoughtless chatter made up by the same expressions. While the former acts are instances of living activity, the others are movements.

5 Language as Shaping Our Form of Life

5.1 Wittgenstein does not content himself to point to an analogy between life and language. He assumes that whoever thinks-and-speaks is, as such, a living being. I will not argue for this, here. Taking it for granted, I will rather focus on how living a life and speaking a language hang together, i.e. on Witggenstein's claim that speaking a language is living a life *of a certain form*. I start from two well-known passages:

> (1) The word "language-*game*" is used here to emphasize the fact that the *speaking* of language is part of an activity, or of a form of life. (PI: §23)
> (2) Can only those hope who can speak? Only those who have mastered the use of a language. That is to say, the manifestations of hope are modifications of this complicated form of life. (PPF: I, §1)

It might seem contradictory that Wittgenstein characterizes speaking both as "a part of a form of life" (1) as well as "a complex form of life" (2) rather than a part of it. The apparent contradiction can be resolved by taking into account that 'form' is what accounts for the unity of what it is the form of.[19] Speaking can thus be seen as an integral part of what accounts for the unity of the lives

---

[19] That such an understanding of form is at work in the *Investigations* might be substantiated by recourse to §123, §§134–136 and §217.

of *those who can speak*. It can thus both be characterized as a form of life (insofar as it is an integral part of what accounts for the unity of the lives of *those who can speak*) as well as a part of it (insofar as speaking is *one type* of activity which those who can speak engage in amongst others, which do not consist in speaking).

When Wittgenstein refers to speaking as an activity, which is "part" of a "form of life", he doesn't mention any further parts.[20] This might strike one as an omission. It isn't one, if what he thereby points to is that the other parts, *whatever they may be*, must be internally related to speaking.[21]

The solution to the apparent contradiction can be substantiated by a closer look at the passages just quoted. Wittgenstein refers to the "*speaking* of a language" as part of the form of life of a speaker, while characterizing the form of life of "who has mastered the use of a language" (*die Verwendung der Sprache beherrscht*) as a complicated one. Accordingly, he doesn't identify the *activity* of speaking with a form of life (it is only a part of the life of those who can speak), but the mastery of the use of a language, thereby implying that the *capacity* to speak informs even those parts of the lives of speakers, which do not consist in speaking.[22] That he characterizes *speaking* as a *part* of that form of life,

---

20 In §25 Wittgenstein refers to walking, eating, drinking and playing as parts of "our natural history". This remark cannot be read, however, as hinting at further parts of the form of life of those who can speak beyond speaking. What Wittgenstein calls "our natural history" cannot be identified with the form of life which we partake in *qua speakers*, but refers to a *specification* of this form. For, if to imagine a speaker is to imagine a living being (cf. PIr: §19), a speaker is someone, who moves and nourishes himself. However, a self-mover doesn't have to be a *walker*, and nourishing oneself isn't, necessarily, *eating and drinking*. Accordingly, what Wittgenstein refers to as "our natural history" is a material specification of the form of life of speakers as such, albeit one, which is situated on a very high level of abstraction. It does not refer to a specific historical or cultural manifestation of this form of life, but to its *human* manifestation. That it is not a cultural manifestation doesn't mean that it would be a biological one – i.e. a topic for biology as a natural science. For, it is the specification of a form of life, which involves the forceful use of language in *thinking*-out as an integral part.

21 Throughout this paper I rely on the formal concept of an internal relation. This might require some discussion, which I cannot provide here. It must suffice to note that later Wittgenstein continued to rely on that notion, cf. PPF, xi, §247.

22 This observation might help one to see the *unity in topic* between (what was formerly called) "the first and the second part" of the *Investigations*. Roughly speaking, it might seem, at first, that part one deals with logic and language, while part two is concerned with *independent* issues in the philosophy of psychology. Contrary to that, Wittgenstein points out, in the very first section of part two, that only the one "who has mastered the use of a language" is someone who can hope. This remark needs to be seen as emblematic. Accordingly, part two doesn't deal with psychological phenomena, which would be *independent* of the fact that those, who experience them, are speakers of a language; it rather deals with perception, imagination etc. as parts of

which is identified with the *capacity to speak*, implies that this capacity includes actual speaking as a part of itself, and is, accordingly, a living rather than a bare potential.

5.2 Even after some clarification of what it might mean to say that speaking is "part of a form of life" it might still seem mysterious, how the expression "language-*game*" could, according to quote (1) from §23, serve to emphasize *that*. It can only do so, if "game" points to a form of life.²³ This seems to imply that only someone, who can play, can acquire a language. The activities, in virtue of which tools of language are introduced and acquired (i.e. language-games in the sense of "those games by means of which children learn their native language", §7) will have a playful character, accordingly. It is important to become clear about what this playful character consists in. It minimally consist in that the activities, in virtue of which tools of language are introduced, must involve prototypical uses, i.e. they must exhibit how to use these tools properly, i.e. in acts of speaking, which are recognizably true or valid. Under real circumstances, it is possible, to use tools of language in acts of speaking, which are false or invalid. Therefore, the activities, in virtue of which tools of language are introduced, must involve some abstraction from real circumstances. Such abstraction is effected, if prototypical uses of linguistic tools count as what they claim to be, i.e. if appearance and reality coincide. Such coincidence is characteristic, for instance, of a game of roles, whose participants count as who they claim to be. While, under real circumstances, who claims to be an inventor can be revealed

---

that form of life, which consists in the mastery of a language, and, hence, as "informed" by that capacity. – However, as long as the capacity to speak, in virtue of its spectral inversion, presents itself as a bare potential rather than a living one, it remains mysterious, how this capacity might "inform" psychological states, which aren't linguistic in character. One might rightly be confused about what it might mean to speak of a "passive actualization of conceptual capacities in perception" (McDowell), *if conceptual capacities are linguistic capacities*. Are words written by an invisible hand into what those who master the use of a language perceive? – There is, accordingly, a *parallel* between the perplexity about what appears as the "superlative fact" (PIr: §192) of grasping the meaning of a word and the perplexity that expresses itself in the question "How is it possible to *see* an object according to an *interpretation*?" and to which such seeing appears "as a strange fact" (PPF: xi, §164). – Getting clear about following rules is, accordingly, a precondition of getting a grip on what "information of perception by linguistic capacities" might be. – That thinking-out allows for an occurent and a non-occurent mode makes it less absurd to assume that the use of language can "inform" psychological states and activities. For, if, *once undertaken*, acts of thinking-out *are in force*, they can be that "in light of which" something is perceived, even though no magical tokenings of signs do have to occur while (or "in what") we perceive.
23 Notice that "playing" (*spielen*) is mentioned in §25, which deals with what distinguishes us thinkers-and-speakers from *mere* animals.

not to actually be one, within such a game, who assumes the role of an inventor thereby counts as one. – If activities in virtue of which tools of language are introduced have a playful character in this sense, they presuppose other activities, which the players engage in seriously. For, playing at something cannot come first, but presupposes serious engagement in other activities. The expression "language-game" seems therefore particularly fit to emphasize that the activity of speaking is part of a form of life, insofar as who can engage in such games, must already be seriously engaged in a bunch of life-activities *and* capable of playing at them.

5.3 So far, I have attempted to *clarify* what it might *mean* to say that mastery of the use of a language is a form of life. It still needs to be *justified* that this capacity is to be seen as a *form*, i.e. as what accounts for the unity of what it is the form of.[24] A living activity is such as to bring about its own unity or form. For, a living activity *establishes* the potential for its continuation rather than merely actualizing it. Acts, which actualize a living potential, aren't isolated, therefore, in the way in which, say, repeated acts of humming might be, but tied back to the series of acts, which precede them. The acts, which actualize a living potential, are thus continuous with each other in a way which acts that actualize a bare potential aren't. Insofar as they are continuous with each other *qua acts of thinking-out*, they partake in a logical form, which runs through all of them.

5.4 It can now be *justified* why speaking or thinking-out cannot be an independent part of the form of life which it is part of, but must integrate the other parts. As shown, the potential for thinking-out is a living rather than a mere potential. Whatever *can* engage in a living activity *is* engaged in it. In this sense, the actualization of the potential for thinking-out is constitutive of who can think-out. For the same reason, the actualization of a further living potential, which belongs to the form of life of one who can think-out, is likewise constitutive of that individual. If the potential for thinking-out and that further potential were independent of each other, who is actively engaged in what one potential is a potential for, would not have to be actively engaged in what the other is a potential for. This cannot be the case, however, since both potentials are supposed to be living potentials. Therefore, different living potentials of one and the same crea-

---

24 That Wittgenstein takes language and "the activities with which it is intervowen" to make up a unified whole is indicated by his choice to call "the whole, consisting of language and the activities, into which it is woven, the 'language-game'" (PIr: §7). It would be nonsense, for instance, to call the whole of card games "the card game". (The point is blurred by Hacker and Schulte, who (mis)translate "das 'Sprachspiel'" as "a 'language-game'").

ture cannot be independent of each other. Insofar as they have their ground in corresponding activities, if such potentials depend on each other, their actualizations must depend on each other as well. Accordingly, there seems to be good reason to *identify* mastery of a language with the form of life of a speaking being, insofar as it *informs* whatever else belongs to this form.

6 The Unity of the Form of Life of a Speaker

6.1 In sections 23–24 of the *Investigations* Wittgenstein points out (1) that the form of life of a speaker comprises a variety of "types of language" (*Typen der Sprache*) or "language games" such as the ones listed in §23[25] (2) that these types cannot be defined, i.e. that they are irreducible (3) that they are not fixed once and for all, but make up a developing whole (4) that in the course of its development certain types are forgotten, while new ones come into existence.

6.2 It might seem that Wittgenstein's claims about the irreducibility and variability of the types of language, which make up the form of life of a speaker, are based on linguistic observation and, hence, empirical in form. However, if these claims had a matter-of-factual character, they could be reasonably contradicted (contrary to what is characteristic, according to §128, of philosophical reminders). Even if they were in fact true, we might imagine languages, for which they don't apply. In what follows, I want to show that claims (2)–(4) are formal (*begrifflich*) rather than matter-of-factual (*sachlich*) in character, i.e. that they elucidate the form of a linguistic practice *as such*. I will try to do so by exhibiting them as consequences of the first claim, according to which the form of life of a speaker comprises a variety of types of language. I will start by giving an account of why such types cannot be defined in terms of other types.

6.3 That a type of language, which is part of the form of life of a speaker, is indefinable and, in particular, indefinable by recourse to other types, cannot be shown by recourse to the sheer variety of such types. Wittgenstein *might seem*

---

[25] "Giving orders, and acting on them, describing an object by its appearance, or by its measurements, constructing an object from a description (a drawing), reporting an event, speculating about the event, forming and testing a hypothesis, presenting the results of an experiment in tables and diagrams, making up a story; and reading one, acting in a play, singing rounds, guessing riddles, cracking a joke, telling one, solving a problem in applied arithmetic, translating from one language into another, requesting, thanking, cursing, greeting, praying" (PIr: §23).

to attempt this insofar as he claims that someone "who doesn't have the manifold of language-games clearly before his eyes" (§24) might be inclined to search for definitions of some such games in terms of others. However, recourse to the sheer variety of language-games would make the indefinability claim a mere conjecture, which is contingently true, at best. Wittgenstein would not have shown that search for definitions of certain "types of language" in terms of others is empty, in principle.

6.4 A starting point for showing that a type of language, insofar as it is a part of the form of life of one who can think-and-speak, cannot be defined, is that what is part of the form of life of a thinker cannot be additively composed, i.e. its formal concept cannot consist of independent traits. If it did, neither could it nor *all* of the parts, which it is composed of, be *parts of a form*, i.e. of what *accounts for the non-additive (internal) unity* of what it is the form of. What accounts for the internal unity between acts of thinking-out, or between further life-activities, or of a life, can do so only, if it is marked by a non-additive unity itself. If a type of language consisted of *independent* parts, it wouldn't dispose of the internal unity, which is required for its being a *dependent* part *of a form* of life. Therefore, types of language, insofar as they make up parts of a form of life, cannot be definable.

6.5 That a type of language, *which is part of the form of life of a speaker as such*, cannot be defined, does not imply that one cannot define *any* types of language or "speech act". It only implies that if a definition can be achieved, the type of act under consideration, while *partaking in* the form of life of a speaker, cannot be a *part of that form*. It must rather be a type of act, which non-formally or materially *specifies* this form and is, accordingly, part of a *specific way of living* or a *particular* culture. It might consist (1) in a specification of the *content* of a type of language (2) in an external relation between a type of language and something else or (3) in an *optional concatenation* of types of language, which make up the form of life of a speaker.

(1) "Proposing to someone", for instance, might be defined as "asking someone whether (s)he will marry one". This doesn't amount to defining one part of the form of life of a speaker *as such* in terms of another. It rather exhibits the speech act at issue as a specification of the *content* of a type of language use – asking –, which is such a part, indeed.

(2) Strawson, in his review of the *Investigations*, aimed to exhibit Wittgenstein's list of language-games as lacking a principle and, hence, as arbitrary, by ironically proposing that one might as well add the game of "sending an

old man to sleep by reading aloud from the translation of a play" to the list.[26] However, this 'type of act' cannot even count as a *species* of the *living activity* of thinking-out. For, the intention to send an old man to sleep makes it a *movement* (an attempt to actualize the bare, soporific potential of dramatic art), rather than an instance of the living activity of thinking-out.

(3) If one abstracts from the perlocutionary intention of Strawson's act, what remains is the act of reading from the translation of a play. This act consists in an *external* and, hence, optional concatenation of types of act, which are already on Wittgenstein's list. Insofar as this concatenation is optional, the kind of act under consideration cannot reasonably count as a part of the form of life of a speaker *as such*, but as a non-formal specification of this form, only. Accordingly, one can coherently think of a community of thinkers-and-speakers, to which the act of reading from the translations of plays is unknown. Therefore, Strawson is misguided in assuming that it might as well be added to the list.

6.6 Insofar as form is what accounts for the unity of what it is the form of, types of language, qua parts of the form of life of speakers, cannot be defined. That they are irreducible cannot mean, however, that they would be logically simple and, hence, independent of each other. For, in this case, they could not be parts of a form, since parts of a form are, as such, *dependent* parts and, hence, internally related to each other. – Sense has its actuality in determinate contributions to the content of acts of thinkings-out – contributions, which can be continued or taken up in further acts of thinking-out of *some type or other*. Sense is thus internally related to force and can only be abstracted from it, rather than subsisting independently of it. That what contributes to the content of an act of thinking-out of one type can be taken up or continued in acts of another type is possible only, if these types are internally related or continuous with each other. For, the continuability of sense across acts of different type can only be accounted for, if what the sense of an act of thinking-out is internally related to – i.e. the type of this act, which is characterized by its force – is itself internally related to other 'types of language' characterized by other forces. Otherwise, there couldn't be a continuity of sense across acts of different force. In consequence, it would be impossible, for instance, *to answer* a question, or to make an assertion, a command or a joke *pertaining to the same subject matter*.

6.7 In the first part of this paper I had suggested that the (constitutive) knowledge in virtue of which we distinguish an act of thinking-out of one type from

---

26 Cf. Strawson 1954: 72.

its dual twin (an act of another type, whose sentential sign is indistinguishable from the sign of the former) involves knowledge of an asymmetry in their relations to acts of a further type. It follows from this suggestion that types of language, which are characterized by their forces, are internally related rather than logically independent. – The suggestion that different types of language or force are internally related to each other has now been argued for *independently*. This argument is based on a premise, which had been established in parts 3 and 4, namely that content is internally related to force. If this is the case, the continuability of sense across acts with different force can only be accounted for, if forces (qua dependent parts of the form of life of a speaker) are internally related to each other.[27]

6.8 The internal relation between forces or types of language, which make up the form of life of a speaker, can manifest itself in three ways. (1) The formal concepts of such types are internally related, i.e. it must be possible to *concretely* exhibit that they mutually point to each other (2) Acts of thinking-out, insofar as they posit themselves as valid, come along with requirements on their unity with other acts, i.e. on which acts they cannot or must go together with. Insofar acts of thinking-out of different type are logically related, there must be requirements pertaining to how acts of *different* type, which share (part of) their content, cannot or must go together.[28] That there is an internal connection between different types of force will manifest itself, accordingly, in logical rela-

---

[27] What can be defined in terms of a certain trait A and a further, independent trait B, can be called an "accidental species" of the genus A (cf. Ford 2011, Martin 2015). I have tried to show that types of language, insofar as they are parts of the form of life of a speaker, cannot relate *to each other* as accidental genus and species. They can neither be accidental species of a supposed genus of "speaking in general", which might be grasped without recourse to its species. For, in this case, these species would likewise lack the internal unity which is required for something to be a *dependent* part of a form. In consequence, the types of language, which are parts of the form of life of a speaker, can each have their own *specific* character in virtue of their mutual interrelation only, while the genus "type of language" will be nothing but the (evolving) system of these interrelations. If specific types of language have their own *specific* character in virtue of their internal relations only, these relations must be asymmetrical.

[28] That later Wittgenstein conceived of logic in this broad sense comes out, clearly, by reading the following passages together: "Aristotelian logic brands a contradiction as a non-sentence, which is to be excluded from language. But this logic only deals with a very small part of the logic of our language" (LW: §525). "When a sentence is called senseless, it is not, as it were, its sense that is senseless. Rather, a combination of words is being excluded from the language, withdrawn from circulation" (PIr: §500). "Let us remember that it doesn't make sense to say '(it is raining) or (is it raining?)'. If I write the assertion that p is the case as '$\sqrt{p}$' and the question whether p is the case as '?p' [...] one cannot write '($\sqrt{p}$)&(?p)'" (MS 113: 49r).

tions between acts characterized by such forces. Variating a phrase of Frege's, one might say that laws of logic, in this extended sense, 'unfold' the form of life of a speaking being as such. They are formal, necessary conditions of unity between acts of thinking-out of *some type or other*. (3) As indicated, there might also be *formal* sufficient conditions of unity between acts of thinking-out *of different type*, e.g. that an affirmative statement can count as the answer to a complement-question, while a negative cannot.

6.9 In the final sections of this paper I will be concerned only with how one might *concretely* exhibit the internal relation between the (formal) concepts of different types of language, i.e. establish that they belong to the form of life of speakers as such. If the types of forceful thinking-out, which Wittgenstein mentions in §23, are indeed both irreducible and mutually interrelated, there must be a way to conclusively exhibit their interrelation. If the form of life of speakers is an evolving rather than static one, what belongs to this form, *at a certain stage of its evolution*, cannot be established without taking this evolution into account. Insofar as this evolution is the evolution of a *form*, it cannot simply be contingent. I will argue, accordingly, that it is possible to exhibit the internal relation between different types of language by *non-empirically* exhibiting the 'evolution' of the form of thinking-out.

6.10 The attempt to non-empirically exhibit the evolution of the form of life of a speaker can only make sense, if it can (1) be shown that inchoate engagement in thinking-out is engagement in as yet undifferentiated activity, which differentiates itself into activities of different type and if (2) this development has a necessary rather than contingent side to it, in virtue of which it can be non-empirically reconstructed.

Types of language, qua parts of a form, are internally related. This relation cannot merely pertain to the formal *concepts* of these types. For, insofar as they are types of living activity, acts, which instantiate them, do not actualize bare potentials, which could obtain independently of their actualization. Accordingly, the potential to engage in a certain type of language use obtains in virtue of *actual engagement*, only. One cannot, however, come to be engaged in acts of *different* type all at once, i.e. in one act. Accordingly, one can neither start to engage in one type of forceful thinking-out while not yet actualizing one's potential for engagement in acts of other types nor start to engage in acts of all types, all at once. Therefore, there must be some kind of inchoate thinking-out, engagement in which precedes the differentiation of thinking-out into different, interrelated types of thinking-out.

6.11 In a retrospective remark on the language-game of the builders, i.e. game No. 2, Wittgenstein stresses that one *can* imagine their thinking and their language as "primitive" or "rudimentary".[29] There is, accordingly, a way of looking at what they are engaged in as *preceding* our distinction between different types of language, i.e. as too indeterminate, in itself, to count, for instance, as a game of *commanding* rather than, say, *asking* or *praying*.[30] From the vantage point of our non-rudimentary form of life with language, what A and B are engaged in, might likewise be characterized as a game of giving and fulfilling orders (to bring a number of building stones), a game of asking (whether there is a slab) and answering (by bringing a slab), or a game of praying (involving A's 'invocation' of a slab and B's performance of a rudimentary 'ritual' with it). In itself, i.e. without the introduction of further distinctions, which would make it no longer rudimentary, the game cannot be seen as instantiating one *specific* type of language use, while it can be seen, indeed, as coming along with the potential to unfold into a whole system of games of various type.

6.12 It has been pointed out that the types of language, which make up the form of life of a speaker, can only come into existence in the course of a development that starts from what Wittgenstein calls "the primitive form of the language-game" (*die primitive Form des Sprachspiels*[31]), i.e. a form, which cannot be adequately characterized in terms of one specific type of language *in distinction to others*, while coming along with the potential to evolve into a whole of games of various types. Accordingly, when Wittgenstein speaks of "development",

---

29 "The important thing is precisely that I can imagine their language, and their thinking too, as rudimentary; that there is such a thing as 'primitive thinking' which is to be described via primitive behaviour" (MS 136: 53b, cf. Z: §99 and RPP II: §205). The "can" is important. It points to the fact that we are *free* to imagine the game as rudimentary or not. *Not* to imagine it as rudimentary requires filling in a lot of details, for we cannot, in this case, imagine what A and B are engaged in as the only type of language use, which they are engaged in. – On the topic of primitive thinking cf. also Wittgenstein's remark in PIr: §554: "We can easily imagine human beings with a 'more primitive' logic [...]".
30 When Wittgenstein introduces game No. 2, he *indeterminately* refers to what A utters as a "call" (*Ruf*). While exclamation marks are absent from §2, they are casually introduced in §6 and from §8 onwards A's calls are explicitly referrred to as "commands". We are thus smoothly led to take it as self-evident that what the builders are engaged in is a game of *commanding*. That the evidence is apparent only comes to the fore, when Wittgenstein asks, in §21: "Now what is the difference between the report or assertion 'Five slabs' and the order 'Five slabs!'?"
31 "The origin & the primitive form of the language-game is a reaction; only from this can the more complicated forms grow. Language – I want to say – is a refinement, 'in the beginning was the deed'" [PO: 395 (= MS 119: 146 (21.10.1937))].

"growth" or "refinement" of language,[32] which starts from a primitive or rudimentary form of thinking-out, his reminders aren't empirical, but formal in character.

6.13 The internal expansion of the *form of life of a speaker*, which starts from rudimentary thinking-out, cannot proceed in a contingent manner. For, the expansion of *form*, qua unifying, cannot consists in an introduction of *independent* differences from without. This is not to deny that the historical development of languages involves contingent changes of all kind. Such changes, however, do not belong to language qua *form* of life. In consequence, a *philosophical* account of the internal expansion of the primitive form of life of a speaker can do no more than bring an *expanding system* of language-games into view, which might serve as an "object of comparison", rather than a model of the *matter-of-factual* development of *natural languages*.

6.14 Insofar as the *form* of life of a speaking being, *qua unifying*, can only *differentiate itself from within*, its development must go hand in hand with the establishment of an order between different types of language. For, what differentiates *itself*, can do so only insofar as what the specification proceeds from is itself retroactively modified in contrast to what it results in. Otherwise, unity would be lost. The differentiation of form cannot, accordingly, proceed by means of a *parallel* introduction of *independent* differences, but of a difference only, which opens up a contrast between what is thus specified and what is thereby *posited as not thus specified*. Therefore, even though a rudimentary language-game as the one of the builders cannot be adequately characterized as *instantiating* one type of language use in distinction to others, it can nevertheless be seen as *closer* to one such type rather than another. Language-game No. 2, for instance, is closer to commanding than to prayer, insofar as, in order to count as a game of prayer, further specifications beyond the ones contained in its initial characterization would be required, while no further specifications (over and above a contrast to games, which are further specified, indeed) seem to be required in order for it count as a game of ordinary, prosaic commanding.

6.15 The expansion of the system of language-games, which make up the form of life of a speaking being, is itself part of that form. The form which the expansion takes can be illustrated by paying attention to Wittgenstein's remark that "the metamorphoses of mathematics" (*die Wandlungen der Mathematik*) can serve

---

32 Cf. fn. 30.

as a "rough picture" (PI: §23) of it. Insofar as elswhere, in the *Investigations*, he compares the extension of the concepts of game and language to that of the concept of number, it doesn't seem too far fetched to think of the metamorphoses, which he refers to, paradigmatically, albeit not exclusively, in terms of transitions from a 'primitive' to a more complex arithmetic.[33]

6.16 Wittgenstein says about our concept of number that we "expand" it (*ausdehnen*).[34] The following points might be noteworthy with respect to the form of this expansion:

(1) A primitive arithmetic is not incomplete, i.e. it isn't, in and by itself, characterized as a fragment of a more complex one.[35] The transition to a more complex arithmetic isn't, accordingly, somehow anticipated or foreshadowed in a more primitive one.

(2) Nevertheless, such transitions (e.g. the transition from the arithmetic of natural numbers to the arithmetic of integers) are not arbitrary, i.e. discontinuous with what they proceed from.[36] They can be accounted for *ex post*, e.g. by the fact that in the more primitive system certain operations (e.g. subtraction) were inapplicable to certain combinations of numbers, while being applicable in the extended system. This account is *ex post* insofar as specifications of what an operation cannot be applied to are not part (of the rules) of the system which it is part of.

(3) A more complex arithmetic doesn't contain a more primitive one as an *independent* part, e.g. the arithmetic of natural numbers is *modified* in virtue of its 'incorporation' into the arithmetic of integers:[37] There are operations applicable to the 'counterparts' of the natural numbers within the integers, which were not applicable before (e.g. subtracting 7 from 4).

---

33 This interpretation has a foothold in a remark from the precursor of PIr §23 in the *Big Typescript*: "We can also imagine a language that consists only of commands. Such a language relates to ours as a primitive arithmetic does to ours. And just as that arithmetic is not essentially incomplete, neither is the more primitive form of language" (BT: 162).
34 Cf. PIr: §67.
35 Cf. fn. 32 as well as PIr: §18.
36 Cf. PIr: §67: "Why do we call something a 'number'? Well, perhaps because it has a direct affinity with several things that have hitherto been called 'number'; and this can be said to give it an indirect affinity with other things that we also call 'numbers'".
37 In PIr: §18 Wittgenstein speaks about the fact that "the symbolism of chemistry and the notation of the infinitesimal calculus" were "incorporated" (*einverleibt*) into our language. The metaphor seems apt, more generally, to shed light on the form of expansion which is characteristic of language *qua form of life*, insofar as a growing organism does not merely modify *that which it incorporates* (e.g. food) but thereby modifies *its overall shape*.

(4) With respect to a more complex arithmetic, it is possible to distinguish between numbers (e. g. the positive integers), which have 'counterparts' in the more primitive system (e. g. the natural numbers) and numbers (e. g. the negative integers), which do not have such counterparts, but "come into existence" in virtue of the extension, only.[38]

6.17 Insofar as the extension of the concept of number can indeed serve as a picture of the internal growth of language qua form of life, Wittgenstein's remark that new language-games "come into existence, and others become obsolete and are forgotten", refers to events, which go hand in hand, rather than occuring independently of each other. For, if what the expansion starts from (the system of language-games already in place) is itself modified in the course of that expansion, it leads to a whole new system of language-games, rather than a motley, which would consist of an *arbitrary* subset of the games, which had been played before, as well as further ones, which hadn't.

6.18 If the form of life which we speakers of a language partake in, at present, is the result of the internal expansion of the form of life of a primitive thinker, and if this expansion has its source *in what expands* and is, *insofar*, non-arbitrary, it should be possible to *philosophically* recapitulate it[39]. The aim to recapitulate stages of the expansion of the form of life of a rudimentary thinker-and-speaker and, thereby, to exhibit a whole bunch of types of languge, which are characterized by different forces, as internally related and, hence, non-arbitrary parts of that form of life, is not an aim, which would be empty from the outset. Obviously, it is not an aim Wittgenstein pursues in the *Investigations*. This work is focused, rather, on exhibiting differences between parts of the *non-rudimentary* form of life of speakers in order to dissolve philosophical perplexities, which have their sorce in confusions between these parts, confusions, which consist, for instance, in conceiving of the expression of pain or talk about the meaning of words as though they had the form of quasi-empirical descriptions.

---

[38] The expression "counterpart" serves to indicate that it would neither be apt to say that a numeral has *the same* meaning in the context of a primitive and a complex arithmetic nor that it has simply *different* meanings. For a general discussion of this issue see PIr: §§555 ff., where Wittgenstein points out that the question whether "negation had the same meaning" to people, who don't know double negation, "as to us would be analogous to the question as to whether the figure '5' meant the same to people whose number series ended at 5 as to us".
[39] I have undertaken this task to a certain extent in my forthcoming book *Die Einheit des Sinns. Untersuchungen zur Form des Denkens und Sprechens*, cf. Martin expected 2019.

6.19 It might seem, however, that non-empirically envisaging the form of rudimentary thinking-out and exhibiting its internal expansion into more developed stages of the form of life of a speaker, is not merely an aim, which Wittgenstein does not pursue in the *Investigations*, but an aim, which he would conceive of as deeply misguided. In §130 of that work he states that "our clear and simple language-games are not preliminary studies for a future regimentation of language as it were, first approximations, ignoring friction and air resistance". What he rejects, in this passage, is the temptation to think of the investigation of "clear and simple language-games" as expandable into a more refined explanation of our form of life as speakers, which is modeled on scientific explanations. Such explanations are reductive, i.e. explanations of certain complex phenomena in terms of something else (e.g. theoretical entities). As seen, the idea of non-empirically exhibiting the expansion of the form of life of a primitive speaker is *not* the idea of a kind of reductive explanation.

6.20 If the aim to philosophically exhibit the expansion of the form of life of a thinker-and-speaker could be realized, it would result in a more transparent understanding of what belongs to us just *insofar as we are beings who think-and-speak*. It would thus amount to *another* way of dissolving confusions of the sort Wittgenstein seeks to dissolve in the *Investigations*, i.e. confusions which have their roots in a temptation to conceive of certain uses of language as of another form than they actually are. Exhibiting the expansion of the form of life of a primitive thinker-and-speaker seems to be the *only* way to conclusively reject an assumption, which appears to be pretty widespread, namely, that there is one type of language use, assertion, which is both *independent* of and *privileged* with respect to other types, insofar as it allows for objective validity. Contrary to this, it would be shown that different types of language equally belong to the form of life of a thinker-and-speaker. Rejecting the allegedly autonomous status of assertion by non-empirically exhibiting the expansion of the form of life of a rudimentary thinker-and-speaker wouldn't result in chaotic speech act pluralism, which proponents of assertion as an "autonomous discursive practice" have good reason to abhor as long as advocates of 'pluralism' rely on linguistic *observation* to justify their view.[40] It would rather be non-empirically shown that it belongs to the form of life of a *thinker-and-speaker* to differentiate itself into a system of different types of thinking-out. The types of language-game, which this system is made up by, would thereby be exhibited as all partaking in logical form. Types of language such as commanding, thanking, storytelling or praying

---

40 Cf. e.g. Brandom 2008: 41–42.

would thus be exhibited as of equal philosophical respectability, insofar as each partakes, *in its own way,* in the form of life of a being who thinks-out, and is, accordingly, a possible locus of objective validity[41].

References

Aristotle (1926) *Nicomachean Ethics*, with an English translation by Harris Rackhham, Cambridge, MA: Harvard University Press. [NE]
Aristotle (2014) *Metaphysics*, with an English translation by Hugh Tredennick, Cambridge, MA: Harvard University Press. [Met]
Baker, Gordon (ed.) (2003) *The Voices of Wittgenstein. The Vienna Circle*, London: Routledge. [VW]
Brandom, Robert (2008) *Between Saying and Doing*, Cambridge, MA: Harvard University Press.
Diamond, Cora (2002) "Truth before Tarski: After Sluga, after Ricketts, after Geach, after Goldfarb, Hylton, Floyd and Van Heijenoort", in: Erich H. Reck (ed.): *From Frege to Wittgenstein*, Oxford: Oxford University Press, 252–279.
Diamond, Cora (2014) "The Hardness of the Soft: Wittgenstein's Early Thought About Skepticism", in: Andrea Kern and James Conant (eds.): Varieties of Skepticism. Essays after Kant, Wittgenstein, and Cavell. Berlin: de Gruyter, 145–181.
Ford, Anton (2011) "Action and Generality", in: A. Ford, J. Hornsby and F. Stoutland (eds.): *Essays after Anscombe's Intention*, Cambridge, MA: Harvard University Press, 76–104.
Frege, Gottlob (1960) *Translations from the Philosophical Writings of Gottlob Frege*, Max Black and Peter Geach (eds.), Oxford: Blackwell.
Geach, Peter (1982) "Truth and God", in: *Proceedings of the Aristotelian Society*, Suppl. Vol. 56, 83–97.
Kosman, Aryeh (2013) *The Activity of Being*, Cambridge, MA: Harvard University Press.
Martin, Christian (2015) "Four Types of Conceptual Generality", in: *Graduate Faculty Philosophy Journal* 36, 397–423.
Martin, Christian (2019) *Die Einheit des Sinns. Untersuchungen zur Form des Denkens und Sprechens.* [unpublished manuscript, publication expected in 2019]
Strawson, Peter (1954) "Critical Notice", in: *Mind* 63, 70–99.
Travis, Charles (2008) *Occasion-Sensitivity*, Oxford: Oxford University Press.
Wittgenstein, Ludwig (1980a) *Remarks on the Philosophy of Psychology*, Vol. I, G. E. M. Anscombe and G. H. von Wright (eds.), transl. G. E. M. Anscombe, Oxford: Blackwell. [RPP I]

---

[41] I am grateful to audiences at the University of Chicago, the Instituto de Investigaciones Filosóficas (UNAM, Mexico City) and LMU Munich for critical comments on earlier versions of this paper. Special thanks to James Conant, Marcela García, Irad Kimhi, Mathis Koschel, André Laks, Ryan Simonelli and Tom Schulte.

Wittgenstein, Ludwig (1980b) *Remarks on the Philosophy of Psychology*, Vol. II, G. H. von Wright and H. Nyman (eds.), transl. C. G. Luckhardt and M. A. E. Aue, Oxford: Blackwell. [RPP II]

Wittgenstein, Ludwig (1982) *Last Writings on the Philosophy of Psychology*, Vol. I, G. H. von Wright and H. Nyman (eds.), transl. C. G. Luckhardt and M. A. E. Aue, Oxford: Blackwell.

Wittgenstein, Ludwig (2004) *Tractatus Logico-Philosophicus*, transl. B. F. McGuiness and D. Pears, London: Routledge. [TLP]

Wittgenstein, Ludwig (2005) *The Big Typescript: TS213*, German-English Scholar's Edition, ed. and transl. C. G. Luckhardt and M. A. E. Aue, Oxford: Blackwell. [BT]

Wittgenstein, Ludwig (2009) *Philosophical Investigations* (the German text, with an English translation by G. E. M. Anscombe, P. M. S. Hacker and Joachim Schulte), rev. 4th edition, P. M. S. Hacker and Joachim Schulte (eds.), Oxford: Wiley-Blackwell. [PIr][PPF]

Form(s) of Life: **the Very Idea**

Jocelyn Benoist
Our Life with Truth

Abstract: This article opposes the idea that it is possible to extract a theory of forms of life from Wittgenstein's *Investigations*. It puts forward instead the elucidatory – not explanatory – nature of the concept of 'forms of life' in Wittgenstein's work. To this end we first return to the original context in which Wittgenstein introduced this expression: the discussion of Russell's *Limits of Empiricism* to be found in *Ursache und Wirkung*. The analysis of this text allows to reassess what the primacy of 'deed' means in Wittgenstein's analysis. Wittgenstein's 'primitivism' is discussed and it is shown that we should absolutely distinguish between deflationism – which Wittgenstein endorses as a method – and reductionism – which he rejects. 'Forms of life' are at the same time a tool for such deflation and such anti-reduction. Wittgenstein's purpose is not to found truth and other normative accomplishments in a life without truth, but to disclose normativity at work in very basic performances of our lives. On this basis, in a second step, we return to the famous passages of the *Philosophical Investigations* that make use of the notion 'forms of life' and show how these remarks should not be understood along the lines of any 'relativism', but as a pedagogical attempt at making us aware of the open variety in the ways of truth. In this pedagogy, 'forms of life' have an essentially methodological function.

1 Introduction

The huge popularity of the theme of 'forms of life' in philosophy after and beyond Wittgenstein is somehow misleading. First because it seems that it is very common to make it a positive, and so to speak constructive theme, as if the so-called forms of life made up a field of their own, to be studied for itself. As if, so to speak, philosophy had one more time found its definition as a (quasi) science: as it were, a science of forms of life, even in order to conclude that, thus, as such, it cannot be a science *proper*.

Now, this use of the notion supposes that one grants the concept of 'form of life' an explanatory power and something like a theoretical import. As if something like a theory of forms of life were possible and desirable – even an essentially negative one, one that discloses the forms of life as the limit on more traditional theoretical ambitions nourished by philosophy.

This temptation to understand 'forms of life' as something we can and maybe must make a theory of is perfectly understandable. After all, is it not the case that: "What has to be accepted, the given, is – so one could say – *forms of life*"? (PI: p. 226) – To be *given*, is this not essentially to be a possible object of theory?

However, *one point I want to make* is that as much legitimate the desire for some theoretical approach to forms of life might be, as it is nowadays currently expressed on the side of sociology or anthropology, this is not Wittgenstein's point. In fact, as much as for every concept in his toolbox, the philosopher makes a strictly elucidatory – and not explanatory – use of this notion. Forms of life are not any things to be registered and described for themselves as if they constituted a field of givenness of their own that philosophy had to explore and to survey. This does not mean that, locally, to describe or maybe more exactly to imagine one such 'form of life' cannot help to relieve us of some philosophical perplexity. As a matter of fact, this is exactly what this concept is about within Wittgenstein's framework. This does not mean that there would be any point in making a theory of forms of life as such. It seems the concept of 'form of life' is essentially a therapeutic tool that helps us relieve the urge for an explanation in a particular theoretical situation in which we mistakenly believe that we need one. Of course, it is not the same as to provide us with such an explanation – as if, in the first place, there were anything there to explain.

The *second misgiving* I want to express about the current inflation of philosophical or semi-philosophical constructions about forms of life is the following: it seems that this notion is very commonly understood not only explanatorily, but reductively. Life is supposed to be something basic – as it certainly is. Thus, to talk of 'forms life', is to talk of something to which allegedly more complex activities or realities could be reduced. This is what I would call the reductionist use of the notion, which seems to be widespread, even if and because it takes on numerous forms. As a matter of fact, this misunderstanding might be induced by some aspect of Wittgenstein's text itself, as it is so easy to mistake deflationism for reductionism. If one misses that Wittgenstein, with his notion of 'form of life', makes a deflationist point, one will readily fall prey to the temptation to think that he makes a reductionist point, or, at least, to draw reductionist consequences from his point, whether with a naturalistic constructionist agenda or with a relativist post-modern one.

Then, the question seems to be what is 'life' in Wittgenstein's 'forms of life'. There are maybe two concepts of life: what one might call a narrower naturalistic concept of life versus a wider one that would involve the social dimension of life. Depending on which kind of life one has in view, it is not the same to bring back every human accomplishment to 'life'.

In particular, if the question is about our linguistic activity, it makes a whole difference whether the life at stake is a life *with or without language*. Of course, if it is a *life with language*, then, at least the spectre of one reduction vanishes: that is to say the one of items of linguistic behaviour to items of non-linguistic behaviour.

Then, what should it mean to bring our activities – inclusively linguistic activities – back to 'forms of life', but to adopt on these activities a take that does not reduce them to anything but themselves, but lets them appear so as they are: in their actuality. This would not be as much a reduction as an aspectual variation that helps make visible what was too close to be visible.

Now, then, both points would be connected. Because, it will result from this that the question is not so much: *what is human life?* and the problem to build a theory of it, as if it made sense to answer this question *in abstracto* – as if for instance the biological answer would *not* turn out to be the adequate one in some contexts. Rather, the task is to look at some human accomplishments from a renewed point of view, such as to capture them precisely as 'accomplishments'. Then, the dispute about human life is not any more a metaphysical one, but a question of method: a question about what I should look at when I ask certain questions. It is not exactly the case that one cannot answer certain questions in a certain way because human life absolutely is as it is. It is rather that these questions themselves involve a concept of human life as being thus and so and to some extent *constitute* this concept. Thus, 'what human life is' really depends on what we ask about. Perhaps Wittgenstein's concept of 'forms of life' has no other purport but to draw our attention to this point. From this point of view as well, there is no global or partial theory of forms of life to establish, but rather something like a sensibility to acquire to what is at stake in what we are really doing on particular occasions and to the particularity of these deeds.

2 Forms of Life in *Cause and Effect: Intuitive Awareness* (1937)

If one wants to address the question of forms of life in Wittgenstein seriously, the first thing to observe is that the connection that the philosopher makes between *the given* and *forms of life* in chapter XI of the second part of the *Philosophical Investigations* is in no way incidental.

In order to make sense of this point, as it is always the case with Wittgenstein, it is really helpful to trace the source of the problem. The philosopher introduces the notion of form of life explicitly in a series of notes of 1937 that have been edited under the title *Ursache und Wirkung* (*Cause and Effect*). These notes are essentially a reaction to Russell's paper *The Limits of Empiricism*, presented at a meeting of the Aristotelian Society on April 6, 1936, and then published in the *Proceedings of the Aristotelian Society* in the same year. Of course it is highly significant that the text that is the primary source of Wittgenstein's discussion of forms of life is dedicated to that question of *the limits of empiricism.*

As a matter of fact, Russell's paper, as such, is a reflection on the Given. Its focus is the demarcation between what is given, in the sense of *sense-given*, and what is not. According to the British philosopher a great deal is 'given': far more than what is *known*, since knowledge always appears as some kind of selection of what is given. To know is primarily to notice some aspect of the given.

At the same time, however, not *so much* is really given. For instance, according to Russell's analysis, when I see a cat, what is really given is only *the appearance of a cat*. In fact, it might turn out to be something else than a cat – e. g., the hallucination of a cat. Thus, the only thing that is really *given* is *the appearance*. In some sense, this restriction is the whole point of the notion of 'given'.

On the other hand, there is something that is essentially *not* given in the sense of 'sense-given', that is to say *that we should apply to what is given the word we apply to it* – where this application is not just some kind of automatism resulting from mere association and memory.

It is, however, something we *know*. How do we know that?

Russell's answer is: by some kind of non-empirical intuition. This answer is Platonic in its essence. As a matter of fact, this reveals something: that Platonism, as this word is commonly used in epistemology – that is to say the doctrine that there is a non-empirical intuition – is, so to speak, the other side of empiricism. Once you have restricted the domain of the Given – and the notion of 'Given' has exactly this restrictive purpose – you feel compelled to introduce some kind of extra-empirical sight of ours in order to make up for that.

This is Wittgenstein's starting point in his remarks of 1937 about "intuition" (*intuitives Erfassen*). He deconstructs the Russellian mythology of intuition by showing that we do not *need* that, without relapsing into empiricist reductionism. Surely, that we should apply the word 'cat' to some object is not 'given' in the sensible appearance of that object. It is nevertheless nothing we should grasp by any extra-empirical intuition. As a matter of fact, it is not so clear whether it is something we know – i.e. whether it really makes sense to say that we *know* that sort of things – but it is at any rate something we *do*, and this is what we should keep in view.

The story about forms of life surfaces in this context. Thus, this story concerns the linkage between the linguistic and the non-linguistic, the way we can connect language with reality. Russell's idea is that, in order to make this connection, we already need to be in some knowing relation to reality, on which the linguistic relation supervenes, and that we need grasp 'intuitively' the way in which the latter relation (from some definite words to what is given) is founded on the former (from our mind to what is given).

Behind this scenario (even if Russell insists that this distinction can here be neglected) one finds a distinction to be made between the *private object* as that mere part of some sensory given that I privately notice – which, according to the British philosopher, is the pre-linguistic form of knowledge – and the *public object* of knowledge as an object fit to be captured by a linguistic act of reference – an object that, as such, is exactly as little 'given' as the reason why we should call it the way we call it.

What Russell is at grips with, is the apparent mystery that language always takes us beyond 'the given'. By the simple fact that we talk of the given and apply some words to it we are already beyond it. How to justify this *leap into the ungiven?* At this point, some 'metaphysical intuition' just drops in. It is as if we *felt* that we should call this so and so.

In his 1937 notes Wittgenstein takes up the problem where Russell has left it. He does not deny that something like that 'feeling' exists. Now, the problem is whether such feeling should be assimilated to any kind of *knowledge*, let alone intuitive knowledge. Wittgenstein asks: "Isn't that like saying: Before recognizing something as 2 m long by measuring it, we have to recognize something as 1 m long by intuition?" (Wittgenstein 1993: 373) This example is known to play an important role in Wittgenstein's later philosophy, thus it is interesting that he makes use of it in this exact context.

The comparison helps to better understand Russell's problem. We can certainly measure something that is one meter long, by applying to it a stick of one meter for instance. Usually we know that this stick itself is one meter long because we have measured it already by another stick that is in turn one meter long, etc. But, this is possible only if we have some sense for *what it is to be one meter long:* some sense on which the measure relies and that is not its product. If we follow Russell, only *intuition* can provide this sense. It would be by intuition, as it were, that we should *know,* not that this or that piece of wood is one meter long but that in general that which is one meter long is one meter long.

The problem with this story is that it makes things that are in fact logically different too much similar. It is as if to know what it is to be one meter long was something on a par with knowing that a certain object is one or two meter long. However, since measurement cannot give us this, we need an extra-faculty: intuition, in order to know it. Wittgenstein, on the other hand, shows that the right question is whether what it is to be one meter long is something we *know* in the same sense in which we *know* that a particular object is one or two meters long. Is there really anything like a *fact to know* in that?

According to the Austrian philosopher, rather than to make room here for a primitive form of knowledge, we should pay attention to the primitive behaviours on which the language-games within which it makes sense to say we know that kind of things feed. For instance, when it comes to causality – this crux of empiricism: the 'cause' is essentially what *cannot* be given – we should have in view our instinctual tendency *to look out for a cause* (*Ausschauen nach einer Ursache*), when something happens, and, if it is possible, to "get rid of the cause if we don't want the effect" (Wittgestein 1993: 373).

Here certainly what could be called 'Wittgenstein's primitivism' finds its expression. An essential aspect of the picture is that what we find at the basis of the game is *instinctual*. In some sense, there is something right in Russell's hunch. Behind 'causality', something like a primordial experience of causality is to be found: i.e. the experience of my drive to suppress what hurts me, or, in an even more interesting scenario, what hurts the other:

"In its most primitive form it is a reaction to somebody's cries and gestures, a reaction of sympathy or something of the sort. We comfort him, try to help him." (Wittgenstein 1993: 381)

These are basic *reactions* – to use Wittgenstein's word – of human life, and to some extent, it is possible to say that we reason in causal terms *because* we have that kind of experiences.

This does not mean that the language game of cause and effect finds its *confirmation* in those experiences – as if we had finally found the missing 'experience of causality' as the missing empirical epistemic counterpart to causality –, but rather that they are to some extent just *part of this game*, that it is very difficult to picture what this game could mean without such experiences at its root. It is all right to call them 'experiences of the cause', but this is *analytic*: they are such because the language game of cause and effect is built on such experiences.

On the other hand, it is essential to observe that if the philosopher suggests here a kind of *genesis* – there are experiences that are 'basic' in that language game – this genesis should not be understood in the sense of a reduction. What we find at the root is, somehow, very primitive and, as Wittgenstein puts it, 'instinctual'. However, as simple as it might be, the primordial 'reaction' that the philosopher invokes *already involves a sense for the cause as such*. The point is not to translate causality into something more elementary in which it would not be already present – to translate our causal language into a primitive non-causal language – but to put to the fore a very basic form of causal thinking: to look out for a cause. The very notion of 'looking out for a cause', obviously, already involves, even if in a very basic and primitive way, the concept of cause.

Thus, the whole point of the analysis is to look up for simple, basic cases of use of the causal relation, but not at all to attempt to reduce this relation to something essentially different, to derive a causal structure from a non-causal one – like for instance a repeated correlation. Primitivism – if something like that is to be found in Wittgenstein's observations – is definitely not empiricism.

This is the context in which forms of life surface, and, as such, they are just part of this story, or, let us say, a working concept that helps formulate this story. Talking of 'forms of life' obviously puts the emphasis on *deeds:* on what we do and on primitive 'reactions' that constitute the background against which what we say has the meaning it has. For instance, one more time, what would we mean by 'causality' if we had not this instinctual drive to remove from our body the object that hurts us? Thus our – very abstract – language game of causality is so to speak rooted in simple experiences of life.

It seems, thus, that in order to be meaningful language has to be rooted in something more primordial than language. This primitivism is to be heard in the use that the philosopher makes of Goethe's famous saying: "Am Anfang war die Tat." It may sound as if deeds were 'in the beginning' (with the biblical echo) in the sense of: before the word. The reminiscence of Saint John is blatant: it is as if Goethe substituted 'Deed' for John's 'Word', maybe as some kind of correction. The primacy of Deed over Word makes full sense at least on some intellectualist interpretation of what 'Word' is.

Now, does Wittgenstein really say that deeds come *before* words? Another interpretation of Goethe's substitution is possible. By substituting Deed for Word, the German poet maybe suggests on the contrary some kind of deeper identity. In the beginning was the Deed because in the beginning was the Word, but this Word was just Deed – as, to some extent, maybe word always is. Then, to go back from words to deeds essentially means to adopt another take on words: to see them as *deeds*.

Thus, the return to deed or life should certainly not be interpreted as a pure and simple reduction to the pre-linguistic. The problem is not to reduce the sense that can be linguistically expressed to any mute pre-linguistic experience and deed, but to relocate the linguistic activity in which such sense is expressed within the context of life, in which we speak, and to pay particular attention to some basic situations in which we use the words that we use to express this sense.

To emphasize that it is always essential to take some basic 'reactions' of ours (one essential aspect of what Wittgenstein calls 'life') into account in order to make sense of what our words mean should not necessarily lead us to take words away so as just to stay with what could be called 'the silence of action'. A remark from *Ursache und Wirkung* sheds a different light on the role of 'action':

> Isn't this how it is: It is very fundamental to the game we play that we utter certain words and regularly *act* according to them [*daß wir gewisse Worte aussprechen und regelmäßig nach ihnen* handeln]. (Wittgenstein 1993: 379)

This is about *Handlung*, so action properly speaking. In order to make sense of a language game, one should look at what the players do – *wie sie handeln*. However, deed here does not come by itself: it is always already deed in relation to words. We act *according to* words. That is the whole point.

Thus, to put the emphasis on 'forms of life' does not mean to focus on *life without words*, or *as opposed to words*, but on *our life with words*. The fact that genealogically we use our words in the first place in very concrete situations of life, in ways that shape the further uses of these words, and that in these uses some very practical and mute happenings of our life play a part is important. However, the converse is important as well: that is to say that this life of ours is, even at this basic level, a *life with language*.

When Wittgenstein says that 'looking out for the cause' is a primordial ingredient of our language game of causality, it is clear that this behaviour is akin to a very basic natural reaction, triggered for instance by pain, that is essentially prelinguistic: even beings without language tend to suppress the stimulus that hurts them by targeting its source and trying to modify their own situation in relation to this source (either to destroy the source or to create some distance to it). However, of course, this is not enough to make this reaction part of the notion of causality. It becomes a part of it only when we become able to talk of the source as we talk of a cause. When for instance we make a difference between suppressing the effect and suppressing the cause (to treat the symptom and to treat the cause). This distinction is an essential feature of the language game of causality as we practice it. It is very simple and already present in what we could call *the primitive language game of causality:* the one according to which we call 'a cause' precisely what we look out for in certain circumstances – when we want to know on what we should act in order not to risk being hurt again, for instance. In the same way, the distinction between changing oneself and changing the cause seems to be essential, even if both moves have exactly the same effect. As long as we cannot make these distinctions, on which our simplest quest for a cause rests, but which raise as many questions that it is essential that we can formulate (they define the logical space of 'what we look out for'), there is no cause, but a mere succession of events only. The fact that my hand does not hurt anymore when I remove it from the flame does not mean *by itself* that this flame is the 'cause' of my pain. We are back to the main point: it seems that 'the cause', as such, is *not given*. To call it a cause is always already to exceed the limits of the given: to place it in a logical space. However, when we 'look out for a cause', we already do that: we look out for something that is not a mere concomitant but that we want to be able to take for the real cause of what we wish to change or to control. If it is not possible to take it this way, i.e. to take that it is *truly* the cause, there is no 'cause'. 'Cause', essentially, is 'the true cause'. Now, this possibility essentially presupposes language and this capacity that it saddles us with to take some distance from the given. The fact that, at a very primitive level of our interaction with our surroundings, we treat things around us as *causes* of some happenings – and not only as something that 'comes with them' –, means that, at that very primitive level, we already put ourselves in the position to call them 'causes': to *claim* more for them than concomitance. Now, a claim, in its essence, is linguistic – in some sense to say so is not to articulate any property of claims but rather to put forward *a mere definition of language*.

It is just as much essential that this claim, in the basic scenario, be *satisfied therefore justified*. Wittgenstein highlights the fact that what is basic in this story is *certainty*. We should first be adamant that some given things are causes of some definite happenings in a lot of cases for it to be possible that we sometimes question whether one thing that we have taken to be the cause of something else really is. So to speak, the language game of causes is, like every language game, installed by its success. In the first place there is no doubt for us that there are causes; the doubts come later, in some particular cases and, so to speak, at a second stage. Causality in general is not anything we can establish from nothing – from an initial situation in which it were unclear to us whether there is such thing as causality or not. The question arises in some particular circumstances because we already reason in causal terms precisely, and we do so inasmuch as, in some basic cases, we have already been able to make it work, inasmuch as *'it does'*, in the sense of: we do it. I.e.: we do it actually, successfully. What comes first is success.

When one says so, the transcendental philosopher frowns and suspects dogmatism: how can you be sure that it is success? Is it really cause, what you take naively to be a cause? Isn't causality a metaphysical prejudice – like philosophers and maybe to some extent 'the author of the *Tractatus*' took it? However, the point does not consist in shielding any particular content of knowledge from rational scrutiny and proclaiming the evidence of some pieces of knowledge – as if, precisely, we knew them by intuition rather than by measurement. It is much more a grammatical point, about the grammar of norms in general: there is no norm where we are not already able to apply it in some way. Thus, if we are not able to say, in some cases, that some A is positively the cause of some B, in such a way that there is no doubt about it, there is just nothing like cause. However, in this case, there would be nothing to doubt about either: what would it mean, to doubt that C is the cause of D, if we did not know what a cause is? And how do we know what a cause is if we were not able sometimes to recognize one?

Thus, Wittgenstein's point about the primitive language game, which is the language game of certainty (*Sicherheit*) is above all a point about the primacy of application, more precisely of successful application, in the definition of norms. From this point of view we have certainly to acknowledge a primacy of *what we do*. However, this does not amount to any primacy of what we do – the 'mere deeds' – over norms. Our deeds play a part here essentially because they are already normative: what we do, in this story, *we do it according to norms*. What Wittgenstein is after, when he pays attention to the basic instinctual reactions of life, is not the non-normative ('natural' in this sense) origin of a norm, but rather the *original form* of this norm – something that still plays a role in the fully developed version of the norm, as the shape of the norm is determined by its primitive applications.

That is not to say that no tension is to be found in Wittgenstein's primitivism. On the one side, undoubtedly, one finds naturalistic remarks. When Wittgenstein writes: "The primitive form of the language game is certainty, not uncertainty. For uncertainty could never lead to action" (Wittgenstein 1993: 397), it sounds as if certainty were some kind of instrumental external condition (a state, maybe?) required for and by action. How could we act if we were not certain? However, this is because *certainty is a part, here, of the form of our action*. The being that takes some things to be the cause of some other things and the being that does not certainly do not act the same way, and probably not even in the same sense. Not in the sense that the theory one buys about action necessarily alters one's action, but rather in the sense that one's non-theoretical immediate assessment of some definite thing as the cause of something else is just a part of *one's way to do* with things.

Thus, this is Wittgenstein's answer to Russell: the leap that Russell is worried about is just *the step we ordinarily make*. Causality is not a late theoretical construction that we apply from outside onto experience, and that would take us beyond what we were initially certain of. Quite the opposite: it is just *a form of our certainty*, in the sense that it is a basic part of our actual way to deal with reality. Our relation to causality does not amount to a hypothesis (a belief) to be confirmed. It is rather a way to proceed with some basic concrete cases. It is because in these cases we do understand some things as the causes of some other things that the notion of causality may have any sense and more specifically the normative sense it has. We cannot make the claim – i.e. use causality as a normative notion – and not buy the certainty, because the certainty is part of the claim.

Thus, it does not make any sense to ask for some warrant of the possibility for us to reason causally, because this is just something we *do*, at a very basic level, and we cannot withdraw from this doing in order to inquire into its possibility so to speak from outside: if we ask about the possibility of causality, it is because we already reason causally and have a sense for it rooted in some actual way to behave. If we did not do so, thus did not primarily recognize 'causes', there would never be any question whether, in a particular case, this thing is *really the cause of* some other thing. As such, some *use* is the condition of causality, and the warrant of causal relation (of the possibility for the causal relation to really obtain) is on the side of this use, not of any 'intuition' – even if the familiarity of the use may exactly come under the guise of this intuitive impression that is at stake in Russell's meditation.

3 The Methodological Function of 'Forms of Life'

It is clear that Wittgenstein's story about 'forms of life' concerns what might be called the hinge of the natural and the normative. This level necessarily has a naturalistic flavour. When one reads these texts, one cannot ignore the biological dimension of the concept of 'life'. To put back our language games into forms of life, as the philosopher suggests us to do, means to take into account the biological function of these language games as well and, in some sense, first:

> The game doesn't begin with doubting whether someone has a toothache, because that doesn't – as it were – fit the game's biological function in our life. In its most primitive form it is a reaction to somebody's cries and gestures, a reaction of sympathy or something of the sort. We comfort him, try to help him. (Wittgenstein 1993: 381)

The reaction of which Wittgenstein speaks: to answer the other's distress call, is however already a reaction on behalf of the other, so, in some sense, on the side of language. We could describe it as *the first step in language*. Life as it is as stake in Wittgenstein's 'forms of life' is from the start an interlocutive matter: when one calls and the other answers the call, making it by so doing a call to him or herself.

When Wittgenstein asks: "Isn't this how it is: It is very fundamental to the game we play that we utter certain words and regularly act according to them" (Wittgenstein 1993: 379), of course, one more time, the emphasis is on action (*Handlung*). However, what is fundamental is still that we utter certain words (*gewisse Worte aussprechen*), and that we regularly act according to them (*regelmäßig nach ihnen handeln*). Thus, the words have the lead.

Two dimensions play a part here, of equal importance. *Regelmäßigkeit* and *Regelgemäßsein:* respectively *regularity* and *conformity to the rule*. In order to have the norms we have, it is fundamental that we regularly do all sorts of things. Without these repetitive patterns of behaviour these norms would just be pointless – we could not even imagine them, or more exactly, we would just imagine them so as to become aware of the fact that they would not be anymore what they are, that, then, *we would play another game*. It seems that the philosopher uses the word *Lebensform* exactly in order to designate these *regularities:*

> I want to say: it is characteristic of our language that the foundation on which it grows consists in steady ways of living, regular ways of acting [*daß sie auf dem Grund fester Lebensformen, regelmäßigen Tuns, emporwächst*]. (Wittgenstein 1993: 397)

Forms of life make their appearance here as *steady forms of life*, i.e. as the mere name of this regularity that any norm seems to require there to be. As such, this regularity seems to be infralinguistic. In the following sentence, is language not called the mere accompaniment (*Begleiterin*) of action?: "Its function is determined *above all* [*vor allem*] by action [*Handlung*], which it accompanies." (Wittgenstein 1993: 397)

The initial phrasing of the problem, however, suggested something different. That is to say that the regularities that are at issue come down to the regular application of some norm, as expressed by some words. "We utter certain words and regularly *act* according to them." (Wittgenstein 1993: 379)

Thus, *Regelmäßigkeit* here is in the first place *Regelmäßigkeit* of the *Regelgemäßsein*. Wittgenstein's point is that, if we did not regularly comply with some norms in some basic situations it would be very difficult to make sense of them as the norms they are. In this sense, conformity to the norm depends on regularity, but on the regularity of something that is already normative[1] – such that we simply *do* in accordance to the norm: the doubts about its application or misfires in applying it are, at this basic level, exceptional.

That *Regelgemäßsein* takes on the aspect of *Regelmäßigkeit* at this level is certainly essential, but this fact does not deactivate *Regelgemäßsein* as such. Then, it is not surprising that, even at that basic level, language is already in.

---

[1] In the sense that it does not come down to the mechanical recurrence of a happening, but is the return in the fabric of our life of some configuration of action, in which we do have reasons to act as we do. Cf. the following remark from the second part of the *Philosophical Investigations*, chapter I (PI: p. 174): "*Grief* describes a pattern which recurs, with different variations, in the weave of our life. If a man's bodily expression of sorrow and of joy alternated, say with the ticking of a clock, here we should not have the characteristic formation of the pattern of sorrow or of the pattern of joy."

We regularly act according to words. The fact that our primary relation to these words is to act according to them and that this pattern of action according to them is in some sense immediate and very regular, thus intrinsically robust, of course, sheds a new light on words that we should not interpret immediately along the lines of the intellectualist fallacy. Action, in some sense, comes before meaning, if by meaning we understand descriptive (theoretical) meaning. However, the action that is here at stake is the action that answers to some words in such a way that this answering is definitional of that sort of action. Thus, from this point of view, if it is clear that "the simplest plough existed before the complicated one" (Wittgenstein 1993: 397), it is still useful to stress that even "the simplest plough" is yet a plough.

In fact, this story about ploughs introduces the theme of a hierarchy (in complexity), but also of a continuity between the different things we call 'forms of life' when it is about a specific game. "We have an idea [a concept: *Begriff*] of which ways of living [*Lebensformen*] are primitive, and which could only have developed out of these." (Wittgenstein 1993: 397)

It is noteworthy that 'form of life' here is not opposed as what is supposed to be 'primitive' to what is not, but that the contrast between what is primitive and what is not rather crosses the realm of forms of life. Of course, there is nothing that human beings do that is not done within a form a life. However, in our forms of life, some things are more primitive than others. That is to say: they play a more primitive role in some games. In fact what makes them 'primitive' is not their mere anteriority from the point of view of an external natural history, but precisely the extent to which these games have naturalized them in making them an intrinsic part of themselves. If "ordering, questioning, recounting, chatting are as much a part of our natural history as walking, eating, drinking, playing" (PI: §25), that means that our language games are just part of our 'nature' as much as our 'nature' is part of them. There is no 'natural history' of language games but an *internal* history.

Hence, it is necessary to relativize the primitiveness essentially involved in every language game. There is no other definition of what is 'primitive' here than 'what we usually do', in the sense of: *what we do without having to think about it*. In this, the biological necessities certainly help. However, from this point of view, it would make no sense to reduce what is primitive to those necessities.

In this respect, it is highly significant that, in every important discussion of 'forms of life', in Wittgenstein's work, the mathematical practice (or *praxis*, a word the philosopher uses not so much, but he does in the case of mathematics) plays a paradigmatic role. It might sound strange by the standard of some *reductionist* primitivism. Mathematics seems rather to be a higher-order practice, even if the simple activity of counting certainly plays a role at a very basic level of our life.² It is, however, not necessarily this elementary mathematics (what Frege would have called "kindergarden-mathematics") that Wittgenstein has in view when he finds in mathematical practice the paradigm of what he calls 'forms of life', but precisely any mathematical practice as an *established practice:* a way to proceed or calculate that is shared by mathematicians, with some *agreement* in the results that goes *without saying*.

> Disputes do not break out (among mathematicians, say) over the question whether a rule has been obeyed or not [*ob der Regel gemäß vorgegangen wurde oder nicht*]. People don't come to blows over it, for example. That is part of the framework on which the working of our language is based [*zu dem Gerüst, von welchem aus unsere Sprache wirkt*] (for example, in giving descriptions). (PI: §240)

Maybe, to translate this more exactly: that kind of agreement in our language – the fact that in some given circumstances we just judge in the same way about things, state *the same things to be true* (thus: apply the norm in the very same way) – belongs to the framework of our language itself, exactly like the fact that in the same theoretical situation the calculations of the mathematicians give the same result is a part of the sense of their calculation.³ This story definitely does not run below the level of calculation or language.

As an echo, we find this in chapter XI of the second part of the *Philosophical Investigations*, before the famous statement that makes, in answer to Russell, forms of life the real locus of the 'given':

> There can be a dispute over the correct result of a calculation (say of a rather long addition). But such disputes are rare and of short duration. They can be decided, as we say, 'with certainty'.
>
> Mathematicians do not in general quarrel over the result of a calculation. (This is an important fact.) – If it were otherwise, if for instance one mathematician was convinced that a figure had altered unperceived, or that his or someone else's memory had been deceived, and so on – then our concept of 'mathematical certainty' would not exist. (PI: p. 225)

Thus, mathematical games (such as the one that, for instance, consists in formulating, then solving a particular kind of problem), insofar as they do not grow

---

2 See *Remarks on the Foundations of Mathematics* I §4 (Wittgenstein 1978: 37): "For what we call 'counting' (*zählen*) is an important part of our life's activities."
3 See *Remarks on the Foundations of Mathematics* III §67 (Wittgenstein 1978: 193): "This consensus belongs to the essence of *calculation*, so much is certain. I.e.: this consensus is part of the phenomenon of our calculating."

from nothing, but are always based on some usual basic ways to proceed (for instance a particular kind of calculation from which i.e. as well *in the context of which* arises a particular kind of problem), suppose something like 'mathematical forms of life'. To talk like this is not to hand over mathematics to some kind of anthropological external explanation – as if mathematics was some kind of consequence of our non-mathematical life, which it might be, but this is just not the point – but to recognize the priority of some not formless life – that is to say: some regular way to do – within mathematics itself.

Thus, mathematics as such is not based on ink and paper. It is not to be 'naturalized' in this reductionist sense, at least if we want to deal with it as mathematics. However, it is essentially true that it is based on what mathematicians *do* with ink and paper, on their way to write out an operation and on the fact that when anyone of them carries it out, it always gives the same result. This is what, if we do mathematics, 'has to be accepted, the given': *the form of our life with mathematics* – as something very analogous to, and maybe a part of, *the form of our life with language*.

In this respect, it is obviously of the highest importance that the paragraphs 241 and 242 of the *Philosophical Investigations* put on a par the idea of an "agreement in the form of life" (*Übereinstimmung der Lebensform*), as opposed to an "agreement of opinions" (*der Meinungen*), and the one of an "agreement in judgments" (*Übereinstimmung in den Urteilen*). Thus, judgements as such – when it comes to commit oneself to what is true or false as opposed to envisaging mere 'opinions' – are clearly made part of 'forms of life'.

To conclude with this, this does not mean that we cannot do otherwise, or that somebody (some being) does not do otherwise. There is no necessity in the fact of doing multiplications. Thus, maybe, we can imagine beings that would calculate without doing so – this is not complicated after all, because there is a logical leap from addition and subtraction to multiplication and division: one can build a machine that can carry out the former without being able to carry out the latter. The whole point is that, however, this would not be what we call calculate: just because we *do* multiply and divide. Of course things are getting worse if we try to imagine beings that do not add or subtract either, or at least do not do it in the sense in which we do it, and that still 'calculate'. The only thing we can say in that case is that we cannot see exactly what calculation should mean then. This does not mean that it is *per se* impossible, but that *we do not have made it possible*. Of course the history of mathematics is full of cases in which things that were impossible had finally been made possible. That is the way it works.

> New types of language, new language-games, as we may say, come into existence, and others become obsolete and get forgotten. (We can get a *rough picture* of this from the changes in mathematics.) (PI: §23)

However, this is a change in our form of life. In this respect, the possibility of a new kind of truth is always the sign that we have started to do something that we did not do before, in the sense that *we did not want to do it:* that we have started to judge what was not even judgeable before.

Thus, the primary outcome of an analysis in terms of 'forms of life' is that we should not be too much in a hurry to reject the other's truth as mere bullshit. This not because truth would be 'relative' to forms of life in the sense of causally dependent on them, therefore nothing to be ever shared. Shareability, on the contrary, is of course an essential feature of any truth, as different as it might look from our truths in its purpose. But the simple fact that we proceed in some way in establishing our truths – we actually do so and it is constitutive so to speak of the physiognomy of our truths – does not mean that it is not possible to proceed in another way, of course with different results then. When we become aware of this – and philosophy is nothing but a way to become aware of this – we can envisage to de-naturalize our ways to do, as, after all, they are nothing but *what we do,* and look at the others as maybe doing something of their own. This supposes to relax this mental cramp by which we stick to practices of truth that become the exclusive horizon of our truths.

Thus, the philosopher writes in the Manuscript 160:

> Ich sage: Gewöhne Dich daran eine Mannigfaltigkeit Techniken der Zeichenverwendung (also des Denkens) zu sehen. Ich will nicht ein Vorurteil der Meinung sondern der Technik beseitigen. Erschrick z. B. nicht prinzipiell vor einem Widerspruch.
> I say: Get used to see a diversity of techniques in using signs (therefore in thinking). I do not want to eradicate a prejudice of opinion but of technique. For instance, do not be on principle afraid of a contradiction. (Wittgenstein 2003: MS 160 26v)

To eradicate a prejudice of technique means to make human beings aware that there are always different ways to do – this is something that is intrinsic to the notion of doing. This does not suppress truth, but opens in it a real diversity. Now, in front of an activity that we do not understand, it remains always to be seen whether a 'technique' is involved: if, in this case, anything is to be found that these people *usually* do. If nothing like *usual results* is to be found in this action, it makes just no sense to look for a normative framework in it, and to make room for some truth that would be conquered on its terms. There are an infinity of mathematical operations we cannot even imagine (of course, to say this already supposes a sufficient community of practices to call them 'mathematical'). However, there is no operation without definite results. I.e.: there is no operation except one defined by the fact that there is a way to concur in carrying it out.

To understand 'other forms of life' is just to become capable to make them parts of ours: to project ourselves in the position of *those who agree in these judgements*. This is not to reject truth in favour of consensus (as if consensus was an ersatz to truth), but to open up new dimensions of truth in becoming able to share *new* truths.

References

Russell, Bertrand (1935–36) "The Limits of Empiricism", in: *Proceedings of the Aristotelian Society* 36, 131–150.
Wittgenstein, Ludwig (1958) *Philosophical Investigations*, 2nd edition, transl. G. E. M. Anscombe, Oxford: Basil Blackwell. [PI]
Wittgenstein, Ludwig (1978) *Remarks on the Foundations of Mathematics*, 3rd edition, Oxford: Basil Blackwell.
Wittgenstein, Ludwig (1993) "Ursache und Wirkung: Intuitives Erfassen", in: Ludwig Wittgenstein: Philosophical Occasions, 1912–1951, James C. Klagge and Alfred Nordmann (eds.), Indianapolis/Cambridge: Hackett, 370–405.
Wittgenstein, Ludwig (2003) *Wittgensteins Nachlass*, The Bergen Electronic Edition, Charlottesville, Virginia, USA: InteLex.

Martin Gustafsson
Language-games, *Lebensform*, and the Ancient City

Abstract: This paper explores Wittgenstein's method of language-games, by discussing how simple language-games are related to language of real-life complexity. It is argued that Wittgenstein rejects as unintelligible an atomist conception of this relation, according to which the step from simple language-games to complex language is a matter of mere accumulation of individually self-standing building-blocks which are supposed to remain substantively unchanged throughout the process. The upshot of Wittgenstein's non-atomism is that his method involves as a crucial element the consideration of how simple language-games themselves undergo transformations when we build up complicated forms of language from rudimentary starting-points. In this connection, it is investigated how the notion of "form of life" enters Wittgenstein's discussion. It is considered why the connection made between his method and Goethean morphology in Waismann's *The Principles of Linguistic Philosophy* is absent in PI, and then argued at some length that a different analogy that he does make use of – that of language as an ancient city – sheds more light on his method than is usually appreciated.

1 Introduction

The terms "form of life" and "language-game" are closely associated in the *Philosophical Investigations*. In Part I of the book, the term "form of life" occurs only three times, and in two of these it is used precisely to explain the significance of simple language-games such as those of the builders in §§2 and 8.[1] In §23, Wittgenstein says "[t]he word 'language-*game*' is used here to emphasize the fact that the speaking of language is part of an activity, or of a form of life". A few paragraphs earlier, in §19, the term occurs in the midst of a discussion where he

---

[1] I prefer the old headings, "Part I" and "Part II", of the *Investigations*, and thus take exception to the renaming of Part II by Peter Hacker and Joachim Schulte in their revised translation of the book (they call it *Philosophy of Psychology – A Fragment*). As Hugh Knott has convincingly shown in a recent paper (Knott 2017), there are good reasons – both historical and philosophical – to stay with the old titles.

seems to insist that simple language-games can be conceived as self-standing languages:

> It is easy to imagine a language consisting only of orders and reports in a battle. Or a language consisting only of questions and expressions for answering Yes and No – and countless other things. – And to imagine a language means to imagine a form of life.

Many commentators have felt uncomfortable with this passage, arguing that it is not at all easy but in fact hardly possible to imagine a genuine *language* consisting only of orders and reports in a battle. Such commentators have claimed that we cannot really make sense of the meager language-games in §§2 and 8 as self-standing languages. "The trouble", says Rush Rhees, "is to imagine that [the builders in §§2 and 8] spoke the language only to give these special orders on this job and otherwise never spoke at all. I do not think it would be speaking a language" (Rhees 1960: 177). More recently, Peter Hacker has come to a similar conclusion:

> It is [...] doubtful whether one can coherently imagine a language consisting only of orders in a battle, but no orders and reports before or after the battle, and no orders and reports at home or in the fields. [...] It is none too easy to imagine such a language, any more than it is easy to imagine language-game (2) as a complete primitive language. (Hacker 2015: 5)[2]

Wittgenstein, however, seems to want to forestall precisely this sort of reaction. For, in §18 he writes:

> Do not be troubled by the fact that languages (2) and (8) consist only of orders. If you want to say that this shews them to be incomplete, ask yourself whether our own language is complete; – whether it was so before the symbolism of chemistry and the notation of the infinitesimal calculus were incorporated in it[.]

In a recent paper, Oskari Kuusela argues that the reason why Wittgenstein urges us not to worry about the extreme sparseness of his simple language-games is that such worry displays a misapprehension of their methodological purpose. Kuusela notes, "the method of language-games [...] is a method for isolating and describing particular aspects or facets of language use for the purpose of philosophical clarification, but involves no claim that such a description captures language use in all its actual complexity" (Kuusela 2014: 151). Hence, he

---

[2] It should be noted that Hacker, like Oskari Kuusela (see below), does not take this objection to be of much relevance for Wittgenstein's central, methodological points. However, it should also be noted that Hacker's conception of Wittgenstein's method is quite different from Kuusela's.

concludes, "nothing depends on whether we acknowledge [Wittgenstein's] primitive language-games as proper languages, as long as we accept that those systems bear enough similarity to actual language in order for it to be compared with them to clarify its particular aspects" (Kuusela 2014: 147). According to Kuusela, the reason why Wittgenstein nonetheless insists that we conceive of a simple language-game such as that of the builders "as a complete primitive language" (PI: §2) is that the language-game can have a determinate function as a model or an object of comparison only if we think of it as completely described: "it would be problematic, if the model had hidden dimensions on which [its] comprehensibility as [an] example of language or as comparable to language depended" (Kuusela 2014: 148).

I think Kuusela is right that language-games are primarily meant to function as tools for clarification, and that Wittgenstein's insistence that they be conceived as complete and self-standing (cf. BB: 81) must be read as methodologically motivated rather than as involving some sort of theoretical claim about what is sufficient for something to be a *language* proper. However, Kuusela does not address one of the principal objections which commentators such as Rhees have raised against Wittgenstein's conception. What such commentators argue is not merely that more parts must be added in order to get a genuine language. Their claim is not that we need to aggregate sufficiently many individual language-games in order to reach a critical mass such that the total sum is extensive enough to count as a full-blown language. Rather, they are making a more thoroughly holistic point: the enrichment they are asking for is not a matter of mere aggregation, but of a wider surrounding of linguistic practices in relation to which a simple "game" is understandable and describable as a *language-game* in the first place. Thus, what they claim is that we cannot speak, say, of orders in a battle, or of the naming of objects, without *already* presupposing that the simple activities we describe stretch beyond themselves as integrated within a rich array of linguistic practices. The point these commentators make is that if we think we can separate and treat as complete a simple language-game such as that of the builders, while at the same time continuing to use notions such as "giving an order" and "pointing at and naming an object" to characterize the moves within that game, we must be working under the illusion that language can be conceived as a merely analytic sum of individually self-standing patterns of activity. As Warren Goldfarb puts it, "[t]he trouble comes when we segment the description, i.e., when we take 'naming', 'wishing to point', and so on, as if they picked out isolatable phenomena, whose character can be given independently of any surrounding structure" (Goldfarb 1982: 272).

Why is this point of methodological significance? Why could not Kuusela's Wittgenstein respond simply by repeating his apparently non-committal claim, that it suffices if the simple language-game we introduce as a tool of clarification bear enough similarity to actual language in order for the specific comparison we want to make to fulfill its purpose?

The problem is that this response fails to explain how there can *be* "enough similarity" between simple language-games and actual language for the envisaged comparison to be illuminating. More precisely, the worry is that there is an unacknowledged tension between the demand for self-standing simplicity and the aim of philosophical illumination. On the one hand, we have seen Kuusela emphasizing that the usefulness of simple language-games in such comparisons presupposes that they have no hidden dimensions on which their comprehensibility as examples of language or as comparable to language depends. On the other hand, it is unclear how such comparisons can be illuminating if they do not allow that the activities involved in the language-games be characterized in at least rudimentary semantic terms, such as "naming", "wishing to point", "ordering", and so on. However, if Rhees and Goldfarb are right, such characterizations presuppose that the simple language-games are *not* treated as complete and self-standing. The upshot seems to be that Kuusela's method of language-games involves inconsistent demands on the model used. In order to handle this sort of holistic worry, it is not enough to insist on a purely methodological conception of how simple language-games are supposed to function. For the point about the holistic interdependence between different parts of language will matter to the question how the envisaged method of clarification itself is supposed to work.

My aim in this paper is to explore this connection between holistic interdependence and Wittgenstein's method of language-games. I will argue that Wittgenstein rejects as unintelligible an atomist conception of the relation between language-games and language in its real-life complexity, and that the methodological significance of language-games is therefore more intricate than Kuusela's discussion sometimes suggests. In particular, I argue that the method will have to involve as a central element the consideration of how simple language-games themselves undergo transformations when we build up complicated forms of language from such rudimentary starting-points. In this connection, I consider how the notion of "form of life" enters Wittgenstein discussion. I discuss why the connection he makes between his method and Goethean morphology in Waismann's *The Principles of Linguistic Philosophy* is absent in the *Philosophical Investigations*, and then consider at some length how a different analogy that he does make use of – that of language as an ancient city – says more about his method than is usually appreciated.

2 Two Different Targets: Essentialism and Atomism

Doesn't Wittgenstein himself conceive language as a mere aggregate of simpler and individually self-standing language-games? Consider the following passage from *The Blue Book:*

> If we want to study the problems of truth and falsehood, of the agreement and disagreement of propositions with reality, of the nature of assertion, assumption, and question, we shall with great advantage look at primitive forms of language in which these forms of thinking appear without the confusing background of highly complicated processes of thought. When we look at such simple forms of language the mental mist which seems to enshroud our ordinary use of language disappears. We see activities, reactions, which are clear-cut and transparent. On the other hand we recognize in these simple processes forms of language not separated by a break from more complicated ones. We see that we can build up the complicated forms from the primitive ones by gradually adding new forms. (BB: 17)

Again, the holistic worry arises: How can Wittgenstein take it for granted that "these forms of thinking" – truth-telling, assertion, assumption, and so forth – appear in the sort of primitive language-games that remain once the "confusing background of highly complicated processes of thought" has been taken out of the picture? Will not the "activities" and "reactions" he talks about be merely non-semantic stimulus-response patterns or "signals", deprived of linguistic significance? (Rhees 1960: 177) If so, how can the isolation of these patterns of reaction shed any light on such "forms of thinking"? In fact, isn't it clear that Wittgenstein is working with a highly questionable, atomistic picture of language according to which the step from the simple to the complex, or from the primitive to the less primitive, is a matter of mere accumulation of individually self-standing games which are supposed to remain substantively unchanged throughout the process?

Similar questions can be raised with regard to some of Kuusela's descriptions of the methodological function of language-games in Wittgenstein's philosophy. Consider the following passage:

> Language-games in the capacity of primitive and simple forms of language use can be used, so to speak, to isolate and study specific aspects of the functioning linguistic expressions. Hence, they can be characterized, in a certain sense, as a tool by means of which the logic of language (or the function of expressions) can be analyzed. By means of simple language-games we can abstract from and take apart complicated uses of linguistic expressions with

> the purpose of clarifying their specific aspects. The shopping language-game [in PI §1] can be used to explain the sense in which we might speak of analysis here. (Kuusela 2014: 139)

How, exactly, are we to make sense of the "analyzing", "isolating", "taking apart" and "abstracting from" that Kuusela is talking about? Again, an atomistic reading seems near at hand: by taking apart our complicated language and studying its building-blocks – individual and self-standing language-games – we isolate specific aspects of our usage from the surrounding complexities and thereby get a clear view of how they function. In response to Rhees's objection against using the word "analysis" to describe the functioning of language-games – "If we call them 'more primitive' or 'simpler' languages, that does not mean that they reveal anything like the elements which a more complicated language must have" (BB: ix) – Kuusela says, "Rhees is right that the language-game method doesn't aspire to reveal any underlying elements in this sense. But the notion of an analysis need not be understood in this way" (Kuusela 2014: 157, n. 12). However, Rhees's objection is not directed against the view that Wittgenstein's simple language-games are to be seen as elements *underlying* linguistic practice, but against the view that they constitute elements that can be *isolated from* the rest of language and yet retain those linguistic features and the "logic" that we want to understand. Rhees is worried about the very idea that we can "take apart" language in this analytic, atomistic sense. Kuusela's remarks do little to alleviate *that* worry.

At this point, it is important to distinguish between two forms that a criticism of an atomistic picture of the relation between language-games and language can assume. One form of criticism is based on some general ideas of what makes language *language*. In its attack on the atomistic picture, this form of criticism invokes ideas of when patterns of activities can be properly counted as genuinely linguistic. An important part of Rhees's criticism seems to be of this sort. He lists a number of things that he takes to be crucial to language proper. Language, he says, must involve *conversation* between speakers (where "conversation" is different from mere game-playing); he claims that "[l]anguage is something that can have a literature"; and he suggests that language is something that can be understood only in relation to how it is anchored in humanly basic customs of farming, building, marrying, and so forth (Rhees 1960: 180–183, 185). So, one argument he uses against the idea that Wittgenstein's simple language-games can be conceived as self-standing and isolatable linguistic practices is that they do not fulfill these conditions for being a language: Wittgenstein's builders are not engaged in proper conversation, their signaling is not something that could have a literature, and so on.

I think this is a genuine point of disagreement between Wittgenstein and Rhees. As we have seen, Wittgenstein insists that we can recognize his simple language-games as forms of language not separated by a break from more complicated ones, and he wants us to see that we can build up complicated forms from more primitive ones by gradually adding new forms. This gradual transition is difficult to make sense of from Rhees's point of view. It seems to me that Wittgenstein would find in Rhees's argument a residual form of essentialism that is better abandoned.

However, does this mean that Wittgenstein must therefore embrace the sort of atomistic picture that Rhees rejects? Or is there a way of resisting the atomistic picture without embracing any essentialist criteria for what makes a language a language? I think so; and this will then constitute a second, non-essentialist criticism of the atomistic picture. The key here is to find a way of conceiving the gradual process of building up complicated forms from more primitive ones, not as the mere accumulation of self-standing practices that remain the same throughout the process, but as a process in which the building-blocks themselves undergo changes as the process goes along, so to speak. Conversely, the "isolation" of a simple language-game will be seen as involving changes in this very game, so to speak: the isolated, primitive game will nowhere be found intact in more complicated structures, but can still somehow be used to shed light on aspects of these structures. This non-atomistic conception of how simple language-games are related to languages of real-life complexity will have to be given in terms that involve no essentialist presuppositions. In what remains of this paper, I will explore this non-atomistic and non-essentialist possibility as it is developed in Wittgenstein's reflections on language-games and their methodological significance.

3 Language-games and Morphology

One of the clearest indications that Wittgenstein does not have an atomistic conception of how simple language-games are related to languages of real-life complexity is his recurring attempts to clarify this relation by reference to Goethe's thoughts on morphology.[3] The most extensive discussion is in a work of which Wittgenstein was not formally the author, but whose content is so directly shap-

---

3 For illuminating discussions of Wittgenstein's relation to Goethe, see Rowe 1991 and various essays in Breithaupt, Raatzsch and Kremberg 2003. For Wittgenstein's thoughts on Goethean morphology, see Schulte 2003.

ed (sometimes literally dictated) by him that it should be given a central position in the present discussion. In the section "Language Games" in Friedrich Waismann's *The Principles of Linguistic Philosophy*, it is emphasized that simple, rule-governed language-games are to be used merely as objects of comparison. According to Waismann – and, I think we can assume, Wittgenstein – we should resist the temptation to "try to arrange the reality of language according to a particular pattern, if not to alter it to fit the pattern" and instead "simply place the pattern beside language and let it throw as much light upon its nature as it can" (Waismann 1997: 77). Waismann notes that the method bears similarity to a method proposed by Boltzmann, namely,

> that of describing a physical model [...] without making any claim that it conformed to something in the real world. It is simply described and then whatever similarities exist between it and reality will reveal themselves. [...] There is no temptation to counterfeit reality, for the model is, so to speak, given once and for all, and it can be seen how far it agrees with reality. And even if it does not, it still retains its value. (Waismann 1997: 77)

Waismann then goes on to contrast this comparative method with that of looking for an explanation:

> [W]e are not dealing here with an explanation of phenomena; [...] but I silence the questionings which seem to resemble a problem by setting a number of similar cases side by side. It is remarkable that the mere bringing together of cases gets rid of perplexity. (Waismann 1997: 80)

And then, strikingly employing the method itself to clarify its own character, he sets his approach side by side with Goethe's. The relevant passage is worth quoting at length:

> Our thought here marches with certain views of Goethe's, which is expressed in his *Metamorphosis of Plants*. We are in the habit, whenever we perceive similarities, of seeking some common origin for them. The urge to follow such phenomena back to their origin in the past expresses itself in a certain style of thinking. This recognizes, so to speak, only a single scheme for such similarities, namely the arrangement as a series in time. [...] But Goethe's view shows that this is not the only possible form of conception. His conception of the original plant implies no hypothesis about the temporal development of the vegetable kingdom such as that of Darwin. What then *is* the problem solved by this idea? It is the problem of synoptic presentation. Goethe's aphorism 'All the organs of plants are leaves transformed' offers us a plan in which we may group the organs of plants according to their similarities as if around some natural centre. We see the original form of the leaf changing into similar and cognate forms, into the leaves of the calyx, the leaves of the petal, into organs that are half petals, half stamens, and so on. We follow this sensuous transformation of the type by linking up the leaf through intermediate forms with the other organs of the plant.

> That is precisely what we are doing here. We are collating one form of language with its environment, or transforming it in imagination so as to gain a view of the whole of the space in which the structure of our language has its being. (Waismann 1997: 80–81)

This is a rich and difficult passage, and I cannot here give anything like a full interpretation of it. What I want to point out, first of all, is that the parallel drawn between Goethe's morphology of plants and the method of language-games seems clearly incompatible with an atomistic conception of the relation between language-games and language in its real-life complexity. Notice that Goethe's aphorism is "All the organs of plants are leaves *transformed*". Even the *leaves* of real-life plants are to be conceived as "leaves transformed", according to Goethe. He thought of the simple original plant as a single leaf, but this single leaf is not fully similar to any leaf of a real-life plant. Rather, the original plant would be "the strangest creature in the world" (Goethe 2009: 310), and transformations of this strange creature are required not only to generate stamens and petals but also to generate the leaves of plants we actually encounter in the world. Similarly, Waismann explicitly says that a "transformation in imagination" is required in order to see the relation between the simple language-games and those aspects of real-life language use that they are supposed to illuminate.

It is worth remembering, more generally, that the living organism is a favorite analogy among holists. The relation between an organism and its parts (its organs) is *the* standard case of a non-atomist relation. The very unity of an organ is tied to its function in the organism: it is by reference to this function within the organism as a whole that we identify and re-identify something as the kind of organ it is, distinguish it from other organs, and identify the organ's own vital parts. So, organs are precisely not self-standing objects, and an organism is not a mere aggregate of such objects.

All in all, it would be peculiar indeed if Waismann (and Wittgenstein) had drawn such a close parallel between Goethean morphology of plants and the method of language-games, had he conceived of the relation between a language and its parts in atomistic terms.

So, the Goethe connection speaks clearly in favor of a non-atomist reading of Wittgenstein. However, what about Wittgenstein's alleged non-essentialism? Here, the situation is less clear-cut. My aim is not to engage in Goethe exegesis, but it would not seem too far-fetched to interpret Goethe's conception of the original plant as a form of essentialism. For isn't the original plant conceived by him as a sort of fundamental archetype in virtue of which plants are conceivable as plants at all, and without which botany would not have any formal unity? At some point, Goethe even thought that such an original plant must actually exist (he hoped to find it somewhere in Italy); but even as he abandoned that assumption, it seems natural to read him as saying that the original plant is the *Urform* that any careful morphologist *must* arrive at after a suitably deep and wide-ranging consideration of how the plants of the earth resemble each other.

In this connection it is also worth pointing out that the overall parallel between language and living organisms invites a sort of essentialism – not necessarily in terms of a common *Urform*, but of organisms qua exemplars of *species*. It is at least arguable that a holistic conception of how a living organism is related to its parts involves the idea that this relation is intelligible only by reference to the species of which the individual organism is a member. The eyes of Tim, the Siamese, are the eyes of a *cat*, and their proper functions are identified accordingly. For example, those eyes are not working properly if Tim does not have night vision. And if Tim does not see at all, he is blind. By contrast, not having night vision is not a way of being incapacitated for a human being – for night vision is not a capacity humans have *qua* humans. And an earthworm is not blind, although it does not see – for an earthworm *qua* earthworm has no organs of sight, not even malfunctioning ones. Thus it would seem that the individual organism and its organs form a unity in virtue of a teleological pattern delineated by reference to the species of which the organism is an exemplar – a pattern of which it seems natural to say that it constitutes the organism's essence. This also means that there is a certain notion of *completeness* associated with living organisms. A blind cat lacks something, namely, properly functioning eyes. By contrast, the fact that an earthworm has no eyes does not mean that it is incomplete – for having eyes is not something that belongs to an earthworm *qua* the kind of creature it is. In this sense, fully worked out botanical and anatomical pictures can be said to depict complete living organisms – organisms that have all those properly functioning organs that are essential to them *qua* exemplars of the relevant species.[4]

All in all, whereas the parallel with Goethean morphology of plants strongly supports a non-atomist reading of Wittgenstein, it does not by itself offer any clear support for a non-essentialist interpretation. However, if one looks at how Waismann (and Wittgenstein) spells out the parallel, the non-essentialist

---

[4] Among Anglophone philosophers, Michael Thompson and Philippa Foot have developed this Aristotelian kind of essentialism in detail, cf. Foot 2001, Thompson 2008. Arguably, it is also present in Anscombe's works – see Gustafsson 2017. Of course, many philosophers of biology argue that such essentialism is scientifically primitive and unacceptable – for a recent influential rejection, see Godfrey-Smith 2009. Given my purposes in this paper, I do not have to take a stand in this debate.

reading still seems motivated. For Waismann clearly pushes the parallel in a non-essentialist direction. Here is how he describes what the method of language games can achieve, just a couple of paragraphs before he brings in Goethe:

> As long as we are familiar only with actual language, we tend to make all sorts of dogmatic assertions, such as 'Aristotelian logic governs every language', or 'Every language must contain the alternatives true or false', or 'In every language a sentence is composed of words', etc. In such a case it is better not to enter into a discussion but simply to describe the language-games which contradict these principles. Suppose that a certain tribe of people possessed a language comprising only commands and commands of a sharply defined type, such as those which direct people from place to place. [...] Exploring such possibilities would finally focus a new light on this function of our language; we would then see that our language can be contrasted with an infinite number of other possible languages which may be adapted to other possible empirical worlds. (Waismann 1997: 79–80)

A little later, and right before he introduces the comparison with Goethean morphology, he says:

> It is remarkable that the mere bringing together of cases gets rid of perplexity. What happens in such cases is similar to what happens if we imagine that some phenomenon in the physical world is unique (e. g. if we imagine that the earth is unique among the heavenly bodies) and are then tempted to attribute metaphysical significance to it but are finally satisfied by seeing this phenomenon in a context of similar ones which take from it its appearance of uniqueness.
> Our thought here marches with certain views of Goethe [...].
> (Waismann 1997: 80)

In fact, Waismann seems to go out of his way to downplay any essentialist tendency in Goethe. As we saw above, he says that Goethe's aphorism, "All the organs of plants are leaves transformed", offers "*a* plan in which one may group the organs of plants according to their similarities *as if* around a natural centre" (Waismann 1997: 81, italics added). He sees Goethe's plan as only one among a large or infinite number of alternatives, and his "as if" clearly suggests that the "natural centre" is not "natural" in any essentialist sense, but only one among many possibilities the suitability of which depends on for which particular purpose of clarification the "synoptic presentation" is being made.

4 The Ancient City

Waismann and Wittgenstein worked on *The Principles of Linguistic Philosophy* during the first half of the 1930's. This is the period during which Wittgenstein was most influenced by conventionalist ideas, and it is arguable that this conventionalist strand is one (of many) ways in which the book differs significantly from his mature later works, and in particular the *Philosophical Investigations*. It is also arguable that the term "form of life" is used in the *Investigations* at least partly to undermine such conventionalist ideas. I believe there is more than a grain of truth in these observations. However, I see no reason to believe that Wittgenstein's later questioning of various conventionalist ideas led him to embrace any form of essentialism about language. After all, he explicitly rejects such essentialism (PI: §65). His view seems rather to be that both conventionalism and essentialism involve confusions that need to be disentangled.

In line with this non-essentialist reading, it should be noticed that even if Wittgenstein associates the terms "language" and "language-game" closely with the term "form of life", he nowhere in the *Philosophical Investigations* tries to clarify the relation between these terms by using an analogy with the nature or morphology of living organisms. Apparently, that is *not* where he wants to go with his notion of "form of life". The organism analogy is conspicuously absent from his discussion, and the only explicit mentioning of Goethe (in Part II, vi) has little relevance for the present discussion.

Instead, the analogy Wittgenstein uses in this connection is that between language and an ancient city. As we saw earlier, in PI §18 Wittgenstein asks his reader not to worry about the fact that his simple language-games (2) and (8) consist only of orders. He acknowledges the temptation to think that these languages are "incomplete", but then wonders what notion of "completeness" we are working with here. He asks, was *our* language complete or incomplete before chemical symbolism and the notation of the infinitesimal calculus became part of it? And then the city analogy is introduced:

> for these [the symbolism of chemistry and the notation of the infinitesimal calculus] are, so to speak, suburbs of our language. (And how many houses or streets does it take before a town begins to be a town?) Our language can be seen as an ancient city: a maze of little streets and squares, of old and new houses, and of houses with additions from various periods; and this surrounded by a multitude of new boroughs with straight regular streets and uniform houses. (PI: §18)

Wittgenstein uses the city analogy to resist the philosophical urge to draw a line between complete and incomplete languages; he wants us to ask ourselves if we really have any clear idea of what the complete/incomplete distinction would amount to in this case. Given this purpose, notice how misplaced it would be for him to instead compare language to a living organism. As we have seen, the notion of a living organism lends itself naturally to an intelligible notion of completeness. Indeed, it is arguable that we can identify a living organism only insofar as we have at least a rough and ready conception of what a "complete" organism of its kind would be like. As Wittgenstein uses it, the city analogy goes in the opposite direction: it is meant to help us realize that the idea of a "complete" language is a philosophical fantasy.

Now, it may of course be argued that Wittgenstein is wrong about cities. Perhaps they are more like living organisms than he would acknowledge. In fact, talk of cities as organisms is common, and some have wanted to draw the parallel so close as to say that there is a kind of completeness to a city, in that there are certain vital functions that define a city *qua* city. Plato comes to mind here – he seems to take the analogy between a city and an organism *very* seriously (for a compelling discussion of exactly how seriously, see Ford and Laurence, forthcoming). One may argue, though, that what Plato is discussing is the nature of a polis *qua* human society, whereas Wittgenstein speaks of cities in more narrowly architectural terms. However, it is an interesting question whether this distinction is really so clear-cut, and whether Wittgenstein would want to make such a separation. I cannot pursue this issue here; for my purposes, it is sufficient to note that in using the city analogy, Wittgenstein seems to count on the reader's agreeing with him that essentialist ideas about what constitutes a "complete" city make little sense.[5]

It may seem as if Wittgenstein's use of the city analogy shows not only that he rejects essentialist ideas about language, but also that he has an atomist conception of how language is built up from self-standing language-games by mere aggregation. For isn't this how he describes the ancient city in PI §18: First there was the mazelike inner city, then newer houses were added, and finally the modern suburbs with straight streets and uniform houses were built? If we are supposed to think of language in similar terms, then mustn't we end up with a conception that is not only non-essentialist, but also atomist?

No. Cities are not mere aggregates of separable elements, and Wittgenstein's description implies no such thing. The character and functions of streets, parks, squares, bridges, residential buildings, libraries, schools, shopping centers, and so on, cannot be understood independently of the surroundings in which they are situated, and those surroundings are in their turn affected by the addition of such structures. Indeed, this mutual interdependence between the elements of a city is crucial to city planning, and a failure to take it into due consideration

---

[5] Of course Wittgenstein would acknowledge that purpose-relative talk of the completeness of a city can make perfectly good sense: "Paris has everything that a lover of tasteful Christmas decorations can wish for".

can have disastrous results. Consider Jane Jacobs's reflections on parks in her classic *The Death and Life of Great American Cities:*

> Too much is expected of city parks. Far from transforming any essential quality in their surroundings, far from automatically uplifting their neighbourhoods, neighbourhood parks themselves are directly and drastically affected by the way the neighbourhood acts on them. (Jacobs 1994: 105)

In some surroundings, a park may indeed provide the sort of benefits that are commonly associated with it, but in other surroundings it may become a deserted, dangerous place. As Jacobs convincingly shows, the holistic interdependence between the park and its surroundings is staggering and pervasive:

> Any single factor about the park is slippery as an eel; it can potentially mean any number of things, depending on how it is acted upon by other factors and how it reacts to them. How much the park is used depends, in part, upon the park's own design. But even this partial influence on the park's design upon the park's use depends, in turn, on who is around to use the park, and when, and this in turn depends on uses of the city outside the park itself. Furthermore, the influence of these uses on the park is only partly a matter of how each affects the park independently of the others; it is also partly a matter of how they affect the park in combination with one another, for certain combinations stimulate the degree of influence from one another among their components. In turn, these city uses near the park and their combination depends on yet other factors, such as the mixture of age in buildings, the size of blocks in the vicinity, and so on, including the presence of the park itself as a common and unifying use in its context. (Jacobs 1994: 446–447)

Thus, adequately planning the construction of a park is a difficult task, and "there is no use wishing it were a simpler problem or trying to make it a simpler problem, because in real life it is not a simpler problem" (Jacobs 1994: 447). Jacobs calls such problems "problems of organized complexity", and she says the same kind of pervasive holism is characteristic "of all other parts or features of cities" (Jacobs 1994: 447).

After having read Jacobs's book, thinking of a city as "a collection of separate file drawers" (Jacobs 1994: 450) is virtually impossible. Strikingly, the convincingness of her discussion is not due to the presentation of some new and sophisticated theory, but largely a matter of her assembling a mass of simple but detailed and pertinent reminders of how everyday city life works. These reminders are perhaps too humdrum to attract the attention of more fanciful visionaries, but once Jacobs has put them before you their collected force is virtually irresistible. I do not know if Jacobs ever read Wittgenstein, but this is one of the ways in which the spirit of her book strikes me as Wittgensteinian.

Jacobs says problems of organized complexity are problems of a kind that the life sciences deal with, and she occasionally talks of cities as organisms (witness the very title of her book). However, she also distinguishes the two:

> Because the life sciences and cities happen to pose the same *kinds* of problems does not mean they are the *same* problems. The organizations of living protoplasm and the organizations of living people and enterprises cannot go under the same microscopes. (Jacobs 1994: 453)

In general, Jacobs's emphasis is always on the holistic character of cities, whereas essentialist notions of what constitutes a "complete" city are of little or no importance in her discussions. I suggest that Wittgenstein's use of the city analogy is congenial to Jacobs's conception of cities: he employs the analogy to criticize essentialist conceptions of what makes a language "complete", but this criticism by no means commits him to an atomist conception of language.

There are two other but related ways in which Jacobs's discussion resonates with Wittgenstein's. To begin with, she emphasizes that the parts of a city hang together in virtue of the human life that goes on there, the *activities* of real-life people: working, traveling, playing, socializing, shopping, and so on and so forth. To understand what a city is, she says, *processes* are more fundamental than objects – for the objects of a city (buildings, streets, parks ...) "can have radically differing effects, depending on the circumstances and contexts in which they exist" (Jacobs 1994: 454). Similarly, in Wittgenstein, the terms "language-game" and "form of life" are used to make us see language in terms of human activity rather than as a formally specifiable structure separable from the various concrete circumstances of human communication and interaction.

Second, Jacobs expresses a worry that her holistic conception of cities may invite the idea that city planning is somehow impossible to deal with in a fully rational manner – as if the intricate hanging-together of the city's parts can be grasped only via some special, intuitive capacity or gaze whose insights do not lend themselves to rational discussion and criticism. However, she vehemently protests against such mystification: "Although the interrelations [...] are complex, there is nothing accidental or irrational about the ways these factors affect each other" (Jacobs 1994: 447). The idea that we are dealing here with something irrational stems, she suggests, from an overly narrow conception of what constitutes a rationally solvable problem – a conception which takes its paradigm of rationality from what she calls the "two-variable problems" of classical physics and the problems of "disorganized complexity" of probability theory and statistical mechanics (Jacobs 1994: 443 ff.).

Similarly, even if Wittgenstein distinguishes the philosophical collection of reminders from the methods of empirical science, his point is not that philosophy is irrational. One may in fact speculate that one reason he prefers the city analogy to the organism analogy is that the organism analogy lends itself more easily to a sort of mystification that Wittgenstein wants to avoid at all costs. Even if he admired Spengler, he seems to have sensed that Spengler inflates the analogy between cultures and organisms into metaphysical theorizing and conceives the application of Goethean morphology as a sort of sublime insight in to the necessary character of cultural development.[6]

5 The Method of Language-games

Where does all this leave us with regard to the methodological significance of language-games? How should their philosophical import be conceived, if not only essentialism but also atomism turn out to be unintelligible? After all, the atomist picture of language as a mere aggregate of self-standing language-games had the apparent advantage of making the methodological function of such games seem pretty straightforward: by isolating one feature or aspect of language use, treating the surrounding practices as disturbing noise, the atomist thinks he can get that feature or aspect into clear, undistorted view. But now, if such isolation cannot be intelligibly pursued, since what gets "isolated" is in fact a product of the simplification process rather than something that was somehow already present as a self-standing building-block of real-life language use – then how can simple language-games be philosophically illuminating?

In the *Blue Book*, we saw Wittgenstein saying that his simple language-games are not separated by a break from more complicated ones, and that we can build up the complicated forms from the primitive ones by gradually adding new forms. I have argued that he rejects the atomist conception of what this process of "addition" amounts to. According to Wittgenstein, such addition is not a matter of mere aggregation, but must be conceived as a process of *transformation*. The simple language-games get transformed as surrounding patterns of use develop. Now, the key to understand the methodological significance of such simple games is to see that *describing and reflecting on these processes of gradual transformation is itself a crucial part of the method*. This is precisely the point at which the method

---

[6] The similarity between Jacobs and Wittgenstein at this point should not be exaggerated. Jacobs would not distinguish her investigation from the methods of empirical science in general, but says that her observations *are* empirical and that she employs the inductive method in drawing her conclusions.

of language-games is close to Goethean morphology. It is not a study of fixed games, but an investigation into the dynamics or potentiality of such games: What developments can we imagine such that more complex forms of language "grow" from these simple starting-points? Thus, the simple language-games provide philosophical illumination, not because they isolate one feature already present in real-life language use, but because they allow us to see a possible development of that feature from more rudimentary stages.

In this paper, I have repeatedly expressed the worry that simple language-games such as those of §§2 and 8 of PI are not similar enough to languages of real-life complexity to provide philosophical illumination. However, once we realize that the methodological significance of language-games is tied to how they must be transformed in order to develop into something like real-life language, we see that how they *differ* from language of real-life complexity can be just as illuminating as the ways they are similar. As Waismann says in a passage I have already quoted, where he compares the method of language games with a method proposed by Boltzmann: "the model is [...] given [...] and it can be seen how far it agrees with reality. *And even if it does not, it still retains its value*" (Waismann 1997: 77; italics added). The same is true of language-games in relation to language of real-life complexity: Since what we want to understand is not a feature "captured" by the rudimentary language game, but a feature that will come clearly into view only once we ponder potential *transformations* of the language-game, the differences between the language-game and real-life language will be just as important as the similarities.

The city analogy may be helpful in order to understand what this means. Suppose we want to get clearer on what a park is. One method would be to imagine a very rudimentary park – say, simply an open commons in the countryside, surrounded by three or four farmhouses. Someone may object: But this is not a proper *park!* However, our aim here is not to draw a line between parks and non-parks, by identifying what properties are essential to a park. Rather, we want to understand the functions of a park, what significance a park may have in different circumstances. Therefore, we start with this very rudimentary "park". What do the people in the farmhouses use this park for? Perhaps the children play there; the families arrange festivities; the farmworkers rest in the grass on a sunny Sunday afternoon; in the evening it may be a place for amorous adventures; and so on and so forth. And then we start imagining various developments. Suppose the small village grows; someone opens a small pub in one of the corners of the field; some pathways are laid out; and so on. Eventually, the village grows into a small town, and a gardener is hired to take care of the pathways and lawns, lay out flower beds, and so on. The park is now, non-controversially, a *park* – but the question when, exactly, it became one is of little interest. Rather, what is interesting is the details of the gradual developments, the ways in which the role of the park hangs together with its changing surroundings. Suppose the town grows into a large city, and the park thrives, as it is used by all kinds of people in all kinds of ways. But then the city council decides to use half of the park to build a mall and a big parking lot, and much of the park's allure is gone. Eventually, people become afraid of visiting it at night. It gradually develops into a hangout for drug dealers and prostitutes. The city decides to close it, the mall is extended, and the park is gone.

I do not mean the analogy to be perfect, of course. In the city case, how its various elements interact will in the end be an empirical matter (perhaps the mall attracts even more people to the park, and the park therefore continues to thrive). The methodological role of language-games is not empirical in this sense. Rather, Wittgenstein says it suffices if the imagined transformations are *possible*, for their purpose is not to offer speculations about what might plausibly happen in a process of actual development, but to display a possible series of transformations in such a way that certain claims about what (say) language *must* be like, or certain questions about what makes (say) language *language*, no longer seem significant. (Of course, considerations of such transformations may have many different purposes, depending on what specific philosophical problem or confusion we are dealing with; I focus here on the essentialist worries about what makes language language.) Still, I think the example with the park sheds light on how the method of language-games is supposed to work. For what we get to see in the park case is the pointlessness of drawing a line between what is a park and what is not, or of trying to identify the necessary and sufficient conditions for being a park. Of course, there might be particular purposes for which such a line needs to be drawn – legal or administrative purposes, say. However, if what we are seeking is an understanding of how a park can have the significance it has in the life of a city, what we need is not to draw such a line. Rather, what we need is an understanding of how the park's significance varies with and depends on the park's wider surroundings. Similarly, my claim is that Wittgenstein's method of language-games provides a perspicuous view of patterns of variation and transformation, and thereby undermines the felt need to identify what is necessary to language *qua* language, or to draw the line between activities that are properly linguistic and activities that are not.

So, when Wittgenstein urges us not to worry that the language of the builders consists only of orders and that it is therefore incomplete, what he urges us to resist is the essentialist tendency to think that a detailed investigation of the sort imagined is unnecessary. An essentialist about parks may object that the simple commons surrounded by three or four farmhouses imagined above is not a proper park. In a sense he might have a point! – But he would miss the opportunity to engage in a profoundly illuminating discussion where the various functions that a park may have come into detailed and perspicuous view. Similarly, the essentialist about language will miss the lessons that can be drawn by considering the "growth" of language from simple language-games such as those in §§2 and 8 in the *Investigations*.[7] In the end, I am not sure how much my view of Wittgenstein's method differs from Kuusela's. Kuusela is clear that Wittgenstein uses language-games as "centres of variation", arguing that "such centers of variation are exemplary or prototypical cases that the varying actual uses of an expression can be related to in order to achieve perspicuity or create order into our knowledge of actual use" (Kuusela 2014: 151–152). This may seem close to my talk of how the transformations of language-games matter to Wittgenstein's method. On the other hand, Kuusela wants to distinguish between Wittgenstein's method of describing language-games as games played according to rules, and other methods where "language is regarded as intertwined with actions and activities or as part of a form of life". He goes on:

> However, the description of these activities may also assume a natural historical form, whereby it is described, not by means of statements of a rule but in terms of pictures of forms of behavior or forms of life. (Kuusela 2014: 153)

I do not want to separate these methods. I believe the natural-historical form is more essential to the method of language-games than Kuusela suggests. For the natural-historical form is, precisely, a matter of describing the sort of transformations I have talked about in this paper. If I am right, the importance of taking such transformations into consideration will be clear as soon as we consistently reject the atomist picture of how language-games are related to language in its real-life complexity.

One may worry that I make the method of language-games too difficult. From an atomist viewpoint, it all seems relatively simple: You isolate that aspect of real-life language use that confuses you, and by looking at it as it is displayed in a simple game, without the disturbing noise that surrounds it in ordinary life, you get clear about its logic. What I have argued is that this cannot work, and that the method can be illuminating only if it includes as a crucial element reflection on the transformations needed for such simple language-games to develop into languages of real-life complexity. This may seem to make everything

---

[7] I cannot here engage in extended exegesis of how Wittgenstein uses the language-games of the builders to shed light on problems about naming, compositionality and so forth. For a very illuminating discussion, see Goldfarb 1983. In the end, I think my position here is close to the interpretation of Wittgenstein given by Goldfarb in that paper.

murky again, and one might feel that the problems we thought we had gotten hold of have once again become "slippery as an eel". However, I think Wittgenstein would defend my stance. After all, there is no use wishing that a philosophical problem were a simple problem or trying to make it a simple problem – because it is not a simple problem.

References

Breithaupt, Fritz, Richard Raatzsch and Bettina Kremberg (eds.) (2003) *Goethe and Wittgenstein*, Frankfurt am Main: Lang.
Foot, Philippa (2001) *Natural Goodness*, Oxford: Oxford University Press.
Ford, Anton and Benjamin Laurence (forthcoming) "The Parts and Whole of Plato's *Republic*", in: James Conant and Sebastian Rödl (eds.): *Practical Reason: Historical and Contemporary Perspectives*, Berlin/Boston: De Gruyter.
Godfrey-Smith, Peter (2009) *Darwinian Populations and Natural Selection*, Oxford: Oxford University Press.
Goethe, Johann Wolfgang (2009) *On the Metamorphosis of Plants*, Cambridge, MA: MIT Press.
Goldfarb, Warren (1983) "I Want You to Bring Me a Slab: Remarks on the Opening Sections of the *Philosophical Investigations*", in: *Synthese* 56, 265–282.
Gustafsson, Martin (2017) "Notes on Life and Human Nature", in: Kevin Cahill, Martin Gustafsson and Thomas Schwarz Wentzer (eds.): *Finite but Unbounded: New Approaches in Philosophical Anthropology*, Berlin/Boston: De Gruyter, 67–95.
Hacker, Peter M. S. (2015) "Forms of Life", in: *Nordic Wittgenstein Review* 4, Special Issue: Wittgenstein and Forms of Life, 1–20.
Jacobs, Jane (1994) The Death and Life of Great American Cities, London: Penguin.
Knott, Hugh (2017) "On Reinstating 'Part I' and 'Part II' to Wittgenstein's *Philosophical Investigations*", in: *Philosophical Investigations* 40 (4), 329–349.
Kuusela, Oskari (2014) "The Method of Language-games as a Method of Logic", in: *Philosophical Topics* 42, 129–160.
Rhees, Rush (1960) "Wittgenstein's Builders", in: *Proceedings of the Aristotelian Society* 60, 171–186.
Rowe, M. W. (1991) "Goethe and Wittgenstein", in: *Philosophy* 66, 282–303.
Schulte, Joachim (2003) "Goethe and Wittgenstein on Morphology", in: Fritz Breithaupt, Richard Raatzsch and Bettina Kremberg (eds.): *Goethe and Wittgenstein*, Frankfurt am Main: Lang, 55–72.
Thompson, Michael (2008) *Life and Action*, Cambridge, MA: Harvard University Press.
Waismann, Friedrich (1997) *The Principles of Linguistic Philosophy*, 2nd edition. Houndmills, Basingstoke: Macmillan.
Wittgenstein, Ludwig (1958) *The Blue and Brown Books*, Oxford: Blackwell. [BB]
Wittgenstein, Ludwig (1958) *Philosophical Investigations*, 2nd edition, transl. G. E. M. Anscombe, Oxford: Basil Blackwell. [PI]

Felix Mühlhölzer
Language-games and Forms of Life in Mathematics

Abstract: In §332 of PPF Wittgenstein writes: "The kind of certainty is the kind of language-game". What he has in mind are mainly language-games of simple calculations, like adding and multiplying, including our characteristic ways to make sure that we calculated correctly. Later on, however, in the much-quoted §345 of PPF and still within discussions of calculations, Wittgenstein suddenly mentions 'forms of life': "What has to be accepted, the given, is – one might say – *forms of life*". What is the function of the term "form of life" in this context? For Wittgenstein, the 'kind of certainty' involved in a language game, and the specific concept of certainty corresponding to it, are constitutive of the language-game because they are intimately connected with our actions characteristic of the game. The term "form of life", on the other hand, does not aim at certainty, at least not directly. It has different functions. In the context of calculations as discussed in PPF, there are at least the following two: (a) "form of life" refers to the *presuppositions* of the respective language-game of calculation, and (b) it sheds light on *other concepts* – like the concept of number, for instance – that are important in connection with our understanding of the language game.

1 Wittgenstein's Multiplication-problem

In §77 of *On Certainty* Wittgenstein raises a nice question:

> Perhaps I shall do a multiplication twice to make sure, or perhaps get someone else to work it over. But shall I work it over again twenty times, or get twenty people to go over it? And is that some sort of negligence? Would the certainty really be greater for being checked twenty times?

Let us call this "Wittgenstein's multiplication-problem". What is the answer?

Before giving it, we should clarify the situation that is presupposed in Wittgenstein's formulation of his problem. It obviously concerns multiplications of numbers that are not too small and not too great, so that calculation-checking is appropriate. If the numbers are sufficiently small, like those of the multiplication tables, we accept the results without further ado, and when the numbers are quite large, calculations normally do not make sense from the outset. Let us consider, as an example, the multiplication of 265 and 463, performed with the usual technique:

$$
\begin{array}{r}
265 \times 463 \\
\hline
795 \\
1590 \\
\underline{1060} \\
122695
\end{array}
$$

This technique reduces the multiplication of the numbers 265 and 463 to the multiplication tables up to ten, supplemented and followed by addition, and Wittgenstein might have actually formulated his problem for the case of addition alone. However, I will stick to multiplication. Wittgenstein does not seem to take into account the use of calculating machines. The form of our mathematical practice certainly changes when calculating machines are used, but in what follows I will be content with a narrower point of view which only allows for calculations by humans. I don't think that this restriction is important for what Wittgenstein wants to convey with OC: §77.

Furthermore, in Wittgenstein's formulation it is obviously presupposed that our checking of the multiplication of two numbers always gives the same result if the numbers are the same; or at least that after a certain point in our checking the result remains the same – that is, it remains stable. Otherwise the question of whether checking twenty times makes the certainty *greater* – at least from the point when said stability is reached – wouldn't make sense. We also should be aware that Wittgenstein's multiplication-problem is not a special case of his rule-following problem. That the multiplication of numbers *is* a case of rule-following and that we *understand* the rules of multiplication, including the usual techniques of multiplying, is not problematized in OC: §77. The problem in this section does not concern rule-following as such but rather our ways to make sure that we have not made *mistakes* by applying the rules. Furthermore, it is important that we allow for checks that make use of different techniques applied to the same numbers. Wittgenstein doesn't explicitly say so, but his mentioning of other people performing the checks can easily be understood as allowing these people to apply different techniques. Also the original calculator (i.e., the person doing the calculating), of course, can do that, and this is actually a common way of making sure that no miscalculation occurred. But there are only a few different techniques that we actually make use of when checking a given multiplication, and their existence and allowance do not alter Wittgenstein's problem but belong to it.

This problem lives on a presumed contrast with cases, and especially non-mathematical cases, where the certainty really becomes greater when the number of checks increases from only a few to twenty times or more. An especially good example is circumstantial evidence in legal proceedings where the increase in evidence also increases the certainty of the accused's guilt or innocence. What about scientific experiments? Take, as an especially prominent and well-known example, the Michelson-Morley experiment with its result that the speed of light remains the same in different spatial directions. As described in the elaborate Wikipedia article about it, Michelson-Morley type experiments have been repeated many times with steadily increasing sensitivity, always confirming the original result.[1] Should we say that these repeated confirmations increased our *certainty* that the result is correct? Perhaps, but more important is the fact that this result is the basis of Special Relativity, and it is actually the importance and success of this fundamental theory in its entirety that backs our certainty with respect to the experiment's result. On the other hand, quite recently doubts have arisen about this entire theory from the angle of quantum gravity, and these doubts may give precise Michelson-Morley type experiments new importance. When these new experiments would again confirm the original result, the new theoretical setting would certainly lead to an increase in our certainty about the result's correctness. The situation is rather complex, however, and I cannot say more about it here. But it is clear that this situation is deeply different from the Wittgensteinian one concerning his multiplication-problem, and differences of this sort are the background of his problem.

2 Solution to the Multiplication-problem

What can we say about this problem? Temporarily ignoring what Wittgenstein himself writes, we may offer the following answer: As already explained, when repeating the multiplication of the same numbers we want to make sure that we have not made *mistakes* when applying the rules of multiplication. Therefore, there is a certain asymmetry between the first calculation and the subsequent ones: the first calculation aims at a certain result and the recalculations aim at confirming this result, while being careful to watch out for possible mistakes we may have made. It is this, in the case when we do not get divergent results, that explains our checking the multiplication only a few times or that only a few

---

[1] There are cases where such confirmations seemed to be lacking but all of them proved to be unconvincing.

other persons work it over, and not twenty times or twenty people, because what we have in mind is only a rather restricted spectrum of possible mistakes and only these are to be taken into account. They include mistakes by oversight, caused by a lack of attentiveness, say, or certain characteristic mistakes of a more systematic character (concerning carrying over, for instance). In order to exclude these mistakes it can be appropriate to simply repeat a multiplication once more, or to vary the method of multiplication, or to get someone else to work through one's multiplication, but at the same time it seems pointless to extend this sort of checking beyond what is usually done. We check whether this or that mistake may have occurred, and how should the repetition of our usual checking make the certainty greater?[2] So, when we have confirmed the original result of a multiplication in the usual way, we are satisfied, and this satisfaction can be easily justified in the way just described. In this way we treat our usual way of checking as sufficient, and the cases in which we have reason to retract our judgment are rare exceptions. This is different in the empirical cases mentioned above: new evidence often overthrows our previous judgment on the accused's guilt or innocence, and new versions of Michelson-Morley type experiments, sparked by quantum gravity, say, may show that the previously accepted results should be retracted in the end. This is not so in the case of multiplication, where our usual way of checking can normally, and without any qualms, be treated as a checking 'for all time'.

This is the answer to Wittgenstein's multiplication-problem we may think of initially. What is Wittgenstein's own answer? It is given, or at least suggested, in OC: §82:

> What counts as an adequate test of a statement belongs to logic. It belongs to the description of the language-game.[3]

---

[2] There is, by the way, also no theoretical 'certainty measure' that would work here; neither Bayesianism, for example, nor Wolfgang Spohn's 'ranking theory' are applicable in this case. (Both approaches are presented and discussed in Spohn 2012.) The reason is that the usual certainty measures are attributed to what people call "propositions" and that, at the same time, all propositions of mathematics are considered as 100% certain. Therefore there is no way to talk about 'greater certainty' in the case of mathematical propositions.

[3] This general claim is mainly aimed at empirical statements but without doubt refers to §77 as well. The German original reads: "Was als ausreichende Prüfung einer Aussage gilt, – gehört zur Logik. Es gehört zur Beschreibung des Sprachspiels", and by using the word "ausreichend" Wittgenstein makes the connection to §77 clear enough. In the official translation this word is rendered as "adequate", but to my mind "sufficient" might be a better choice.

This is a tightening of the answer just given. And a tightening may seem desirable because the reasons offered so far could be rejected as insufficient if one is thinking in a very strict way: our attentiveness, and the attentiveness of our helpers, may remain insufficient when working the multiplication over, and we may not have considered all systematic mistakes that are possible. Our normal way of checking may be adequate from a pragmatic point of view, sufficient with regard to our actions, but what about a stricter one? That normal ways of checking appear satisfying from a pragmatic point of view, but *only* from such a view, is emphasized by Locke in a different context, the context concerning our "certainty of things existing *in rerum natura*", as Locke says. When we have the testimony of our senses in favor of something, this certainty is, according to Locke, "not only as great as our frame can attain to, but as our condition needs".[4] The same might be said with respect to our multiplications, with the further remark, that it doesn't stand up, however, to a stricter view.

Wittgenstein in a way seems to agree with Locke when he says in "Cause and Effect: Intuitive Awareness":

> The primitive form of the language game is certainty, not uncertainty. For uncertainty could never lead to action. (PO: 397)

But Wittgenstein's attitude is not to depreciate this certainty as 'merely pragmatic', with the consequence that we should look for something beyond the pragmatic level. When talking about the 'primitive' form of the language game what he has in mind is not the contrast with less primitive language games where this certainty may be less important. What he means is that *all* language games have this 'primitive' or, as one might also say, 'primary' character of involving specific forms of certainty. Only then are they oriented towards action, which is one of their defining characteristics. In other words, he interprets this certainty not as something merely pragmatic but as belonging to *logic*.[5] With re-

---

[4] I quote this from Austin's *Sense and Sensibilia* (Austin 1962: 6), where it occurs in a passage quoted from Ayer's *The Foundations of Empirical Knowledge*.
[5] This reaction is similar to Austin's with respect to the Lockean passage just quoted. Austin replies that in this passage it is "taken for granted, that there is *room* for doubt and suspicion, whether or not the plain man [that is, the man who regards the usual ways of testing as sufficient] feels any. The quotation from Locke [...] in fact contains a strong *suggestio falsi*. It suggests that when, for instance, I look at a chair a few yards in front of me in broad daylight, my view is that I have (*only*) as much certainty as I need and can get that there is a chair and that I see it. But in fact the plain man would regard doubt in such a case, not as far-fetched or over-refined or somehow unpractical, but as plain *nonsense*; he would say, quite correctly, 'Well, if that's not seeing a real chair then *I don't know what is*'" (Austin 1962: 10). Wittgenstein would agree

spect to our ways of testing, he explicitly says this in OC: §82 where, as throughout OC, the word "logic" is meant in a rather general sense: a *logical* proposition "describes the conceptual (linguistic) situation", as explained in §51. In other words, it is "the description of the language game", as said in §82. In other passages, Wittgenstein presents a thought of this sort not only with respect to *testing* and to what we regard as a sufficient test, but he also explicitly says that the presupposed kind of *certainty* characterizes a language-game; see OC: §§446–448 and especially §497, where he writes that the relevant certainty "defines a game", that is, a language-game. In PPF: §332 it is expressed as follows:

> Am I less certain that this man is in pain than that 2 × 2 = 4? – Is the first case therefore one of mathematical certainty? – 'Mathematical certainty' is not a psychological concept.
> The kind of certainty is the kind of language-game.

I am *not* 'less certain' that this man – whose hand had just touched the red-hot cooktop and who is now crying – is in pain than that 2 × 2 = 4, or that, if sufficiently checked, 265 × 463 = 122695, but the *kind* of certainty is obviously different. Normally I am certain with respect to this man's pain, but at the same time I know that there exist certain specific situations in which my certainty may after all be shaken by the suspicion that his hand is numb and he's only pretending to be in pain. Wittgenstein even says with respect to a possible uncertainty of this sort, which is characteristic with respect to pain, that it is 'constitutional' of 'pain' and 'not a shortcoming'. Nevertheless in normal circumstances I *am* certain.[6] But my certainty that a certain multiplication is correct – in the case of 2 × 2 = 4 anyway, but also in the case of 265 × 463 = 122695, if sufficiently checked – is of course tremendously different. And the same is true in the case of other language games and the kinds of certainty they involve.

I think that Wittgenstein's answer to his multiplication-problem as just presented, an answer essentially making use of his notion of a language-game, is *prima facie* rather plausible. To someone who doesn't wholeheartedly accept our checking of multiplications in the way indicated in OC: §77, we may simply say:

---

with Austin's 'plain man', and with regard to his multiplication-problem he agrees with the plain man as well. In fact, Wittgenstein formulates the Austinian sort of reply almost verbatim in OC: §495: "One might simply say 'O, rubbish!' to someone who wanted to make objections to the propositions that are beyond doubt. That is, not reply to him but admonish him". But Wittgenstein gains more philosophical depth than Austin by the way he then brings into play his conception of a *language-game*.

6 RPP II: §657. See also the thorough discussion of the kind of certainty we exhibit with respect to sensations, feelings and motives in Hertzberg 1989.

Obviously, you do not understand what 'multiplication' is; you do not understand that it is a mathematical notion belonging to a mathematical language-game with its own standards of certainty, standards that, as it were, *define* what 'calculation' in the sense of mathematics is.[7]

However, this answer, plausible as it may sound, can nevertheless seem too rash, in particular from a philosophical point of view, and we may remain tempted to present and to defend a view that tries to dig deeper. I will come back to that later. But before this I want to consider another possible Wittgensteinian answer to his multiplication-problem, an answer that doesn't make use of the notion of a *language-game* but of a *form of life*. Instead of saying that the kind of certainty concerning 'multiplications' is characteristic of the respective language-game, couldn't we also say, and didn't perhaps Wittgenstein himself say, that this kind of certainty is characteristic of the respective form of life? And what would be the difference between these two answers? As we have seen, Wittgenstein definitely gave the first one – what about the second? Or doesn't there exist a noteworthy difference between them?

One might think that the second answer is included in OC: §358:

> Now I would like to regard this certainty, not as something akin to hastiness or superficiality, but as a form of life.

Could the certainty addressed here not be the certainty in the case of multiplications as dealt with in §77? Strictly speaking, as shown by its context in OC: §358 is about my certainty that what I see in front of me and what is familiar to me is a chair; but isn't Wittgenstein's remark also appropriate for the situation described in §77? Couldn't it in fact be meant by Wittgenstein also with regard to his multiplication-problem?

Such an interpretation, however, would go too far. In the subsequent section, §359, Wittgenstein presents what appears to be an elucidation of §358:

> But that means I want to conceive it [= this certainty as mentioned in §358] as something that lies beyond being justified or unjustified; as it were, as something animal.

---

7 This accords with Wittgenstein's pithy saying in MS 169: "With 'mathematical certainty' falls 'mathematics'" ("Mit der 'mathematischen Sicherheit' fällt die 'Mathematik'"; translations of manuscript passages are always my own). Unfortunately, p. 38v of MS 169, which contains this passage, shows a vertical line from top to bottom that looks like a crossing out. Vertical lines of this sort occur on several pages of MS 169. It seems that Wittgenstein was dissatisfied with them, but I do not know his reasons. These lines should make us cautious when quoting, but on the other hand many of the respective passages are rather illuminating and I think they shouldn't be ignored.

It is true that, if we inquire sufficiently long, the certainty in the case of a multiplication may in the end prove to lie beyond being justified or unjustified, but should this certainty be really called "animal"? Would Wittgenstein himself describe it in this way? One's certainty regarding perceptible objects like chairs may be seen as something animal-like, similar, say, to the beaver's certainty that there is a branch in front of him which he can use to build his dam, but this is far from the kind of certainty with multiplications that are checked as described in OC: §77. Furthermore, OC: §358 ends with the following statement in brackets that comes immediately after the statement quoted above: "That is very badly expressed and probably badly thought as well". I do not know what precisely Wittgenstein deems 'bad' in what he had just expressed,[8] but this acutely critical judgment should give us pause. And as if this wouldn't be enough, §358 turns out to be the only section in *On Certainty* in which the expression "form of life" occurs at all. So we definitely shouldn't consider this section as supporting an answer to Wittgenstein's multiplication-problem that makes use of the notion "form of life". Furthermore, I do not know any other Wittgensteinian passage that may suggest an answer of this sort. Let us therefore discard it and try to understand why it may be inappropriate.

3 A Vicious Circle?

But we should also understand in which way the expression "form of life" may nevertheless prove to be important in the context of multiplications. For it occurs in the much-quoted §345 of PPF amidst remarks about calculations and about mathematics in general:

> What has to be accepted, the given, is – one might say – *forms of life*.

What does Wittgenstein mean with the expression "form of life" here? What is its function here and what its relation to "language-game"?

An appropriate starting point in order to answer these questions is §332 of PPF, already quoted above, in which Wittgenstein pithily says: "The kind of certainty is the kind of language-game". The subsequent sections, up to §341, contain elaborations of this statement, followed by considerations that lead to §345.

---

[8] Hacker comments on this statement as follows: "This is, indeed, rather badly expressed, for the expression 'form of life' obscures rather than reveals the point, which is indeed much better expressed in §359" (Hacker 2015: 14). I do not know, however, what precisely he finds obscuring in the expression "form of life" here.

In the second paragraph of §339, Wittgenstein explicitly states his methodological guideline with respect to what we call "certainty":

> Don't ask: "What goes on in us when we are certain that ...?" – but: How is 'the certainty that this is so' manifested in people's action?

And in §340 he comes back to the end of §332 with its reference to language-games:

> "While you can have complete certainty about someone else's state of mind, still it is always merely subjective, not objective, certainty." – These two words point to a difference between language-games.

As I understand him, Wittgenstein does not reject the statement in quotation marks, but he interprets it in a way that may not be intended by people who are putting it forth. What does his interpretation look like? That is, how do the words "subjective" and "objective" point to a difference in language games in the situations presupposed? In view of the next section, and also in view of passages in the MSS 137 and 169, Wittgenstein can be understood as follows: Although the situations in which we assess someone else's state of mind very often do not go along with uncertainty, there are other situations – and they are such that we recognize them as essentially belonging to our talking about 'someone else's state of mind' – in which an enduring dispute about this state may arise, a dispute that may not be decided even in the long run, let alone decided with certainty. We then have the tendency, as suggested with the first statement of §340, to lay the blame on the fact that we cannot "look into the other's mind" (MS 169: 37r – 37v), as we might say, or that "the inner" of another person (MS 137: 60b) is something irreducibly subjective and as such ultimately hidden. According to Wittgenstein, however, this is a reversal of the actual conceptual situation: talk in this metaphorical manner – "look into the other's mind", "the inner" – is in reality *derived* from the fact that unresolvable disputes as just mentioned are always recognized by us as important possibilities, and not the other way round. In this way the respective 'subjectivity' pertains to the language-game in question, a language-game with its characteristic kind of certainty that essentially allows those cases of unresolvable uncertainty. This is Wittgenstein's view of the *subjective* certainty mentioned in §340.

In the next section, §341, he then looks at the certainty that is characteristic of calculations and which, in contrast to 'subjective' certainty as just understood, can be called *objective:*[9]

> A dispute may arise over the correct result of a calculation (say, of a rather long addition). But such disputes are rare and of short duration. They can be decided, as we say, 'with certainty'.
>
> Mathematicians don't in general quarrel over the result of a calculation. (This is an important fact.) – Were it otherwise: if, for instance, one mathematician was convinced that a figure had altered unperceived, or that his or someone else's memory had been deceptive, and so on – then our concept of 'mathematical certainty' would not exist.

The kind of certainty about results of calculations is obviously different from the kind of certainty about someone else's state of mind. Disputes over the correct results of calculations are not only rare, but almost always of short duration and they can be decided conclusively.[10] In the second paragraph of §341 Wittgenstein emphasizes that this characteristic sort of not quarrelling over the results of calculations is an important fact, and he then imagines a community of people in which it is otherwise. His example is drastic: he describes people who not only quarrel over whether the calculations presented were performed correctly, but who consider whether or not the figures have been unperceptively altered, whether their memories are faulty, and so on. And Wittgenstein is certainly

---

9 Wittgenstein himself calls it "objective" in MS 169: 35r–35v. Unfortunately, these pages again show cancellations by vertical lines from top to bottom as already mentioned in a previous footnote with respect to p. 38v of MS 169. Nevertheless, I think that in view of PPF: §§340 f. There can be no doubt that Wittgenstein accepts the claim that the certainty of calculations is of the 'objective' kind.

10 One could mention, of course, a lot of other characteristics of language-games of calculating which, from Wittgenstein's point of view, make them different from language games concerning states of mind and, for that matter, different from many other language games. So, for example, a calculation, like a proof, should be surveyable (see RFM III: §§1–20); 265 multiplied by 463 not only *is* 122.695 but *must be* 122.695 (see RFM III: §§30–41, VI §§7 f.); a calculation is deeply different from an experiment (throughout RFM); not only is multiplication itself a rule, but also sentences like "265 × 463 = 122.696", and in most cases mathematical sentences in general, are rules (throughout RFM, but see especially RFM I: §7), or they are at least *akin to* rules (RPP I: §266). (All this is discussed in Mühlhölzer 2001, 2006 and 2010.) It would go too far to consider these other aspects in the present paper. In the context of the sections of PPF that I am dealing with, Wittgenstein is exclusively concerned with our concept of 'mathematical certainty' and its connection with the sort of agreement we show when performing and checking calculations.

right: in such a community our concept of 'mathematical certainty' would not exist.[11]

This applies to *our* concept of 'mathematical certainty', that is, to *our* way of dealing with multiplications, say, and judging them to be correct. We are satisfied when having done what is described in OC: §77, and we then are in fact certain. But couldn't there be a stricter concept? Can't we imagine that, in the case of the uncertain people just described, there always *were* specific numbers and calculations they originally had in mind, albeit only for a very short time until their uncertainty sets in, and couldn't one then bring forward what Wittgenstein's interlocutor (even someone belonging to these people, as it seems) says in §342?:

> Even then it might be said: "While we can never *know* what the result of a calculation is, for all that, it always has a quite definite result. (God knows it.) Mathematics is indeed of the highest certainty – though we possess only a crude likeness of it."

One might say that this view corresponds to a concept of 'mathematical certainty' that is, as it were, *God's concept*, and why not think of it as the concept that actually accords with the essence of mathematics in its purity?

In order to see 'mathematical certainty' in this way one need not, in fact, consider the drastic scenario imagined by Wittgenstein. To look at our actual practice may be enough. When in §342 Wittgenstein uses the expression "a crude likeness" ("*ein rohes Abbild*"), I do not know whether it really suits the drastic scenario described in §341. Perhaps the uncertainty of these people is far too drastic and the ensuing practice too chaotic to allow us to speak about a 'likeness' at all. But this way of speaking may very well appear appropriate regarding *our* practice as it actually looks like. After all, our familiar behavior as described in OC: §77 could be easily assessed as insufficient if one is thinking in a really strict way: our attentiveness may remain insufficient even when working the multiplication over, and we may not have considered all mistakes that are possible. Our normal way of checking may be sufficient from a pragmatic point of view, but wouldn't a stricter view be appropriate? Isn't what we are considering only a hotchpotch of possibilities and shouldn't there be a more principled and uniform way to say what it really is that makes up the correctness of a multiplication?

---

11 In spite of this, Wittgenstein describes these people as "mathematicians". The best way to understand him here may be to imagine that these people had formerly been mathematicians but then developed the strange behavior just described. Their former mathematical practice would become impossible then.

Many mathematicians, and perhaps non-mathematicians as well, in fact have the following idea of the multiplication-algorithm: that it is an abstract, ideal, hyper-rigid machine with two input slots for the insertion of two numbers and an output slot that emits the product of these numbers. And our understanding of the algorithm then consists in having 'grasped' this machine and its mechanism.[12] It then suggests itself that the *correct* way of calculating is nothing but a sort of mirroring of this mechanism and that a *mistake* consists in a deviation from that. Such would be the general, uniform idea of calculating and miscalculating that may be seen as underlying our normal, hotchpotch practice.

This picture, beautiful as it may seem, of course contradicts Wittgenstein's rule-following considerations which request us to be content with our actual practice, hotchpotch as it may be, and not to look for an underlying ground. I take this Wittgensteinian insight for granted here.[13] So, what we must do is to look at our actual practice. – But doesn't this practice have the resources to justify our certainty regarding our multiplications *beyond* what I have presented as an answer to Wittgenstein's multiplication-problem? At this point one may think, first, of our practice to construct *foundational systems* like logicist or set-theoretical ones. Whatever may be the merits of these systems, however, they do not heighten our *certainty* regarding ordinary calculations. This is admitted, for example, by Russell and Whitehead already in the second paragraph of the preface to the first edition of *Principia Mathematica*, and I will not say more about it. But, secondly, there is also our *scientific* practice, and shouldn't we ex-

---

12 In precisely such a way the so-called 'metric tensor', for example, which is omnipresent in differential geometry, is characterized on p. 22 of Misner et al. 1973: "the *metric tensor* [...] is a machine with two input slots for the insertion of two vectors [...]. If one inserts two vectors [...] one gets out a number".

13 It pervades Wittgenstein's later philosophy but seems to be expressed in a particularly pithy way in the following passage in the *Remarks on the Foundations of Mathematics* which makes use of the expression "way of living" ("Lebensweise" in Wittgenstein's German): "Language, I should like to say, relates to a *way* of living. | In order to describe the phenomenon of language, one must describe a practice, not something that happens once, *no matter of what kind*" (RFM VI: beginning of §34). And Wittgenstein immediately adds the impressive remark: "This is a very difficult insight". (This is my translation of Wittgenstein's German sentence in BGM: "Das ist eine sehr schwierige Erkenntnis". The official translation by Elizabeth Anscombe reads: "It is very hard to realize this", which however changes the sense of the German original.) For a long time I liked this whole passage, but then I discovered that in the manuscript Wittgenstein actually crossed it out (it is a diagonal crossing out; see MS 164: 98 f.)! Quite characteristically, the editors of the published version overlooked this crossing out. And I must admit that I do not really know why Wittgenstein is discontent with this passage. His crossing out should make us reluctant to quote it, but of course this does not alter his insights concerning rule-following as presented in other places.

pect scientific, theoretical justifications of our usual practice of calculating and checking our calculations? In other words, why shouldn't there be a *naturalistic* justification of this practice?

If I understand her correctly, this is Penelope Maddy's point of view in her recent book *The Logical Must*.[14] Maddy hesitates in her usage of the word "justification", but she talks about what *grounds* our rule-following, in the sense of an *explanatory* grounding. The following is a pertinent passage from her book:

> [W]hy shouldn't the [naturalist[15]] provide an explanatory account of what grounds the practice of rule-following, or more specifically, the practice of inferring – indeed an account that simply fills in the various types of facts that Wittgenstein agrees do form its basis? [...] if reliably formed belief is enough, presumably our rudimentary logical beliefs do count as justified. What's wrong with providing this sort of explanation/justification? (Maddy 2014: 117)

Instead of "logical beliefs" she might also have written "mathematical beliefs", at least with respect to our familiar practice of elementary calculations and its usual applications.

A view of this sort may in fact seem rather obvious to people who restrict their philosophizing to naturalistic ways of thinking, and Wittgenstein himself explicitly comments on a variant of it in his next section, PPF: §343:

> But am I really trying to say that the certainty of mathematics is based on [*beruhe auf*] the reliability of ink and paper? *No.* (That would be a vicious circle.) – I have not said *why* mathematicians do not quarrel, but only *that* they do not.

Why is this remark placed immediately after §342 in which someone argues for a sort of God's point of view with respect to 'mathematical certainty'? – It is clear that Wittgenstein doesn't accept this point of view and that, when thinking about 'mathematical certainty', he concentrates on our actual mathematical practice and its conditions in the world. And now someone like Maddy, for example, may think it highly relevant to this certainty that ink and paper are reliable (§343) and also that we are convinced of this reliability (§341), because the important fact of our not quarreling over most of our calculations would not per-

---

14 As the book's subtitle "Wittgenstein on Logic" indicates, it is intended as an investigation of Wittgensteinian thoughts about logic. In what follows, I will show how distant Maddy's approach is from a genuinely Wittgensteinian one. See also Gustafsson 2015 for illuminating remarks in this vein.

15 Maddy's term is "Second Philosopher", but this refers to a person that adopts a specific version of naturalism as elaborated in her book and in other texts of hers.

sist without such fundamental stabilities of the world and our confidence in them.

In §343, however, Wittgenstein puts forward three important clarifications: (1) he does *not* want to say[16] that the certainty of mathematics is based on the reliability of ink and paper; (2) to say so would involve a *vicious circle*; (3) he hasn't said (in §341) *why* mathematicians do not quarrel, but only *that* they do not. Let us discuss these points one after the other. Wittgenstein's extremely condensed text in §343 certainly requires a thorough explanation.

As for (1), this of course is implied by (2), but it is plausible also independently of (2). What Wittgenstein is concerned with is our *concept* of 'mathematical certainty', which would in fact not exist without the fundamental stabilities of the world and our confidence in them as just mentioned, but these stabilities are only the *preconditions* of the way we treat mathematics as certain. They are the preconditions of our concept of 'mathematical certainty' but do not characterize it. And when we talk about 'the certainty of mathematics', we make use of this concept and do not refer to its preconditions. In MS 168, p. 22a, Wittgenstein makes this point by considering physicists, who essentially rely on mathematics and its certainty, and he lets someone say: "The physicist calculates because paper and ink are more reliable than his instruments". This is obviously absurd (and very funny at that).

But in (2) Wittgenstein goes further by even diagnosing a *vicious circle* in our saying that the certainty of mathematics is based on the reliability of ink and paper. What precisely does he have in mind here? One may think that he explains it in the next section, §344:

> It is no doubt true that one could not calculate with certain sorts of paper and ink, if, that is, they were subject to certain strange alterations – but still, that they changed could in turn be ascertained only through memory and comparison with other means of calculation. And how, in turn, are these tested?

The thought presented in this passage seems to be this: In order to perform a calculation with paper and ink – and, as we might add, to be justifiably certain about its result –, the paper and ink should not be subject to strange alterations. But to test whether this is the case, we rely on our memory and other means of

---

[16] In Wittgenstein's German §343 begins with the words: "Aber will ich etwa sagen", which in Anscombe's translation is rendered as "But am I trying to say" and in Hacker/Schulte's (which I'm using) "But am I really trying to say". I do not know why they haven't translated it simply as "But do I really want to say", which to my mind would be closest to Wittgenstein's text.

calculation; and to test the reliance of this, we again rely on our memory and calculations, sometimes calculations performed with ink and paper; and so on.

Is there a vicious circle in this, or maybe a (vicious) infinite regress? To my mind, Wittgenstein here merely hints at the familiar holism concerning our testing of hypotheses. However, such testing allows bootstrap procedures and need not involve anything vicious. If Wittgenstein had been of the opinion that his remark in §344 hints at a vicious circle, this was too rash. However, there is another interpretation of this remark that suggests itself:[17] In spite of the described possibility to repeat tests without end, our *actual* testing-practice lets us stop after a finite number of steps, and this is the basis of *our concept of 'reliability'*. In analogy to what is said in §341 about our concept of 'mathematical certainty', Wittgenstein now could say: "Were it otherwise – that is, if we remained unsatisfied with our tests without end – then our concept of 'reliability' would not exist". And he need not go so far to diagnose anything circular.

Nevertheless, I think that in the present context there does exist some sort of vicious circle as claimed in §343. One should look for it not in §344 but in the first paragraph of §346, where Wittgenstein hints at it with the example of judgments of color and color-words.[18] After §346 he instantly comes back to mathematics, and it is clear that mathematics is his actual target. The first paragraph of §346 reads as follows:[19]

> Does it make sense to say that people generally agree in their judgements of colour? – What would it be like if it were different? – One man would say that a flower was red, which another called blue; and so on. – But with what right could one then call these people's words "red" and "blue" *our* 'colour-words'? –

When Wittgenstein here asks about the sense of the statement "People generally agree in their judgements of color", what he means is a *substantial* sense that also allows the negation of this statement: "People generally do not agree in their judgements of color". But this statement is an extremely dubious one, for if people do not agree in their judgments of color, with what right are these judgments then still to be called judgments 'of color'? These people no longer seem

---

[17] I do not know whether it accords with Wittgenstein's intentions, but it is certainly not far away from them and it makes perfect sense in the context at hand.
[18] The close connection between §343 and §346 is confirmed by the first occurrence of these passages on pp. 26a–26b of MS 138, in which the text of §345 is missing. Wittgenstein there writes down the texts of §§343&344 immediately followed by the text of §346. The text of §345 has been inserted only afterwards, on pp. 57–58 of MS 144.
[19] I omit the second paragraph, which is the rest of this section, because it doesn't present anything new regarding the possible vicious circle.

to use our color-words. In PPF: §351, Wittgenstein says this explicitly: "There is, in general, complete agreement in the colour statements of those who have been diagnosed normal. This characterizes the concept of a colour statement". But then one can diagnose some sort of vicious circle with respect to the statement "People generally agree in their judgements of color": the concept of a color statement seems to be used in it in order to make a substantial claim, but this alleged claim does only say something about this concept itself. That is, what we have is a circle from the concept of a color statement back to this concept itself.

How can this throw light on the vicious circle mentioned in §343? Not in an immediate way,[20] but I would nevertheless offer the following – admittedly rather loose – interpretation inspired by §346: The *concepts* that Wittgenstein now considers are the concepts of 'certainty' and 'reliability', and when someone says, as in §343, that the certainty of mathematics is 'based on' facts like the reliability of ink and paper, and on the corresponding fact that in general mathematicians do not quarrel over the result of a calculation, this looks like a really substantial claim, even like an *explanation*. It would be an explanation, or at least a partial explanation, of *why* mathematics is certain. But what does "certainty" mean here? And what does "reliability" mean? These words do not possess a particular metaphysical weight and we should consider *our* concepts of 'mathematical certainty' and 'mathematical reliability'. But an important criterion concerning the use of these concepts is that mathematicians in general do not quarrel over the result of a calculation (and similar things). In other words: the *sense* of what we say concerning 'mathematical certainty' and 'mathematical reliability' depends on the mathematicians' not quarreling, which in turn is one of the criteria for what we call "mathematical certainty/reliability". So we are in fact landing in some sort of vicious circle. It is vicious because an explanatory claim should allow the possibility that a different situation obtains, a situation where the claim is false, but just this is excluded by the sense of our claim. Consequently, it is a pseudo-explanation.

In this way I understand Wittgenstein's clarification (2): to say that the certainty of mathematics is based on the reliability of ink and paper would involve a *vicious circle*. And it immediately explains his clarification (3): he hasn't said (in

---

20 An immediate way, totally analogous to the way regarding color-concepts, would center around the concept of 'calculation' and the statement "People generally agree in their calculations". Wittgenstein suggested considerations of this sort at the end of RFM III, beginning with §65 (see the commentary in Chapters 7 and 8 of Part II of Mühlhölzer 2010), but in our present context it is not the concept of 'calculation' but the concepts of 'certainty' and 'reliability' he is concerned with.

§341) *why* mathematicians do not quarrel, but only *that* they do not, because to say "why" means to give an explanation, but as just argued what we actually come across here is only a pseudo-explanation. In this way Wittgenstein rejects naturalist positions that aim at such explanations, and this applies in particular to the Maddyan version.[21]

4 Form of Life as Presupposition of a Language-game and as Constitutive of Specific Concepts

The type of argumentation just presented certainly should be discussed in more detail. I cannot do that, however, in the present paper. Instead, my aim now is to use this argumentation in order to interpret PPF: §345 which contains the expression "form of life":

> What has to be accepted, the given, is – one might say – *forms of life*.

Why does this statement appear at precisely this point in PPF?[22] What does the expression "form of life" refer to at this point and what is its function? – It seems rather clear that what Wittgenstein has in mind here is what is mentioned in §341: the important fact that mathematicians don't in general quarrel over the result of a calculation, and if a dispute concerning the correctness of a result does come up, it is typically dispelled rather quickly and normally without remaining uncertainties, at least – as we should add to PPF: §341 at this point – if checked in the way described in OC: §77. That this quarrelling doesn't exist belongs to the form of life meant in PPF: §345. And this fact is to be accepted as something simply given because the attempts to explain it – by referring to

---

21 As it happens, Maddy thinks that the later Wittgenstein would be in the same boat with her, were he not prevented from this by his anti-scientific prejudices; see pp. 123–125 of Maddy 2014.
22 It is precisely the point where it also appears in its original German version in MS 144: "Das Hinzunehmende, Gegebene – könnte man sagen – seien *Lebensformen*" (MS 144: 57v). Strictly speaking, PPF is not directly taken from this manuscript but from the typescript TS 234 which in turn is based on MS 144. Unfortunately, TS 234 is lost. Furthermore, there is MS 138 which can be seen as a sort of precursor of MS 144, and in MS 138, as already mentioned before, the texts of PPF: §§344 and 346 directly follow each other whereas the text of §345 is missing. So, Wittgenstein added it afterwards, which makes the question all the more interesting what precisely he wants to say with it in the present context.

our trust in the stability of the figures written down, the reliability of the ink and paper used, our memories, and similar seemingly more basic things – involve vicious circles and therefore prove to be pseudo-explanations. It is this not-quarreling and our way to treat things as reliable that Wittgenstein has in mind when referring to a '*form of life*' in PPF: §345. So this form of life consists, first, of the language-games of calculating, which include specific ways of checking and which characterize our concept of 'mathematical certainty', *and*, second, of our not-quarreling and our considering things as reliable, which have not yet been mentioned when the language-games of calculating alone are described. This at least is the interpretation of "form of life" in PPF: §345, suggested by the context in which it occurs, that I would propose: the language-games of calculating, like the language-game of multiplication mentioned in OC: §77, are part of this form of life.

What is the function of Wittgenstein's emphasis on our not-quarreling in the case of the language-games of calculation? It is mentioned in §341: "Were it otherwise [...] then our concept of 'mathematical certainty' would not exist". And this concept would not exist because the relevant language-games would not exist. So, the form of life as mentioned in PPF: §345 is a *presupposition* of the language-games in question. This function of stating a presupposition of the language-game is not mentioned in sections §§19&23 of the PIr. At first glance these sections may seem to *introduce* the expression "form of life" into the PIr, but upon closer examination they leave us rather at a loss because they do not at all clarify what the actual role of this expression may be. Nevertheless, one may at least get a glimpse of what Wittgenstein may have in mind when reading §19 in the way von Savigny does in his commentary on *Philosophical Investigations:* we need a form of life surrounding the language-games mentioned at the beginning of §19 – "a language consisting only of orders and reports in battle" or "consisting only of questions and expressions for answering Yes and No" – in order to really make sense of them. Without such a surrounding we would not understand them as language-games consisting of 'orders and reports' and of 'questions and expressions for answering Yes and No' (Savigny 1994: 51). In a similar vein we may understand then Wittgenstein's speaking of language-games being 'parts' of forms of life in §23:

> The word "language-game" is used here to emphasize the fact that the *speaking* of language is part of an activity, or of a form of life.[23]

---

[23] See again von Savigny's commentary in Savigny 1994: 59–61.

Prima facie this doesn't say very much about Wittgenstein's understanding of "form of life", because already in PIr: §7 he had made it sufficiently clear that language-games are languages woven into activities. §23 contains the addendum that a language-game is embedded into a context of activities which is *more inclusive*, but what, beyond what has already been said in §7, is the point of such an embedding? Wittgenstein remains silent about this question in §23, and it is quite strange that in this section he presents a rather long list of language-games without suggesting a parallel list of corresponding forms of life into which the language-games may be embedded.

Nevertheless, we can interpret him here in von Savigny's way, and the relationship between language-games and forms of life may then be seen as follows: The 'pure' language-game, as it were, which functions as an object of comparison in order to clarify a philosophically puzzling situation (see PIr: §§130 f.), is typically rather meager, but in order to really make sense of it we should embed it into an appropriate surrounding, and this is the form of life of which it then is a 'part'. This relationship is already evident in the case of the paradigmatic language-game of the builders in PIr: §2. In its pure form it consists of the interaction of a so-called 'builder' A with his so-called 'assistant' B; and in this form it is offered as a model of the Augustinian description of language. As such it need not involve any idea about the aim of this interaction. We primarily think of the ordinary building of houses, but this sort of 'building' may also have quite another purpose, for example a ritual one. There are different possible surroundings of the language-game which are not necessary for its functioning as an object of comparison with respect to the Augustinian picture, but which provide the language-game with a 'more complete sense', as one might say.

It is noteworthy, by the way, that among the many language-games listed in PIr: §23 there is only one *mathematical* language-game and that, furthermore, this game is explicitly characterized as belonging to *applied* mathematics: "Solving a problem in applied arithmetic".[24] The mathematical language-games considered by Wittgenstein in our present context, however, are purely mathematical ones: the disputes or non-disputes over the correct result of a calculation

---

24 "Ein angewandtes Rechenexempel lösen", in Wittgenstein's German. This formulation goes back to MS 115: 88. It is taken over, in handwritten form, to the *Big Typescript* (see page 208v), with an interesting twist: Wittgenstein there first wrote: "Eine Rechnung machen", but then crossed this out and replaced it by: "Ein angewandtes Rechenexempel lösen". I do not know why it was important to him to make this sort of change. It may be that in this phase of his philosophical development – MS 115 was written in 1933 – he was still too skeptical of non-applied mathematics and that he dogmatically refused to apply his newly invented term "language-game" to games that are purely mathematical. But this is only speculation.

discussed in PPF: §§341–343 only concern calculations as such, irrespective of their relevance outside mathematics, and the same is true of the multiplication mentioned in OC: §77. It is irritating that in the long list of examples of language-games presented in PIr: §23, Wittgenstein mentions only a single mathematical game and that this game is explicitly described as one of 'applied arithmetic'. This constriction may be a relic of former phases of his philosophical development (see my footnote above), but even when one takes this into account, the constriction remains striking in view of several other examples in §23 that show great liberality ("Constructing an object from [...] a drawing": where is the 'language' here?; "cursing": must this involve 'language', must it involve rules of a 'game'?). There is no doubt that in his mature later philosophy Wittgenstein accepts purely mathematical language games;[25] see, for example the following simple language-game mentioned in RFM VI: §20:

> A further language-game is this: He gets asked "How much is '365 × 428'?" And he may act on this question in two different ways. Either he does the multiplication, or if he has already done it before, he reads off the previous result.

And there are many other places in Wittgenstein's texts, besides this one and besides PPF: §§332& 341–345 and OC: §77, where such purely mathematical language-games are referred to.[26]

Let us come back to the question about the precise role of the notion of a form of life in Wittgenstein's texts. Up to now we have seen that in PPF: §345 the form of life into which a language-game is embedded states an important presupposition of this language-game. Furthermore, what is visible in PIr: §§19&23 is the role of a form of life to present a surrounding that gives the language-game a 'more complete sense', as I said above. This latter point may seem a bit lame and a bit vague, but it is considerably strengthened in two important passages outside the *Philosophical Investigations*. The first passage is in §47 of RFM VII (and goes back to remarks in MS 127: 91f., and MS 124: 150, both written in March 1944):

---

25 And to be precise: practically any mathematical language-game that deserves this name, whether purely mathematical or not, does not only concern the *speaking* of language, as said in PIr: §23, but also the *writing* of symbols.

26 See RFM I: Appendix III §6; RFM VI: §15; RFM VII: §25 and 52 ("Following a rule is a particular language-game", which does not exclude purely mathematical cases of following a rule); and in the *Nachlass:* MS 115: 182 and 185f.; MS 123: 49v and 57r–67r; MS 124: 41 ("im 'rein mathematischen Sprachspiel'"!); MS 133: 10v–11r; MS 161: 52r–52v; MS 173: 47v–48r.

But how then does the teacher interpret the rule for the pupil? (For he is certainly supposed to give it a particular interpretation.) – Well, how but by means of words and training? And the pupil possesses the rule (interpreted *thus*) if he reacts to it thus and thus.[27] But *this* is important, namely that this reaction, which is our guarantee of understanding [*Verständnis*], presupposes as a surrounding particular circumstances, particular forms of life and speech. (As there is no such thing as a facial expression without a face.)
(This is an important movement of thought.)

Here Wittgenstein goes beyond the actual rule-following considerations and the relevant language-game of rule-following by talking of the rule-follower's *understanding*, something that need not be done in the 'pure' rule-following context (as one might say). To talk in this way presupposes, as Wittgenstein says, as a surrounding particular forms of life. Imagine, for example, that the rule-following scenario is not realized in the surrounding of a teacher-pupil but of a master-servant or master-slave relationship. Then what is at issue is not the rule-follower's understanding but her obedience. The respective language-game of rule-following with its characteristic problem – how is it determined what the rule-follower should do from case to case? – can be seen as remaining the same, but the different surroundings present different foci: on understanding or on obedience. This important movement of thought – to use Wittgenstein's own words – of course also applies to our language-games of calculating. It is natural to associate with them a surrounding – to wit: form of life – that gives sense to our talking about the calculators' 'understanding' of the relevant rules; but in another surrounding – form of life – it would not be understanding but 'obedience' that is involved. In this way the notion of a form of life not only gets its importance via its relation to the language-game that is embedded in it – by stating the presupposition of the language-game or by giving it a 'more complete sense' – but by constituting new concepts that are important in their own right.

The other illuminating passage making a similar point is §630 of RPP I:

Instead of the unanalysable, specific, indefinable: the fact that we act in such-and-such ways, e.g. *punish* certain actions, *establish* the state of affairs thus and so, *give orders*, render accounts, describe colours, take an interest in other's feelings. What has to be accepted, the given – it might be said – are facts of living//are *forms of life*.//[28]

---

27 In Wittgenstein's German: "Und der Schüler hat die Regel (*so gedeutet*) inne, wenn er so und so auf sie reagiert". I have changed Anscombe's official translation of this sentence which shows a misunderstanding of the German "innehaben".
28 I have changed the official version of this remark in RPP I, which presents "facts of living" in the main text and moves "*forms of life*" into a footnote, seemingly favoring "facts of living". In MS 133: 28r, the end of this remark reads: "seien *Lebensformen*//seien Tatsachen des Lebens.//". On page 333 of TS 229, which is the typescript that emerged from MS 133, Wittgenstein has inter-

What is remarkable, of course, is the fact that the last sentence is exactly the same as in PPF: §345 but appears in a different context. To be more precise, it is actually two things that are noteworthy here: Firstly, this passage originally occurs in MS 133: 28r, written on November 7, 1946, which is earlier than the manuscript-passage on page 102 of MS 144 where PPF: §345 comes from. The exact date when this particular passage was written is unknown, but MS 144 in its entirety is from 1949. Furthermore, the surrounding of this passage in PPF, ending with §344 and beginning with §346, stems from MS 138, also written in 1949, but a bit earlier than MS 144, and the text of PPF: §345 is missing there (see MS 138: 26a–26b), as already said in a previous footnote. It was specifically added when Wittgenstein resumed the relevant passages of MS 138 in MS 144. Secondly, not only is the context of this sentence in MS 133, which has been taken over to RPP I, not a mathematical one, as in the case of PPF: §345, but the function of the notion of a form of life is very different. According to my interpretation of the passage in PPF, "form of life" there aims at the presupposition of the language-game involved – including a glance at the concept of 'reliability' which is intimately connected with the concept of 'certainty' – whereas in RPP I (MS 133) it is put forth with respect to our ideas "of the unanalysable, specific, indefinable" as they are discussed in its surrounding sections, especially regarding colors and color-impressions (see RPP I: §§628&63: "'Colours are something specific. Not to be explained by anything else'" and "'How does it come about that it seems to me that this colour-impression that I am having now, is recognized by me as the specific, the unanalysable?'"). It is true that also the section immediately after PPF: §345 is about 'color', but not with respect to the seeming specificity, etc., of colors, but to the presupposition of our language-games involving judgments of color.

In RPP I: §630 Wittgenstein proposes not to talk about this seeming specificity, etc., of colors but about the relevant form of life, and he not only applies this philosophical strategy to our concept of color but also to other concepts: *punishing* actions, *establishing* states of affairs, and so on. He doesn't mention mathematical contexts, but he could have done so as well. In other words, he could have referred also to concepts of mathematics and our respective acting in such-and-such ways, concepts which are characteristic of certain forms of life that have to be accepted as something simply given.

Let me mention only one very elementary concept that might be considered here, a concept that actually suggests itself in our language-games of calcula-

---

changed "seien *Lebensformen*" and "seien Tatsachen des Lebens". I do not know whether this occurred intentionally, and I don't think that it is of any importance.

tion: the concept of *number*, understood in the simple sense of 'natural number' (0, 1, 2, ...). It is remarkable that the word "number" occurs neither in the surrounding passages of PPF: §345 – from §330 to §350, say – nor in OC: §77.[29] What Wittgenstein has in mind there is mainly the concept of 'mathematical certainty' together with the relevant language-games of calculating (and at least implicitly also the concept of 'reliability'), but without doubt we automatically think that these language-games are about 'numbers'. This, however, need not be the case, at least not when, so to speak, our *full* concept of number is meant. All these language-games, the respective concepts of 'certainty' and 'reliability' included, could be realized, for example, within a practice of producing wallpaper patterns, as discussed by Wittgenstein himself in several places.[30] This could be a practice in itself according to which the norms of doing things right – of 'calculating' – are the same as ours, but without any sort of application of these so-called 'calculations' and their results to the world outside the wallpapers. With respect to *our* concept of number, however, the practice of 'counting things', like apples, say, and other extra-mathematical applications of arithmetic, are certainly important, and we need to embed the language-games considered in PPF: §§330–350 and OC: §77 into the relevant form of life: into our form of life which includes the counting of things, the measurement of their lengths, and so on. Only then, we might say, will 'numbers' be involved.[31]

Let us now take stock. What we have found are three sorts of role that the notion of a form of life may play with regard to the language-game of calculations considered in this paper. Firstly, in PPF: §345 it refers to certain *presuppositions* of this language-game, and these are at the same time presuppositions of

---

29 In PPF: §341 Wittgenstein mentions a 'figure' ("Ziffer" in German), but figures are not numbers.
30 See MS 117: 159; MS 124: 137; MS 127: 195; and LFM: 34 and 59f.
31 This does not mean that I subscribe to what Wittgenstein wrote in the notorious 'mufti' passage in RFM V: §2: "I want to say: it is essential to mathematics that its signs are also employed in *mufti*. | It is the use outside mathematics, and so the *meaning* of the signs, that makes the sign-game into mathematics". In its generality – "mathematics" *tout court*! – this remark is too dogmatic to be taken at face value, and it is in fact not the result of Wittgensteinian investigations but the beginning of them in RFM V, or more precisely: in the manuscripts MSS 126 and 127 on which RFM V is based. When starting this remark with the words "I want to say", Wittgenstein formulates a tendency he feels in himself but which now requires a multifaceted examination. To my mind, Wittgenstein never arrived at a stable view of it; to this point, see Chapter 3 of Floyd and Mühlhölzer 2018. On the other hand, it seems uncontroversial to me that the *concept* of number – not 'mathematics' *tout court*, as referred to in Wittgenstein's 'mufti' passage, but our familiar concept of number which belongs to our familiar methods of calculation as considered in PPF: §§330–350 and in §77 of OC – is based on our counting of things in the world.

the concept of 'mathematical certainty' realized in this game. Secondly, and in a rather inchoate way, the role of forms of life in PIr: §§19&23 is to make the language-games that are seen as embedded in them *more familiar* than they are when considered in their pure form. In this form they serve as objects of comparison in order to make certain philosophical points, but it is certainly helpful to bestow greater familiarity upon them. Thirdly, and in a way that gives this second point more strength, the form of life into which a certain language-game is seen as embedded is constitutive of *specific concepts* – "to understand a rule", "to punish certain actions", "to establish a state of affairs", "number", and so on – which we may be concerned with beyond what interests us regarding the language-game as such.

Seen in that way, we may in the end better understand why Wittgenstein solved his multiplication-problem of OC: §77 with the help of the notion of a language-game and not of a form of life: This problem concerns our notion of 'mathematical certainty' and Wittgenstein has good reasons to locate this notion in our *language-game* of calculating, with our characteristic ways of checking as described in OC: §77. The notion of a *form of life* is simply not needed in order to come up to 'mathematical certainty'. But it *is* needed if we want more: if we want to say something about the presupposition of the language-game of calculation and about its relation to other concepts, like 'understanding' the rules of calculation or like the concept of 'number'. This, then, is the role of "form of life".[32]

Of course, in saying that I restrict myself to the specific mathematical activity of calculating as considered in PPF: §§330–350 and OC: §77, and I do not claim to have captured all the roles that the expression "form of life" actually plays or may play in Wittgenstein's work. So, I haven't said anything about "meaning", at least not explicitly, let alone about something like a Wittgenstein-inspired 'theory of meaning', as envisaged, for example, in Eike von Savigny's heroic paper "Sprachspiele und Lebensformen: Woher kommt die Bedeutung?". This is a subject to be dealt with on another occasion.[33]

---

32 I'm not sure whether this sort of view may help to explain Wittgenstein's critical concluding sentence in OC: §358, after having used the expression "form of life" immediately before, and I prefer to refrain from speculations about Wittgenstein's actual motives when writing it down.
33 In writing this paper I have not only profited from the discussions on the occasion of my presentation of the original – and very different – version at the conference *The form of our life with language*, but also from comments by and discussions with Marianne Mühlhölzer, Dolf Rami, Joachim Schulte, Julian Small and Hannes Worthmann. Furthermore, I am particularly grateful to Almut Kristine von Wedelstaedt who in her Magisterarbeit *Zum Begriff der Lebensform bei Wittgenstein* gave an extremely useful survey of all the relevant Wittgensteinian passages. And for correcting my English I am grateful to Tyler Q. Sproule who, however, in no way is responsible for the remaining Germanisms.

References

Austin, J. L. (1962) *Sense and Sensibilia*, Oxford: Oxford University Press.

Floyd, Juliet and Felix Mühlhölzer (2018) *Wittgenstein and the Real Numbers: Annotations to Hardy's A Course of Pure Mathematics*, New York: Springer.

Gustafsson, Martin (2015) "Review of Penelope Maddy, *The Logical Must: Wittgenstein on Logic*", in: *Notre Dame Philosophical Reviews*, 8.5.2015, http://ndpr.nd.edu/news/57606-the-logical-must-wittgenstein-on-logic/.

Hacker, Peter (2015) "Forms of Life", in: *Nordic Wittgenstein Review* 4, Special Issue: Wittgenstein and Forms of Life, 1–19.

Hertzberg, Lars (1989) "'The Kind of Certainty is the Kind of Language Game'", in: D. Z. Phillips and P. Winch (eds.): *Wittgenstein: Attention to Particulars*, London: Macmillan, 92–111.

Maddy, Penelope (2014) *The Logical Must: Wittgenstein on Logic*, Oxford: Oxford University Press.

Misner, Charles W., Kip S. Thorne and John Archibald Wheeler (1973) *Gravitation*, San Francisco: W. H. Freeman.

Mühlhölzer, Felix (2001) "Wittgenstein and the Regular Heptagon", in: *Grazer Philosophische Studien* 62, 215–247.

Mühlhölzer, Felix (2006) "'A Mathematical Proof Must Be Surveyable' – What Wittgenstein Meant by This and What It Implies", in: *Grazer Philosophische Studien* 71, 57–86.

Mühlhölzer, Felix (2010) *Braucht die Mathematik eine Grundlegung? Ein Kommentar des Teils III von Wittgensteins Bemerkungen über die Grundlagen der Mathematik*, Frankfurt am Main: Klostermann.

Savigny, Eike von (1994) *Wittgensteins "Philosophische Untersuchungen": Ein Kommentar für Leser*, Vol. 1, Sections 1–315, 2nd edition, Frankfurt am Main: Klostermann.

Savigny, Eike von (1998) "Sprachspiele und Lebensformen: Woher kommt die Bedeutung?", in: Eike von Savigny (ed.): *Ludwig Wittgenstein, Philosophische Untersuchungen*, Berlin: Akademie Verlag, 7–39.

Spohn, Wolfgang (2012) *The Laws of Belief: Ranking Theory and Its Philosophical Applications*, Oxford: Oxford University Press.

Wedelstaedt, Almut Kristine von (2007) *Zum Begriff der Lebensform bei Wittgenstein*, Magisterarbeit, Bielefeld University.

Wittgenstein, Ludwig (1974) *On Certainty*, G. E. M. Anscombe and G. H. von Wright (eds.), transl. D. Paul and G. E. M. Anscombe, Oxford: Blackwell. [OC]

Wittgenstein, Ludwig (1976) *Wittgenstein's Lectures on the Foundations of Mathematics, Cambridge 1939*, C. Diamond (ed.), Ithaca, NY: Cornell University Press. [LFM]

Wittgenstein, Ludwig (1978) *Remarks on the Foundations of Mathematics*, rev. edition, G. H. von Wright, R. Rhees and G. E. M. Anscombe (eds.), transl. G. E. M. Anscombe, Oxford: Blackwell. [RFM]

Wittgenstein, Ludwig (1980a) *Remarks on the Philosophy of Psychology*, Vol. I, G. E. M. Anscombe and G. H. von Wright (eds.), transl. G. E. M. Anscombe, Oxford: Blackwell. [RPP I]

Wittgenstein, Ludwig (1980b) *Remarks on the Philosophy of Psychology*, Vol. II, G. H. von Wright and H. Nyman (eds.), transl. C. G. Luckhardt and M. A. E. Aue, Oxford: Blackwell. [RPP II]

Wittgenstein, Ludwig (1984) *Bemerkungen über die Grundlagen der Mathematik*, in: *Werkausgabe*, vol. 6, Frankfurt am Main: Suhrkamp. [BGM]
Wittgenstein, Ludwig (1993) *Philosophical Occasions, 1912–1951*, James C. Klagge and Alfred Nordmann (eds.), Indianapolis: Hackett. [PO]
Wittgenstein, Ludwig (2000a) *Manuscripts from Wittgenstein's Nachlass*, in: *The Bergen Electronic Edition*, Charlottesville, VA/Oxford: Intelex Corporation/Oxford University Press. [MS]
Wittgenstein, Ludwig (2000b) *Typescripts from Wittgenstein's Nachlass*, in: *The Bergen Electronic Edition*, Charlottesville, VA/Oxford: Intelex Corporation/Oxford University Press. [TS]
Wittgenstein, Ludwig (2005) *The Big Typescript: TS 213*, German-English Scholars' Edition, ed. and transl. C. Grant Luckhardt and Maximilian A. E. Aue, Oxford: Blackwell [BT]
Wittgenstein, Ludwig (2009a) *Philosophical Investigations* (the German text, with an English translation by G. E. M. Anscombe, P. M. S. Hacker and Joachim Schulte), rev. 4th edition. P. M. S. Hacker and Joachim Schulte (eds.), Oxford: Wiley-Blackwell, [PIr]
Wittgenstein, Ludwig (2009b) *Philosophy of Psychology – A Fragment*, in: Wittgenstein 2009a, 182–265. [PPF]

Matthias Haase
The Representation of Language

Abstract: The contemporary debate on the metaphysics of language is dominated by two positions. According to the one, languages are not things in the world; they are abstract objects. According to the other, a language consists in the historical chain of causally interrelated acts and states of its speakers. The later Wittgenstein would reject both positions. A natural language is neither an abstract object nor a singular happening of any kind; it is something general that is actual or concrete. The difficulty to understand the peculiar kind of actuality of a language is, I argue, the source of the rule-following puzzle. Its solution consists in an investigation of the logical grammar of the statements with which speakers of a language describe their use of words. When we say what 'we' or 'one' says, the pronouns exhibit a kind genericity that cannot be treated within the quantificational model of generality.

1 The Metaphysics of Language

In *Remarks on the Foundations of Mathematics* Wittgenstein writes: "In order to describe the phenomenon of language, one has to describe a practice, not something that happens once, *no matter of what kind*." And he adds: "It is very hard to realize this" (RFM: VI, §34, translation changed). To the innocent ear, the addition sounds surprising. What should be so difficult here? Who would be tempted to affirm what Wittgenstein denies? An utterance of an English sentence may perhaps be classified as a singular event. Or an evening's conversation between two people. But English, the language spoken on those occasions? Why should anyone think that it belongs to the order of datable happenings?

The remark hasn't received a lot of attention in the literature. And it doesn't seem to sit well with a widespread assumption about the role that talk of such things as 'practices', 'language-games', 'uses', 'institutions' or 'forms of life' plays in the *Philosophical Investigations*. The claim that thought and language are to be conceived through those notions is commonly taken to present the formula for the solution of the philosophical puzzles labored in the passages where these terms are introduced.[1] In the light of this, it seems surprising to be told that

---

[1] Of course, it is highly controversial how this bare bone structure is to be filled in. The main divide in the literature concerns the role assigned to the concept of a social practice. The "con-

there is a supreme difficulty connected with realizing that to describe a language is to describe a practice. In what follows, I argue that this should indeed surprise and that reflection on this point reveals that problem and solution are in a different place than the assumption would suggest.

One can begin to see what difficulty Wittgenstein might have had in mind, once one notices that what he says doesn't seem to have a place in the landscape of the philosophical options recognized in the standard debate about what kind of thing a language is.

As far as formal semantics is concerned, a language is individuated by giving a set of types of expressions, rules for their concatenation and a function that assigns semantic value to every well-formed concatenation. As David Lewis puts it, the task is to give a "description of possible languages or grammars as abstract semantic systems whereby symbols are associated with aspects of the world" (Lewis 1983a: 190). According to Donald Davidson, this exhausts what can sensibly be said about the metaphysics of language:

> [W]e talk so freely about language, or languages, that we tend to forget that there are no such things in the world; there are only people and their various written and acoustical products. [...] The existence of the French language does not depend on anyone's speaking it, any more than the existence of shapes depends on there being objects with those shapes. [...] [T]here is nothing about the existence of a particular language that imbues it with anything more than the sort of interest any abstract object may have; as logicians we can study it as one example among countless others of a formal pattern. (Davidson 2001: 108–109)

---

structive" camp suggests that in a proper development of the thought that Wittgenstein hints at the notion of a practice figures as *explanans* in a non-circular account of language and thought. Accordingly, the notion of practice is taken to be logically independent of the concepts of meaning and understanding. The task is to define the particular structure a social practice has to exhibit, if it is to count as a specifically *linguistic* practice. (See, for instance, Brandom 1994, Dummett 1993: 34–91, Horwich 2002: 260–273, Wright 1980.) The "quietist" camp, by contrast, insists that the whole point of Wittgenstein's appeal to practices is to make us see that such explanatory ambitions are fundamentally misguided. Accordingly, it is argued that one must *not* conceive of a 'practice' as something that is intelligible independently from being represented as the practice of using words in accord with their meaning. In this kind of approach, the notion of a practice is often presented as a bit of common sense appealed to in order to bring out that it is illusory to adopt a standpoint outside of our life with meaning. (See, for instance, Diamond 1989, Goldfarb 2012, McDowell 1998c: 221–262, Stroud 2000: 170–192.) What the two approaches seem to have in common is the assumption that the notion of a practice can be taken for granted while doing philosophy of language – either because it is given to the philosophy of language from elsewhere (its definition belongs to another part of philosophy or perhaps the social sciences); or because the question 'What is a practice?' is taken to be a misguided demand for a non-circular explanation. I want to suggest that this assumption is mistaken.

Delimited in this way, the class of languages includes not only natural languages such as English, French or Urdu. There is an infinite number of languages no one has ever spoken or ever will speak. A natural language is, strictly speaking, not any more *real* or *actual* than Lewis' 'possible languages'. What exists in reality are datable utterances and their speakers. The types, of which those utterances are the tokens, are abstract. And so is the language to which they belong: it is neither subject, nor cause of change. The difference between French and those countless possible languages comes down to this: there are tokens of its types. Davidson famously combines this claim with the thesis that there is no philosophically interesting notion of a natural language. Lewis denies the latter. But the account he puts forward abides by Davidson's restriction on what kinds of linguistic 'things' can be said to exist in the world. A given language L is actual, if it is "*used by*, or is a (or the) language *of*, a given population P" (Lewis 1983b: 166); and what makes a language *the language of* a population is spelled out in terms of conventions. A convention, in turn, is defined in terms of social constellations of the speech acts, beliefs and intentions of the individuals that make up the population.[2]

It seems safe to say that this is not what Wittgenstein had in mind when he denied that a language belongs to the order of datable happenings. In the *Philosophical Investigations*, he writes: "We are talking about the spatial and temporal phenomenon of language, not about some non-spatial, non-temporal phantasm" (PI: §108). One might think that what we talk about must thus be the acts and states of particular speakers. But Wittgenstein adds: "But we are talking about it as we do about the pieces in chess when we are stating the rules of the game, not describing their physical properties." Within the framework just sketched, stating the rules of the game is to describe the abstract patterns of possible behavior that would occupy particular space-time positions. The game of chess, by contrast to our playing it on an evening, would thus have to be classified as an abstract object.[3]

One might think that the bone of contention is a disagreement about the notion of an abstract object. That is what Michael Dummett suggests: "in general, the existence of abstract objects depends upon what concrete objects there are: for instance, sets or sequences of concrete objects" (Dummett 1981: 504). On his view, the idea of 'pure abstract objects' – abstract objects that are independent of correlated concrete objects – is unintelligible. Wittgenstein seems to disagree.

---

[2] Very roughly speaking, a convention C is in place in a population P if and only if each member of P, or at least most of them, has a set of beliefs and intentions concerning C and the correlated beliefs and intentions of the other members of P. See David Lewis 2002.
[3] See, for instance, Dummett 1981: 487.

He grants that a person could invent a game that is never played or a language that is never spoken. In *Zettel* he writes:

> How did I arrive at the concept 'sentence' or at the concept 'language'? Surely only through the languages that I have learnt. – But they seem to me in a certain sense to have led beyond themselves, for I am now able to construct a new language, e. g. to invent words. – So such construction also belongs to the concept of language. But only if that is how I want to fix the concept. (Z: §325)

One can use the term 'language' in such a way that it also applies to what an individual may invent in her head or on a piece of paper by setting down a system of rules. And since this can be done by merely mentioning the words, such a notion will encompass languages that are not, in fact, spoken by anyone. Wittgenstein doesn't take issue with that idea, as long as one notices that it is an expansion of what one might call the *original* concept of language. At the latter, I arrived by learning a particular language. And that can only be done by actually using its words.

How, then, are we to understand the notion of a spoken language? In order to illustrate the point of the remark I quoted at the outset Wittgenstein asks us to imagine a country that existed only for two minutes and is the exact replica of a part of England. For those two minutes its inhabitants do just what people in, say, Sussex, do on a sunny afternoon: sit in school, write a mathematical calculation on the blackboard etc. The question is whether there is something to imagine here. The section as a whole appears as an elucidation of Wittgenstein's statement that he would like to say that "language [...] relates to a *way* of living". This suggests the following analogy. Two minutes is a little short for the cycle of self-maintenance and reproduction characteristic of a lifeform to take hold. A lifeform or species is not abstract; it is a real object with an origin, a past, a present and an uncertain future. Analogously we may think of French as an actual or concrete object that can be subject to change and might cease to exist like an endangered species.

The thought that a language is a kind of actuality is, of course, not alien to contemporary philosophy. David Wiggins calls it the "common sense view" (Wiggins 1997). But what kind of object are we talking about? The analogy with lifeforms or biological species hardly settles the issue. After all, one might think that a biological species is just as abstract as French is according to Davidson. Moreover, it is not obvious what the alternative is supposed to amount to. Ruth Millikan deploys the analogy with biological species in order to argue that a language is not an abstract object, but "consists of actual utterances and scripts, forming crisscrossing lineages" (Millikan 2003). A language is here identified with the historical chain of causally interrelated acts and states of its speakers. Similarly,

Wilfrid Sellars proposes that reflection on biological kinds can figure as a model for how the "talk about any abstract entity can be unfolded into talk about linguistic or conceptual tokens" (Sellars 1996: 96). Accordingly, expressions like 'the lion' that seem to refer to the species or lifeform are best interpreted as "distributive singular terms" (Sellars 1996: 76). The envisioned analysis is supposed to establish "a sense in which *ones* are *reducible* to *many, the lion* to *lions*, and, in general, *the K* to *Ks*" (Sellars 1967: 54).

On the syntactic level, David Kaplan has proposed an equivalent account of the individuation of words. Kaplan proposes to replace the type-token model with what he calls the "stage-continuant model" (Kaplan 1990: 98). Several utterances or inscriptions are reappearances of the same word *not* in virtue of being tokens of a type, but rather in virtue of being causally related to each other. This connection between them is what makes them phases or "stages" of the continuing existence of the word. Taking Kaplan's account of words as his model Timothy Williamson describes the approach as the general strategy to explain the identity of an object in terms of the history of the causal interactions of its parts:

> What binds together uses of a word by different agents or at different times into a common practice of using that word with a given meaning? This is an instance of a more general type of question: what binds together different events into the history of a single complex object, whether it be a stone, a tree, a table, a person, a society, a tradition, or a word? In brief, what makes a unity out of diversity? Rarely is the answer to such questions the mutual similarity of the constituents. Almost never is it some invariant feature, shared by all the constituents and somehow prior to the complex whole itself – an indivisible soul or bare particular. Rather, it is the complex interrelations of the constituents, above all, their causal interrelations. (Williamson 2006: 35)

On this view, the relation between language and utterance is not the relation between the general and the particular, but rather the relation between a whole and its parts. Rather than having a history, a language *is* the historical succession of utterances. But this doesn't seem to be neither what Wittgenstein had in mind. For, if a language consisted in nothing but the complex causal interrelations of actual utterances, then it would seem that it belongs to the order of happenings. But a language is "not something that happens once, *no matter of what kind*".

What the Type-Token Model and the Stage-Continuant Model have in common is the assumption that all we need to introduce into the philosopher's collection of kinds of things or ways of being in order to account for the metaphysics of *spoken* languages are individual speakers, their acts and states, and the relations between them. I call this the *Quantificational Model* of language. Within this framework, there are only two options: either 'French' picks out a subclass of the class of all languages in the realm of abstract objects, or it is to be identified with the interrelations between the various written and acoustical products of French speakers. The underlying assumption may be put like this: what is general can only be abstract. If something is to be actual and causally efficacious, it must be a dated particular. What Wittgenstein characterizes as a "very difficult insight" is the denial of this assumption. In order to describe a language one must describe something *general* that is *actual* and *not abstract*.

The passage mentioned above stands in the context of what has come to be called the rule-following considerations. I want to suggest that one of its main targets is the conception of generality that makes it seem like the only alternative to conceiving language in the register of datable happenings is to conceive of it as something in the order of abstract objects. Accordingly, the question what kind of *actuality* one describes when one describes a language goes to the heart of the matter. Talk of 'practices', 'uses', 'institutions' or 'forms of life' just names the very thing that is 'very hard' to get into focus. That the Type-Token Model and the Stage-Continuant Model may not exhaust the philosophical options is suggested by an alternative take on the notion of a life-form or biological species. Michael Thompson argues that understanding the actuality of such a thing requires recognizing that its description exhibits a form of generality that doesn't fit into the quantificational framework of predicate logic. On his view, natural historical judgments are neither universally quantified or statistical judgments about what *all* or *most* exemplars of a lifeform do nor normative judgments about its *good* exemplars. They are generic judgments *sui generis:* what they describe is something *general* or *universal* that is not *abstract*, but rather *actual* or *concrete* (cf. Thompson 2008: 25–82). Of course, the analogy to lifeforms or biological species has its limits. It can't illuminate the idea of following a rule and the peculiar kind of knowledge or understanding that is connected with it.

2 The Epistemology of Language

In the framework Davidson puts forward, the notion of an actual language has its original home in the interpretation of the observed utterances of others. Assigning semantic value to certain strings of graphic marks can be understood as empirically constrained if we conceive of the notion of an actual language as a theoretical term belonging to an empirical theory:

> The concept of a language is of a sort, and depends on, concepts like name, predicate, sentence, reference, meaning [...]. These are all theoretical concepts, and the items to which they apply are abstract objects. [...] The main point [of these concepts] is to enable us to

give a coherent description of the behavior of speakers and of what speakers and their interpreters know that allows them to communicate. (Davidson 2001: 109)

The formal calculus is supposed to acquire an *actual* subject matter by being treated as an empirical theory that can be confronted with the observable linguistic behavior of people. Since a theory of meaning, as Davidson conceives it, is a deductive system, it "may be tested by comparing some of its consequences with the facts" (Davidson 1984: 24). In this way, the paradigmatic scene in which the concepts *sentence* and *language* have a role is the scenario in which a 'radical interpreter' works towards arriving at a systematic theory of meaning for a language that is not her own. What it is to be a speaker of a language is then explained by reference to this scene. Even though a native speaker of the language doesn't need to have a theory of meaning for her own language, *what she knows in being a competent speaker can be articulated by such theory.*

Wittgenstein's remark from *Zettel* that I quoted above suggests the reverse order of understanding. Rather than beginning with a notion of language defined as an abstract object that can be instantiated in order to then ask in a second step what it means for a language to be spoken or used by an *observed* individual or a group, the kind of description or articulation of language that Wittgenstein has in mind is not *radical*, but rather *domestic*. To begin with, it is concerned with one's own language. This contrast has often been pointed out. And philosophers following Wittgenstein often stress that in the basic case understanding can't be an interpretation, but must be immediate and for this reason requires a language that speaker and hearer share. But the focus on perception is often retained in this context. It is suggested that understanding, properly conceived, is the capacity to *directly* perceive the meaning of what is said such that the identification of the material sign is not separable from the intake of its meaning.[4] This is supposed to correct empiricist distortions of what giving a theory of meaning would amount to. But it is not clear what follows from this correction for the question whether the language manifested in the perceived utterances is abstract or concrete.

A different picture arises when one focuses on the first personal perspective of the passage from *Zettel*. I learned a language by speaking it. So, originally, a *sentence* is what I form in performing a speech act. And *language* is what I speak in doing so. The idea of a language different from mine is a reflective achievement that comes later. So, if one were to speak of semantics here, it would not only be *domestic*, but also *naïve*. The plural only enters the passage, because

---

4 See McDowell 1987, 1997; Hornsby 2005.

there are several languages that were learned. If one only gets initiated into one 'first' language, then one's original concept of language has no plural. To begin with, language is *my* language.

Of course, it is not 'mine' in a sense where this is opposed to what is 'yours'. Language is learned by speaking with others. So, it's 'ours'. By the same token, a *sentence* is from the very beginning also what others form when they address a speech act to me. This obviously involves perception on my part. But the perceptual relation to something given to me is not the register of the naïve perspective. When someone speaks to me, this is an interaction in which I am involved as interlocutor. A conversation is an exchange of thoughts in which both are active. In the naïve perspective of a linguistic transaction the perceptible character of the material sign is, as it were, not salient. It comes to the foreground when something goes wrong and I can't quite hear what you are saying or when I listen in on a conversation between others. But just like the idea of language that is not mine, this comes later. That is not how I got into it. My original relation to language is, as Irad Kimhi once put it, not *perception*, but *participation*.

The point is well familiar from Wittgenstein's discussion of primitive language games like that of the builders. A language is originally something in whose actuality one partakes as agent and not primarily something whose instantiations are 'out there' given to one by the senses. The remarks on the builders have given rise to all kinds of intricate debates. But the central point is often left aside: the peculiar kind of actuality characteristic of a language. In its original conception, language is the reality of *what we do*. The difficulty is to hold on to this conception when doing philosophy. It seems to elude the familiar categories of kinds of things or ways of being. That is what gives rise to the puzzle about rule-following.

Given the Type-Token Model of the relation between language and utterance, it holds that for each datable utterance of a string of graphic marks or sounds, considered in isolation, there is an in principle unlimited number of languages of whose types it could be a token. Davidson suggests that this difficulty has a "relatively simple answer": "The longer we interpret a speaker with the apparent success as speaking a particular language, the greater our legitimate confidence that the speaker is speaking that language" (Davidson 2001: 111). But the question about how I can find out whether a given utterance is an instance of this or that language, presupposes that the utterance is determinately connected to one of those infinitely many patterns. But what does this come to? The connection cannot be elucidated by appeal to the language itself. As abstract objects, languages "cannot be called on [...] to explain linguistic behavior", as Davidson points out himself. So, what makes the connection? And how does the speaker "show it to himself", as Wittgenstein would put it? (See RFM: IV, §32.)

It seems that the connection can't be explained by appeal to yet another utterance. A further element seems to be required – something over and above the 'various written and acoustical products' of people. In passing Davidson introduces what he describes in the following way: "the speaker's dispositions to go on are not shadowy or mysterious: they are real features of brains and muscles" (Davidson 2001: 111). Somehow the abstract semantic system must be 'embodied' in the speaker so that it can enter into the explanation of her acts. The same sort of issue arises in the Stage-Continuant Model of the relation between utterance and language. The approach is designed to avoid "attributing causal force to an abstraction", as Sellars puts it (Sellars 1991b: 326). But it is clearly not sufficient to just have a succession of causally related utterances. Something in the speaker – and somehow present to her – must figure as underlying unity of the elements in the series.

Illustrating precisely this issue, Wittgenstein asks us to imagine the scenario of a student extending a number series according to the formula '$(n, n + 2)$'.[5] In interpreting his writing numbers on the paper as an act of calculating, we refer his present behavior to the rule of addition which already sorts all his potential steps into those that would and those that would not be in accord with it. In saying *what* he is doing, we bring his acts to something general that figures at the same time as the standard of correctness. Our description of each step he takes implicitly points ahead to an in principle unlimited series of potential acts of adding. In this way, the numbers on the paper appear like "a visible section of rails laid out to infinity", as Wittgenstein's interlocutor puts it (PI: §218).

Nothing hangs on the mathematical nature of the scenario. The example of extending a number series is just a vivid way to bring out something that holds for every act of using a word in accord with its meaning or, for that matter, applying a concept to an object. "A thought", Frege says, "always contains something reaching out beyond the particular case so that this is presented to us as falling under something general" (Frege 1989: 189, Kernsatz 4). In this way of putting it, the focus is on the relation between a concept and the range of objects that fall under it. Leaving aside the special use that Frege makes of the word '*Begriff*' and focusing on the realm of *sense*, one might say that 'concepts' have to be conceived as *components* of thoughts which are not features of any particular mind, but are that which different minds can grasp and affirm. A concept is thus what unifies all the thoughts of which it is a component into a series of items that can be grasped and affirmed. Take the simple singular judgment

---

5 The following paragraphs present a condensed version of some considerations I developed in Haase 2011.

'*a* is *F*', framed by a particular subject. If '*F*' is to figure as a predicate in this judgment, it must be such that it can also appear in indefinitely many other judgments. The predicative element reaches beyond any given act of mind in which it is deployed. It is not that it must be possible for other objects to fall under the concept – that might not always be the case. Rather, it must be possible to deploy the concept in other judgments of affirmation and denial. A concept is thus something inherently general insofar as it sets no limit to how often it can be deployed. Each act of judgment therefore points to an in principle unlimited series of possible judgments. The elements of the series are united under a principle or 'rule' – namely, the concept that is applied in the judgment and determines whether the object brought under it actually falls under it.

Gareth Evans termed this the "*Generality Constraint*" (Evans 1982: 100). He immediately links it to what I will call the *Explanation Requirement*. Evans says that there must be a "single state" of the judging subject that provides a "common partial explanation" of all her acts of mind in which the predicative element '*F*' figures (Evans 1982: 101–102). The reason is this. As I presented it in the last paragraph, the Generality Constraint seems to leave open how the individual has to be related to that space of possibilities if she is to count as making a judgment. As long as one only looks at the behavior exhibited by the pupil so far, there seems to be an infinite number of patterns or 'rules' with which his behavior accords. For his acts to be connected in a determinate fashion with any one of them, the pattern or rule cannot figure only as that with which his acts accord. Somehow, it must enter into the explanation of his acts. As Sellars points out, there is a world of difference between behavior that *merely conforms* to a pattern and behavior that is *governed* by the pattern (cf. Sellars 1991b: 322 ff.). Unless there is a sense in which the pupil's behavior happens *because of the rule*, it might as well be a mere coincidence that it exhibits the pattern specified by the rule. On the assumption that the rule is something abstract, it cannot provide the relevant explanatory connection itself. What underwrites the 'because' must be something actual or 'real' in the pupil. When we ascribe the judgment that *Fa* to a subject we implicitly refer her act to an infinite series of potential judgments *by that subject* and thus to something *about her* that underwrites our reaching ahead in this way. Only by being conceived as springing from such a common source are the acts of an individual intelligible as acts of judgment.

On further reflection, it should be clear that we cannot leave the sense of the 'because' unspecified. There may be some 'real features of brains and muscles' that underwrite a non-accidental accordance between a subject's behavior and some abstract pattern. But that doesn't mean that her acts come under the heading of repeatedly deploying a concept. The connection might even involve what is sometimes called 'primitive normativity'.[6] Arguably, the complex patterns that bees exhibit in flight are *governed* by a pattern. What each of them is doing happens *because of a rule*, as Sellars puts it. And a bee that fails to exhibit the pattern is defective. But that doesn't mean that they are *following a rule*. In order to count as extending a number series by repeatedly executing the operation of addition, one must somehow conceive of oneself as continuing in the same way, where the relevant respect of sameness is defined by the concept of addition. Somehow, the general must be 'understood' or 'represented' in the acts that instantiate it. Let's call this the *Apprehension Requirement*. As one only judges that *Fa* if one knows that one does, the judging subject must conceive of her act as an instance of an in principle infinite series of acts containing the predicative element *F*. In framing the judgment, the subject must act on an understanding of the concept she deploys in the judgment.

Things get puzzling as soon as one enquires into the nature of that 'understanding' or 'representation'. What is its content? It seems that our description of the pupil's act can only implicitly reach ahead to an unlimited series of acts, if his own conception of his act somehow does. In consequence, it is tempting to think that in understanding the concept his 'soul' must, as Wittgenstein puts it, "as it were fly ahead and take all the steps before [he] physically arrived at this or that one" (PI: §188). And then it looks as if his 'soul' has already done what he could never hope to do with the pen in his hand – namely extend the series up to infinity. Obviously, the pupil's understanding of the *plus*-function cannot consist in the whole extension of the number series being present in his mind. There would be no space anymore for the idea of *executing* the operation of addition. So, it seems that his 'understanding' of the rule must somehow be such that it does not already represent the rule's application at each point in the series. This threatens to lead to the picture in which the rule as it is 'represented' or 'understood' by the pupil is an item in her mind that is, at each step, in need of an act of interpretation if it is to issue a determinate result. But that picture is just as hopeless. For, the act at any particular point in the series only has a determinate content in virtue of its connection to the other acts.

At this point it can look like there are only two options. Either one rejects the Generality Constraint and denies that the whole extension of the series is determined by rule. Or one rejects the Apprehension Requirement and holds that what is called 'understanding' is something below the level of thought – something 'tacit' or 'unconscious'. Each view has been ascribed to the later Wittgen-

---

6 See Ginsborg 2011.

stein, in a number of guises. But both are just a rejection of the very idea of following a rule.

In the light of this mess, it is tempting to simply insist on the irreducibility of the phenomenon. John McDowell argues that all that is needed to dissolve the alleged paradox is a reminder of "a bit of common sense about following a sign-post [or a rule]" – namely: that doing so is "not acting on an *interpretation*" (McDowell 1998b: 276). As McDowell suggests, the source of the puzzle is the assumption that a person's mind is "populated exclusively with items that, considered in themselves, do not sort things outside the mind, including specifically bits of behaviour, into those that are correct or incorrect in the light of those items". That this assumption is false and counterintuitive, is easy to see, McDowell contends, when one applies it to "intentionality in general". For, that would amount to the denial that "an intention, just as such, is something with which only acting in a specific way would accord" and that "generally, a thought, just as such, is something with which only certain states of affairs would accord". Once we realize how implausible this is as a *general* thesis about intentionality, the more restricted claim about the understanding of "the principle of a series" equally looks "quite counter-intuitive". In this way, the alleged puzzle is "revealed as illusory": it rests on a "thesis that we have no reason to accept" (McDowell 1998b: 264, 270–272).

At the center of McDowell's remedy stands the analogy between (a) the way an order is related to its executions, an intention to what fulfills it, etc., and (b) the way in which a concept or the 'principle of a series' is related to its applications. But, as I presented it, that analogy is precisely what leads into the puzzle. It suggests that we could take the following appearance of the 'surface grammar' of our language at face value: The word 'understanding' as it occurs in 'He understands the concept F' seems to function in the same way as when it occurs in 'He understands the thesis that a is F.' In the latter case, the verb is used to ascribe what Frege would call the grasping of a thought. So, if the grammatical role of 'understanding' is the same, then we should expect that in the former case as well: here too there must be a propositional object of the understanding. But that assumption was precisely what led into trouble: it seemed that that object of the understanding must be either the whole extension of the series or something that still needs to be applied. Our difficulty is thus *not* that there is some *definite* mental item that seems 'normatively inert' if one adopts the wrong perspective, but rather that it is unclear *which* 'item' we are supposed to be talking about.

3 The Ability to Speak a Language

In the second half of §201 Wittgenstein gives a formal characterization of the element that would allow us to avoid the dilemma sketched above: "What this shows is that there is a way of grasping a rule which is *not* an *interpretation*, but which is exhibited in what we call 'following the rule' and 'going against it' in actual cases." Wittgenstein regards the rule-following paradox as a *reductio* of the conception of understanding according to which the subject's apprehension of a concept is in an act of mind in the same order as the deployment of a concept in a judgment.[7] Instead we are told to look for something *general* that is *instantiated*, *manifested* or 'exhibited' in 'actual cases' of 'following the rule'.

The remark picks up an earlier consideration about how the surface grammar of our language can mislead the philosopher's investigation of what it is to understand a concept or a language. We are told that it is crucial to recognize that in the sentence "I know how the word 'game' is used" the words 'know how' figures in a different role than in the sentence "I know how high the Mont-Blanc is." (See PI: §79) Wittgenstein suggests that assimilating these two cases is what leads into confusion. In the context of ascribing the possession of a word or concept, the verbs 'understanding' and 'knowing' are *not* deployed in order to ascribe an act or state that could be called the grasping of a thought or proposition. Their grammar is rather akin to the role of 'being able to' or 'having mastered (a technique)' (see PI: §§146–151). In stating the Generality Constraint, Evans makes what looks like the same point. He expresses it in terms of the 'ability' the judging subject must be credited with: if a subject is to count as framing a judgment involving the concept *F*, her act must be the exercise of a capacity which she can exercise elsewhere, again and again – in judging that *b* is *F*, that *c* is *F* etc. The understanding of a sentence of the form '*Fa*', or the grasping of the thought expressed by it, results from the joint exercise of 'two abilities': the understanding of the object-term '*a*' and her understanding of the predicate-term '*F*'. As Evans has it, each of them figures as a 'single state' of the judging subject that provides a 'common partial explanation' of all her acts of mind in which the respective element figures (see Evans 1982: 101–102). The idea of an

---

[7] As many authors have pointed out, the fact that the skeptical paradox figures in PI §201 as a *reductio* suggests that the "skeptical solution" that Saul Kripke tentatively ascribes to Wittgenstein cannot have anything to do with how Wittgenstein conceived of what he was doing. Kripke's reading rests on the assumption that Wittgenstein *accepts* the skeptical paradox and then tries to show us how we can live with the consequences. See Kripke 1982: 55 ff.

ability is supposed to enable us to meet what I called the 'Explanation Requirement'. Intuitively, a capacity, ability or disposition of an individual is something that doesn't exhaust itself in any particular act, but can be exercised in a potentially *unlimited series of acts by this individual*. At the same time, it is not something abstract, but rather something actual or concrete insofar as it exists in an individual and is, as Anthony Kenny puts it, "a positive explanatory factor in accounting for [his] performance" (Kenny 1975: 135).

A number of philosophers have suggested that all that is needed to solve the alleged paradox about rule-following is the introduction of the notion of ability, capacity or power and the idea of 'normative regularity' that comes with it.[8] McDowell is skeptical about this sort of approach:

> [I]t is useless to invoke the notion of ability as a response to the difficulty in the case of understanding in particular. Of course, it is not wrong to say that understanding is something in the nature of an ability; I am not suggesting it would be anything but an egregious category-mistake to assimilate, say, my standing knowledge of what 'careen' means to an episode in consciousness. But why should that seem to help with the difficulty that arises about accord? (McDowell 1998a: 301)

It is not wrong to characterize understanding a concept or a language as an ability. But the appeal to the generic idea of an ability cannot be sufficient. There are all kinds of abilities – for instance, my ability to digest food. And, arguably, the latter also introduces a kind of normative regularity. But my exercise of such an ability is not an act of following a rule or deploying a concept. And if our problem is a puzzle about acts of the latter kind, then it stands to reason that the correlated notion of ability is just as puzzling.

In this connection, it is worth looking at what Wittgenstein says on the matter:

> The criteria which we accept for [...] 'being able to', 'understanding', are much more complicated than might appear at first sight. [...] [T]he role of these words in our language [...] is what we need to understand in order to resolve philosophical paradoxes. And hence definitions usually fail to resolve them; and so, a fortiori does the assertion that a word is 'undefinable'. (PI: §182)

The passage is instructive in two respects. First, it suggests that simply rejecting reductive ambitions won't do.[9] Secondly, it suggests that investigating the gram-

---

8 See, for instance, Baker and Hacker 1984: 95–96.
9 It is often argued that Wittgenstein's solution consists in the insight that the kind of ability or capacity we are after is the one that one acquires by being initiated into a "practice" or "form of

mar of 'understanding' and the way in which it is akin to 'being able to' is precisely what is required to 'resolve philosophical paradoxes'.

But what is the confusion that requires a grammatical investigation? There is an intuitive difference between having mastered a word or concept and understanding a sentence or proposition in which it occurs, just as there is an intuitive difference between the ability to digest food and the ability to deploy a concept. But when we leave these differences intuitive – or, if you will, as a matter of 'common sense' – while doing philosophy, then they seem to point in opposite directions. Focusing on the latter difference, it seems like there must be *something* that he who has mastered a concept or a language 'understands' or 'represents' – a proper intentional object akin to the thought grasped when one understands a sentence. But the original reason to introduce the talk of ability, capacity or *know how* was that it seemed that there can't be such an intentional object – a proper thought or system of thoughts that one grasps when one has mastered a concept or language. On the fundamental level, the only way to display the mastery of a concept or a language is to use it in speech acts and judgments. And then it looks like we are dealing with an 'understanding' of a queer kind – one whose intentional object seems to be elusive: the understanding or knowledge must somehow be 'implicit' or 'tacit', in that strange way where it doesn't require that one can make it explicit upon being asked.

It is a peculiar feature of the literature that stating what ought to strike one as puzzling is often presented as the lesson to be learned: on the fundamental level, we 'follow the rule blindly'. The slogan just presents the knot to be untangled. Early on, in discussing the kind of understanding that guides the deployment of a concept or the extension of a number series, Wittgenstein writes:

> Nothing would be more confusing here than to use the words 'conscious' and 'unconscious' for the contrast between states of consciousness and dispositions. For this pair of terms covers up a grammatical difference. (PI: §149)

The literature on the role that the notion of an ability, capacity or disposition plays in the dialectic of the rule-following considerations tends to exhibit the

---

life". But when one asks what a "practice" is, or a "form of life" in the relevant sense, one is told that the only thing that *can* and *may* be said is that it is the practice to follow rules and that the lifeform in question is a life with meaning. In consequence, it seems that, strictly speaking, the talk of "practice" and "form of life" is just as "useless", as McDowell claims the appeal to the notion of ability to be. What the proposed solution ultimately comes to is the insistence that understanding a concept or a rule is irreducible and so are the notions of ability and social practice that may be connected with it. The talk of the latter doesn't really do any work. It just illustrates a point that can also be made without mentioning them.

same structure as the discussion about the role of the notion of a social practice or customs. There seem to be only two options. Either the notion of a disposition is taken to supply the conceptual resources for a non-circular or reductive explanation of meaning and understanding. Or it is said that the crucial point is to realize that understanding is an ability *sui generis* that has to be accepted as basic and irreducible. In both cases, the notion of ability doesn't seem to belong to what we are investigating in the context of the rule-following considerations. In the former case, because it is assumed that its definition is the task of another discipline (either another branch of philosophy or perhaps psychology), in the latter case, because the rejection of a demand for explanation is taken to be the whole point. But there may be a third option. On this view, the discussion of the grammar of 'being able to' is a first step in the dismantling of a conception of generality that makes it impossible to understand the actuality of language.

What originally motivated the introduction of the talk of abilities or dispositions was that it seemed to provide the resources to meet the Explanation Requirement. An ability or disposition is something *general* insofar as it doesn't exhaust itself in a particular act, but can be actualized in an in principle unlimited series of acts. At the same time, it is not something abstract, but rather something *real* or *concrete* insofar as it (partially) explains its instances. That abilities or dispositions have these two features is widely recognized. But the established quantificational conception of generality puts severe restrictions on the shape that an account of dispositional sentences can take. It requires that the truth value of dispositional statements like 'Peter *walks* to school in the morning' is determined by the truth value of the corresponding statements about ongoing happenings like 'Peter *is walking* to school.' The usual way to meet this demand is to take the latter statement as a sentence that includes a time-specification as part of its content. Then one quantifies over these points in time. Accordingly, the dispositional statement is either read as a counterfactual or as a judgment about what *mostly* or *normally* happens.[10]

In both cases, the predicate appearing in the singular statement and the predicate appearing in the general statement must have the same grammatical form. But then it becomes unclear, why a disposition is not something abstract and causally inert.[11] If dispositional statements can be reduced to counterfactual conditionals, then it looks like we are talking only about *potential* acts. The stan-

---

10 For the former see Ryle 1949: 116 ff., for the latter see Fara 2005: 43–82.
11 Elisabeth Prior, Robert Pargetter and Frank Jackson think that the causal inertness of dispositions follows from the fact that dispositional statements are to be analyzed as counterfactuals, see 1982: 251–257.

dard reaction to this problem is to claim that the disposition has a 'causal basis' – an underlying *state* that can be described in categorical statements.[12]

Wittgenstein is famously skeptical about rendering understanding as an underlying state that guides the rule-following subject. The problem is supposed to be that "we cannot [...] find anything which we should call such a state".[13] One might think neuroscience will take care of that. But the problem is that the subject *herself* can't seem to find it in perspective of judging. If the subject is to be 'guided' in the way required to warrant talk of following a rule, the item that provides the common explanation of her multiple acts can't be anything that she has to discover. But that is precisely what the received analysis suggests. Wittgenstein's diagnosis of the source of the trouble is that we have been misled by the tense of the verb phrases by means of which we ascribe a capacity:

> There are [...] various reasons which incline us to look at the fact of something being possible, someone being able to do something, etc. as the fact that he or it is in a particular state. [...] And his way of representation, [...] is embodied in the expressions 'He is capable of ...', 'He is able to multiply large numbers in his head', 'He can play chess': in these sentences the verb is used in the *present tense*, suggesting that the phrases are descriptions of states which exist at the moment when we speak. (BB: 117)

The first step is to realize that there are judgments about an individual that are properly expressed by sentences in the present tense that are neither about a process that the individual is going through nor about a state in which it is during a certain period of time. The relevant dispositional statements have the form of *habituals:* they say what the individual does in general. Their temporality is, as it were, time-general. That is to say, their generality does not consist in quantification over acts at a time. Rather, it consists in the way in which subject and predicate are united: the predicate appearing in the general judgment 'Peter *walks* to

---

12 How the relation between the counterfactual and the state ascription is conceived in detail varies. Some suggest that we need *both* a counterfactual description of the disposition and a categorial description of its "causal basis". (See, for instance, Lewis 1997: 143–158.) Others think that dispositions can be reduced to their causal basis. (See, for instance, Armstrong 1968: 88 ff.) Yet others think that even though dispositional statements *cannot* be *reduced* to state ascriptions, they will ultimately be *eliminated* in favor of statements about microphysiological states in a proper scientific description of the world. (See, for instance, Davidson 2004: 96 and Quine 1974: 10.)

13 Cf., for instance, Wittgenstein: "[...] B is guided by the particular combination of words in one of our three sentences if he could also have carried out orders consisting in other combinations of dots and dashes. And if we say this, it seems to us that the 'ability' to carry out other orders is a particular state of the person carrying out the orders [...] And at the same time we cannot in this case find anything which we should call such a state" (BB: §43), see also PI: §146 and §149.

school in the morning' does not have the same grammatical form as the predicate appearing in the corresponding particular judgment 'Peter *is walking* to school now.' The former statement describes, no less than the latter, something that is real and concrete; it just concerns another level of actuality, if you will.

4 The Practice of Language

These considerations alone are, of course, not sufficient. They don't articulate the difference between the possession of a concept and a mere habit. Accordingly, they don't provide the resources to meet the Apprehension Requirement. What we need is an account of a special kind of power, ability or disposition – a conceptual capacity. Wittgenstein appears to suggest that this can be accomplished, if we see the individual against the background of a 'custom' or 'form of life'. The difficulty is to understand how this is supposed to help.

In PI §199 Wittgenstein accompanies his remark that to follow a rule is a 'custom' with the commentary that it should be read as "a note on the grammar of the expression 'to follow a rule'". Philosophical problems, we are told, "arise through the misinterpretation of our forms of language" (PI: §111), and they can be solved by "giving prominence to distinctions which our ordinary forms of language easily make us overlook" (PI: §132). A 'grammatical remark', then, is a remark about the proper interpretation of the grammar of our language. Accordingly, the difficulty to which Wittgenstein alludes in the passage from *Remarks on the Foundations of Mathematics* I quoted at the outset pertains to the interpretation of the grammatical form that the statements exhibit with which we describe a language. So, if we want to know what the alleged insight is, then we need to investigate their grammar. Appreciating the specificities of this kind of description is what is supposed to put us in the position to realize that what appears to be a problem about the very possibility of conceptual content is in the end nothing but 'grammatical confusion', as Wittgenstein would put it. But what is in this case the 'surface grammar' that tends to lead the philosopher astray?

The first step is to establish what statements we are to look at. The Apprehension Requirement can be put like this. In order to count as having mastered a concept or the meaning of a word, one must, at the very least, be able to give an example for how it is used. This may seem trivial. But in giving an example one presents one's act as an instance of something general. Against this background, we can articulate the contrast between a conceptual capacity and a mere habit in the following way. A habit can operate behind the back of an individual. In that case, having a habit does not go together with being able to put an act forward as an example. Of course, there can be conscious habits. In this case, the habit will come with the ability to give an example of what one is in the habit to do. But here, giving an example points to something that is specific to *me* as *this* individual. A mere disposition explains the acts of one subject. It does not point beyond it. What makes it no accident that you are acting in this way is your habit, not mine. This is not how it is in the case of the mastery of a concept or a language. In judging that *a* is *F*, I exclude the opposed act of any other thinker. If you judge that *a* is not *F*, then our acts are in contradiction. And in judging that *a* is *F*, I know this. That is what it means to put '*a* is *F*' forward as true.

Since the Apprehension Requirement determines the sense of '*because of the rule*' introduced by the Explanation Requirement, we get a further specification of the generality of a concept. For it to be possible for our acts to be in contradiction, it must be the *same* concept that is deployed in your act and in mine. The predicative element '*F*' that figures in my judgment must be such that it can also figure in acts of mind of an *in principle unlimited series of subjects*. The generality of a concept points not only *beyond any particular act of mind* in which it is deployed; it also points *beyond any particular mind*. But according to the Explanation Requirement it holds that what figures as the standard of correctness must be such that it can explain the acts that are in accord with it. So, if there is to be an act that due to its apprehended, reflexive or self-conscious character excludes any opposed acts by another, then that which explains it must be such that it can also explain the acts of others that are in agreement with it.

This introduces the notion of a practice in the abstract. Just as a capacity can be described as a kind of actuality that exists in a single individual and figures as the *common source* of an *in principle unlimited multiplicity of acts* by that individual, a practice can be described as an actuality that is exhibited by an *in principle unlimited multiplicity of subjects* and figures as the *common source* of their acts. That may also be said of a lifeform and the 'primitive normativity' it involves. In the case of the bees, it holds that the act of a multiplicity of subjects is governed by a pattern that acts at the same time as a standard for their correctness. The difference between primitive and conceptual normativity is marked by the relation between the acts of the respective individuals. In the case of the normativity of a sub-rational life-form, the acts of each individual bearer are judged as sound or defective in relation to the relevant kind of feature or activity characteristic of the lifeform. But the sound act of this individual does not itself exclude the defective one of another individual. In an act of following a rule, by contrast, one takes one's acts as exemplary for the proper way to instantiate the 'pattern' that can be instantiated by others as well. This can be made explicit by presenting one's act as an example. To offer the sentence '*Fa*' as an example for the use of the word '*F*' is an act of mind that can be expressed in a sentence of the form "'*F*' is used like this ...' or 'We use '*F*' like this ...'

This is the kind of statement we need to investigate in order to understand what it is to describe a language – namely: the sort of thing a speaker of the language would say when, to put it in familiar Wittgensteinian terms, the explanations have come to end and she has reached bedrock so that the only thing left to do is to articulate her own language by giving examples for the use of words: '*This* is what I do.' But now said against the background of the idea that if I am not confused *what I do* is fundamentally *what is done* in the practice to which the respective word belongs. So, the subject matter of the grammatical investigation is the speech act of saying what we say.

In the last section, we looked at the peculiar kind of generality expressed by the deployment of a verb phrase with habitual aspect. Let us then turn to the generality expressed by the subject term of the statement at hand. Even though 'we' tends to play a prominent role in the writings of philosophers, its logical features have received much less attention than that of the first person singular. It tends to be overlooked that 'we' exhibits a different logical grammar depending on the context in which it figures. Take a simple sentence of the form 'We are φ-ing.' It can express three logically distinct thoughts.

Imagine you and I are playing tennis on court 3 while others are also playing tennis on courts 1 and 2. A bewildered bystander asks you what all these people are doing, running around in this peculiar way. You respond: 'We are playing tennis.' Here, 'we' figures *distributively:* it signifies an *aggregate* or *collection* of individuals that all exhibit a certain feature. To make that explicit you could have also said: 'We are *each* playing tennis.' Further inquiry into what it is to play tennis will bring out that there are several senses in which this action verb can't be said of one individual unless it is also said of others. But in the case of the statement at hand these implications of the predicate don't determine the logical grammar of 'we'. For, the fact that you and I are playing tennis on court 3 is independent of the fact that those people over on court 1 are currently doing the same. And perhaps on court 2 there is just one person practicing her serve on her own. Still she is 'playing tennis' – in one way of taking the term. Heard in this way, the truth-value of 'We are φ-ing' is determined by the truth-values of the singular judgments contained in it. Accordingly, the we-statement can be presented as a conjunction of a first person singular statement with several statements in the third person singular. In the example, it is implied that each of them knows that the predicate applies to her. But this special character of the activity of tennis playing just informs the grammar of the singular judgments brought together in the 'we'-statement; it doesn't inform the distribution expressed by 'we'. The latter is the same as in 'We have reds dots on the nose' when I say it upon looking in the mirror and at the other people in the room.

In both cases, 'we' signifies a group or set of individuals of which I'm an element. Let's call the general category the *Distributive We*.

A moment later, you might utter the same string of words with respect to the two of us on court 3 and mean it in a way that the 'we' could not include those people on court 1 and on court 2. The two of us are playing a match. Accordingly, your playing is linked to my playing in a way in which it is not to their playing. Making that explicit you could say: 'We are playing tennis *against each other.*' This statement can't be analyzed as a conjunction of singular judgments with independent truth values. Given the implied reading of 'playing tennis', it would not be true that you are playing, unless it is also true of another: your opponent. Consequently, the 'we' is not distributive; it signifies the poles of *relation* expressed by the verb phrase – in the present case, the agents of a *transaction*. Specified in this way, this usage of the first person plural is also exhibited by 'We are fighting each other' or 'We are bumping into each other'. Let's call the general category the *Dyadic We*.

This usage of the first person plural admits of categorial sub-specifications. When it is deployed in connection with a predicate like 'bumping into each other' where the transaction described is not intentional, 'we' can be analyzed in terms of 'I' and 'her' or 'him'. For, this kind of transaction can also take place without the awareness of the agents involved. So, when it does come to consciousness, the awareness of the one may be independent of the awareness of the other. It is different in our tennis example where the relation of transaction takes a special turn. Here, the self-conscious character of the activity expressed by the action verb informs the logical grammar of the 'we'. For it to be true that we are playing tennis against each other, the thought that we are must somehow be operative on both sides of this relation. And we must be aware of being related to each other in this way. So here the 'we' contains that the poles of the relation think towards each other in terms of 'I' and 'you'.

These two uses don't exhaust the ways in which 'we' may be deployed. On another day, you and I are playing doubles against another team. Once again, you might utter the same string of words, but this time mean it in a way that it can only include the one who is with you on the same side of the court. Making that explicit you could say: 'We are playing tennis *together.*' This statement can't be analyzed distributively either: 'playing doubles' could not be true of you unless it also true of another. But this time this is not because the two of us are the opposed poles of a relation in which we do something to each other. The other pole of the transaction expressed by the action verb is on the other side of the court. That is what our common endeavors are directed at. The 'we' expresses our being united in this effort. We are pursuing a project that involves a distribution of labor and assigns different roles to those involved. Currently, I am covering the net while you are serving. That in doing so we are also involved in a transaction with another team is a feature of the activity we are engaged in, but it doesn't inform the logical grammar of this 'we'. The latter is the same as in 'We are playing Beethoven's Ninth' said by a member of the orchestra or 'We are forming the letter S' said by someone who is lying together with others in a certain formation on the beach. Let's call this general category the *Cooperative We*.

If you want, these three uses of 'we' present three forms of plurality: *collection*, *relation* and *cooperation*. Arguably, being a full master of tennis requires competence in all three forms of judgment in the first person plural. In any case, it should be clear that each of the facts described by these three uses of 'We are playing tennis', presupposes something that can also be articulated by statements deploying 'we'. An individual could not be playing tennis – whether it is doubles, singles or just training the serve – unless there was that game or practice. And if you were to explain to the bewildered bystander what playing tennis is, what its rules are and how it is done well, you might find yourself uttering sentences about what *a tennis player does* or *what tennis players do* – or, for instance, giving a description of how *one* hits a forehand. However, since you *are* a tennis player you could also put it in terms of what *we* do.

In describing the art of tennis, you are not talking about these particular individuals and their actions on a specific occasion. What you are describing is that which is manifested or actualized by their actions and in the light of which we have to see their current behavior in order to understand what they are doing, running around in this peculiar way. And as the art of tennis is open to infinitely many new apprentices, it would seem that the 'we' you deploy in your statement does not signify any determinate number of persons. It includes you not as this particular individual, but as representative of this sport. Deployed in this way, 'we' is general or impersonal. Let's call this the *Generic We*.

Despite the grammatical features just noted, one might think that the 'we' that figures in the description or articulation of a practice is to be read in one of the registers of plurality just considered. For, each of them can occur not only in the description of action on a particular occasion, but also in the ascription of dispositions to the respective kind of manifold of individuals. Say, everyone who is on the courts at the moment has the habit of playing tennis on Tuesdays. Accordingly, you could utter the habitual statement deploying the Distributive We: 'We *each* play tennis every Tuesday.' The same holds for the Dyadic We ('We play *against each other* on Tuesdays') and the Cooperative We ('We play *together* on Tuesdays'). And if one deletes the time specification 'on Tuesdays' and the respective marker of the specific form of plurality, what one retains is a sentence exhibiting the schema 'We φ'. And that just looks like the statements describing the practice. On the surface, they are all the same.

Given the framework of what I called in §1 the Quantification Model, the 'we' that figures in the description of a language or practice must be cast in one of the registers of plurality. For the underlying assumption is that the existence of a *spoken* language has to be rendered in terms of the truth of statements about the particular acts and states of a group of speakers and causal interrelations between them. It is this assumption that shapes the received positive proposals for how to understand the notion of a custom or social practice in the context of the rule-following considerations. Roughly speaking, there are three competing accounts. Each takes one of the three forms of the plurality as defining the grammar of 'we' and consequently interprets the articulation of a language in the light of it. In each case, the proposal is confronted with considerable problems.

What is sometimes called the 'Simple Community View' is shaped by the distributive rendering of 'we'. A version of this view is endorsed by Crispin Wright in his initial take on the rule-following material. He argues that the normative status of my act of rule-following is determined by nothing but the 'community verdict' on the matter. What is 'right' in the light of a rule is what the community is disposed to take to be right:

> None of us unilaterally can make sense of the idea of correct employment of language save by reference to the authority of securable communal assent on the matter; and for the community there is no authority, so no standard to meet. [...] we shall reject the idea that, in the sense requisite for investigation-independence, the community goes right or wrong in accepting a particular verdict; rather, it just goes.[14]

On closer inspection, it turns out that what Wright calls a 'community' is not some entity over and above its members; the 'community assent' about whether some given act accords with the rule is nothing but the view that the majority of its members are disposed to hold.

As the practice is nothing but a constellation of the *actual* dispositions of its practitioners, the proposed account could be said to meet the Explanation Requirement. But the upshot is a rejection of the Generality Constraint when it is understood as the thesis that it is the concept or rule that determines the whole extension of the series. For, it is an implication that a change in the dispositions of the majority will change what number comes next in the series. In consequence, the dispositions whose collection constitutes the 'community verdict' cannot themselves be understood as the mastery of a concept. Ultimately,

---

[14] Wright 1980: 220, see also Peacocke 1981: 73.

they have to be conceived as "basic reactive propensities, primitive classificatory dispositions", as Wright puts it (Wright 1986: 72). On the fundamental level, there is no difference between having a conceptual capacity and having a mere habit. It is only through the position that the individual occupies in a social network that its acts and states acquire a semantic significance. The elements making up the social network are features of our sub-rational natures. But it is hard to see how such a notion of a social practice should supply us with anything that the bare notion of disposition hasn't already. For, the 'community' is modeled on the distributive conception of 'we' and thus conceived of as a mere aggregate of individuals. Just adding individual dispositions to each other can't introduce the idea of the members being in 'agreement' – in a sense of the word connected with the logical notion of contradiction. There seems to be only the matching or mismatching of brute dispositions.

It has often been remarked that the Simple Community View is alien to the later Wittgenstein.[15] He must be working with a different conception of the social – a different rendering of the 'we' of linguistic community. But which one? The dyadic rendering of 'we' underlies Robert Brandom's attempt to fix the shortcomings of the Simply Community View. The alternative Brandom recommends focuses on the relations between the individual members that make up a linguistic community:

> [What we treat as fundamental is] *I-thou* sociality rather than *I-we* sociality. Its basic building block is the relation between an audience that is attributing commitments and thereby keeping score and a speaker who is undertaking commitments, on whom score is being kept. The notion of discursive *community* – a 'we' – is built up out of these *communicating* components. (Brandom 1994: 508)

On this view, the 'we' of linguistic community is instituted by what its members do to each other. As Brandom conceives it, the 'we' of linguistic community belongs to the same category as the 'we' used in 'We are playing tennis against each other.' It is just that the relevant transaction verb – 'keeping score' – allows for indefinitely many others to figure as the other pole of the relation. In discussion, Brandom once characterized the first person plural as a "recognitional quantifier". Its domain is defined by a certain respect in which I recognize myself in others. His example was 'We pragmatists believe that *p*.' And the point was that the use of 'we' enables me to attribute a commitment to others that I undertake myself with this very statement. The judgment so expressed cannot be con-

---

15 See, for instance, McDowell 1998c and Cora Diamond 1997: chapter 7.

ceived as a conjunction of singular judgments, since it contains the concept of a *relation:* the attribution of commitment and entitlement.

In certain respects, Brandom's approach is very similar to Wright's. Just as Wright, Brandom thinks that 'normative statuses' have to be explained in terms of 'normative attitudes'. For, only the latter are in the 'causal order': "What is causally efficacious is our practically taking or treating ourselves and each other as having commitments" (Brandom 1994: 626). The new idea is that focusing on the perspectival difference in reciprocal scorekeeping is supposed to allow us to specify a social structure where the inference from 'Everyone believes that *p*' to '*p*' is *not* valid so that the norms implicit in the practice of using words "extend beyond the practitioners' actual capacity to use them correctly" (Brandom 1994: 633). This is supposed to make space for an idea of objectivity required to understand the notion of conceptual content. But, on the face of it, it just shifts the place of the puzzle. On the assumption that the norm of the practice resides in the perspectival difference between attributing and endorsing commitments, it looks like it *systematically* eludes the capacities of its practitioners. In consequence, it is hard to see how the Explanation Requirement can be met.

Another way in which one might attempt to avoid the consequences of the Simple Community View is to insist on a cooperative rendering of 'we'. That is what Sellars proposes:

> [T]he fundamental principles of a community, which define what is 'correct' or 'incorrect', 'right' or 'wrong', 'done' or 'not done', are the most general common *intentions* of that community with respect to the behaviour of members of the group. [...] Thus the conceptual framework of persons is the framework in which we think of one another as sharing the community intentions which provide the ambience of principles and standards (above all, those which make meaningful discourse and rationality possible) within which we live our own individual lives. (Sellars 1991a: 39–40)

On this view, 'we' doesn't signify a mere aggregate or collection: "Community intentions ('One shall ...') are not just private intentions ('I shall ...') that everybody has" (Sellars 1991: 40). And it cannot be build up from what the individual members of the group do to each other. Rather, it expresses "membership in an embracing group each member of which thinks of itself as a member of the group" (Sellars 1991a: 39). As Sellars conceives it, the 'we' of linguistic community belongs to the same category as the 'we' in 'We are playing tennis together.' It is just that the respective communal enterprise encompasses an indefinite number of partners.

The proposal is not without difficulties either. On the face of it, it is not easy to see how the appeal to a special kind of intention could help to solve a puzzle about the constitution of conceptual content. However, this is precisely what Sellars claims. The appeal to the notion of we-intentions is supposed to introduce a kind sociality that is constitutive of thought: "As Wittgenstein has stressed, it is the linguistic community as a self-perpetuating whole which is the minimum unit in terms of which conceptual activity can be understood" (Sellars 1969: 512). Sellars is well aware of the difficulty. The solution is supposed to become available by way of the distinction between two interrelated levels of a social practice: the 'game' and the 'meta-game'. The former consists of mere 'pattern governed behavior', the latter of 'rule obeying behavior'. Sellars suggests that the primitive or basic pattern-governed behavior can be conceived as occurring *because of conceptual norms* if we relate it to the 'meta-game' by considering the scenario of language acquisition. On the assumption that the trainer's conditioning of the trainee is 'rule obeying behavior', we can extend the normative reach of the rules articulated on the level of the 'meta-game' to the patterned governed behavior on the basic level: "Trainees conform to *ought-to-be's* because trainers obey corresponding *ought-to-do's*" (Sellars 1996: 67).

The problem is that it is unclear how the transition from 'pattern governed behavior' to 'rule obeying behavior' is to be understood. Somehow it is supposed to involve becoming aware of the uniformities that already govern one's primitive behavior so that one can articulate them in the 'meta-game' and, in turn, form the relevant we-intentions manifested, *inter alia*, in the conditioning of trainees. However, Sellars stresses (1) that the training is nothing but stimulus-response conditioning that, taken by itself, is "essentially identical with that in which the dog learns to sit up when I snap my fingers" and (2) that those "learned habits of response […] remain the basic tie between all the complex rule-regulated symbol behavior […] and the environment in which the individual lives and acts" (Sellars 1980: 122). Given these assumptions, it is hard to see how a dispositions acquired in this way could be the source of its own representation. And even if I somehow come to be aware, what I am aware of will be a mere habit.

Each of these three accounts of linguistic community is confronted with a specific set of problems. However, the difficulties have a common root. The assumption underlying all three approaches is that the relevant concept of a social practice is to be elucidated through some notion of *agreement* or *disagreement* between the members of a multiplicity of subjects. They differ with respect to the question how exactly the relevant talk of agreement is to be understood on the fundamental level. Wittgenstein rejects the common assumption:

> It is no use […] to go back to the concept of agreement, because it is no more certain that one action is in agreement with another, than that it happened in accordance with a rule. (RFM: VII, §26)

Talk of agreement between acts (or dispositions) of different individuals cannot provide the solution to the rule-following paradox. For it is just the other side of the very thing that is puzzling: the idea of agreement between act and rule. What makes it seem appealing "to go back to the concept of agreement with another" is the assumption that 'we' deployed in the articulation of practice can only express a form of plurality. But that is a misinterpretation of surface grammar. Alluding to the passage I quoted at the beginning of this paper, one could put the point like this: "To describe the phenomenon of language one must describe a practice *and not a group of individuals, no matter of what kind.*" This negative point implies a positive one. Judgments that neither refer to a particular individual nor to a group of individuals are judgments that are not only time-general but also what one might call '*subject-general*'. The Quantificational Model of language rests on a confusion between generic predication and plural predication.

The logical contrast between the Generic We and the three forms of first personal plurality – the Distributive We, the Dyadic We and the Cooperative We – can be brought out by considering a feature of the grammar of English that can seem peculiar as long as one assumes that 'we' always signifies a multiplicity of individuals. In certain contexts, 'we' can be replaced by a certain way of deploying the word 'you'. In English, 'you' can be used in two ways. One can use it to address an individual or a group. But there is also a usage where what is said is independent of it being said *to* anyone (at least on that occasion). Linguists call it the *Generic* or *Impersonal You* and oppose it to the *Addressee-Referring* or *Personal You*. The Impersonal You can be deployed in order to say, for instance, how we use this word in English, how one plays Solitaire, how to make an omelet, how the city looks from the hill or how long it takes to recover from a flu. Here, 'you' doesn't pick out a particular person or group; it presents a situation for an unspecific person to confront – or a procedure to put into work by anyone, no one in particular.

In Maghrebi Arabic, or Darija, the difference between Impersonal You and Personal You is grammaticalized. The second person pronoun can occur in masculine or feminine form. In the addressee-referring or personal use it takes on the gender of the addressee. In the generic or impersonal use, by contrast, it takes on the gender of the speaker instead of the person spoken to. In English, the difference is exhibited by the fact that in its impersonal use 'you' can be replaced *salva sensu:* what *you do*, what *we do*, what *one does* and what *is done* – it's all the same here. So are 'he', 'she' or 'she*he' and 'they' when they refer back to generic noun phrases such as 'the English speaker' and 'English speakers'. In certain contexts, the exemplifying use of 'I' familiar from the 'what I do' of cooking shows on TV can get the same job done. The contrasts between the first, second and third person as well as the contrast between singular and plural all collapse in the *generic* use of the pronouns. And that is because the *impersonal* pronoun in all its expressions is formally distinct from each *personal* pronoun. The Generic We no more signifies a determinate multiplicity of individuals of which the speaker is (in one way or other) a part than Generic One picks out a particular individual or Generic You expresses the act of address.

Depending on the form of activity or practice described, the statement involving Generic We may entail that a multiplicity of subjects, including the speaker, make judgments deploying Dyadic We or Cooperative We. It doesn't follow that the logical grammar of the former is determined by the latter. For, the same could be said of the Distributive We. When you say 'We are playing tennis' and mean to include the two of us playing on court 3 as well as the people over on court 1, then your statement entails that each of us is deploying the Dyadic We. Still, the 'we' that figures in your statement is distributive.

Just pointing out that there is a generic or impersonal use of what look like standard first, second or third personal pronouns is, of course, not sufficient to challenge the Quantificational Model of generality. For, one might try to give an account of the generic pronouns that fits into the quantificational framework. Friederike Moltmann, for instance, proposes an analysis of Generic One according to which it can be treated as a generalization from one's own case (see Moltmann 2010). Taking her cue from statements like 'One can see the whole city from the castle', Moltmann argues that 'one' is internally connected to the first person singular. It quantifies over a range of individuals defined by the operation of simulation: the subject attributes properties to the individuals in that range by putting herself into their shoes.

It is an implication of Moltmann's account that the correlated judgment in the first person singular – e. g., '*I* can see the whole city from the castle' – is prior to and independent of the respective general judgment articulated by using 'one'. And it is just the other side of this point that this use of 'one' leaves open whether the speaker thinks that there *actually* are or ever have been others in the range delimited by the operation of simulation. As Moltmann defines it, Generic One could also be deployed by someone who denies that there is or ever has been anyone but herself. All that is required is that she allows the possibility of other subjects like her. It is hard to see how this treatment of 'one' is supposed to work where the ascription of an act to an individual – whether to oneself or another – is *mediated* by an apprehension of the practice that is instantiated in performing such an act. A subject could not conceive of herself as playing tennis without understanding what *one* does with a racket and the ball when *one* plays tennis. Where an understanding of *what one does* is required for the intelligibility of the very thought of what *I am doing*, the former cannot be reached by a generalization from my own case. This use of 'one' implies that there are (or at least have been) other individuals who do that sort of thing too. But that doesn't mean that I am speaking *about* these individuals when I articulate what it is to do what they do.

The original or first generic pronoun – whether it is marked by 'one', 'we', 'you', 'he', 'she', 'she*he', 'they' or the correlated use of the generic passive 'what is done' – is the one that one acquires by learning a language. The use of the personal pronouns that occurs in the articulation of the use of words of the language I speak does not signify or refer to *any* particular individual or group whether actual or possible. And it is not a logical category that can be defined by isolating the features of a form of thought or predication. For, the statement in which it occurs does not express a further thought I think in addition to the judgments in which I deploy the respective concepts. Rather, it articulates what is understood or co-represented in my thinking any thought at all. Its grammar is what we have to get into focus in order to understand the relevant notion of a 'practice' that, according to Wittgenstein, is required to solve the puzzle about following a rule.

References

Armstrong, David (1968) *A Materialist Theory of Mind*, London: Routledge.
Baker, Gordon and Peter Hacker (1984) *Skepticism, Rules and Language*, Oxford: Basil Blackwell.
Brandom, Robert (1994) *Making It Explicit*, Cambridge: Harvard University Press.
Davidson, Donald (1984) "Truth and Meaning", in: *Inquiries into Truth and Interpretation*, Oxford: Oxford University Press, 17–36.
Davidson, Donald (2001) "The Second Person", in: *Subjective, Intersubjective, Objective*, Oxford: Oxford University Press, 107–121.
Davidson, Donald (2004) "Representation and Interpretation", in: *Problems of Rationality*, Oxford: Oxford University Press, 87–99.
Diamond, Cora (1989) "Rules: Looking in the Right Place", in: D. Z. Phillips and P. Winch (eds.): *Wittgenstein: Attentions to Particulars*, Basingstoke: Macmillan, 12–34.
Diamond, Cora (1995) "Wright's Wittgenstein", in: *The Realistic Spirit*, Cambridge, MA: MIT Press, 205–224.
Dummett, Michael (1981) *Frege: Philosophy of Language*, Cambridge, MA: Harvard University Press.
Dummett, Michael (1993) "What Is a Theory of Meaning? (II)", in: *The Seas of Language*, Oxford: Oxford University Press, 34–91.
Evans, Gareth (1982) *The Varieties of Reference*, Oxford: Oxford University Press.
Fara, Michael (2005) "Dispositions and Habituals", in: *Noûs* 39 (1), 43–82.
Frege, Gottlob (1989) "17 Kernsätze zur Logik", in: *Nachgelassene Schriften*, Hamburg: Meiner, 189.

Ginsborg, Hannah (2011) "Primitive Normativity and Skepticism about Rules", in: *Journal of Philosophy*, Vol. CVIII, No. 5, 227–254.
Goldfarb, Warren (2012) "Rule-Following Revisited", in: J. Ellis and D. Guevara (eds.): *Wittgenstein and the Philosophy of Mind*, Oxford: Oxford University Press, 73–90.
Haase, Matthias (2011) "The Laws of Thought and the Power of Thinking", in: *Canadian Journal of Philosophy*, Suppl. Vol. 35 (Belief and Agency, ed. D. Hunter), 249–297.
Hornsby, Jennifer (2005), "Semantic Knowledge and Practical Knowledge", in: *Proceedings of the Aristotlelian Society*, Supplementary Volumes, Vol. 79, 107–145.
Horwich, Paul (2002) "Meaning, Use and Truth", in: A. Miller and C. Wright (eds.): *Rule-Following and Meaning*, Montreal and Kingston, Ithaca: McGill-Queen's University Press, 260–273.
Kaplan, David (1990) "Words", in: *Proceedings of the Aristotelian Society*, Suppl. Vol. 64, 93–119.
Kenny, Anthony (1975) *Will, Freedom and Power*, London: Barnes and Noble.
Kripke, Saul (1982) *Wittgenstein on Rules and Private Languages*, Cambridge, MA: Harvard University Press.
Lewis, David (1983a) "General Semantics", in: *Philosophical Papers*, vol. 1, Oxford: Oxford University Press, 189–232.
Lewis, David (1983b) "Language and Languages", in: *Philosophical Papers*, vol. 1, Oxford: Oxford University Press, 163–188.
Lewis, David (1997) "Finkish Dispositions", in: *Philosophical Quarterly* 47, 143–158.
Lewis, David (2002) *Convention*, Oxford: Blackwell.
McDowell, John (1987) "Anti-Realism and the Epistemology of Understanding", in: H. Parret and J. Bouveresse (eds.), *Meaning and Understanding*, Berlin: Walter de Gruyter, 225–248.
McDowell, John (1997) "Another Plea for Modesty", in: R.G. Heck (ed.): *Language, Thought and Logic: Essays in Honour of Michael Dummett*, Oxford: Oxford University Press, 105–129.
McDowell, John (1998a) "Intentionality and Interiority in Wittgenstein", in: *Mind, Value and Reality*, Cambridge, MA: Harvard University Press, 297–321.
McDowell, John (1998b) "Meaning and Intentionality in Wittgenstein's Later Philosophy", in: *Mind, Value and Reality*, Cambridge, MA: Harvard University Press, 263–278.
McDowell, John (1998c) "Wittgenstein on Following a Rule", in: *Mind, Value and Reality*, Cambridge, MA: Harvard University Press, 221–262.
Millikan, Ruth Garrett (2003) "In Defense of Public Language", in: L. M. Antony and N. Hornstein (eds.): *Chomsky and his Critics*, New York: Blackwell, 215–235.
Moltmann, Friederike (2010) "Generalizing Detached Self-Reference and the Semantics of Generic 'One'", in: *Mind and Language* 25, 440–473.
Peacocke, Christopher (1981) "Rule-Following: The Nature of Wittgenstein's Arguments", in: S. H. Holtzman, and C. M. Leich (eds.): *Wittgenstein: To Follow a Rule*, London: Routledge, 72–95.
Prior, Elisabeth, Robert Pargetter and Frank Jackson (1982) "Three Theses about Dispositions", in: *American Philosophical Quarterly* 19, 251–257.
Quine, W. V. O. (1974) *Roots of Reference*, La Salle, IL: Open Court.
Ryle, Gilbert (1949) *The Concept of Mind*, Chicago: Chicago University Press.

Sellars, Wilfrid (1967) "Abstract Entities", in: *Philosophical Perspectives. Metaphysics and Epistemology*, Atascadero, CA: Ridgeview, 49–89.
Sellars, Wilfrid (1969) "Language as Thought and as Communication", in: *Philosophy and Phenomenological Research* 29, 506–527.
Sellars, Wilfrid (1980) "Language, Rules and Behavior", in: *Pure Pragmatics and Possible Worlds*, Atascadero, CA: Ridgeview, 115–134.
Sellars, Wilfrid (1991a) "Philosophy and the Scientific Image of Man", in: *Science, Perception and Reality*, Atascadero, CA: Ridgeview, 1–40.
Sellars, Wilfrid (1991b) "Some Reflections on Language Games", in: *Science, Perception and Reality*, Atascadero, CA: Ridgeview, 321–358.
Sellars, Wilfrid (1996) *Naturalism and Ontology*, Atascadero, CA: Ridgeview.
Stroud, Barry (2000) "Mind, Meaning and Practice", in: *Meaning, Understanding, and Practice*, Oxford: Oxford University Press, 170–192.
Thompson, Michael (2008) "The Representation of Life", in: *Life and Action*, Cambridge, MA: Harvard University Press, 25–82.
Wiggins, David (1997) "Languages as Social Objects", in: *Philosophy* 72, 499–524.
Williamson, Timothy (2006) "Conceptual Truth", in: *Proceedings of the Aristotelian Society*, Suppl. Vol. 801–41.
Wittgenstein, Ludwig (2001 [1981]) *Remarks on the Foundations of Mathematics*, 3rd edition, Oxford: Blackwell.
Wittgenstein, Ludwig 1984) *Zettel*, in: *Werkausgabe*, vol. 8, Frankfurt am Main: Suhrkamp.
Wright, Crispin (1980) *Wittgenstein on the Foundations of Mathematics*, London: Duckworth.
Wright, Crispin (1986) "Rule-Following, Meaning and Constructivism", in: C. Travis (ed.): *Meaning and Interpretation*, Oxford: Blackwell, 271–297.

Form(s) of Life after Wittgenstein

Avner Baz
Wittgenstein and the Difficulty of What Normally Goes Without Saying

Abstract: What Wittgenstein calls 'form of life' might initially be characterized as the *background* apart from which a human utterance, or anything else that a person might do, would not have whatever sense it has for us. I argue that this topic belongs in a region of Wittgenstein's thought that presented him with real difficulties that he never came to resolve to his own satisfaction. The basic difficulty is just the difficulty of phenomenology – the difficulty of bringing out and elucidating, without *thereby* distorting, what is, normally and in essence, not attended to, reflected upon, or articulated. I suggest, however, that Wittgenstein's struggles in this area reveal not only the inherent difficulty of phenomenology, but also inherent limitations of his method of *grammatical* investigation. This is brought out by contrasting that method with Merleau-Ponty's *phenomenological* treatment of non-objectivized, perceptual experience, where that includes our perceptual relation to what Wittgenstein calls 'our form of life'.

1 'Form of Life' and the Conditions of Sense

I do not know what exactly Wittgenstein meant by 'form of life'. But if there is anything I've learned from Wittgenstein, it is that attempts to answer that question by trying to identify a *something* – some worldly constellation, or type of worldly constellation, that is there anyway and to which Wittgenstein's 'form of life' may simply be attached as a label – are more likely to lead to confusion, and to illusions of sense sustained by enticing pictures, than to insight. If we want to see what Wittgenstein meant by 'form of life', he himself has taught us, we need to ask ourselves what work that notion was meant to do in his articulation of his thoughts – what he was trying to get at when he invoked the notion of 'form of life'.

And I don't think there is a simple answer to *that* question. My own sense is that the notion of 'form of life' belongs in a region of Wittgenstein's thought that presented him with real difficulties that he never came to resolve to his own satisfaction. I might initially characterize that region by saying that it has to do with the *conditions* (*Bedingungen*) of sense – the *background* apart from which a human utterance, or anything else that a person might (intentionally) do, would not have whatever sense it has for us. (And let me emphasize at the outset that I take, and take Wittgenstein to take, the distinction between sense and non-sense to be basic – not groundable in anything else and therefore, in an important sense, inexplicable. "I must *begin*", Wittgenstein says, "with the distinction between sense and nonsense. Nothing is possible prior to that. I can't give it a foundation" (Wittgenstein 1974: 81). So when I talk about the conditions of sense, I'm not talking about conditions for *generating* sense out of what is senseless.)

What is the background apart from which some given utterance, or series of utterances, would not have the sense it has for us? The answer to this question turns out to be *very* complicated. Take, for example, an everyday exchange in which someone – call him Austin – wishes to find out whether such and such. Someone else – call her Informer – tells Austin that such and such. Austin then asks 'How do you know?'; and Informer responds by telling Austin her basis for thinking, and saying, that such and such. Austin may then be satisfied, and proceed as if such and such, or unsatisfied, in which case he may challenge Informer's basis, or its adequacy for supporting her claim, or turn to look for a different source of information, or proceed without assuming that such and such, taking suitable precautions... What is the background apart from which this imagined exchange would not have the sense it has? What must one be familiar with, and moreover somehow *alive to* – in a sense that will later be explicated – in order to understand the exchange?

Keeping in mind that sense comes in various degrees of determinacy, and that understanding too comes in degrees, I think we could here usefully distinguish between things one would need to be familiar with and alive to in order to understand *such* exchanges, and things one would need to be familiar with and alive to in order to understand *this* exchange. The latter may include such things as Austin's practical interests and what is at stake for him in whether such and such, and what he *already* knows, or takes for granted, and the nature of his relationship with Informer and why he turned to *her* for information. The former include such things as the human practice of asking others for needed information and relying, or else deciding not to rely, on the information they provide; and the related practice of giving others assurance, and the significance of accepting, or rejecting, another person's assurance; and the practice of asking 'How do you know?' or otherwise inviting others to give us their basis for saying that such and such, and of challenging other people's bases, and responding to such challenges ...

These are only *some* of the things one would need to be familiar with and alive to in order to understand the imagined exchange; and we have barely begun to so much as indicate the background apart from which the exchange would not have the sense it has. The list could be extended indefinitely, and in any number of directions. There is, for example, all that one would need to be familiar with and alive to in order to understand 'such and such' as uttered by Austin and Informer on *that* occasion; and similarly with respect to the words Informer uses to give her basis, and the words Austin then uses to challenge that basis, and so on. And since the proper understanding of those words is partly a function, not of meanings separable from use – Wittgenstein has shown us that *those* are theoretical posits incapable of doing that for which they were posited – but of the history of their employment, that history too is part of the background apart from which Austin and Informer's exchange would not have the sense it has, and therefore part of what they, and anyone who understands them, must be drawing and relying upon, however distantly or indirectly.

Also part of the background of the exchange that affects its sense are what we might call general facts of human nature, such as the fact that different people have different risk tolerances, and that our practices normally allow for a range of acceptable tolerances (though in any actual exchange, the difference between what's acceptable to some particular participant and what isn't may be slight); or the fact that some people are more trusting of other people than others, and that here too our practices normally allow for a range of acceptable levels of trust (though, again, in any actual exchange, the difference between what's acceptable to some particular participant and what isn't may be slight).

And then, at the background of all of *that*, there are what we might call metaphysical facts that contribute, distantly but essentially, to the sense of the exchange, such as the fact that we are embodied and finite – bound to a particular point of view, epistemically (as well as, of course, morally) fallible, susceptible to such things as injury, disease, fatigue, hunger, and death. And there are what we might call phenomenological facts that contribute to the sense of this, or any other exchange, such as the fact that from the moment we open our eyes to the world we find ourselves sharing it with others, whose bodies we almost immediately perceive and respond to as intentional and expressive unities, whose points of view may be more or less similar, but never identical, to ours, and with whom we may come to have various kinds of relationships, which may then be challenged, broken, and restored in indefinitely many ways ... (I note that though I follow Wittgenstein here in using the notion of '(very general) *facts*', I take this talk of facts to be, not wrong, but potentially very misleading, for it encourages an objectivist, third personal perspective; and from that perspective neither the sense of an utterance, nor the way that sense is affected by the utterance's background, may truly come into view.)

I have tried to give some sense, however rough, of what I mean when I talk about the background apart from which an utterance, or an exchange, would not have its sense for those capable of perceiving and responding to that sense. I think this background is what Wittgenstein means to gesture at when he talks about 'form(s) of life'. And I think it is clear why he says that our form of life – as opposed, say, to the builders' – is "complicated" (PPF: i, §1): any direction one might go to bring out, and spell out, the background contributing to endowing some particular human utterance with some particular, more or less determinate, sense, immediately branches off into indefinitely many others; and the different branches may then be seen as internally related – each contributing to the sense, or significance, of the others. This is the deep truth in Stanley Cavell's referring to our form of life as "a whirl of *organism*" (Cavell 1969: 52, my emphasis). To understand a sentence, Wittgenstein says, is to understand a language (PIr: §199); and to understand a language, he more or less also says, is to understand a form of life (see PIr: §19). That is what my opening example of the exchange between Informer and Austin was meant to illustrate.

Wittgenstein also says that a form of life is "what is to be accepted", "what is given" (PPF: xi, §345), in the sense, I take it, that every time we speak or think, or perceive and respond to the speech of others, we are *always already* responsive and beholden to it, and drawing upon it – playing with it, so to speak, more or less creatively. Even when we attempt to throw the whole of our world into doubt, as Descartes did in his first Meditation, we rely on a background of worldly conditions of sense that cannot, as such, be doubted.[1] The topic of this paper is the difficulty of seeing aright our relation to that background. In particular, this paper concerns Wittgenstein's difficulties in doing justice to that relation.

2 Stage Setting: Kant and the Difficulty of Understanding Our Relation to the Worldly Conditions of Sense

I said that the notion of 'form of life' belongs in a region of Wittgenstein's thought that presented him with real difficulty. The bulk of this paper will be devoted to elucidating the difficulty, as I see it. One way to characterize the difficulty goes through Kant's *Critique of Pure Reason*, which argues that seemingly unavoidable but at the same time apparently insurmountable traditional philosophical 'antinomies' arise when we imagine that it should be possible for words such as 'cause', 'effect', 'part', 'whole', 'one', 'many', 'simple', 'divisible', 'begin-

---

[1] This is one central lesson of the 'Cogito' chapter in Merleau-Ponty's *Phenomenology of Perception* (PP).

ning', 'end', and so on, to apply, truly or falsely, to the world 'as it is in itself'– that is, as it is apart from *our* making true or false empirical judgments about it, and apart from certain conditions that according to Kant make such judgments possible. When we attempt to employ our words apart from those conditions, Kant says, we produce not judgments (true or false), but "nonsense" (Kant 1998: A 485/B 513), which Kant at one point glosses in terms of our failing to put our words to any "use" (*Gebrauch*) (Kant 1998: A 247/B 304). So for Kant, as for Wittgenstein, philosophical problems arise when "language goes on holiday" (PIr: §38) – when we imagine ourselves to be employing our words even though the conditions for their felicitous employment are missing (or not properly drawn upon). Kant likens those sense-conditions to the air resistance that makes it possible for birds to fly, and likens the philosopher to a bird who thinks she could fly (even better) in a vacuum (see Kant 1998: A 5/B 8). Strikingly similarly, Wittgenstein likens those conditions to the friction that makes walking possible, and likens the philosopher to someone who thinks he could walk (even better) on slippery ice (see PIr: §107).

For the Kant of the first *Critique*, however – and herein lies a fundamental difference between him and Wittgenstein[2] – the successful employment of words is understood in terms of what he calls 'judgments', which he understands as not-essentially-linguistic mental acts, performed by some not-essentially-embodied transcendental subject, of subsuming sensible intuitions under concepts. The conditions of (making) sense, for Kant, are the "conditions of sensibility" (Kant 1998: A 240/B 300; see also A 239/B 298), by which he means space and time – the 'forms' to which sensible intuitions must conform if they are to become subsumable under *concepts*, in judgment. For the author of the first *Critique*, sense is essentially *conceptual*, and therefore *general:* though a concept would be 'empty' apart from its link to sensible intuitions, it essentially transcends any one, or any finite set, of its instances; and it abstracts from indefinitely many differences among its instances.[3]

What Kant calls 'judgment' is not *essentially* – or at least he does not seem to take it to essentially be – a worldly act that depends for its sense on a background of shared linguistic practices and on its particular place in history (both the history of the judger herself and the history of her community, and culture), and which positions the judger significantly in relation to others, in a world that she *already* shares with them. Not only does Kant make it seem as

---

2 I elaborate on this difference in Baz 2016a.
3 It should be noted that in the third *Critique* (Kant 2000), Kant clearly recognizes the possibility, and reality, of non-conceptual but nonetheless inter-subjectively sharable, perceivable unity and sense. It's the possibility, and reality, of what he calls "beauty".

if all that's required for sense is an encounter between a lonely transcendental subject armed with a priori categories and sensible intuitions, but there are moments, most notably perhaps in the 'Second Analogy of Experience', in which he argues that it is only by way of the application of concepts in judgment that we move from a "merely subjective succession" of *Vorstellungen* with no "relation to an object" to a world we can share with others (Kant 1998: A 196–197/B 241– 242).[4]

A way of putting an insight shared by Wittgenstein and Austin, on the one hand, and phenomenologists such as Merleau-Ponty and Heidegger on the other, is that what may plausibly and intelligibly be thought of as the application of concepts in judgments takes place in a world that is *already* shared with others. Merleau-Ponty refers to that world as the "ante-predicative" "phenomenal world" – the world we must already be responding to, and engaged with, in order to produce true or false judgments, or predications; and Heidegger famously protests, in response to Kant and the philosophical tradition that culminated with him, that the real scandal of traditional philosophy is the continued attempt to think of the human subject as not essentially tied to an intersubjectively shared world that is "ready-to-hand" before it becomes "present-at-hand" – that is, before it becomes the object of true or false assertions (Heidegger 1962: 249).

In the *Phenomenology of Perception*, Merleau-Ponty says that there are moments in the Transcendental Dialectic in which Kant seems to recognize the worldly and intersubjectively-sharable background of the application of concepts. Merleau-Ponty says that this is an important insight that Kant seems to "forget" in the Transcendental Analytic (PP: 304). Though he doesn't expand on this last remark, I believe Merleau-Ponty has in mind moments in the Dialectic in which reason's demand for the 'unconditioned' or 'absolute' – the demand that, when combined with the idea of the empirical world as a thing in itself, generates the antinomies – is presented not merely as the demand to transcend the conditions of sensibility, but also, even primarily, as the demand to transcend the *temporal unfolding* of empirical investigation, or, as Kant refers to it, "the successive synthesis of the manifold of intuition" (Kant 1998: A 417/ B 444). Later on, he refers to it – to the natural home, as it were, of our transcendental categories and empirical concepts – as "the advance of experience [*Fortschritt der Erfahrung*]" or as "empirical advance [*empirische Fortschritt*]" (Kant 1998: A 493/B 521; see also A 479/B 507). On (what I would regard as) a charitable reading, Kant is here alluding to the intersubjectively shared *practice* of empirical inquiry – a practice whose temporal unfolding, or succession, is *neither* cau-

---

[4] A similar idea may be found in Frege (cf. 1956: 309).

sally determined *nor* merely subjective, or metaphysically private. He is thereby also tacitly alluding to the worldly, historical background apart from which that practice would not be the practice that it is, would not have the sense it has for us.

What matters for present purposes, however, is not whether Kant recognizes the worldly, inter-subjectively sharable conditions of (making) sense. What matters is that *the Kantian account of what he calls "Erfahrung" does not give us the resources for understanding our relation to that worldly background.* "We can understand", Kant says, "only that which brings with it, in intuition, something corresponding to our words" (Kant 1998: A 277/B 333), and that may be fine as far as our relation to the world we speak *of* is concerned; but it does not help us recognize, let alone understand, our relation to the world we speak *in*. And yet, it is a world that we evidently perceive and respond to with (at least some) *understanding* – albeit not the sort of understanding that formulates itself in objective, true or false, judgments. "The Kantian subject posits a world", Merleau-Ponty writes, "but, in order to be able to assert a truth, the actual subject must in the first place have a world, that is, sustain round about it a system of meanings whose reciprocities, relationships, and involvements do not require to be made explicit in order to be exploited" (PP: 129). "The world", he writes in another passage that alludes to Kant, "is not what I think, but what I live through" (PP: xvi–xvii).[5] Now of course, one could presumably turn one's attention to any element of the world we live through and speak in, and form judgments or make assertions about it; but one would thereby do nothing to elucidate the nature of *our relation* to the worldly background of any such judgment or assertion. And this brings us back to Wittgenstein.

3 Wittgenstein and the Difficulty of What Normally Goes Without Saying

Wittgenstein, I suggested at the opening of this paper, was struggling in his final years to articulate an understanding that would satisfy him of our relation to the worldly background conditions of sense – in particular, the sense of human discourse. Before I say more about Wittgenstein's difficulty as I see it, let me emphasize that for much of his later work clarity about the nature of that relation

---

5 This last passage strikingly echoes Emerson who wrote in *Experience*, almost a hundred years earlier, in a passage that also seems to have Kant in mind, "I know that the world I converse with in the city and in the farms is not the world I *think*" (Emerson 1983: 491).

is not essential. The Wittgensteinian work of grammatical investigation and dissolution of philosophical difficulties is carried out from *within* the perspective we all occupy as competent speakers of our language. As competent speakers, we rely, draw, and play upon features of our form of life; and so we do as well when we engage in the sort of work exemplified in the first part of the *Investigations*. And for *that*, it is not essential that we be clear on the nature of our relation to what we rely, draw, and play upon, *as we rely, draw, and play upon it*. When we do wish to clarify that relation, however, the Wittgensteinian grammatical investigation can only take us so far.

The remarks from Wittgenstein's final years collected in *On Certainty* and elsewhere, show him struggling with questions concerning our relation to the worldly conditions of sense. One source of difficulty is his tendency to think of that relation as a relation to *propositions*, or to something that is *propositionally articulated* – a tendency encouraged, no doubt, by the fact that he was responding, in part, to G. E. Moore's *Defense of Common Sense* (in Moore 1993). But, as Wittgenstein himself sometimes acknowledges (cf. Wittgenstein 1969: §204 and §402), the worldly background against which we make this or that judgment, or commit ourselves to the truth of this or that proposition – though it is a background apart from which that judgment or proposition would not have had the sense it has for us – is not, for us, there and then, the object of judgment or propositionally articulated.

Another, related source of difficulty for Wittgenstein is the (broadly Kantian) dichotomy between what he calls "seeing" and what he calls "acting". When he finds that talking about our relation to the background of our language-games in terms of "seeing"– which he in turn understands in terms of "propositions striking us immediately as true" (Wittgenstein 1969: §204) – falsifies that relation, he tends to recoil into putting it in terms of "acting" (cf. Wittgenstein 1969: §204 and §402). But while it is true, and important, that our relation to the worldly conditions of sense is not aptly thought of in terms of certain propositions striking us as true, and also true, and important, that making and responding to sense – verbally expressed or otherwise – is an *activity* that positions us in a world shared with others and would be impossible apart from a suitable worldly background, neither of these two points does much to illuminate the nature of our relation to these conditions, or that background.

Moreover, if it could be shown that, and how, perception makes present to us a world that has more or less determinate sense for us, and to which we immediately respond in one way or another, *even apart from making judgments about what we perceive, or otherwise representing it truly or falsely*; and if it could also be shown that the world *as perceived* and *responded to* prior to being *thought*, or *thought (or talked) about*, always has the structure of figure and background that are *internally related* – in the sense that how the figure presents itself to us is not independent of its perceived background, and vice versa; and if it could further be shown that perception is not the merely passive reception of stimuli, but that we play an active role in generating and sustaining that pre-objective perceived sense – where that includes effecting its structure of figure and background; then we may find that we may aptly be said to *perceive* the worldly background of linguistic sense, and that only certain deeply entrenched notions about what perception *must* be (what 'perception' *must* mean) have prevented us from seeing this. When Merleau-Ponty speaks, in the passage quoted above, of our ability to sustain round about us "a system of meanings whose reciprocities, relationships, and involvements do not require to be made explicit in order to be exploited", he means to be telling us something about *perception*, and about *the world as perceived* – "the phenomenal world", as he calls it. But he is well aware of the fact that he is working against three long-standing philosophical proclivities: the empiricist-naturalist prejudice of supposing that what we perceive is, or is essentially determined by, what physically impinges on our sense organs; the rationalist prejudice of supposing that what we perceive is essentially propositionally articulated, or has the sort of 'content' that propositions may have; and the tendency, shared by both empiricists-naturalists and rationalists of various stripes, of thinking about perception from an objectivist, third personal perspective – a perspective from which the perception of *meaning*, or *meaningfulness*, cannot truly come into view. The perception of Wittgensteinian aspects, I will now turn to suggest, effectively undermines all of the above prejudices, and thereby provides important clues about our relation to the background conditions of sense.

4 Bringing the Phenomenal World into View by way of Aspect Perception

Our relation to our form of life, or to what I have been calling the worldly background conditions of sense – being a relation to *meaningful phenomena in their meaningfulness* – may not aptly be understood, or even so much as recognized, from the objectivist, mechanistic perspective of empirical science. From that perspective, sense, or meaning, does not come into view, and neither does its perception. Nor, I have argued, may that relation aptly be understood as a cognitive, judgment-based relation, in the Kantian sense. If we are to make sense of that relation, we need to find room for – and recognize the reality of – perception of (and response to) *sense* that is not cognitive, not propositional or conceptual. In other words, and following Merleau-Ponty, we need to find room for, and recognize, the *phenomenal world* – the world *as perceived* and *responded to* prior to, and apart from, being *thought*, or thought (or talked) *about*, or otherwise *represented* truly or falsely.

One type of experience that brings out in a rather dramatic way the difference between the phenomenal world and the objective world, and brings out the role we play in effecting the non-discursive unity and sense of the former, is the dawning, or lighting up, of what Wittgenstein calls "aspects". When an aspect dawns, we see the object differently – its perceived *overall unity and sense*, its *physiognomy*, changes; and yet we *know* that, objectively, it hasn't changed. That is the sense in which "everything changes and yet nothing changes" when an aspect lights up for us (see Wittgenstein 1980b: 474). And seeing aspects is "subject to the will": not so much, or primarily, in the sense that we can see them at will, but rather in the sense that it makes sense both to *call upon others* to see something under this or that aspect – see it *as* this or that – and to *try* to see this or that particular aspect (PPF: xi, §256).

Moreover, when an aspect dawns on us, what dawns on us is not "a property of the object", Wittgenstein remarks, but rather "an internal relation [*interne Relation*] between it and other objects" (PPF: xi, §247). The notion of internal relation, I wish to suggest, is key to understanding our relation to the background against which things – including human utterances – present themselves to us as having some particular (more or less determinate) sense. The notion, as used in this context, is drawn from Gestalt psychology and is, importantly, a *perceptual* notion, not an objective, third personal notion. (Among elements of the objective world, only external relations may hold; and those are precisely the relations that empirical concepts enable us to capture. In the objective world, an object's being blue and its being made of wool are two separate properties; but in the phenomenal world, the blue of a carpet (for example) "would never be the same blue were it not a woolly blue" (PP: 313).)

Two (or more) perceived things (objects, elements) stand in an internal relation to each other when their perceived qualities are not independent of the perceived relation between them. The duck-rabbit provides a simple and clear illustration of this: when you see it as a rabbit, say, you see the two "appendages" as ears; but your seeing them as ears is not independent of your seeing the whole thing as a rabbit. Perceptually, the ears are (seen as) ears only when the whole thing is (seen as) a rabbit, which means that the ears – when seen *as ears* – are internally related to the other parts of the rabbit-aspect.

According to Gestalt psychology, and this much it shares with Merleau-Ponty (cf. PP: 3–4), what we perceive, at the most basic level, is not atomic sensations that by themselves are devoid of any sense, or significance, and which we then somehow synthesize into significant, intelligible wholes. Rather, we (normally) perceive unified, significant wholes, where the perceived qualities of the elements of a perceived whole, and so the specific contributions those elements make to the overall perceived significance of that whole, are not perceptually independent of that perceived overall significance, and so are internally related to each other. This reaffirms Kant's anti-empiricist dictum that synthesis comes before analysis and is not mechanically given, but rather is actively projected and sustained by the subject (cf. Kant 1998: B 130), except that the synthesis here does *not* take the propositional form of empirical judgment, and so is *not* secured by empirical concepts.⁶

In order to appreciate the way in which the notion of 'internal relation' can help us understand our relation to the background conditions of sense, however, we need to see that the notion applies much more broadly than the duck-rabbit illustration suggests. To begin to see this, recall that Wittgenstein refers to the dawning aspect as an internal relation between the object one is looking at and *other* objects. Take the experience Wittgenstein uses to introduce the concept of "noticing an aspect": being struck by the similarity between two faces (PPF: xi, §113). What dawns here is an *internal* relation between the one face and the other, as Wittgenstein suggests, precisely because the perceived relation – of similarity – is inseparable from the perceived change in the overall physiognomy or expression of the face. One *sees* the other face *in* the face one is looking at, so the perceived qualities of each of the two faces that make them bear a similarity to each other are not independent, perceptually, experientially, from our perception of the similarity.⁷

The next thing to note is that internal relations hold not just among the perceived elements of perceived objects, or between one perceived object and some other, particular object (as in the case of the two faces), but also between the perceived physiognomies of objects (broadly construed) and the background against which they are perceived. The internal relation between some perceived figure and its background is illustrated in Wittgenstein's remark that "a smiling mouth smiles only in a human face" (PIr: §583). In the *Brown Book*, Wittgenstein

---

6 I argue at some length that Wittgensteinian aspects may not aptly be identified with, or in terms of, empirical concepts, in Baz 2016b.

7 Of course, they *could be:* we could recognize an objectively establishable similarity between the faces – a similarity that may be *known* to be there, objectively, and which does not depend on anyone's visual experience of the face (that's just what it means for it to be objective). But that would not be the seeing of a Wittgensteinian aspect – the *seeing* of one thing *as* another. As Wittgenstein notes, even the person he calls "aspect-blind" and defines as someone "lacking in the capacity to see something *as something*" should be able to recognize objective similarity and "execute such orders as 'Bring me something that looks like *this*'" (PPF: §257).

gives a similar example of friendly eyes in a friendly face (cf. Wittgenstein 1958: 145). He notes that even though the eyes *are* (perceived as) friendly, and even though their friendliness does contribute essentially to the (perceived) friendliness of the face, those very same eyes – or eyes objectively, geometrically, identical to them – could feature in a face that was not (perceived as) friendly, in which case they would not be (perceived as) friendly.

The context-sensitivity of the perceived overall significance, or physiognomy, of anything we perceptually attend to, and the internal relation between figure and background, manifest themselves at every level: just as a mouth has its particular expression only in the context of a particular face, so is the perceived expression of a face internally related to a worldly context, however indeterminate, apart from which it would not have been, for the perceiver, *that* expression.[8] When, for example, some particular schematic drawing of a face strikes you, as it struck Wittgenstein, as having the expression of "a complacent businessman, stupidly supercilious, who though fat, imagines he's a lady killer" (Wittgenstein 1958: 162), the picture-face is, for you, internally related to a suitable worldly context: its having *that* expression, and therefore its invoking *that* context for its perceiver, is not separable from its relation to that context.

Wittgenstein gives another clear, if also characteristically non-theoretical, expression to the internal relation between perceived figure and its background, in the following remark:

> Look at a long familiar piece of furniture in its old place in your room. You would like to say: "It is part of an organism". Or "Take it outside, and it is no longer at all the same as it was", and similar things. And naturally one isn't thinking of any *causal* dependence of one part on the rest. Rather it is like this: [...] [I]f I tried taking it *quite* out of its present context, I should say that it had ceased to exist and another had got into its place.
>
> One might even feel like this: "Everything is part and parcel of everything else [*Es gehört alles zu allem*]" (*external and internal relations* [my emphasis, AB]). Displace a piece and it is no longer what it was. Only in this surrounding is this table this table. (Wittgenstein 1980a: 339)

In the next section, I will say something about Wittgenstein's tentative tone here, and in similar moments in which he is moved to describe perceptual experience. But for Merleau-Ponty, what Wittgenstein says here is just right *when said about the phenomenal world*, and may be said without the tentativeness: in the world *as perceived*, prior to reflection and objectification, everything *is* part and parcel

---

8 Creators of comics know that it is possible to change dramatically the perceived expression of a drawn face – however realistically it is drawn – just by changing what the character is given to say, or think.

of everything else – everything is internally related to everything else, however remotely and indeterminately. This, Merleau-Ponty suggests, is the phenomenological truth in Leibniz's *Monadology* (PP: 67–68).

And this, I wish to propose, is how we should think of the relation between an utterance and the context in which it has the sense it has for us: they are internally related. Just as friendly eyes are only friendly in a friendly face, and the table you are looking at would not be what it is, *perceptually, experientially*, if moved to a different context, so would some uttered form of words not have quite the same sense in a different context.

This, if you will, is just the context-sensitivity of linguistic sense that semantic 'contextualists' such as David Lewis, Charles Travis, Robyn Carston, and François Recanati, have argued for, sometimes following Wittgenstein and Austin. A good way of summarizing some of the work I have done thus far in this paper, as well as some work I have done elsewhere, would be to offer the following additions and amendments to the basic and (I assume) familiar contextualist account:

1. Contemporary contextualists have tended to be representationalist about language: they have focused exclusively on utterances assessable in terms of truth and falsity, and have thought about linguistic sense exclusively in terms of that assessment. I have argued elsewhere (Baz 2012 and 2017) that this representationalism follows neither Wittgenstein nor Austin, and has led contextualists to misrepresent, in philosophically significant ways, the ordinary and normal functioning of philosophically troublesome words such as 'know' and its cognates.
2. In this paper, I have made explicit a crucial point that has remained implicit in extant contextualist accounts: on the contextualist account, just as on mine, we *must somehow* be perceptually alive to the context against which our own words, and those of others, have their particular sense for us; but, I have argued, whether we are using our words representationally or not, their relation to the context against which they have their particular sense for us – and therefore *our* relation to that context as we employ them – *cannot itself be one of representing it truly or falsely*. In other words, even when our words represent this or that truly or falsely, they do not represent the context that makes it possible for them to successfully do so. Nor can *our* perceptual relation to that context, *as* we attend to *that* utterance, be one of representing it truly or falsely, on pain of infinite regress of representations of contexts of representations of contexts; but also, even more importantly, on pain of dissolving the figure-background

structure that is essential to the perception of anything, including linguistic sense.⁹

3. Whereas contemporary contextualists have focused on contextual features that *change* between one utterance featuring some word or expression and another utterance featuring that same word or expression (in order to bring out the context-sensitivity of linguistic sense), I have, in this paper, expanded significantly the scope of 'the context of an utterance', to include worldly conditions that remain stable, or anyway *relatively* stable, over time and across different speech situations. In my initial example of the exchange between Austin and Informer, I drew a (rough) distinction between things one would need to be familiar with and alive to in order to understand *such* exchanges and things one would need to be familiar with and alive to in order to understand *that* particular exchange. Contemporary contextualists have (for good reason) tended to focus on the latter. But, as I understand Wittgenstein, it's background conditions of the former sort that constitute what he calls 'our form of life'.

4. The tendency in analytic philosophy has been to think of the context of an utterance as something like an objectively present container that is identifiable apart from the utterance itself, and to think about the determination of utterance-sense by the context of the utterance as an objective matter as well: utter *that* form of words in *that* context, the thought typically goes, and you'll get *that* sense (typically understood in terms of truth conditions and truth value).¹⁰ I believe the tendency has also been to think in a similar way about what Wittgenstein refers to by 'form of life'– to think, that is, that for any community of speakers, it should, *in principle*, be possible to identify and describe their form of life objectively. If, as I have suggested, the relation between an utterance and its context, or worldly conditions of sense, is *internal*, however, this common way of thinking about context, and about the relation between an utterance and its context, cannot be right. The perceived

---

9 As Merleau-Ponty puts it, "Even if I knew nothing of rods and cones, I should realize that it is necessary to put the surroundings in abeyance the better to see the object, and to lose in background what one gains in focal figure, because to look at the object is to plunge oneself into it, and because objects form a system in which one cannot show itself without concealing others. More precisely, the inner horizon of an object cannot become an object without the surrounding objects' becoming a horizon [...]" (PP: 67–68).

10 This way of thinking about the context of an utterance is perhaps most explicit in Lewis and his followers. Though Lewis came to despair of the possibility of *actually* being able to list all of the features of the context of *every* utterance that affect its sense – he called such features "indices" – and to say how each of them contributes to the utterance's sense, he never doubted that such a list may *in principle* be had (see Lewis 1980).

context of an utterance is not independent of its perceived sense: come to understand an utterance differently and you'll come to see its context differently, and vice versa.[11]

5. The context of an utterance is not a set of objectively establishable facts, but a set of *significant facts*, or better yet, a constellation of internally-related meaningful phenomena in their meaningfulness, as I earlier suggested. That we are mortal, and fallible, and dependent on each other in any number of ways, and have certain needs and desires and sensitivities, and have developed certain complex practices of passing information, and challenging it, and so on, are all facts that contribute to the sense of the exchange between Austin and Informer; and at least some of those facts may be seen as empirical and objective. But to the extent that those facts affect the *perceived sense* of the exchange, they do so as *significant, meaningful* facts; and significance or meaning is not, at bottom, empirically, objectively, establishable.

6. This in no way means that anything goes in the realm of sense. It is true, and important, that there is an ineliminable indeterminacy in the perception of sense (see PP: 6) – whether linguistically expressed or otherwise – and, relatedly, an ineliminable role for creativity in the perception (and production) of sense (cf. PP: 189; and Cavell's *Excursus on Wittgenstein's Vision of Language* in Cavell 1979). And it is also true, and important, that nothing ensures our agreement in what makes (what) sense to us, and under what conditions (see Cavell 1969: 52) – nothing is deeper than the fact, or extent, of our mutual attunement in what makes (what) sense to us and how (see Cavell 1979: 32). But for all that, one can no more choose or decide what sense some utterance has, and hence what will present itself as its context, and how, than one can choose or decide what expression someone had on her face when one saw her. Though the sense of an utterance is, ultimately, where we competent speakers find it, what sense we (can) truly and reasonably find in some utterance is "deeply controlled" (Cavell 1979: 183); and so is what presents itself to us as its context, or background, and how it presents itself.

This, in its undeniable sketchiness, concludes what I have had to say 'positively' about 'form of life' in Wittgenstein's later work. I have tried to show how aspect perception, as identified and characterized by Wittgenstein, points us in what I

---

[11] This is also how Sperber and Wilson 1986 have proposed that we think about the relation between the understanding of an utterance and the context of that understanding.

take to be the right direction for thinking about what Wittgenstein calls 'form of life' and our relation to it. In the next and final section, I will say a little more about the limitations of the Wittgensteinian grammatical investigation when it comes to elucidating our relation to the background, worldly conditions of sense, or to what he calls 'our form of life'.

5 The Natural Attitude and the Limitations of the Wittgensteinian Grammatical Investigation

Wittgenstein, I have suggested, was struggling in his final years with questions concerning our relation to the background apart from which what we say (and do) would not have had the sense it has for us. And the questions *are* difficult. The basic difficulty, as I see it, is just the difficulty of phenomenology – the difficulty of bringing out and elucidating, without *thereby* distorting, what is, normally and in essence, not attended to, reflected upon, or articulated. I want to propose, however, that Wittgenstein's struggles in this area reveal not only the inherent difficulty of phenomenology but also inherent limitations of his method of grammatical investigation.

Wittgenstein's method, or set of related methods, is designed to enable us to overcome philosophical difficulties that arise when "language goes on holiday" (PIr: §38) – that is, when we rely on our words to express thoughts, or to otherwise carry determinate commitments or implications (determinate enough, in any case, for generating and sustaining precisely those philosophical difficulties), even apart from *our* meaning them in some determinate (enough) way or another, in a context suitable for meaning them that way. In the face of philosophical difficulties *thus* generated, the best response may well be therapy by way of the deliberate assembling of "reminders" that aim at leading the words of our philosophizing "back from their metaphysical to their everyday use" (PIr: §116), thereby revealing the difficulties as difficulties with "*Luftgebäude*" (PIr: §118) that are sustained by unreasonable and ultimately nonsensical expectations that we have of those words.

The basic source of difficulty for the Wittgensteinian grammatical investigation vis à vis phenomenology in general, and our relation to the worldly conditions of sense in particular, is that *we do not normally talk about, or describe, or otherwise verbally express our relation to the background of our talking about or describing or expressing things*. This is an important truism that applies not just to linguistic expression: one does not normally attend to the background of one's attending to something (verbally or otherwise), and *cannot* attend to it *as background*.

To fully appreciate the significance of this truism, it should be noted that when we talk about or describe something made available to us in perception, our words, or the concepts they embody, being *generally* applicable, *necessarily* leave out some of what makes it the *particular* thing it is (see Wittgenstein 1981: 568);[12] and that something, in its particularity, must have been somehow perceptually present to us, however indeterminately, *prior to* our attending to it with words, for otherwise it would not have *drawn* our attention, and there would have been nothing for us to *try* be faithful (or unfaithful) to with our words (see PP: 28 ff.) (and for science to strive to "translate into precise language", as Merleau-Ponty puts it (PP: xviii)). There is therefore a sense in which even what we do speak of, or describe, belongs to the perceived background against which our words acquire their sense. And it should further be noted that when we talk about or describe something, we are normally not talking about or describing *our perceptual relation* to it.

So while it is true, and important, that *we never attend to the background of our attending to something*, and certainly do not attend to our relation to the *background as background*, I wish to propose that at the root of Wittgenstein's *special* difficulties in this area lies the tendency of our ordinary and normal employment of words to be focused on capturing and objectifying the world that comes into view in perception, rather than on our perceptual relation to that world – where that includes our perceptual relation to the background conditions of sense. It is for *this* reason that reminders about the ordinary and normal employment of our words are not going to shed much *direct* light on that relation, and *might* actually lead one astray.

In its tendency to bypass our perceptual experience in favor of its objects, our ordinary and normal employment of words participates in what Merleau-Ponty, following Husserl, refers to as our "natural attitude". The natural attitude, according to Husserl, is that of being "immersed naively in the world" and "accept[ing] the experienc*ed* as such" (Husserl 1998: 14, my emphasis) – focusing on "objects, values, goals", rather than "on the experienc*ing* of [one's] life" (Husserl 1998: 15, my emphasis; see also Husserl 1970: 119 and 144). Husserl's "bracketing", or *epoché*, is meant to counteract our tendency to focus on objects (broadly understood) and overlook our experiencing of them – to overlook, that is, how those objects actually present themselves to us, and how we relate to them, be-

---

[12] This basic point and its significance have recently been emphasized by Charles Travis (cf. Travis 2013: 187 and 269).

fore we begin to reflect on and theorize about perception from the perspective of the natural sciences, and therefore on the basis of what we take ourselves to already know, objectively, about what we perceive.

Merleau-Ponty invokes the 'natural attitude' and the difficulty it creates for the phenomenologist when he says, in the Preface to the *Phenomenology of Perception*, that "our existence is too tightly held in the world to be able to know itself as such at the moment of its involvement" (PP: xv). He comes back to that idea early in the first chapter of that book, when he says that "we are caught up in the world and [...] do not succeed in extricating ourselves from it" (PP: 5). This natural involvement with the world, which Merleau-Ponty later refers to as our "obsession with being" (PP: 70), culminates in the constitution of an objective world, which (failing to heed Kant's warnings!) we tend to think of as "a world in itself" (PP: 41) – fully and finally determinate, and wholly independent from our experience of it (cf. PP: 47). This, as I earlier noted, is the objectivist prejudice shared by both empiricists-naturalists and rationalists.

The main obstacle to understanding perception, and hence behavior, Merleau-Ponty argues, is the tendency to take the objective world – that is, the world as objectively construed – as the starting point of our theorizing about perception. In trying to reconstruct perception on the basis of what we take ourselves to already know objectively, we commit what Merleau-Ponty, following Köhler, calls "the experience error": "we make perception out of things perceived [...] And since perceived things themselves are obviously accessible only through perception, we end up understanding neither" (PP: 5). "Our perception", he similarly says later on, "ends in objects, and the object once constituted, appears as the reason for all the experience of it which we have had or could have" (PP: 67). The task of phenomenology, Merleau-Ponty writes, is therefore

> to rediscover phenomena, the layer of living experience through which other people and things are first given to us, the system of 'self-others-things' as it comes into being; to reawaken perception and foil its trick of allowing us to forget it as a fact and as perception in the interest of the object which it presents to us and of the rational tradition to which it gives rise. (PP: 57)

Now, if it is of the essence of normal perception to overlook itself in the interest of the object which it presents us – if, in other words, we do not perceive perception, do not perceptually attend to our perceptual relation to whatever it is we are perceiving and to the background against which we attend to it perceptually – then it is only to be expected that our ordinary and normal use of words would participate in, and reflect, that overlooking of our pre-reflective perceptual experience.[13] If that's right, then there is reason to worry that the Wittgensteinian grammatical investigation, insofar as it takes its bearing from the ordinary and normal use of our words, will only take us so far when it comes to elucidating non-objective, or non-objectivized, perceptual experience, where that includes our perceptual relation to what Wittgenstein calls 'our form of life'. And it might, moreover, lead us astray, by encouraging us to take the objectivist use of our words as primary, and to commit the experience error.[14]

To be sure, to project oneself imaginatively into situations of significant speech, as Wittgenstein's reminders invite us to do, necessarily involves making oneself alive to features of our form of life that contribute to the shaping of those situations and to the sense of anything we might say or do in them. I do not deny this. On the contrary, it has been my contention from the start that we must, *somehow*, be alive to the background conditions of sense, both in the course of everyday discourse and when engaged in the Wittgensteinian grammatical investigation. My point here is just that we do not primarily, or commonly, use language in order to represent, or for that matter express, our form of life *as* the background of our language-games, and how we relate to it as producers and perceivers of linguistic sense. And this means that our form of life *as the background of our language-games*, and our relation to it *as that background*, are bound to remain, precisely, *in the background* of the Wittgensteinian grammatical investigation. The difficulty is to make them come to the fore, without distorting them. This, at the most general level, is just the difficulty of phenomenology, and in the present case the difficulty of putting our relation to our form of life – qua the background of our language-games – into words, without thereby distorting it. My more recent proposal has been that the Wittgensteinian grammatical investigation is not best suited for *that* task.

It is worth noting in this connection that the later Wittgenstein was suspicious of phenomenology, and an important tenet of his grammatical investigation is that it is meant, among other things, to turn our attention *away* from our first-personal experiences. This comes out clearly and explicitly in the remarks on aspects, where Wittgenstein again and again calls upon his reader (or himself) to "*forget* that you have these experiences yourself" (Wittgenstein 1980b: 531), to think about aspect perception from a third person perspective (PPF: xi, §241 and §204), and not to try to "analyze your own inner experience"

---

13 In the appendix to Baz 2017, I give some evidence that our ordinary and normal use of words does partake of the natural attitude.
14 In the appendix to Baz 2017, I argue that, in his remarks on aspects, Wittgenstein is sometimes misled by grammar into taking the objectivist perspective on perception as primary – not just grammatically, but phenomenologically.

(PPF: xi, §188). This, I have argued elsewhere (Baz 2011), is an effective and well-motivated approach when it comes to the sort of philosophically troublesome concepts that are the focus of the first part of the *Investigations:* 'learning', 'understanding', 'meaning', 'naming', 'thinking', 'reading', 'intending', and so on. When it comes to concepts such as *those*, the attempt to elucidate them by way of reflection on the experiences we undergo when we learn, understand, think, intend, and so on, is bound to lead us astray. Here, what is needed is what Cavell has insightfully called Wittgenstein's "undoing of the psychologizing of psychology" (Cavell 1969: 91). But when we wish, not to disentangle conceptual entanglements, but to bring out and elucidate our pre-reflective perceptual *experience* – our relation to the world as it perceptually presents itself to us before we put it into words – we need, at the very least, to supplement the Wittgensteinian method of grammatical investigation that proceeds on the basis of "reminders" (PIr: §127) of the "kind of statements we make about phenomena" (PIr: §116); for we do not *normally* make *any* statements or otherwise talk about our pre-reflective, perceptual experience. Even words that might be thought to refer us to that experience – 'see', 'hear', 'feel', 'notice', and so on – are not normally used for describing, or expressing, that experience. On the common, 'primary' use of 'see', for example – that's Wittgenstein's "first use of 'see'" (PPF: xi, §111) – what someone saw, is, as Travis has noted, mostly a matter of what was there, anyway, objectively, to be seen (see Travis 2013: 411; see also 102; and Travis 2015: 47).[15]

Let me emphasize that I am *not* saying that the difficulty of phenomenology may not, in principle, be overcome, or that our language somehow prevents us, in principle, from overcoming it. The work of phenomenology – the work, as we may now put it, of uncovering the background, and our relation to it – might be never-ending (see PP: xiv), but it is not impossible; our words *may* be used for describing, or expressing, our perceptual experience and the world as it presents itself to us prior to being thought, or thought about. *That our words may thus be used is itself part of 'the grammar of our language'*, and therefore part of what the Wittgensteinian grammatical investigation may bring out. It is brought out, for example, in Wittgenstein's remarks on aspect perception. The "second use of 'see'" Wittgenstein describes at the opening of section xi, for example, does refer us to a particular sort of perceptual experience – namely, that of noticing, or being struck by, an aspect.

---

15 In the appendix to Baz 2017, I argue that while the first use of 'see' Wittgenstein describes *is*, grammatically, primary, in the sense that it is acquired first and that you couldn't acquire the second use Wittgenstein describes – that is, the 'seeing' of aspects – if you didn't already master the first, the second use of 'see' refers us to what is *phenomenologically* primary.

Still, it is one thing to bring out and elucidate the grammar of the phenomenological use of our words and its differences from their objectivist, or object-oriented, uses, and another thing to *do phenomenology* (just as it is one thing to bring out and elucidate the grammar of empirical science, or of aesthetic evaluation, and quite another thing to engage in empirical science, or in aesthetic evaluation). And what I've proposed is, first, that Wittgenstein's invocation of 'form (or forms) of life' was prompted by questions that call for the work of phenomenology, and, second, that his grammatical investigation suffers limitations in *that* area.

To be clear, it is open to Wittgenstein, just as it is open to Merleau-Ponty and to everyone else, to try to *describe* perceptual experience, including our perceptual relation to the background conditions of sense.[16] And this, as we saw in section 4, is something Wittgenstein does in some of his remarks. It should first of all be noted that in order to do phenomenology *well* one needs to do more than just recognize pre-objective, pre-conceptual perceptual experience and attempt to describe it (as many people do, at least to some extent and more or less successfully, in the course of everyday life).[17] But my more basic point has been that when Wittgenstein does *that*, he is no longer engaged in the grammatical investigation of philosophically troublesome words or concepts by way of the perspicuous representation of language-games, but rather is moving, as Cavell puts it, "to regions of a word's use which cannot be assured or explained by an appeal to its ordinary language games" (Cavell 1979: 189).

If, as I have proposed, the primary uses, hence meanings, of our words tend to partake of the natural attitude and focus, or focus us, on objects and their objective constellations, rather than on our perceptual experience of those objects and constellations, including our experience of the background against which

---

16 The *Phenomenology of Perception* is full of such descriptions: for example, when Merleau-Ponty describes the human subject as sustaining round about her a system of meanings whose reciprocities, relationships, and involvements do not require to be made explicit in order to be exploited (PP: 129), or when he talks of the phenomenal body as "rising toward the world" (PP: 75), or talks of the hand when used for touching something as "shoot[ing] through like a rocket to reveal the external object [...]" (PP: 92), or talks of our phenomenal body, when we lean with our hands against a desk, as trailing behind our hands "like the tail of a comet" (PP: 100). As I go on to note in the text, it is of the essence of phenomenology that the phenomenologist will need to use his or her words creatively, as Merleau-Ponty does in such passages.

17 I say more about Merleau-Ponty's method of investigation in the appendix to Baz 2017. Importantly, Merleau-Ponty's investigation proceeds on the basis of careful examination of a wealth of empirical findings concerning normal and abnormal perception and behavior – the sort of examination that is almost entirely absent from Wittgenstein's later work.

we attend to them, then it is only to be expected that the phenomenologist will need to use her words creatively – in what Wittgenstein calls their 'secondary meanings'. This, if you will, is part of the Wittgensteinian grammar of 'phenomenology'. But what it means is that when it comes to the work of phenomenology, one's philosophical footing is not going to be secured by reminding oneself how one's words are used "in the language which is their original home" (PIr: §116). That a displaced piece of furniture is no longer what it was, for example, or that everything is part and parcel of everything else, is not a piece of Wittgensteinian grammar. When it comes to the work of phenomenology, one still needs to avoid the "metaphysical" (empty, idle) use of one's words, if one wishes to make real progress; but leading those words *back* to their everyday use (PIr: §116) is not going to satisfy one's real need in this area.

References

Baz, Avner (2011) "Seeing Aspects and Philosophical Difficulty", in: Marie McGinn and Oskari Kuusela (eds.): *Handbook on the Philosophy of Wittgenstein*, New York: Oxford University Press.
Baz, Avner (2012) *When Words Are Called For*. Cambridge, MA: Harvard University Press.
Baz, Avner (2016a) "The Sound of Bedrock: Lines of Grammar between Kant, Wittgenstein, and Cavell", in: *European Journal of Philosophy* 24, 607–628.
Baz, Avner (2016b) "Aspects of Perception", in: Gary Kemp and Gabriele Mras (eds.): *Wollheim, Wittgenstein, and Pictorial Representation: Seeing-as and Seeing-in*, New York: Routledge.
Baz, Avner (2017) *The Crisis of Method in Contemporary Analytic Philosophy*, New York: Oxford University Press.
Cavell, Stanley (1969) *Must We Mean What We Say?* New York: Cambridge University Press.
Cavell, Stanley (1979) *The Claim of Reason*, New York: Oxford University Press.
Emerson, Ralph Waldo (1983) "Experience", in: *Essays and Lectures*, New York: Library of America, 469–492.
Frege, Gottlob (1956) "The Thought", in: *Mind* 65, 289–311.
Heidegger, Martin (1962) *Being and Time*, transl. J. Macquarrie and E. Robinson, New York: Harper & Row.
Husserl, Edmund (1970) *The Crisis of the European Sciences and Transcendental Phenomenology*, transl. D. Carr, Evanston, IL: Northwestern University Press.
Husserl, Edmund (1998) *The Paris Lectures*, transl. P. Koestenbaum, Norwell, MA: Kluwer.
Kant, Immanuel (1998) *Critique of Pure Reason*, transl. P. Guyer and A. Wood, New York: Cambridge University Press.
Kant, Immanuel (2000) *Critique of the Power of Judgment*, transl. P. Guyer and E. Mathews, New York: Cambridge University Press.
Lewis, David (1980) "Index, Context, and Content", in: Stig Kanger and Sven Öhman (eds.): *Philosophy and Grammar*, Dordrecht: Reidel, 79–100.

Merleau-Ponty, Maurice (1996) *Phenomenology of Perception*, transl. C. Smith, New York: Routledge. [PP]
Moore, George Edward (1993) *Selected Writings*, T. Baldwin (ed.), New York: Routledge.
Sperber, Dan and Deirdre Wilson (1986) *Relevance: Communication and Cognition*, Oxford: Blackwell.
Travis, Charles (2013) *Perception*, New York: Oxford University Press.
Travis, Charles (2015) "Suffering Intentionally?", in: M. Campbell and M. O'Sullivan (eds.): *Wittgenstein and Perception*, New York: Routledge, 45–62.
Wittgenstein, Ludwig (1958) *The Blue and Brown Books*, Oxford: Blackwell.
Wittgenstein, Ludwig (1969) *On Certainty*, G. E. M. Anscombe and G. H. von Wright (eds.), transl. G. E. M. Anscombe, New York: Harper and Row.
Wittgenstein, Ludwig (1974) *Philosophical Grammar*, R. Rhees (ed.), transl. A. Kenny, Oxford: Blackwell.
Wittgenstein, Ludwig (1980a) *Remarks on the Philosophy of Psychology*, Vol. I, G. E. M. Anscombe and G. H. von Wright (eds.), transl. G. E. M. Anscombe, Oxford: Blackwell.
Wittgenstein, Ludwig (1980b) *Remarks of the Philosophy of Psychology*, Vol. II, G. E. M. Anscombe and G. H. von Wright (eds.), transl. C. G. Luckhardt and M. A. E. Aue, Oxford: Blackwell.
Wittgenstein, Ludwig (1981) *Zettel*, G. E. M. Anscombe and G. H. von Wright (eds.), transl. G. E. M. Anscombe, Oxford: Blackwell.
Wittgenstein, Ludwig (2009) *Philosophical Investigations*, transl. G. E. M. Anscombe, P. M. S. Hacker and J. Schulte, Malden, MA: Wiley-Blackwell. [PIr, PPF]

Sandra Laugier
Wittgenstein. Ordinary Language as Lifeform

Abstract: The concept of form of life is simultaneously and inseparably overvalued and neglected in Wittgenstein's work. The author aims to understand the concept of form of life, or *lifeform* (as Cavell proposes to translate *Lebensform*), as an alternative to the concept of rules in the exploration of ordinary language. Cavell shows at once the fragility and the depth of our agreements, and he seeks out the nature of the necessities that emerge from our forms of life. Ordinary language philosophy as inherited by Cavell is thus anchored in an attention to language as it is commonly used, as part and milieu of our everyday interactions and conversations. Attention to ordinary language is also attention to neglected realities and to the constant risk of failure of conversation in everyday life. Recognizing the vulnerability of language – excuses, e. g., in their everyday recognition of human vulnerability and tragedy – allows us to recognize the human lifeform as itself vulnerable. Contemporary philosophy often sees recourse to the ordinary, to forms of life (as given), as a too-easy solution to skepticism. But the threat of destruction of forms of life (social and biological) in the present world gives the concept of *Lebensform* renewed reality and relevance:

> It is to turn us toward the unending political evaluation of the confrontation between need and rule, and to compare this with Emerson's recurrence to the collisions of power and form, that I have urged noticing the key ambiguity in Wittgenstein's concept of a form of life. The concept projects simultaneously, as I take it, an irreducibly horizontal ethnological or conventional axis crossing an irreducibly vertical biological axis, which is in effect to picture human existence as that life form which eternally criticizes itself – as it were from below and from beyond – or incessantly declines to. (Cavell 2010: 108)

1 Introduction

In his preface to Veena Das' book *Life and Words* Cavell (2007) notes that our ordinary language is ordinary insofar as we constantly render it foreign to ourselves, uncanny. He invokes the Wittgensteinian image of the philosopher as an explorer of a foreign tribe: as seen by this tribe, it is we who are foreign and strange to ourselves, "at home perhaps nowhere, perhaps anywhere." The intersection of the familiar and strange, shared by anthropology and philosophy, is where the concept of form of life is located:

> Wittgenstein's anthropological perspective is one puzzled in principle by anything human beings say and do, hence perhaps, at a moment, by nothing. (Cavell, *Introduction* to Das 2007: X)

The ordinary does not exactly mean the common. We no more know what is common than what is ordinary to us: it is not determined by a web of beliefs or shared dispositions. Common language nevertheless defines the ordinary: the ordinary (that is, everyday, shared life) is defined by the ordinary language philosophy of Wittgenstein and Austin. The thought of the ordinary is experiential, improvisational; it demands new forms of attention to the human form – and forms – of life. The concept of form of life is simultaneously and inseparably overvalued and neglected in Wittgenstein's work: it is seen either as the key to everything, or as an empty and shifting idea, one that Wittgenstein himself did not take seriously. My aim here is to understand the concept of form of life, or lifeform (as Cavell proposes to translate *Lebensform*), as an alternative to the concept of rules as a tool for exploring ordinary language.

I will follow the progression in Cavell's work from the question of shared language and usages (forms of life) to the question of sharing lifeforms, both of which are remarkably expressed in the Augustine quote that opens the *Investigations*; a sharing that does not merely mean being part of social structures or institutions but rather participating in everything that makes up the texture of human activities and existences. For Wittgenstein it is never enough to answer by saying "this is what we do." Skepticism is inherent in every human practice, especially language: all certitude or confidence in what we do (following a rule, counting, etc.) is modeled on the confidence we have in our shared uses of language.

Mere acceptance of forms of life, often mentioned in a so-called "quietist" tonality, is not enough either. Cavell shows at once the fragility and the depth of our agreements, and he seeks out the very nature of the necessity that for Wittgenstein emerges from our form of life. All of Cavell's work begins from the following three thoughts, which orthodox readings of Wittgenstein have consistently avoided:

– There is a rationality and an objectivity to the procedures founded on/in our "forms of life."
– A rule is neither a foundation nor an interpretation: it is just *there*, but this in no way diminishes its rigor. A unique aspect of Cavell's position is his redefinition of the necessity of ordinary usage and rules of language in terms of lifeforms and nature (the biological sense of life): it is this very particular understanding of nature that defines the ordinary.

– There is not, then, for Cavell, any "answer" to the skepticism that emerges from the fragility of our agreements. That our ordinary language is founded on nothing other than itself is not only a source of anxiety as to the validity of what we do and say, it is the revelation of a truth about ourselves that we do not want to recognize: the truth that "I" am the sole possible source of such validity. To refuse this, to attempt to overcome skepticism, is to end up reinforcing it. This is what Cavell means by his famous saying in *The Claim of Reason* that skepticism is *lived*. This is not an "existential" or romantic interpretation of Wittgenstein but rather an understanding of the fact that language is our form of life.

2 Categories of the Ordinary

Let us start with Cavell's hypothesis in *This New Yet Unapproachable America* that the distinctive feature of American thought, that which enables it to begin philosophy again in America, is its invention of the ordinary. This new frontier for philosophy – which is not a clean slate, but rather, as in Hollywood "remarriage" comedies, a second chance (Cavell 1981) – is a reversal of philosophy's two inveterate tendencies: on the one hand, the tendency to deny our ordinary language and lives as part of the philosophical pretension to transcend or correct them, and, on the other hand, the tendency to pretend that we already know what is common to us. The call to the ordinary, or the return to practices, is neither evidence nor solution: it is shot through with the "uncanniness of the ordinary."

It is from this perspective that we must understand Cavell's return to Emerson and Thoreau. Emerson asserts America's intellectual independence, with its appropriation of the ordinary, and contrasts it with Europe's tradition of sublimities in a passage from *The American Scholar:*

> I ask not for the great, the remote, the romantic; what is doing in Italy or Arabia; what is Greek art or Provençal minstrelry; I embrace the common, I explore and sit at the feet of the familiar, the low. Give me insight into today, and you may have the antique and future worlds. (Emerson 1982: 102)

Admittedly, the practice of turning to the "common" or the "low" has long existed in philosophy. But there is a new emphasis on the ordinary here. It is not a matter of praising common sense but rather of returning thought and attention to the ordinary – to the low, the close at hand, which stands in direct opposition to the great and the remote – which makes it possible to "know the meaning" of ordinary forms of life.

> What would we really know the meaning of? The meal in the firkin; the milk in the pan; the ballad in the street; the news of the boat; the glance of the eye; the form and the gait of the body. (Emerson 1982: 102)

Here Emerson expresses the demand for a distinctive American culture as an alternative to European culture, defined by this positive aspiration for the common. He describes, ahead of his time, the favored objects of American cinema and photography.

> His list in "The American Scholar" of the matters whose "ultimate reason" he demands of students to know – is a list epitomizing what we may call the physiognomy of the ordinary, a form of what Kierkegaard calls the perception of the sublime in the everyday. It is a list, made three or four years before Daguerre will exhibit his copper plates in Paris, epitomizing the obsessions of photography. (Cavell 1972: 150)

Here we see Cavell tentatively elaborating new categories of ordinary life. These are the elements of a "physiognomy," gait, or "look" of the ordinary, which philosophy, as well as cinema and photography, must now describe.

The transcendental question has shifted: the aim is no longer to determine the "ultimate reason" for phenomena of nature, but rather to establish a connection to the human form of life in all its detail and particularity. Note that for Emerson this new particularist and perceptual approach is inseparable from a new relationship between the classes.

> One of these signs is the fact that the same movement which effected the elevation of what was called the lowest class in the state, assumed in literature a very marked and as benign an aspect. Instead of the sublime and beautiful, the near, the low, the common, was explored and poeticized. That which had been negligently trodden under foot by those who were harnessing and provisioning themselves for long journeys into far countries, is suddenly found to be richer than all foreign parts. The literature of the poor, the feelings of the child, the philosophy of the street, the meaning of household life, are the topics of the time. (Emerson 1982: 102)

The poor, the child, the street, the household: these are the new objects that it will be necessary to *see*. Attention to ordinary life undermines the usual hierarchies, whether intellectual or social.

> What we are supplying are really remarks on the natural history of human beings [...] observations which no one has doubted, but which have escaped remark only because they are always before our eyes. (PI: §415)

> Where does our investigation get its importance from, since it seems to destroy everything interesting, all that is great and important? What we are destroying is nothing but houses of cards [*Luftgebäude*]. (PI: §118)

The search for the ordinary acquires its significance from the threat of skepticism – the threat of losing or becoming distant from the world. At the beginning of "Experience," Emerson associates this loss with the failure of speech, an impossibility to be in touch with one's words, to actually mean them – which renders it essentially inadequate, or – to use an Austinian concept – unhappy. It is this inadequacy of language that Emerson calls the conformity of his contemporaries, and that Thoreau denounces as "quiet desperation."

> Their every truth is not quite true. Their two is not the real two, their four not the real four; so that every word they say chagrins us, and we know not where to begin to set them right. (Emerson 1982: 181)

In their defense of the ordinary against the traditional philosophical wish to conceptualize and grasp reality, Emerson and Thoreau are the precursors of ordinary language philosophy, recommending attentive descriptions of reality: being *next* to the world, part of an ordinary life.

> The connection means that I see both developments – ordinary language philosophy and American transcendentalism – as responses to skepticism, to that anxiety about our human capacities as knowers. My route to the connection lay at once in my tracing both the ordinary language philosophy as well as the American transcendentalists to the Kantian insight that Reason dictates *what we mean by a world*. (Cavell 1988: 4)

The concept of form of life is an element of this response to skepticism: a life *in* ordinary language. As Cavell says, "Words come to us from a distance; they were there before we were; we are born into them. Meaning them is accepting that fact of their condition" (Cavell 1972: 64). The meaning of a word is its use: to borrow Cavell's Wittgensteinian phrase, "We do not know what 'Walden' means if we do not know what Walden is" (Cavell 1972: 27). And this applies to all the words employed by Thoreau, to which he gives new sense: morning (morning is when I am awakening and there is the dawn in me), the bottom of the pond (we do not know what the base is, or the foundation, until we have probed, like Thoreau, the bottom of Walden Pond), the sun (a morning star).

"Discovering what is said to us, just like discovering what we say, is to discover the exact place of where it is said; to understand why it is said at this precise place, here and now" (Cavell 1972: 34). This is the method of ordinary language: to see why, when, and in which circumstances we say what we say – because without its use a word is a "dead sign." Everything is already in front of us, before our eyes: we need to *see the visible*. Thus Thoreau, like Emerson, announces the project of the *Investigations:* to see the ordinary, which escapes us because it is too near to us, right beneath our eyes.

> What we are supplying are really remarks on the natural history of human beings; we are not contributing curiosities, however, but observations which no one has doubted, but which have escaped remark only because they are always before our eyes. (PI: §415)

One can turn here to a formulation by Foucault, who connects this ability to "see the visible" to ordinary language philosophy and its project of referring to usage to discover what is actually going on. He proposes *"une analyse critique de la pensée à partir de la manière dont on dit les choses"*:

> We have long known that the role of philosophy is not to discover what is hidden, but to render visible what precisely is visible – which is to say, to make appear what is so close, so immediate, so intimately linked to ourselves that, as a consequence, we do not perceive it. (Foucault 1994: 540–541)

The ordinary exists within this characteristic difficulty of accessing what is right before our eyes, of learning to see it, and is systematically neglected. Neglected because it is ... life itself.

> In other words, how much of a matter of course the given is. It would be the very devil if this were a tiny picture taken from an oblique, distorting angle. This which we take as a matter of course, *life*, is supposed to be something accidental, subordinate; while something that normally never comes into my head, reality! (NB: 44e)

In a democratic inversion of the sublime, the low always has to be reached. It is not a question of correcting the heritage of European philosophy or of creating new categories: rather, it is necessary to give another sense to inherited words such as "experience," "idea," "impression," "understanding," "reason," "necessity," and "condition," to bring them back from the immanent to the common, from the metaphysical to the ordinary. Emerson proposes his own version of categories in the epigraph to *Experience* with his list of "the lords of life":

> The lords of life, the lords of life, – / I saw them pass, / In their own guise, / Like and unlike, / Portly and grim; / Use and Surprise, / Surface and Dream, / Succession swift, and Spectral Wrong. (Emerson 1982: 285)

At first glance, the lords of life resemble categories of our experience, which govern our access to the world, as causality, substance, or totality do in Kant. But the list demonstrates that this cannot be. By identifying the lords as use, surprise, surface, dream, succession, evil, and temperament, Emerson acknowledges that a new list of concepts must be invented in order to describe the ordinary, those diverse materials "strewn along the ground." Forms of life demand new categories but also another sense of "mastery" – one that lets go of the desire to seize and grasp, "the most unhandsome part of our condition" (Emerson 1982: 288).

> This revolution is to be wrought by the gradual domestication of the idea of Culture. The main enterprise of the world for splendor, for extent, is the upbuilding of man. Here are the materials strewn along the ground. (Emerson 1982: 99)

If Emerson were satisfied with carrying on the arrangement of categories, merely replacing the traditional list (the European transcendental heritage) with a modernized, "Americanized" version, his contribution would be insignificant. To imagine categories of ordinary life changes the very idea of category. The idea of domesticating *culture* is not the same as mastering reality, because the ordinary can be neither conceptualized nor grasped. It is not a matter of rewriting the list of categories but rather of redefining their use: they are not meant for grasping reality conceptually, but for neighboring the world, the domestic. The revolution achieved by Emerson consists less in redefining categories than in remodeling what experience is. This is a project that connects him to James, Dewey, and Wittgenstein.

Our relation to the world is henceforth no longer a matter of (actively) applying categories of understanding to experience but of (passively) watching the lords of life pass by in the course of experience. They will emerge from experience – "I find them in my way" – as if the categories, instead of being imposed or posited, are simply to be patiently waited for, and found:

> Illusion, Temperament, Succession, Surface, Surprise, Reality, Subjectiveness – these are threads on the loom of time, these are the lords of life. I dare not assume to give their order, but I name them as I find them in my way. (Emerson 1982: 309)

Cavell subverts Kant through Emerson. The lords of life do not control our experience, but instead come from it, like forms emerging from a background: "I saw them pass." Thus, the categories of the ordinary themselves become the object of exploration. The transcendental question is no longer "How do we know from experience?" but instead "How do we approach the world? How do we *have an experience?*" Emerson expresses the skeptical situation in *Experience* with regard to the experience of grief, and generalizes to an experience of the world as a whole in terms, or under the category, of loss. Skepticism is the inability to have an experience. We are not so much ignorant as inexperienced. William James followed this thread of Emersonian thought in *The Will to Believe*, as did Dewey by exploring experience, and Wittgenstein, too, in his last writings on the philosophy of psychology, explored the "logical" connection of the "inner" to the "outer."

For Emerson, contrary to what "paltry" empiricism tells us, experience cannot teach us anything – not because it is insufficient, as traditional epistemology suggests, but because it does not touch us. Our attempts to master things, to grasp them materially and conceptually, distance us from them. This is what Emerson describes in *Experience* as "the most unhandsome part of our condition" (Emerson 1982: 288) – the fact that fleeting reality slips between our fingers at precisely the moment we clutch at it: it is un*hands*ome. It is our desire to grasp reality that causes us to lose it, that keeps us from an ordinary proximity with it, and cancels its availability or attractiveness (the fact that it is at hand, handsome). Emerson transforms the Kantian synthesis not by going the transcendental route but by doing the opposite, seeking to obtain immanence. This overcoming of synthesis *by the low*, and not by the high, is characteristic of Cavell's ambition of describing and viewing the ordinary world (Cavell 1971).

We need to give up on "cognitive rapaciousness," just as Wittgenstein insists in the *Blue Book* that we must resist our "craving for generality." The attention to the particular that he demands contradicts our tendency to attempt to grasp.

> We feel as if we had to *penetrate* phenomena: our investigation, however, is directed not towards phenomena, but, as one might say, towards the *"possibilities"* of phenomena. (PI: §90)

When Wittgenstein specifies that our "grammatical" investigation is directed not towards phenomena but towards their possibilities, he means to replace the categories with an imaginative and improvised grammar of human concepts, a *grammar of the particular*. The difference from Kant is that in Wittgenstein and Emerson each word of ordinary language, each bit of ordinary experience, each aspect of a form of life requires a deduction to determine its use: each one must be retraced in its application to the world, on the basis of the criteria of its application. A word, for Emerson and for Wittgenstein, must be stated in the particular context where it has meaning, or else it is false (it sounds false): it "chagrins us." Again, the list of lords is not a renovated list of categories, but a grammar of the human form of life. Even speaking of the *given* is inappropriate. What interests Cavell, we may say, is the "found": "finding as founding," as he puts it (Cavell 1991: 79), suggesting that we understand any foundation as discovery. The ordinary, then, is what escapes us, what is distant precisely because we seek to appropriate it rather than let ourselves go to things, and to insignificant encounters: "all our blows glance, all our hits are accidents. Our relations to each other are oblique and casual," writes Emerson (1982: 288). The casual is also misfortune, fatality – hence the irony or pun on casual/casualty: our experiences are both casual and catastrophic; the casual structures ordinary experience, and makes it vulnerable.

3 Vulnerabilities of Ordinary Language

Ordinary language philosophy (OLP) as Cavell seeks to reinvent it after Wittgenstein and Emerson is anchored in *attention* to language as it is commonly used, as part and milieu of our everyday interactions and conversations, necessarily spoken by a human voice. It is this sense of language as human voice that Wittgenstein means by a form of life in the *Investigations*:[1] he no longer conceives of language as representing the world, but rather seeks to "come back to earth" and perceive the practices in which language is *caught*, which collect around our words. Attention to ordinary language is attention to neglected reality. OLP's primary methodological ambition is to arrive at a conceptual analysis that allows us to recognize the importance of *context* in our uses of language, thought, and perception – that is, in our various ways of *engaging* in the real – while at the same time defending a certain form of realism anchored in these practices: in our words, expressions, and thoughts. Ordinary language philosophy assesses its reflection on language on the basis of an adequacy measured no longer in terms of correspondence, but rather in terms of the fineness of adjustment. Wittgenstein and Austin do not encourage us to define the meaning of a term as the set of situations in which the term is appropriate, nor as a group of established uses, but rather to examine how meaning is made and improvised in its integration into practice and expressivity. Just as in Emerson, the exploration of uses is an inventory of forms of life: for Austin, we must examine "what we would say when," what is fitting to the circumstances or allows one to act on them.

Austin is important here for having (more or less) theorized ordinary language philosophy (in his essay *A Plea for Excuses*) and the revolution it aims to effect. He makes clear that in examining ordinary language "we are not looking merely at words, but also at the realities we use the words to talk about. We are using our sharpened awareness of words to sharpen our perception, though not as the final arbiter of the phenomena" (Austin 1962: 182). The language of description is then a tool for focusing and paying attention, and is associated with agreement. Very important here is Cavell's transition from the question of common language to that of form of life in language, which is the sharing not only of social structures but of all that constitutes the fabric of human existences and

---

[1] See Laugier 2015b for this part of our study of form of life.

activities. The theme of the ordinary thus introduces skepticism into practice: certainty, or the trust we have in what we do (play, argue, value, promise), is modeled on the trust we have in our shared uses of language and our capacity for using it appropriately. The enigma of speaking ordinary language – the uncanniness of our use of ordinary language – is the possibility that I may speak in the name of others, and vice versa. It is not enough to invoke commonness; it remains to be determined what authorizes me to speak, what is the real strength of our agreement. Hence the central role of the following well-known passage from the *Philosophical Investigations* in Cavell's work:

> It is what human beings say that is true and false; and they agree in the language they use. That is not agreement in opinions but in form of life. (PI: §241)

It is crucial for Cavell and Wittgenstein (as well as for Austin, who insists on the "method" of agreement) that we agree *in* and not *on* language. That means that language precedes an agreement as much as it is produced by it; we agree *in* form of life prior to any convention, contract, or rule.

> We learn and teach words in certain contexts, and then we are expected, and expect others, to be able to project them into further contexts. Nothing ensures that this projection will take place (in particular, not the grasping of universals nor the grasping of books of rules). (Cavell 1969: 52)

This celebrated passage from *Must We Mean What We Say* is not, as some might claim, an unsatisfying response to skepticism: it is a clear formulation of the *vulnerability of the ordinary*. Austin, Wittgenstein, Cavell want to specify and list the conditions of felicitous language as ordinary practice, to highlight the vulnerability of our uses, and to provide some tools for adequate repair (excuses, arrangements). Hence the theory of speech acts is an element of a global conception of ordinary language and the constraints of forms of life. It cannot be understood independently from Austin's other writings, and relies particularly on his essays *Truth*, *Pretending*, and *A Plea for Excuses*. Austin's theory is not just a theory of speech acts; it is a theory of what it is to say something, a theory of what is said when we agree in a form of life.

Austin claims to have made a nearly empirical discovery, the discovery of a natural phenomenon that in some sense has always been there. A mixture of familiarity and foreignness characterizes his description of the discovery of performatives, just as it characterizes the phenomena of ordinary language: something that has always been there before our eyes, but to which we have never paid enough attention (what Cavell calls the uncanniness of the ordinary). Austinian speech acts thus point the way to a crucial articulation of the relationship between the activity of language and human vulnerability. For Cavell, this is the significance of a theory of excuses, which deals with instances in which I act wrongly or put someone else in danger, whether intentionally or not.

We excuse ourselves from our mistakes, we write them off as bad acts. This is a crucial component of our form of life in language. Excuses are exactly symmetrical to failures of speech acts: it is when one has failed to do something well, when one has underperformed, that one has recourse to an excuse. It is our multiple ways of explaining or justifying our failures that determine the effectiveness of the morality in question. The variety of excuses available to us reveals the impossibility of crafting a general definition of action independent of the detail and diversity of our forms of responsibility and narration. It is thus that Austin describes the complexity of human actions and their possible description and classification in terms of excuses. The existence of excuses indicates the connection between vulnerability and morality.

The connection between failure and the vulnerability of human forms of life is best shown in Erving Goffman's analyses of everyday behavior. Moments of social disorganization, such as moments when interactions/communication break down or, more radically, the irruption of mentally disturbed behavior, are moments of *loss of experience* itself. Recognizing the vulnerability of language allows us to recognize the vulnerability of the whole human form of life, not only of specific (social, local) forms of life. Concern with excuses and reparations due to others is indeed typical of attention to the particulars of *a* social life (forms of life in the social sense), but also to the human lifeform *as itself vulnerable*.

For Austin, the essential failure is a lack of attention and care: thoughtlessness, inconsiderateness, failure at the stage of *appreciating* the situation. Excuses – that is, *what we say when* it appears that we have acted badly (clumsily, inadequately, etc.) – are the site of human vulnerability. The existence of excuses is essential to the nature of action: excuses do not somehow arrive on the scene later; they are implied in human action itself. Action in this sense, Austin notes, is something specifically human: the human form of life as defined by the "linguistic constellation" of excuses. Austin presents the complexity of human actions and their possible classifications in terms of excuses. We can get a sense of this by looking at familiar examples such as the act of killing a donkey: would we say this occurred "by accident"? Or "by mistake" (Austin 1961: 185)?

In a stunning description of a (his?) social form of life, Austin points out that we do not give just any type of excuse for just any type of action. One can excuse lighting a cigarette or covering one's books by "the force of habit," but a killer cannot invoke force of habit to excuse his murdering (an example of Austin's reported by Pitcher). The diversity of excuses demonstrates the diversity and variety of actions, and for any given excuse there is a limit to the acts for which it will be accepted: what Austin calls "norms of the unacceptable." "We may plead that we trod on the snail inadvertently: but not on a baby – you ought to look where you are putting your great feet" (Austin 1961: 142).

Austin, like Goffman, aims to set out the conditions of felicity of language *in all circumstances*, to make clear the vulnerability of our shared usages, and to specify certain adequate tools for making up for our misses (excuses, compensations). Failures are due to failures in *appreciation*, a lack of sensitivity to the particulars.

> So too in real, or rather civilian life, in moral or practical affairs, we can know the facts and yet look at them mistakenly or perversely, or not fully realize or appreciate something, or even be under a total misconception. Many expressions of excuse indicate failure at this particularly tricky stage: even thoughtlessness, inconsiderateness, lack of imagination are perhaps less matters of failure in intelligence or planning than might be supposed, and more matters of failure to appreciate the situation. (Austin 1962a: 142)

Through his emphasis on failure Austin shows the vulnerability of ordinary human action, defined, just like performative utterances, in terms of what can go wrong. Thus, the pragmatic theme is reversed (Austin chose the title *How to Do Things with Words* for his William James lectures in ironic homage to the pragmatist maxim): action is structured by language, defined and regulated by failure, by going wrong. Then, "a wrong construction is put on things," says Austin in *Sense and Sensibilia*, mentioning "misreadings, mishearings, Freudian slips etc."

There is no clear dichotomy between

> things going right and things going wrong: things may go wrong, as we really all know quite well, in lots of different ways [...]. (Austin 1962b: 13)

Here is the main point, and the deeply skeptical element in Austin's view of language as form of life. Action signifies that misfortunes lie in wait for oneself and for others, and that we take risks (threats to oneself or others): it means that our actions have circumstances, which make us, and reality, vulnerable. Human action is precisely that which more often than not needs to be excused, not only because we sometimes act wrongly but also because of what we miss by a close call, what we "do not exactly do": see the conclusion of *Pretending*, where Austin speaks of a general project to describe the failures and vulnerability of human agency and the varieties of "not exactly doing things":

> [...] the long-term project of classifying and clarifying all possible ways and varieties of *not exactly doing things*, which has to be carried through if we are ever to understand properly what doing things is [...]. (Austin 1961: 219)

Ordinary language philosophy thus conceived is not only a study of ordinary usage and the social conventions that govern it, but of the human form of life as vulnerable to others, to ourselves, and to our mistakes. Here we may raise the issue – suggested by Cavell – of the distinction between two senses of form of life, one social and one biological, and the different orders of normativity they involve. Before exploring them, I will give two examples of this difference.

4 Two Concepts of Form(s) of Life

We find an analysis of form of life and of the coupling of failure and excuse, of offense and compensation, in Goffman's analyses and in his examples of failures and inappropriate behavior. Attention to excuses and to the compensation due to others is actually also an essential connection between Austin and Goffman, especially in Goffman's later major work, *Frame Analysis: An Essay on the Organization of Experience*. The point in Goffman is to *see* the human form of life as vulnerable, as defined by a constellation of possibilities for failure and ways we have of making amends, strategies we can use to forgive or forget, to iron things out, to swallow our difficult condition as beings of failure. In his analysis in "To cool the mark out," he examines cases where we have to accompany someone in suffering a radical social failure. Goffman's analysis of interactions gives full place to disorders, turmoil, embarrassment, shame, the stage fright of social interactions, encroachments, intrusions, offenses, and tears in the surface of "normal appearances." These phenomena make us feel the fragility of ordinary life and interactions and cause us to become aware of our vulnerability in the presence of others. Goffman sees this vulnerability as a loss of reality itself, and more precisely of "the minute social system that is brought into being with each encounter" (Goffman 1971: 135). This is a loss of norms that encapsulates the very idea of the form of life, itself defined by what is *under threat:* not only the comfort of seamless social relations.

> Whether crucial or picayune, all encounters present occasions when the individual can become spontaneously involved in the proceedings and derive from this a firm sense of reality. When an incident occurs and spontaneous involvement is threatened, then reality is threatened. [...] The minute social system, that is brought into being with each encounter, will be disorganized, and the participants will feel unruled, unreal, and anomic. (Goffman 1971: 135)

Cavell traces this vulnerability of encounters back to our expressive body, quoting Emerson's phrase "the giant I carry around with me." This means a vulnerability of form of life that connects the social and natural sense of life, the normativity of rules and of life itself, and which is inherent in human encounters.

Excuses, in their permanent recognition of human vulnerability, place the ordinary in the realm of the tragic (Cavell 1989, 1994). The radical vulnerability characteristic of this form of life is equally manifest in small, everyday offenses (the word of excuse that doesn't come, the absence of attention, carelessness) and in radical casualties.

Attention to the ordinary means seeing the fragility of our perceptions with a new understanding of skepticism: our perceptions are fragile not because we fail to perceive or know the world, but because we fail to perceive the situation clearly or accurately. Indeed, Austin himself discusses cases where "a wrong construction is put on things": where there is no difference between misperceiving and misbehaving, simply doing wrong. We miss reality not because it is inaccessible or distant, but because of a lack of care and attention to form of life, evidence of a strong connection between skepticism and form of life.

We can recall here what Cavell says about the importance of film, which resides in the fact that in our ordinary lives we "miss" things because we do not care, do not pay enough attention:

> that a failure so to perceive, to persist in missing the subject, which may amount to missing the evanescence of the subject, is ascribable only to ourselves, to failures of our character; as if to fail to guess the unseen from the seen, to fail to trace the implications of things – that is to fail the perception that that there *is* something to be guessed and traced, right or wrong – requires that we persistently coarsen and stupefy ourselves. (Cavell 1988: 14)

Reality itself is vulnerable to our re-readings and our agreements, to our misperceptions and carelessness, and it is this vulnerability that defines the ordinary, which can be neither "seized" nor defined.

The point here is no longer to identify the conditions for successful performative utterances, it is to *see* all of the human form of life as vulnerable, subject to threat. Excuses, with their permanent and obsessive acknowledgment of human vulnerability, turn philosophy's attention to the unpleasant "fact that human life is constrained to the life of the human body," the fact that "the human body is the best image" of the human mind – not because it represents it but because it expresses it. All human expressions, even ones that are ridiculous, or fail, such as some of the passionate utterances Cavell analyzes in his later work, achieve something by performing, and therefore accepting, human vulnerability, expressing a human form of life.

Here we are in territory opened by Cavell who proposed paying new attention to the perlocutionary and analyzed "passionate utterances." In his essay "Passionate and Performative Utterances," probably the major work of his "later period," Cavell identifies the perlocutionary dimension of language as the domain of the passionate utterance. The performative utterance, as it is defined in *How to Do Things with Words* in reference to the illocutionary, cannot account for the dimension of improvisation and uncontrollability in expression. If a performative utterance is, as Cavell writes, "an offer of participation in the order of law," then perhaps, he suggests, a passionate utterance is "an invitation to improvisation in the disorders of desire" (Cavell 2005: 185). Cavell acknowledges Austin's effort to show how speech *does* things (and is thus a structuring element of forms of lives) as well as states or says things, beginning with social actions such as marrying, betting, christening, and bequeathing. Austin himself interestingly notes that utterances have further effects, ones he calls perlocutionary rather than illocutionary, and which can be named by such verbs as deter, convince, alarm, surprise, upset, humiliate (Austin 1962a: 108; 117). Cavell wonders why Austin mysteriously drops the subject of the perlocutionary:

> Why not suppose that there are conditions to be found for felicitous perlocutionary acts, or for what I call passionate utterances? (Cavell 2005: 180)

That Austin avoids this task has two consequences: "the region of the perlocutionary has gone undefined and uncharted," and has remained an unknown zone or "dark continent" (Cavell 2005: 256); and the domain of the performative remains within the limits of social rules or conventions. Cavell's counter-proposal is to see the perlocutionary as equally *meaningful*, and as revelatory of performativity (in its difference from the descriptive or assertive) as the illocutionary. This thesis of the passionate utterance is no more than an expansion of the analysis of the performativity of discourse.

Cavell's rehabilitation of the perlocutionary, the extension of performativity, "affords a portrait, or scan, of the interactions which constitute a society that is at variance with Austin's portrait of a constitution rationally dominated by established rituals and shared rules" (Cavell 2005: 158) The interactions or encounters named by those perlocutionary verbs are ones that, reversing the conditions of the illocutionary, in effect occasionally challenge the rationality of the reign of rules. Interactions are not only governed by explicit social or moral conventions, but by a different order of rules, the rules of a shared form of life.

Here we might insist again on the double dimension of form of life: Cavell's critique (1989) of common interpretations of "forms of life" deploys the expression "*life forms*" (not simply *forms* of life); that is, the form of life not only in its social dimension but in its biological dimension. Cavell emphasizes this second (he calls it vertical) axis of form of life, while recognizing the importance of the first (horizontal), social agreement. Discussions of this first meaning (conventions, rituals, rules) have occluded the force of the "natural" and biological sense of forms of life in Wittgenstein, which he also defines in his mention of "natural reactions," or "the natural history of humanity" (cf. the opening of the *Investigations*). What is *given* in forms of life are not just our social structures and different cultural habits, but everything that has to do with "the specific strength and scale of the human body, senses and voice" (Cavell 1989: 41–42). This is well known among interpreters, but my thesis here is that these two senses of *Lebensform* are at stake in the dichotomy between passionate and performative utterance.

But how can one propose conditions of felicity for the perlocutionary effects of what Cavell calls passionate utterances if there are no rules and no rationality involved? Cavell ambitiously parallels Austin's conditions for illocutory utterances (procedure, appropriate person …) with a series of his own analogous conditions for the perlocutionary, such as:

> Perlocutionary Condition 1: There is no accepted conventional procedure and effect. The speaker is on his or her own to create the desired effect.
> Perlocutionary Condition 2: (In the absence of an accepted conventional procedure, there are no antecedently specified persons. Appropriateness is to be decided in each case; it is at issue in each. I am not invoking a procedure but inviting an exchange. I therewith *single you out* (as appropriate) in the given case.) (Cavell 2005: 181)

In the case of performative utterances, failures have to do with identifying the correct procedure and the right person, either as performer or addressee ("securing of uptake"). In passionate utterances, failure "puts the future of our relationship, as part of my sense of my identity, or of my existence, more radically at stake." A performative utterance is "an offer of participation in the order of law." A passionate utterance is "an invitation to improvisation in the disorders of desire." An exploration of form of life needs to attend to the rules governing both, even if that means changing the sense of "rules." For the conformist role given to rules by classical analyses of Wittgenstein cannot account for this practice.

5 Rules of Our Lives

This fragility of reality and experience, to speak again in Goffman's idiom (1987), is characteristic of everyday encounters and ordinary experience, which are "structurally vulnerable." The question is now how to find rules that would govern our ordinary ways of behaving together. This is what has guided me to an ethics of care,[2] which is characterized by a reorientation of morality towards importance, attention to others, and a connection to the structural vulnerability of experience. The notion of *care* is indeed inseparable from a whole cluster of terms that comprise a language game of the particular: attention, care, importance, significance, counting, mattering. The ethics of care is not only an alternative ethics, *care* is a concept that transforms the object of ethics. It is in the use of language (choice of words, style of expression and conversation) that a person's moral vision, her *texture of being*, is intimately developed and openly shown. This texture has little to do with rules and moral arguments or judgments but instead with what "matters" and gives expression to the differences between individuals. Moral philosophy must change its field of study, from the examination of general concepts to the examination of particular visions, of individuals' "configurations" of thought and the details of forms of life, as described by Iris Murdoch:

> When we apprehend and assess other people we do not consider only their solutions to specifiable practical problems, we consider something more elusive which may be called their total vision of life, as shown in their mode of speech or silence, their assessments of others, their conception of their own lives, what they think attractive or praiseworthy, what they think funny: in short the configurations of their thought which show continually in their reactions and conversation. These things, which may be overtly and comprehensibly displayed or inwardly elaborated and guessed at, constitute what, making different points in the two metaphors, one may call the texture of man's being or the nature of his personal vision. (Murdoch 1997: 80–81)

The aim of ethics is to perceive "the texture of man's being or the nature of his personal vision." It is in her use of language ("choice" of expressions, style of conversation) that a person's moral vision shows overtly. For Murdoch this *vision* is not a theoretical point of view but rather a texture of being (a texture might be visual, aural, or tactile). This is similar to what Diamond says about ethics and literature:

> But we cannot see the moral interest of literature unless we recognize gestures, manners, habits, turns of speech, turns of thought, styles of face as morally expressive – of an individual or of a people. The intelligent description of such things is part of the intelligent, the sharp-eyed, description of life, of what matters, makes differences, in human lives. (Diamond 1991: 375)

---

2 Laugier 2015a, 2016a.

These are the differences that must be the object of a "sharpened, intelligent description of life." The notion of "human life" is here obviously connected to Wittgenstein's form of life conceived as attachment to ordinary language:

> The familiar physiognomy of a word, the feeling that it has taken up its meaning into itself, that it is an actual likeness of its meaning – there could be human beings to whom all this is alien. (They would not have an attachment to their words). And how are these feelings manifested among us? – By the way we choose and value words. How do I find the "right" word? How do I choose among words? Without doubt it is sometimes as if I were comparing them by fine differences of smell: that is too ... – This is the right one. But I do not always have to make judgments, give explanations; often I might only say: "it simply isn't right yet." (PI: p. 218)

Texture, likeness, physiognomy, being "not right" refer to an unstable reality that cannot be fixed by concepts or identified with determinate particular objects, but only by the recognition of gestures, manners, and styles. From the point of view defined by Diamond, form of life is perceived through attention to moral textures or motifs; reality is "morally expressive." What is perceived is therefore moral expression, which is neither possible nor recognizable without the background provided by a form of life. Literature is a privileged site for moral perception, inasmuch as it creates a background against which important (significant) differences can emerge; "what matters, makes differences, in human lives." This background, again, is the background of the life of the words we use.

> Justification, in ethics as anywhere else, goes on within lives we share with others, but what we may count in that life is not laid down in advance. The force of what we are able to say depends on its relation to the life of the words we use, the place of those words in our lives. (Diamond 1991: 27)

Within such an approach, attention (care), "the way we choose and value words," is at the root of ethics, rather than being a subordinate or marginal element of it. Moral learning defines ethics as attention to the details and particulars of reality. Morality (and politics also, but that is another question[3]) thus concerns our ability to read and assess human moral expression. This ability is not only affective or emotional, but conceptual and linguistic – it is our ability to make good use of words, to use them in new contexts, and to respond/react correctly.

---

[3] See Ogien and Laugier 2014 on democracy as form of life, Ferrarese and Laugier 2015, and Ogien 2016.

Here we can follow earlier reflections proposed by Charles Taylor: the capacity for moral expression is rooted in a malleable form of life, vulnerable to our uses of language. Form of life (in both the social and biological sense) determines the structure of expression, which inversely reworks it and gives it its form.

> This structure can only be put to work against a background that we can never completely dominate, for we remodel it endlessly, without dominating it and without having an overlooking view. (Taylor 1985: 10)

The relationship to the other, the type of interest and care that we have for others, the importance we give them, exist only in their singular and public expression against the background of our form of life. What Cavell describes in a skeptical mode is described by Taylor in a more "hermeneutic" mode, but both approaches lead to moral questioning on the basis of mutual expression, the constitution of style, and an apprenticeship in attention to the expressions of others. This reading of expression, this sensitivity to meaning and to textures of being, which makes *responding* possible, is the product of attention and of care more than rule-following.

We must modify and enlarge our sense of the rationality of rules. The focus on moral notions such as duty or choice leaves out essential ordinary moral questioning and realities, and has been insufficient for thinking through ordinary moral problems. As Diamond remarks, someone who is perfectly rigorous and moral may be petty or stingy, and this unlovable (in the strong sense) trait is something that could, instead of being considered a vague, non-ethical, psychological concept, form an integral part of a moral reflection that can only be carried out in descriptive and normative terms and which resists analysis in terms of rules. This is part of learning a form of life, something Cavell has insisted on as early as in the essays that make up *Must We Mean What We Say?*

> There is a pervasive and systematic background of agreements among us, which we had not realized, or had not known we realize. Wittgenstein sometimes calls them conventions, sometimes rules ... The agreement we act upon he calls "agreement in judgments" (§242), and he speaks of our ability to use language as depending upon agreement in "forms of life" (§241). But forms of life, he says, are exactly what have to be "accepted"; they are "given." (Cavell 1969: 30)

That we agree *in* language means that language – our form of life – produces our understanding of one another just as much as it itself is a product of agreement. Language is natural to us in this sense; the idea of convention is there to at once ape and disguise this necessity. "Beneath the tyranny of convention, there is the tyranny of nature," Cavell writes. At this point, the criticism Cavell formulates of common interpretations of "form of life" can be taken one step further. Cavell opposes these interpretations by using the translation "form of *life*" – or lifeforms – rather than "*forms* of life." What is given is our form of life. What leads us to want to violate our agreements, our criteria, is the refusal of this given, of this form of life in not only its social but also its biological dimension. It is on this second (vertical) aspect of form of life that Cavell insists, while at the same time recognizing the importance of the first (horizontal) dimension, i.e., social agreement (rules). What discussions of the first sense (that of conventionalism and rules) have obscured is the strength Wittgenstein recognizes in the natural and biological sense of form of life, which he points to by evoking "natural reactions." What is given in a form of life are not only social structures and various cultural habits, but the natural necessities that are the background of tragedies, and of philosophy: everything that makes it the case that, just as doves, in Kant's phrase, need the air to fly, so we, in Wittgenstein's phrase, need friction to walk (PI: §107).

Cavell describes with precision and in detail the texture of this necessity in the famous passage already quoted, whose conclusions are widely discussed (the fact than human life and sanity depend on a fragile net), but strangely, the careful details of the form of life shaped by practices of ordinary language are not.

> We learn and teach words in certain contexts, and then we are expected, and expect others, to be able to project them into further contexts. Nothing insures that this projection will take place (in particular, not the grasping of universals nor the grasping of books of rules), just as nothing insures that we will make, and understand, the same projections. That on the whole we do is a matter of *our sharing routes of interest and feeling, modes of response, senses of humor and of significance and of fulfillment, of what is outrageous, of what is similar to what else, what a rebuke, what forgiveness, of when an utterance is an assertion, when an appeal, when an explanation* – all the whirl of organism Wittgenstein calls "forms of life." Human speech and activity, sanity and community, rest upon nothing more, but nothing less, than this. It is a vision as simple as it is difficult, and as difficult as it is (and because it is) terrifying. (Cavell 1969: 52; emphasis mine)

This whirl is both natural, "organic," on the vertical axis of lifeform, and linguistic, on the horizontal axis of the various uses of languages and in particular the performative and the perlocutory – "what a rebuke, what forgiveness, when an utterance is an assertion, when an appeal, when an explanation." Again, the two axes of form of life define ordinary language as lifeform.

By contrast with the overly visual and static analogy of the background, one may prefer that of texture or pattern (Wittgenstein himself speaks of a "pattern in the tapestry of our life"), or the "whirl" of life that Cavell describes here as the whirl of linguistic practices. These connections are in our life, in which nothing is hidden: they are there, before our eyes, like the "figure" in the carpet of James' story. Our concepts and rules get their grip in the unfolding of life.

> Not what *one* man is doing *now*, but the whole hurly-burly [*Gewimmel*], is the background against which we see an action. (Wittgenstein, RPP II §624: 629)

The background of a form of life is neither causal nor fixed like décor, but rather is living and mobile. One can speak here of "lifeform," as Cavell does: the forms that life takes under an attentive gaze, or the "whirl" of our life *in language*, or the life of ordinary language – not, for example, a body of meanings or of social rules.

Here two representations of rules may be opposed: that of the background (cf. Searle, for whom institutions constitute the fixed background that allows us to interpret language, to perceive, and to follow social rules), and that of the perceptual/sensory texture of the whirl of life. The term background appears in Wittgenstein in order to designate a background for description that makes the nature of actions appear, and not, as Searle suggests, in order to *explain* anything. We perceive action, but in the midst of a bustle, the whirl of the form of life out of which it emerges and which gives it its meaning and importance. It is not the same thing to say that the application of a rule is causally determined by a background as to say that it is describable against a backdrop of human actions and connections. This is the heart of the distinction drawn by Cavell in *Conditions Handsome and Unhandsome* between his conception of ethics and a "conformist" conception that aims at justifying our actions in terms of previously agreed-upon rules. The background does not determine ethical meaning (for there is no such thing). Rather, it allows us to perceive what is important and meaningful for us (the important moment). The meaning of an action is given by the way it is perceived against the background of a form of life. The "accepted," given background does not determine our actions but it does allow us to *see* them (as in Emerson's description of the Lords of life: "I saw them pass.")

With this in mind we can turn to what Wittgenstein says about rules: we see rules, the *practice* of following a rule, against the background of human life.

> We judge an action according to its background within human life. [...] The background is the bustle of life. And our concept points to something within *this* bustle. [...] How could human behavior be described? Surely only by showing the actions of a variety of humans, as they are all mixed up together [*durcheinanderwimmeln*]. Not what one man is doing now, but the whole hurly-burly [*Gewimmel*], is the background against which we see an action. (PI: §629)

It is not "our practices" (and what would that mean? See Diamond 1991, introduction) that make up this background, but rather this background is what allows us to describe our practices. So the background is not made of things known or believed, but it is this "hurly-burly" of the form of life.

> We do not learn the practice of making empirical judgments by learning rules; we are taught judgments and their connection with other judgments. A totality of judgments is made plausible to us. (OC: §140)

The pseudo-Wittgensteinian idea (espoused notably by Searle, but quite widely shared in "analytic" discussions of rules) of a *causal* foundation for our judgments and perceptions in a background of practices and rules is thus deeply mistaken and misses the senses of *Lebensform*.

> No: it is the inherited background against which I distinguish between true and false. (OC: §94)

6 Towards a Politics of Forms of Life

One important consequence of Cavell's and Das's criticism of a monolithic sense of forms of life as social practices is that my agreement or my belonging to *this or that* form of life, political or moral, is not given. The form of this acceptance, the limits and scales of our agreement, are not knowable *a priori*, "no more than one can *a priori* know the scope or scale of a word."

> In being asked to accept this, or suffer it, as given for ourselves, we are not asked to accept, let us say, private property, but separateness; not a particular fact of power, but the fact that I am a man, therefore of this (range or scale of) capacity for work, for pleasure, for endurance, for appeal, for command, for understanding, for wish, for will, for teaching, for suffering. (Cavell 1989: 44)

The (conformist) connection between form of life and acceptance needs to be severed. You haven't accepted everything in a form of life. One thing that Wittgenstein is aiming to show – if we follow Cavell's and Diamond's reading – is that one does not say much about a practice (such as language, history, or politics) when one simply states that it is governed by rules. Discussions of rules are distorted by the (philosophical) idea that a rule contains an explanatory or justificatory power – an idea that leads fatally to conformity. We must be done, then, with conformist interpretations of what a rule is and with the idea – found in many contemporary political doctrines, including Rawls' – that certain claims are impossible, or out of place, and do not have meaning in our society because they take place outside of its rules and deny the basic agreement that founds it. But what agreement? This is precisely Cavell's question. What have I agreed to? What is the measure of consent? I cannot have consented to everything that happens in my society, or *in my name*, just because I am a member of this society or part of this practice. Cavell's early discussion, in Chapter III of *The Claim of Reason*, of Rawls' seminal paper *Two concepts of rules* (1955) takes on a later and greater significance: agreement to a practice, and to a set of rules, is never given, but always up for discussion: it is at stake in the conversation of justice.

There is, adjoined to the idea of community and the horizontal normative conception of forms of life (associated with rule-following and social practices), the idea that one must somehow learn to make claims as people generally do, that one must consent to certain *rules* in order to be able to make a claim to anything. But, as Cavell reminds us, there is no rule that tells us how to stake a claim.[4]

Thinking about community and politics from the side of ordinary life leads us to understand the very sense of the given, the *Gewimmel*. So the error of conservatist, conformist, or quietist readings of Wittgenstein is to see rules as governing *us* through practices:

> It is not our aim to refine or complete the system of rules for the use of our words in unheard of ways ... The real discovery is the one that makes me capable of breaking off philosophizing when I want to. – The one that gives philosophy peace. (PI: §133)

This brings us back to the anthropological perspective. What Wittgenstein aims at is "peace," but not by merely following or accepting our practices. This is at the heart of his descriptive project, of really seeing things as they are, and hence changing the way we see them. As Diamond says,

> Our practices are exploratory, and it is indeed only through such exploration that we come to see fully what it was that we ourselves thought or wanted to say. I did speak of stories as capable of changing the ways we look at things. (Diamond 1991: Introduction)

Lifeforms are the forms our life takes under an attentive gaze, the "whirl" of life in language, not a body of meanings or of social rules. Recourse to the notion of community in Wittgenstein and Cavell is in no way a solution to the skeptical problem. The community gives me a political voice, but can equally take that

---

[4] Ogien and Laugier 2010, Ogien and Laugier 2014.

voice back from me, or betray me to such an extent that I no longer wish to speak for it, or let it speak for me (Cavell 1990, 1994). My participation is constantly in question, in discussion – in *conversation*, to take up an essential and shared theme in Rawls and Cavell – in my connection to the community. When Wittgenstein says that human beings "agree in the language that they use," that they agree *in form of life*, he invokes an agreement that is founded on nothing other than the validity of a voice. Wittgenstein seeks to show at once the fragility and the depth of our agreement, and the very nature of the necessities that emerge in agreement in form of life.

We now understand why Cavell, who devoted his first works to Wittgenstein and Austin, later took it upon himself to make Emerson's voice reheard in the field of philosophy, inscribing Wittgenstein in the extension of the Emersonian voice.

> To speak for oneself politically is to speak for the others with whom you consent to association, and it is to consent to be spoken by them – not as a parent speaks for you, i. e. instead of you, but as someone in mutuality speaks for you, i.e. speaks your mind.
>
> Who these others are, for whom you speak and by whom you are spoken for, is not known a priori, though it is in practice generally treated as given. (Cavell 1979: 27)

One acts as if the recourse to the ordinary, to our forms of life (as something given), is a solution to skepticism: as if forms of life were, for example, social institutions that have to be "obeyed" or followed; as if certain claims or actions are impossible, out of place, not part of the "game," or meaningless in our society.

The "accepted," given background of/agreement in form of life does not determine our actions but it does allow us to *see* them clearly if we check, if we pay attention. This means letting things come as they come, but still letting them "come to attention."

> Philosophy is not a culture, not one among others. The locale of its originating form of life is the singular human being dissatisfied with itself, a fate inherent, or say natural, within any civilized human society. (Cavell, Introduction to Das 2007: XI)

This is the most powerful application of the concept of form of life, which goes far beyond scholastic discussions of what Wittgenstein does or does not mean by the expression. We can take the example of Das, who claims to follow Cavell's analysis when she tries to explain the loss of form of life at stake in contemporary violence, mentioning as well

> [...] the two dimensions of the expressions "form" and "life" – or a horizontal dimension corresponding to "forms" and a vertical dimension corresponding to life. The former refers to different societal arrangements and the latter to the idea of how life might be defined as a *human* form of life ... In the latter case the differences alluded to are those of being human or being animal or being bird – thus eating, pawing or pecking – each act meeting a biological need but only in ways that humans or animals or birds do.
> I have elaborated further that what language expresses here is the idea of a *naturalness* of the acts of eating, pawing or pecking as belonging to our lives as humans, as distinct from what is natural for animals or birds. It was this sense of the naturalness of what the human form of life implied that was broken in the terrible violence of the Partition of India that I studied. (Das 2016: 170)

The vulnerability of the ordinary world is obvious in the contexts Das's *Life and Words* describes, where violence destroys the everyday and the very sense of *life* (Das 2007: 89). The human is defined by the permanent threat of denial of the human, of dehumanization, devitalization – loss of the sense of life, or, better yet, of the *form and content* of life. "The blurring between what is human and what is not human shades into the blurring over what is life and what is not life" (Das 2007: 16). Das calls *the everyday life of the human* this new yet unapproachable object of anthropological inquiry, and this core of life may, in some circumstances, be under threat – not only social structures and institutions, but the foundation and activities that insure their continuance and "our life as humans."

Cavell refers to Das's description of the role of women in the preservation/reinvention of form of life in times of disaster,

> [...] her recognition that in the gender-determined division of the work of mourning the results of violence, the role of women is to attend, in a torn world, to the details of everyday life that allow a household to function, collecting supplies, cooking, washing and straightening up, seeing to children, and so on, that allow life to knit itself back into some viable rhythm, pair by pair. (Cavell, *Introduction* to Das 2007: XIII–XIV)

Acknowledging the importance of forms of life means acknowledging a dimension of *life* systematically ignored or undervalued in political and moral philosophy, although, or because, it makes (our) everyday life possible; and it means doing so in present contexts of ordinary and extraordinary life in which human (and non-human) beings find their needs and vulnerability totally exposed, and their natural conditions of life destroyed and transformed – collapsing together the senses of *Lebensform*.

References

Austin, John Langshaw (1961) *Philosophical Papers*, Oxford: Oxford University Press.
Austin, John Langshaw (1962a) *How to Do Things with Words*, Oxford: Clarendon Press.
Austin, John Langshaw (1962b) *Sense and Sensibilia*, Oxford: Oxford University Press.
Cavell, Stanley (1971) *The World Viewed: Reflections on the Ontology of Film*, Cambridge, MA/London, UK: Viking Press.
Cavell, Stanley (1976) *Must We Mean What We Say? A Book of Essays*, Cambridge: Cambridge University Press.
Cavell, Stanley (1979) *The Claim of Reason: Wittgenstein, Skepticism, Morality, and Tragedy*, Oxford: Oxford University Press.
Cavell, Stanley (1988) *Themes out of School: Cause and Effect*, Chicago: University of Chicago Press.
Cavell, Stanley (1989) *This New Yet Unapproachable America: Lectures after Emerson after Wittgenstein*, Albuquerque, NM: Living Batch Press.
Cavell, Stanley (1990) *Conditions Handsome and Unhandsome: The Constitution of Emersonian Perfectionism*, La Salle, IL/Chicago: Open Court/University of Chicago Press.
Cavell, Stanley (1992) *The Senses of Walden*, expanded edition, Chicago: University of Chicago Press.
Cavell, Stanley (1994) *A Pitch of Philosophy: Autobiographical Exercises*, Cambridge, MA: Harvard University Press.
Cavell, Stanley (2005) *Philosophy The Day after Tomorrow*, Cambridge, MA: Harvard University Press.
Cavell, Stanley (2010) *Little Did I Know: Excerpts from Memory*. Stanford, CA: Stanford University Press.
Das, Veena (2007) *Life and Words: Violence and the Descent into the Ordinary*, Berkeley, CA: University of California Press.
Das, Veena (2016) "The Boundaries of the 'We': Cruelty, Responsibility and Forms of Life", in: *Critical Horizons* 17 (2), 168–185.
Diamond, Cora (1989) "Rules: Looking in the Right Place", in: D. Z. Phillips and P. Winch (eds.): *Wittgenstein: Attention to Particulars. Essays in Honour of Rush Rhees (1905–89)*, New York: St. Martin's Press.
Diamond, Cora (1991) *The Realistic Spirit: Wittgenstein, Philosophy, and the Mind*, Cambridge, MA: MIT Press.
Emerson, Ralph Waldo (1982) *Selected Essays*. New York: Penguin.
Ferrarese, Estelle and Sandra Laugier (eds.) (2015) *Politique des formes de vie*, Paris: Presses de Sciences Po.
Foucault, Michel (1994) "La philosophie analytique de la politique [1978]", in: *Dits et écrits*, Vol. 3, Paris: Gallimard.
Goffman, Erving (1952) "On Cooling the Mark Out", in: *Psychiatry* 15 (4), 451–463.
Goffman, Erving (1974) *Frame Analysis: An Essay on the Organisation of Experience*, New York: Harper & Row.
Goffman, Erving (2005) *Interaction Ritual: Essays in Face-to-Face Behavior*, New Brunswick, NJ: Aldine Transaction.
Laugier, Sandra (2009) *Wittgenstein: les sens de l'usage*, Paris: Vrin.
Laugier, Sandra (2010) *Wittgenstein: le mythe de l'inexpressivité*, Paris: Vrin.

Laugier, Sandra (2013) *Why We Need Ordinary Language Philosophy*, transl. Daniela Ginsburg, Chicago: University of Chicago Press.
Laugier, Sandra (2015a) "The Ethics of Care as a Politics of the Ordinary", in: *New Literary History* 46 (2), 217–240.
Laugier, Sandra (2015b) "Voice as Form of Life and Life Form", in: *Nordic Wittgenstein Review* 4, Special Issue: Wittgenstein and Forms of Life, 63–82.
Laugier, Sandra (2016a) "Care, the Ordinary, Forms of Life", in: *Iride* 29, 109–122.
Laugier, Sandra (2016b) "Politics of Vulnerability and Responsibility for Ordinary Others", in: *Critical Horizons* 17 (2), 207–223.
Murdoch, Iris (1997) "Vision and Choice in Morality", in: *Existentialists and Mystics: Writings on Philosophy and Literature*, London: Chatto & Windus, 76–98.
Ogien, Albert (2016) "Wittgenstein's Puzzle. Forms of Life in a Sociological Perspective", in: *Iride* 29, 123–136.
Ogien, Albert and Sandra Laugier (2010) *Pourquoi désobéir en démocratie?*, Paris : Découverte.
Ogien, Albert and Sandra Laugier (2014) *Le principe démocratie: enquête sur les nouvelles formes du politique*, Paris: Découverte.
Taylor, Charles (1979) "Action as Expression", in: Jenny Teichmann and Cora Diamond (eds.): *Intention and Intentionality: Essays in Honour of G. E. M. Anscombe*, Ithaca, NY: Cornell University Press, 73–89.
Taylor, Charles (1985) *Human Agency and Language*, Cambridge: Cambridge University Press.
Taylor, Charles (1995) *Philosophical Arguments*, Cambridge, MA: Harvard University Press.
Thoreau, Henry David (2004) *Walden: A Fully Annotated Edition*, Jeffrey S. Cramer (ed.), New Haven, CT: Yale University Press.
Wittgenstein, Ludwig (1961) *Notebooks 1914–16*, G. E. M. Anscombe and G. H. v. Wright (eds.), New York: Harper & Brothers. [NB]
Wittgenstein, Ludwig (1978) *Philosophical Investigations*, Oxford: Basil Blackwell. [PI]

David Zapero
Hostage to a Stranger

Abstract: On a widespread conception of singular thought, part of what makes a thought singular is the obtaining of certain worldly facts. Had those facts not obtained, the thought wouldn't be a singular one. Which means that for any given singular thought one can conceive of circumstances under which it (*that* thought) would not be singular. In the present essay, I want to trace out the motivations for this view. The story I want to tell is one part of a longer story about the difficulties of coming to terms with an idea that Wittgenstein developed in his later work. The idea may, in very general terms, be put as follows: the world doesn't only determine the truth or falsity of a thought, it also contributes to determining what *counts as* a thought's being true or false. It is by misunderstanding the import of this idea that we can be led to the aforementioned conception of singular thought.

1 Introduction

One way in which reality has a grip on our thought is by its providing us with particular objects to think about. At least on one understanding of "thought", it is trivial to say that we can only entertain thoughts about particular objects when reality bequeaths us those objects – and that no such thoughts can be entertained when reality doesn't so bequeath us. Had Wittgenstein taken to life on the countryside after writing the *Tractatus* there may never have been *Philosophical Investigations* – and there would also be no opportunities to entertain thoughts, true or false, about that work. We could, of course, have entertained thoughts about a possible work by Wittgenstein called *Philosophical Investigations*, but not about the particular piece of philosophy that he did end up producing. No such piece of philosophy would be available for us to think about. If a singular thought is one that represents a particular object as being a certain way – it delimits a certain range of cases, namely those in which the object is *that* way –, there is no way, without the object, that it can represent things as being. Without the object, there is no such thought to be entertained.

The possibility that reality should not be forthcoming has been unsettling for some. Most famously, Russell was concerned to avoid the possibility that we should have the impression that we are thinking a singular thought when, in fact, no such thought can be entertained. Rather than allowing for such a possibility, he radically restricted the domain of things that singular thoughts can be about. Much work has gone into avoiding his outlandish conclusions. One prominent strategy in this respect has been to account for singular thought in terms of the contextual or causal relations between the subject of the thought and what the thought is about. On such a view of singular thought, the singularity of such thoughts is to be explained by the fact that some contextual or causal link obtains between the thought and a particular object.

In this essay, I want to look into one way in which such an outlook can make singular thought seem profoundly enigmatic (once again). The enigma is the following. In trying to account for the singularity of singular thought in terms of intra-worldly relations, such an outlook makes singularity a wholly worldly matter. For a thought to be singular only means that that thought is, in fact, about a particular object. The object that it represents as being a certain way is, in fact, a particular object – but nothing about the thought itself tells us just *which* object it is. The thought is beholden to a certain object, but, from the point of view of the thought, we don't know which object that is. Indeed, on such a view, while a singular thought is about a particular object, it *might* also have been about a different object. Indeed, the singular thought *might* also not have been singular at all. Which of course means that its singularity is of quite a peculiar kind.

There is a case to be made for the claim that no such singularity exists. That is, that *thoughts* can't be singular in that sense of "singular". It isn't a case that I want to make here. I rather want to trace one possible path that can lead to such an idea of singularity – or, depending on how one may see things, to such a *disavowal* of singularity. In other words, I want to look into the considerations that make it seem plausible that a singular thought can be singular without it determining which particular object it is about.

The story I want to tell is one part of a longer story about the difficulties of coming to terms with an idea that, most prominently, Wittgenstein developed in his later work. The idea may, in very general terms, be put as follows: the world doesn't only determine the truth or falsity of a thought, it also contributes to determining what *counts as* a thought's being true or false. In the *Philosophical Investigations*, the point is first presented as a critique of a certain idea of representational identity. (One which Wittgenstein reflects back on in §92 when he writes: "*The essence is hidden from us:* this is the form our problem now assumes. We ask: '*What is* language?', '*What is* a proposition?' And the answer to these questions is to be given once and for all, and independently of any future experience.") It is a mistake, Wittgenstein suggests in his *posthumous* book, to think that the truth and falsity of our representations could be explained by appealing to a representational identity which decides on its own just *when* the world agrees with those representations and when it does not. The truth and falsity of a representation can of course only depend on how the world is – and not in any way on how we take up the relevant representation. But it is a mistake, on this Wittgensteinian conception of representation, to think that this entails that a representation has a structural identity, which determines under which circumstances the representation would be true. Rather, the objectivity of truth is perfectly compatible with the possibility that what instances a representation on a certain occasion doesn't instance it (that *same* representation) on others. The notions of a language game and a form of life are meant, I take it, to help cash out this fundamental way in which thought is beholden to the world.[1] The disavowal of singularity that we will be dealing with in this essay is one way in which one may disavow or misconceive this beholdenness.

2 Referring to the "Object Itself"

Even by Kripke's own lights, the most explicit characterisation that he provides of rigidity in *Naming and Necessity* cannot be entirely satisfactory. His characterisation of rigid terms as terms that refer to the same object in every possible world in which the relevant object exists (Kripke 1980: 48) raises at least two important difficulties. Firstly, and perhaps most crucially, that characterisation fails to capture the kind of necessity that paradigmatic cases of rigidity, namely proper names, exhibit. Kripke's definition suggests that rigidity should be understood in terms of truth-conditions: to say that a designator is rigid is to say that there is an individual such that, with respect to every counterfactual situation, the truth-conditions of any sentence containing the designator involve the individual in question.[2] But it is clear that such a definition of rigidity would not capture what is distinctive, according to Kripke, of the kind of necessity characteristic of the reference of proper names. Proper names don't simply *turn out* to desig-

---

[1] The point that we are interested in is addressed most explicitly in two paragraphs of the *Investigations*, §§241–242. When a thought is true or false, we are told, depends on a certain, particular kind of agreement: an agreement in the form of life. The dependency on such an agreement – in the way that we proceed and in what we do – *seems* to abolish logic, that is, it seems to call into question what we have called the objectivity of truth, namely the idea that the truth of a representation can only depend on how the world is. But, in fact, it does not. The kind of beholdenness to the world that such a dependency involves doesn't require giving up the objectivity of truth. Rather, failing to acknowledge that beholdenness leads us into all kinds of dilemmas. One dilemma which Wittgenstein is particularly interested in concerns singular thought and is discussed in §§36–64.

This point about the concept of a form of life has, most notably, been developed by Charles Travis in Travis (2001) and Travis (2006). See also his contribution to the present volume.

[2] Peacocke 1975: 110–111 proposes to understand rigidity in this way.

nate the same individual under every possible circumstance. In designating the same individual in every possible circumstance, they draw on a particular mechanism which is quite different from the one deployed by the definite descriptions which also designate the same individual under every possible circumstance.

Kripke makes the point quite explicitly when explaining what he understands by "fixing the reference of a term".

> [E]ven in cases where the notion of rigidity versus accidentality of designation cannot be used to make out the difference in question, some things called definitions really intend to fix a reference rather than to give the meaning of a phrase, to give a synonym. Let me give an example. π is supposed to be the ratio of the circumference of a circle to its diameter. Now, it's something that I have nothing but a vague intuitive feeling to argue for: It seems to me that here this Greek letter is not being used as short for the phrase 'the ratio of the circumference of a circle to its diameter' nor is it even used as short for a cluster of alternative definitions of π, whatever that might mean. It is used as a name for a real number, which in this case is necessarily the ratio of the circumference of a circle to its diameter. Note that here both 'π' and 'the ratio of the circumference of a circle to its diameter' are rigid designators, so the arguments given in the metric case are inapplicable. (Kripke 1980: 60)

If one sticks to the characterisation of rigidity presented above, one has to treat both of the terms as rigid. Which is what Kripke does. But it is clear that he cannot leave it at that. If rigidity is meant to capture the kind of necessity that is paradigmatically, exhibited by proper names, one can hardly extend the notion of rigidity to a case such as 'the ratio of the circumference of a circle to its diameter'. For while such phrases (may) refer to the same number in any possible world, they do so in a way that is quite different from the way that is characteristic of proper names.

Indeed, while a definite description may refer to the same object under every possible circumstance because the object instantiates that description under every possible circumstance, a proper name's rigidity does not depend on any sort of discursive instantiation. This is what one may want to point to by saying that in the case of certain definite descriptions it can "turn out" that the description is rigid (cf. McGinn 1981 and Recanati 1993: 11–12). In the context of explaining the kind of reference distinctive of proper names, the notion of rigidity was meant to capture a certain *mode* of reference. This is lost in a definition in terms of sameness of reference in all possible worlds. Such a definition follows quite naturally from a possible world semantics in which a rigidly designating expression is modelled as a certain kind of intension, namely a constant (partial) function from possible worlds to extensions. But it fails to do justice to the kind of use, which Kripke makes of the notion of rigidity in the context of explaining the reference of proper names.

In the preface to *Naming and Necessity*, Kripke himself acknowledges that one may want to draw a distinction between two quite different kinds of rigidity, namely one for which it can "turn out" that a term is rigid and one for which it cannot (Kripke 1980: 21). He calls the former rigidity *de facto* and the latter rigidity *de jure*, and acknowledges that proper names are rigid *de jure*. Yet, while it isn't difficult to provide various negative characterisations of rigidity *de jure*, it is notoriously difficult to provide a precise positive definition of such sort of rigidity. That it doesn't rely on any kind of conceptual or descriptive mediation still leaves open just what such rigidity consists in. The idea is often put by saying that rigidity *de jure* involves reference to the "object itself", not simply to the object under a certain description or specification. But, of course, that can only be a presentation of the *explanandum*, not the *explanans*.

The difficulty here is closely tied to another notorious difficulty, namely the distinction between weak and strong rigidity. When defining rigidity at the point mentioned above (Kripke 1980: 77–78), Kripke allows for a distinction between cases in which the object may not exist under certain circumstances ("weak rigidity") and cases where the object exists under every possible circumstance ("strong rigidity"). The distinction is meant to make room for the inevitable possibility that a rigidly designated object should not exist under certain circumstances. But in acknowledging that possibility, Kripke seems to take a step further, since he claims that a rigid designator wouldn't designate anything in such circumstances. That is, in drawing a distinction between weak and strong rigidity, he assumes that rigid designators only designate their object under circumstances in which that object exists. Which, it seems, goes counter to the central insight that the notion of rigidity is meant to capture. A rigid designator refers to its actual referent *independently* of the circumstances – and it isn't clear why nonexistence of the object should be an exception.

Indeed, Kripke himself at various points acknowledges the issue quite explicitly. For he acknowledges, for instance, that "X does not exist" can be true not simply because under certain circumstances X does not exist (in *that* case, X would lack a reference and the statement would not have a truth-value), but because *what it designated* didn't exist (Kripke 1980: 78). In such passages, the notion of rigidity doesn't simply capture the mere fact that a term designates the same object in every circumstance. Rigidity is taken here to capture a particular *way* in which a term designates the same object in every circumstance. Most crucially, that way involves making the reference *wholly* impermeable to how the world may turn out to be. However the world may turn out to be, whatever circumstances of evaluation one may end up finding, the rigidly designating term designates the object that it designates in the actual circumstances. This conception may be contrasted with a conception of rigidity according to which rigidity simply registers the *fact* that a term refers to the same object in different circumstances. This latter conception does leave room for the possibility that the term should not refer where the object is not available to be referred to because it doesn't exist. If all that matters is the fact that a term refers to the same object in every circumstance, the possibility that there should be no reference at all in certain circumstances isn't inimical to that term being qualified as rigid.

This second set of difficulties is the point of departure of the most influential attempt, in Kaplan's "Demonstratives", to systematize Kripke's insights on reference and provide a precise characterisation of rigidity. Most notably, that attempt involves dissociating the notion of rigidity from the Millian tradition in which Kripke had placed it. Kaplan seeks to show that the kind of reference mechanisms studied by Kripke need not be opposed to those that involve meaning, and that the distinction between rigid terms and definite descriptions need not coincide with the Millian distinction between connotation and denotation. That a term should be rigid – in the interesting sense in which proper names are meant to be rigid (i.e. rigid *de jure*) – doesn't imply that it is devoid of all meaning. That it is an essentially "denotative" term doesn't necessarily mean that it doesn't also "connote". The referential terms of interest can indeed also have a "connotative" dimension and that dimension can even play a role in determining their object of reference.

To see that that is so, Kaplan claims, one must carefully distinguish two sets of considerations that Kripke runs together at times. On the one hand, there are the different uses to which an expression can be put in different contexts. On the other, there is the relation an expression entertains to a reference once its use has been fixed. Indeed, even proper names can be employed differently in different contexts. "Aristotle" can be, and has been, used to designate other individuals than the founder of the peripatetic school. That kind of variability in the use of terms must be distinguished from the relation that a term has to its referent *once* a certain use has been fixed. The interesting feature about rigidity concerns this level of analysis. Rigidly designating terms in the interesting sense (*de jure* rigid terms) refer to the same individual in a particular way once their use has been fixed. Thus, on such a view, indexicals and not proper names are the paradigm of rigidity. For that former class of referring expressions allegedly exhibit most clearly the two different registers just touched upon. On the one hand, they are eminently context-dependent, since their object of reference is fixed by the contextual circumstances of their use. But, on the other hand, they refer to their object of reference in the particular way that is characteristic of rigidity *de jure*.

There is little doubt that Kaplan's argumentation is, in crucial respects, faithful to Kripke's guiding insights about rigidity. The kind of phenomenon that the notion of rigidity was meant to capture cannot simply amount to the fact that certain terms refer to the same object in every possible circumstance, and Kaplan has good reasons to insist on the need to find a more precise characterisation of the particular way in which a rigid designator – in the interesting sense that underlies Kripke's project – refers to its object. It is clearly a mistake to stick too closely to possible world semantics when it comes to conceptualizing the kind of reference mechanisms that interested Kripke. In such semantics, rigid terms are usually distinguished from definite descriptions by the fact that their propositional content is a constant function of circumstance. But the referent of *de jure* rigid terms is wholly independent of the circumstance – and thus not really a function of circumstance at all.

Whether this however involves a return to a Russellian conception of propositions, which explains such reference in terms of the "object itself" being a component of the proposition, is of course an entirely different matter. It is important, in this respect, to start off by recognizing that the main concern driving Kaplan's analysis is different from that driving Kripke's analysis. In his attempt to refute what he takes to be a Fregean conception of reference, Kripke is, of course, concerned to show that we can refer to objects in a more direct way than Frege (allegedly) allows for. But it isn't clear that, in appealing to Mill, Kripke is simply running together two different matters, as Kaplan claims. It isn't clear that Kripke is not distinguishing sufficiently between issues of directness and immediacy, on the one hand, and issues of meaning and "connotation", on the other – and that he is tacitly assuming that directness or immediacy inevitably excludes any kind of meaning or connotation. For Kripke's main concern about the Fregean picture is not that it considers all reference to be mediated or indirect. It is rather that such a picture runs together epistemological and metaphysical considerations.

The fundamental flaw of the Fregean picture, in Kripke's view, is that it fails to recognize the autonomy of certain metaphysical phenomena – amongst which is, of course, the kind of link that is established by a large number of referential terms. Most crucially for Kripke, the reference of proper names is guaranteed by a mechanism that is wholly independent of any knowledge that we may possess about the object of reference. The knowledge may play a role in "fixing the reference" and setting up the link between a term and its referent, but it plays no role whatsoever in determining *which* object is the object of reference of a term. The important point being that that claim cannot be equated with the claim that reference in such cases is particularly direct or unmediated.

This becomes manifest if one reflects, for instance, on the kind of cases that Kripke is most interested in. He is not just interested in cases in which referential terms refer to an object independently of what we know of an object; he is also interested in, perhaps *primarily* interested in, cases where a term refers to an object *despite* the properties that we attribute to the object. One may of course seek to assimilate this latter set of cases to the former set by claiming that the relevant feature for the latter set is still the fact that reference is established independently of any discursive capacity. But it is far from clear that this is how Kripke conceives things. He has a particular interest in the second kind of scenario because it is meant to illustrate that our ability to refer to an object is, more generally, independent of any capacity to discriminate or identify it. Kripke is not just concerned about us being able to refer to an object independently of any descriptive or predicative specification. He is also – and perhaps primarily – interested in another sort of independence, namely an independence from any sort of identification or discrimination. In seeking to distinguish between the epistemological and the metaphysical, he takes a step further – or, at least, a step in a different direction – than Kaplan does. He is interested in the possibility that there should be a referential link to an object that one isn't able to discriminate or identify at all.[3] The issue is not simply the irrelevance of discursive or conceptual capacities – the existence of a referential link that doesn't depend on discursive specification –, but, more generally, the irrelevance of any kind of capacity to identify the object. In the cases in which a term is considered to refer to an object *despite* the beliefs we hold about that object or the properties we attribute to it, the important point – I am suggesting – is not simply that there is a referential link that bypasses any kind of discursive specification. Rather, the important point is that reference is established independently of any kind of discriminatory capacity.

3 Thought and Identification

To see the contrast, let us consider what is perhaps the most detailed attempt to systematically flesh out Kaplan's proposals, namely the account that Recanati has developed, particularly in Recanati (1993). Recanati follows Kaplan in holding that, for the strict variety of rigidity – we will adopt his term from now on:

---

[3] One may of course dispute that this is an objective of Kripke's, as, most notably, Evans (1982: 74–79) does. Evans considers that Kripke himself doesn't seek to challenge the idea that in order to have a thought or a belief about a particular object you must know which object it is about which you are thinking. Such a challenge was only projected into Kripke's work retrospectively by philosophers working – not on language, but – on mental representation. I'll expand below on the reasons why one may think that Kripke's argumentation does already involve such a challenge.

"direct referentiality", or simply "referentiality" –, the "object itself" is part of the proposition. That idea is then cashed out in terms of the capacity to identify the object: in the case of directly referential terms, an understanding of utterances containing such terms involves identifying the particular object being referred to. Recanati avoids claiming that *any* understanding of an utterance with a directly referential term involves identifying the reference of the term (Recanati 1993: 15). But this is just to make room for the kind of understanding involved in grasping utterances containing referential terms without a referent. For instance: I gullibly nod as I'm told that "Ralph Banilla" has entered the room. The discovery that there is no such person presupposes that the relevant statement was not only intelligible, but was actually understood. There is thus understanding of the utterance – and, *ipso facto*, of the proper name – without identification of the (alleged) referent.

This Recanati acknowledges. And we will come back to the way in which he seeks to account for this kind of understanding. The important point for now is that the general strategy of his explanation consists, nonetheless, in accounting for direct referentiality in terms of the capacity to identify the relevant object. To flesh out what that capacity involves, Recanati introduces a certain idea of a proposition:

> The distinction between the proposition expressed and the truth-condition provides the basis for the distinction between rigidity [de facto] and direct referentiality (or rigidity de jure). When the subject-term "α" in the sentence "α is G" is rigid, the truth-condition of the utterance is singular – it includes the reference of "α" as a constituent: there is an object x such that the utterance is true iff x is G. When "α" is a directly referential term, the utterance presents its truth-condition as singular: an utterance "α is G" in which "α" is a directly referential term means that there is an object x, possessing a certain property F (= mode of presentation), such that the utterance is true iff x is G. If such an object is actually identifiable in context, the utterance expresses the proposition that it is G. This is a "singular" proposition, consisting of the reference of "α" and the property expressed by the predicate "G". (Recanati 1993: 27)

On Recanati's account, an utterance containing a directly referential term "presents itself" as having singular truth-conditions. The truth-conditions do not simply turn out to be singular and don't simply turn out to involve a particular object; instead, that singularity is already exhibited by the utterance because it shows that the proposition that it gives expression to "contains" a certain object.

So the idea of a proposition that Recanati draws on involves the notion of a mode of presentation: the proposition is said to be the truth-condition of an utterance "under a certain mode of presentation". Yet, while the notion of mode of presentation is part of the definition of a proposition, the mode of presentation itself is not taken to necessarily be a constituent of the proposition. Indeed, according to Recanati, this is the difference between neo-Russellian and neo-Fregean accounts of direct referentiality:

> Both the neo-Russellian theory and the neo-Fregean theory capture the difference between referential and non-referential terms by introducing the reference into the proposition when a term is referential; and they both take for granted that a referential term may have a meaning and present its reference in a certain way. The difference between the neo-Russellian theory and the neo-Fregean theory is simply the fact that the former takes the content of a referential term to be nothing other than its reference while the latter takes it to be constituted by the reference under a certain mode of presentation. (Recanati 1993: 32)

Of course, Recanati makes here a host of controversial claims, some of which we will return to further below. Most crucially, he claims that a Fregean account of direct reference involves introducing the "object itself" into the proposition.[4] One may ask what remains Fregean about an account that violates the Fregean distinction between sense and reference. For Frege, that distinction is a categorial one: members of one category cannot engage in the kind of business that members in the other category engage in. Yet, by having objects figure directly in propositions, which are presumably the paradigmatic instances of sense, one allows members of the *Bedeutung* category to play a role that is reserved for members of the *Sinn* category. But this too is an issue that Recanati is not unaware of (cf. Recanati 1993: 193–197) and we will come back to it.

For current purposes, the important point is a different one. Recanati is sensitive to the fact that the interesting features of rigidity only come into view at the level of understanding and thinking. He acknowledges that if one wants to capture the difference between rigidity *de facto* and rigidity *de jure*, one has to raise questions about thought and understanding; one must, that is, look into what is involved in understanding utterances containing that designator.

The way that Recanati appeals to ideas of understanding and identification is quite misleading, though. By defining directly referential terms in terms of a capacity to identify the relevant object, Recanati frames the issue in a way that neglects – or at least risks neglecting – one of the main challenges that the notion of rigidity presumably poses for traditional ways of thinking about reference and representation. The notion of rigidity has contributed decisively to propagating the idea that it is possible to think about an object *without* being capable to identify or discriminate it. Whether Kripke already actively entertains this kind of possibility may be up for grabs. But it is certainly central to the use that has been made of his ideas. The existence of directly referential terms has

---

[4] He deals with this in more detail in Recanati 1993: 97–115.

seemed to make room for the idea that simply *being* in a certain contextual, i.e. causal relation to an object is sufficient for a subject to entertain thoughts about that object. And Recanati's treatment of these issues is a case in point: his very way of framing the issue – his presentation of the *desiderata* of an explanation of direct referentiality – makes it seem as though rigidity just *were* the idea that we can entertain thoughts about objects solely in virtue of certain contextual relations.

An adequate definition of direct reference, he claims (Recanati 1993: 38–41), must do justice to two fundamental intuitions. The first one is that understanding an utterance containing a directly referential expression requires that one be able to identify the relevant object. The second intuition concerns the role of "modes of presentation" for directly referential terms: it is not part of the truth-conditions of an utterance containing a directly referential term that the relevant object – the reference of the directly referential term – should satisfy the mode of presentation that the term draws on. Recanati does not say anything about the relation between those two intuitions, but they are presumably meant to capture the central aspects or sides of the essential feature of direct reference – the aspect that, following Kaplan, we have intuitively captured in negative terms by saying that directly referential terms don't simply "turn out" to refer to the same object in different circumstances. There is a particular kind of warranty or guarantee associated with direct reference: a directly referential term does not solely refer to the same object in different circumstances because that object always satisfies a certain specification. The term has a more intimate link with the object: it has somehow latched on to the object and refers to it *independently* of what properties the object may have in different circumstances.

Notice, though, how Recanati glosses the first intuition:

> To identify the reference, in the relevant sense, one must go beyond the descriptive content of the referring expression and equate the reference with a certain object about which one has independent information. [...] Thus you do not understand what is said by my uttering "He is a spy" if you do not go beyond the (meagre) indication provided by the word "he" and identify a certain person, e.g. someone you are currently perceiving, as the person to whom I am referring; likewise, you do not understand what is said by an utterance of "I am French" if you know only that "I" refers to the speaker, without knowing who the speaker is. Directly referential terms such as "he" or "I" prompt the hearer to go beyond the meaning of the sentence and find an object in the world matching the descriptive content of the referring expression. [...] By contrast, the reference of an attributively used definite description need not be identified for the utterance to be understood. (Recanati 1993: 38)

The idea of identifying an object is here introduced as a gloss on the idea of having information about an object that is independent of the descriptive conditions by which one may in fact have referred to it. The notion of identification is thus meant to capture what Recanati in later works has called, perhaps more adequately, an acquaintance condition. The intimate link to an object that direct reference involves is understood in terms of an informational link that is independent of any specification by which one may identify the object.

Whether or not the idea of an informational link to an object or an acquaintance with an object can help capture the crucial feature of directly referential terms is a matter that we will come back to. The important point for now is this. By presenting that link in terms of a capacity for identification, one risks taking for granted the idea that thought can be about a certain object simply in virtue of the thinker standing in a certain contextual relation to the object. Being capable of identifying or discriminating an object is closely tied to being able to entertain a thought about that object – so that if one explains the former capacity solely in terms of an informational link with an object, one implicitly takes a stance on the question of whether one can entertain thoughts about objects that one is unable to discriminate. For that question concerns precisely the relation between discriminatory capacities and informational links. Its significance depends on the possibility that identification should be something distinct from acquaintance or an informational link. If from the outset "identification" is taken to mean something like "informational link", there is no room for the question to arise.

This point is closely tied to another one. Note that the examples that Recanati presents contain indexicals – and not, like in another passage that we mentioned, proper names ("Ralph Banilla"). But, presumably, the point about our being able to understand utterances with directly referential terms even when there is no appropriate referent also extends to indexicals. The scenario is perhaps a more remote one, but not one to be theoretically excluded. One can for instance imagine a situation that could have taken place in Hitchcock's *North by Northwest*. "He is the spy", mutters one of the KGB officers to his comrade as they hear what they take to be footsteps in the neighbouring hotel room. Once they storm into the room, they discover with dismay that no one is there (the shutters were rhythmically clicking against the window). There is no such spy, it was a stratagem devised by the CIA to lure them out of their hiding. That doesn't make the aforementioned utterance unintelligible. As in the case of "Ralph Banilla", here too the discovery that there is no referent presupposes that the utterance could be understood. Of course, in the film, the KGB officers never find out that the spy they call "Kaplan" doesn't exist. Indeed, from a certain point onwards, the life of the advertisement agent (Roger Thornhill) that they "mistake" for that spy depends on their *not* finding out that there is no such person. (The quotation marks are meant to flag that it isn't clear that one may speak of an error of identification. Indeed, *whom* has Thornhill been mistaken for? Kaplan just comes to life when they find Thornhill.) But that is another matter. The basic point that interests us: in the case of indexicals too, one can presumably understand utterances containing referential terms that don't have a referent.

The question is why one might be reluctant to extend the point to such cases. Presumably, when it turns out that the designating expression doesn't have a referent, it turns out that the utterance of which it was a part didn't express a thought or a proposition. That is, the utterance didn't present things as being a certain way such that it was possible for things to be, or not to be, that way. Since there was no relevant object that could have been one way or another, there was no truth-evaluable stance that one could entertain about that object. So while there was something to be understood, there was nothing to be thought – in the sense of "thought" that we've just mentioned. One understands only too well what the comrade meant when he uttered "He is the spy"; it just turns out that he wasn't thereby expressing a thought, namely the kind of stance that is susceptible to being true or false – true or false depending on whether things are, or are not, as that thought presents them as being.

Now, one may consider that while there wasn't a thought to be entertained about a particular spy, the fact that there was something to be grasped shows that there was a certain thought to be entertained – namely one which presents the supposed individual as being a spy in the same way that that would have been the case about Kaplan if he had existed. If Kaplan doesn't exist, then the agent's utterance fails to express a thought about *Kaplan*. There is nothing to be the relevant way, namely a spy, if there is no Kaplan – and, thus, no thought presenting things as being that way, namely as Kaplan being a spy. The utterance fails to express such a thought in bearing the understanding it does. But that understanding, one may claim, purports to present someone as being a certain way. And while there is no such someone, the way in which the utterance presents that someone is exactly the way that *Kaplan* would have been presented if he had existed. The way in which the utterance presented the person is indistinguishable from the way that Kaplan would have been presented in a thought about Kaplan. So while he wasn't giving expression to a thought about *Kaplan*, he was giving expression to a thought – and one which is of the same "type" as the thought that could, had Kaplan existed, have been thought about Kaplan. This might be one path leading from the idea that the agent's utterance is intelligible to the idea that a thought has been expressed.

Of course, Recanati doesn't claim in the passage that a thought has been expressed when an indexical lacks a referent. But he seems to leave no room for the possibility of understanding in cases in which there is no referent. And that involves establishing a close relation between meaning and language on the one hand, and thought and representation on the other. That relation then makes room for a notion of thought which is, so to speak, a few elements short of some way to represent things as being.

4 Object-dependence

Let's begin with the first issue that we flagged, namely the *rapprochement* of identification and acquaintance. Despite using the term "identification" to refer to an informational link or a relation of acquaintance, Recanati ends up dealing, in a different context, with the crucial issue of what role discriminatory capacities play in the thinking of thoughts. The issue comes to a head when he examines the way in which thoughts expressed by utterances containing directly referential terms are dependent on the objects to which those terms refer.

On one conception of an object-dependent sense, it is possible to distinguish between types and tokens of such senses. The fundamental idea is the idea we just sketched. A certain way of thinking of an object may occur in two different contexts – one in which one thinks of one object, another in which one thinks of another or of no object – because it is possible that those objects should be indistinguishable in the way that they were thus thought about. Two apples may be different in several respects, but in the respect in which they were thought about on two occasions, they may be indistinguishable. For instance, if the way of thinking is grounded in the perceptual appearance of the apples, and the appearance is indistinguishable, one has two indistinguishable ways of thinking about what are in fact two different apples. This is what, according to such a line of thought, makes it possible to individuate object-dependent senses without reference to a particular object. The point is often put by saying that the sense can, qua type, be individuated narrowly. Only a particular *token* of that sense-type, in the context of a particular token-thought, is object-dependent in the sense that its individuation requires referencing a particular object.

It is of course surprising to talk about *object-dependent* senses even though such senses aren't, *qua* types, dependent on any particular object. On another conception of object-dependent sense, it is definitional of object-dependent senses that no two different objects can be thought about by means of the same sense. It can only *seem* that one is entertaining the same sense with respect to two, qualitatively indistinguishable objects. But it cannot be the same sense precisely because that sense is individuated with respect to an object. Of course, as long as this notion of object-dependent sense is presented in these terms, it only gets us so far. If it is merely definitional of object-dependent sense that such a sense cannot be entertained to think about two different objects, no substantial claim is being made. A substantial claim only arises to the extent that a partisan of such a conception denies that the conception of sense mentioned above is coherent because what is allegedly in common to the different scenarios isn't a *sense*. Indeed, if no such claim is made, a partisan of the "weak" conception of object-dependent sense can easily take on board the strong idea of object-dependence just outlined.

This is precisely what Recanati seeks to do. Having presented the idea of a strong kind of object-dependence, he goes on to argue that one may still identify a kind of sense which is individuated more narrowly and which can be common to thoughts about different objects. Of course, the issue is not simply whether *something* is common to thoughts about qualitatively very similar or perhaps even identical objects. *Ex hypothesi* there is. The question is whether that common element can qualify as sense and whether one can thus individuate *senses* more narrowly than those that defend a strong kind of object-dependence claim.

Recanati acknowledges the point and goes on to argue:

> The philosophers who say that a de re thought determines a reference only with respect to a context use "thought" or "conceptual content" in the sense of "mental sentence". What [they] point out is that such "thoughts" in the sense of mental sentences (= thoughts$_1$) are not thoughts by Fregean standards (thoughts$_2$): they are putative vehicles of thought, and the fact that they need a context in order to determine a reference (i.e. in order to express a genuine thought$_2$ which will in turn determine a reference) raises no problem for the Fregean picture [...]. This point is well taken, but, again, it is a verbal point concerning the meaning of "thought" or "sense" in Frege's theory. Once this exegetical problem is set aside, nothing prevents one from saying that a de re thought$_1$ determines a reference only with respect to a context, contrary to a descriptive thought$_1$. [...] For an object-dependent thought$_2$ is a thought$_2$ which requires a context for its expression: an object-dependent thought$_2$ can be expressed by a thought$_1$ only with respect to a particular context (a context which includes the reference), contrary to an object-independent thought. (Recanati 1993: 102–103)

For Recanati, the partisans of a strong variety of object-dependence draw a legitimate distinction. They point out that *Fregean* thoughts, as truth-evaluable stances, can only come into play when one takes into consideration contextual relations. But this does not, Recanati claims, invalidate the possibility of a more narrow individuation of another kind of stance which can also plausibly be called a thought.

Now Recanati recognizes that the opposition to such a more narrowly individuated stance is closely associated to dissatisfaction with the idea that contextual relations could determine what a thought is about. Yet, for Recanati, the dissatisfaction is the following: actual, contextual relations with an object are not *sufficient* for determining reference (Recanati 1993: 116). According to him, the authors who reject the "weak" object-dependence do not deny that thoughts about particular objects – singular thoughts – involve actual empirical relations to the relevant object. What they insist on is that in order for a thought to be about a suitably related object the thinker must *also* be in a position to *discriminate* the object in a certain way. But it is not at all clear that that is how the dissatisfaction must be understood. For the authors in question, the issue is not just that empirical relations do not suffice to explain how a thought should be about a certain object. Rather, the issue is that such relations cannot play *any* kind of role in giving such an account. Such relations are, for them, not in a kind of business that can play a role in explaining why a certain thought is about a certain object.

In other words, it is not at all clear that those authors accept what Recanati takes to be the fundamental distinction undergirding the idea of direct reference – the distinction between a satisfactional or descriptive mode of reference determination and a relational or contextual mode of reference determination. On the view that Recanati fleshes out, the object-dependence of thoughts expressed by utterances containing directly referential terms results from the fact that the reference of those terms is determined "relationally" and not "satisfactionally".[5] It is not because an object satisfies some specification or description that it is the reference of such a term. Instead, it is the reference of a directly referential term because some actual relation obtains between the speaker and that object. On such an understanding of the matter, directly referential terms are not simply distinct from definite descriptions; they are in an important sense opposed to such "descriptive" referential devices because they rely on a fundamentally different mechanism of reference determination.

Yet, it is not at all clear that the partisans of a stronger conception of object-dependence want to oppose the kind of mechanism at work in object-dependent

---

5 The terminology is from Bach (1987: 12): "If you could not have *de re* thoughts about things in the world, you could think of them only by description, each merely as something of a certain sort. If *all* your thoughts about things could only be descriptive, your total conception of the world would be merely qualitative. You would never be related in thought to anything in particular. Thinking of something would never be a case of having it 'in mind', as we say colloquially, or as some philosophers have said, of being '*en rapport*', in 'cognitive contact', or 'epistemically intimate' with it. But picturesque phrases aside, just what is this special relation? Whatever it is, it is different from that involved in thinking of something under a description. If we can even speak of a relation in the latter case, it is surely not a real (or natural) relation. Since the object of a descriptive thought is determined *satisfactionally*, the fact that the thought is of that object does not require any connection between thought and object. However, the object of a *de re* thought is determined *relationally*. For something to be the object of a *de re* thought, it must stand in a certain kind of relation to that very thought."

senses to specification or description. Indeed, in allowing for such an opposition, one makes the relation to the object external to the sense in a way that such authors seek to call into question by their idea of a strong object-dependence. If what makes something a sense of *that* particular object is the fact that there obtains a certain contextual or causal relation, there is no feature intrinsic to the sense which makes it dependent on that object. Presumably, when the authors in question insist on the idea that the relation to the object is *constitutive* of or *intrinsic* to the relevant sense, they don't just seek to make a point about one possible notion of a sense. The idea is that the individuation of an object-dependent *sense* cannot rest on a feature that is external to the sense in the way a causal or contextual relation would be. The difference cannot be due to a feature or an entity which, from an internal point of view, could be indistinguishable from another such feature or entity. The individuation cannot rely on something that would allow for the sense component of the relation to be the same in two different situations.

The point about the constitutive or intrinsic nature of the relation is thus another way of dealing with the issue we started off with – the question of how object-dependent senses may be individuated. Of course, if the intrinsic nature of the relation is taken as being merely definitional of a certain conception of sense, the point becomes a trivial one.[6] But the point is not a definitional one. It goes hand in hand with a *denial* that a more narrowly individuated sense is still recognizably a sense. The appeal to a strong sort of object-dependence is tied to the rejection of the possibility of a narrower individuation of sense or thought. The point is not easy to capture, but it can preliminarily be put in this way: a certain thought cannot be about different objects solely in virtue of factors that cannot be distinguished from a point of view that is internal to the thought.

Recanati doesn't acknowledge that talk about the constitutive nature of the relation is just another way of making this "disjunctivist" point, but he nonetheless deals with this latter point and recognizes that an opposition exists, on this matter, between the two conceptions of object-dependent senses. He is indeed

---

6 "Far from denying that *de re* thoughts, or the thinkers who grasp them, are empirically related to the objects of these thoughts, in contrast to what happens in the descriptive case, Evans and McDowell merely emphasize that these relations between thought (or thinker) and objet are *constitutive* or the *de re* thoughts themselves, in such a way that the relational determination of the reference which characterizes *de re* modes of presentation no longer undermines Frege's principle that *intentional content* determines reference (nor, thus understood, does it undermine Russell's principle, that in order to have a thought about an object you must have discriminating knowledge of that object)" (Recanati 1993: 116–117).

particularly explicit about the argument that makes plausible a narrower individuation of senses:

> According to this argument, mental contents (and representations in general, whether mental or not) are essentially fallible: there is no representation without a possibility of misrepresentation. This implies that a fundamental distinction has to be made between two independent aspects of representations: what is represented and what it is represented as. The latter is an intrinsic property of the representation, while the former aspect is a relational, extrinsic property of the representation. What is represented – apple A or apple B, say – depends upon the external environment (it depends on which apple is actually being perceived), but what it is represented as is a feature of the narrow content understood as "the action-guiding intra-individual role" of the representation. (Recanati 1993: 213–214)

So the possibility of being able to distinguish between an internal and an external component is meant to result from what Recanati – following McGinn (1982) – calls the fallibility of representations. The possibility of a certain kind of failure allegedly makes that kind of a distinction inevitable.

Of course, on one understanding of "representation", the possibility of misrepresentation is indeed constitutive of representation. It is the understanding that interests here: one on which the kind of correctness that representation can achieve is the kind of correctness characteristic of truth. If representations involve a claim to truth, it is essential that there should be the possibility that the representation is false, since the status of a claim is decided by something independent of that claim itself. In this kind of representing, when one represents things as being some way, one exposes oneself to a risk of error: things can, but can also not, turn out to be the way that one represents them as being. The most important contrast here being one with factive meaning. If not-P, then nothing factively means that P was the case. If there is no fire behind the hill, the smoke that we saw from the distance doesn't mean that there was a fire – irrespectively of what we may have expected and even if we had good reasons for thinking so. In contrast, when we represent things as being a certain way – for instance, as there being a fire behind the hill –, the achievement of *representing* is independent of whether things are actually or not so. If there is no fire, we represented things incorrectly, but this changes nothing about the fact that we *represented* them as so. (There is a parallel difference also in the kind of reasons that each of these phenomena can provide. That something factive means P may be a good reason for thinking that P. Whereas P being represented as so leaves it entirely open whether there are good reasons to think P as being the case.)

But it isn't clear, of course, that the possibility of representing incorrectly forces one to distinguish between an internal and an external component of representations. Recanati makes the transition very quickly by appealing to a distinction between "*what* is represented" and "what it is represented *as*". Presumably, that distinction isn't merely a distinction between the representation, on the one hand, and what decides about the truth of the representation, on the other. The following sentence of the passage makes it seem as though it were that distinction. But, clearly, if it were, it would not get us far in showing how the possibility of failure requires separating an external from an internal component. Indeed, it is important that "what is represented" be an aspect or element of the representation and not simply, as the phrase may suggest when taken out of context, that to which the representation is answerable. As external as the external component of the representation may be, it is still meant to be a component *of* the representation – and not that which determines the truth-value of the representation.

5 Content and Content-bearers

As Recanati acknowledges in a footnote to the passage, the distinction he has in mind is one that Goodman (1976) draws between pictures *of* black horses and black-horse pictures. For reasons that will become evident shortly, it is best to think about the distinction with respect to photographs. A photograph of a black horse may not exhibit a black horse *as* a black horse. The black speck on some hill in the photograph may in fact be a black horse without being identifiable as one – without it appearing as one – in the photograph. That is, "what is represented" by an element in the picture need not figure in the photograph in a way that makes it identifiable as the relevant object – the black horse need not be represented *as* a black horse.

Thus, "what is represented" doesn't refer to a worldly object; it refers to an element in the photograph, but in as far as that element has a certain relation to some worldly object. "What is represented" by an element in the photograph depends on what that element is "actually" about, what object actually corresponds to – or, to use Goodman's term: is denoted by – the element in question. Of course, what such a relation of "actually" being about an object amounts to is up for grabs. Presumably it is some form of causal relation. The black speck in the photograph represents a black horse despite being identifiable as one because there is some causal story to be told about how that black speck got onto the photographic film, a story that involves a certain black horse.

So the distinction turns on the idea that there can exist a representative relation in virtue of actual or causal links between an element in the representation and a worldly object. Just what such links amount to is a question that we will come back to in a moment. For now, the crucial point is simply this: those relations involve no specification or generality. They hold independently of any of the features of the representative element, e. g. any particular sensible features of the black speck. What makes that element a representation of a certain object is some actual, worldly relation to that object. One could say that the relation is one of bare symbolisation: the element in the representation or photograph is a placeholder for the worldly object; it is a placeholder in virtue of the worldly relation it has to that worldly object. Nothing about the sensible features of the representative element contribute to it playing that role. Its playing that place-holding role is entirely external to it having the features that it actually has.

One might of course object to this last claim. One could insist that that relation isn't entirely external, since there is also a story to be told about why the representative element has the features that it in fact has. In the case mentioned above, the representative element is a black speck because, at the distance from which the photograph was taken, the black horse in fact appears as a black speck. The black speck *in the photograph* is a placeholder for a black horse because from the position from which the photograph was taken the black horse appeared like that. From the point of view of the photographer, the black speck just *was* the horse – and the black speck in the photograph is a record or trace of the black speck that there was to be seen.

It is crucial to note, however, that in such an explanation there is a transition from one black speck to another, quite different black speck. The black speck that the photographer could see – perhaps even by looking through the camera – *was*, presumably, a certain black horse. *That* speck wasn't a placeholder for a horse, it was just the horse as seen at a certain distance. We can't however say of the black speck in the photograph that it is a certain black horse because, quite clearly, it isn't. It is, rather, a patch of ink. Indeed, if there is no way of telling what the speck is by looking at the photograph, only some knowledge of the circumstances in which the photograph was taken can allow us to identify the speck as a black horse. Of course, in that case, one may say something similar about the photographer. It was only by using binoculars or by moving closer to the object that he could know that it was a black horse. As seen from where he was, there was nothing more to be seen than when we now look at the photograph that he took. He also had to "step outside" a certain viewpoint to know that the black speck was a horse. But still: whether he knew it or not, the black speck that he saw *was* a horse. And the black horse that we now see in the photograph clearly isn't a horse in that sense. Once we find out about the circumstances in which the photograph was taken, we can *identify* a certain region of the photograph as a black horse. But that is quite a different matter.

Of course, if we are trained in identifying such horses in the distance, we may be able to identify it as a black horse without knowing anything else. Particular abilities can enable us to see something that others don't see. The forest ranger may look at the photograph and *see* a black horse, not just a speck that turns out to be a black horse. But notice that in this case the particular features of the speck have to do some representational work once again. The ranger sees a black horse because certain features of that speck make it identifiable, to her, *as* a black horse. If for her the black speck in the photograph *is* a black horse, it is that because the black speck isn't simply a placeholder – a *Vertreter* – of a black horse. The representative status of the speck isn't grounded in a relation that obtains independently of how that speck is. And, to that extent, the speck isn't a mere *Vertreter*, which stands for something independently of what features it has.

This doesn't mean that we shouldn't distinguish sharply between the elements that bear representational content and that content itself. There is, on the one hand, the ink on the paper with its particular shape, colour, position, etc., and, on the other, that which that ink allows us to achieve, namely the feat of representing a certain horse as being on a certain hill. (Note the emergence of the "as" here. If representing is an achievement, some such element is required. That is, if representing is an achievement, it involves representing something *as* something. And that already calls into question the distinction that we're considering. More on this in a moment.) This distinction will be particularly important if one holds, as for instance Frege does, that no transition can be made from one register to the other. That is, one may consider that the particular, sensible features of the ink – and, more specifically, of the black speck – cannot determine, however detailed our description of them may be, what they can contribute to representing. On such a view of representation, as close as one may look at the physical features of a painting, there is no way of establishing on that basis whether a certain particular situation counts as the one that that painting is meant to represent. There is thus an unbridgeable gulf between what allows us to make an instance of representing recognizable and the achievement of representing itself. Thus, on such a view, it is a mistake to think that any particular, sensible features of something could explain why something represents as it does. (I take this to be the central import of the critique of correspondence theories of truth that one finds in "The Thought". Cf. on that point, Travis 2011.)

These are not questions that we can deal in detail with here. The important point, for our purposes, is simply the following. That the particular features of a bearer of representational content – e. g. a black speck on a certain photograph – should play a role in our taking something to represent a certain state of affairs doesn't mean that that bearer is itself a representation. Yet, if the black speck is not just to be a *Vertreter*, it is quite relevant that it is, say, shaped in a certain way. The particular features of the speck enable us to recognize something as a certain representation – and, bereaved of those features, it could only entertain a very different sort of relation to whatever it represents. It could of course stand in for something, and be a representation in that sense. But that kind of *Vertretung* relation, that kind of place-holding, is a fundamentally different kind of relation than the one that is characteristic of representation.

Indeed, the fact that particular abilities can come into play when deciding whether the black speck is a horse or not is already a clear indication that the speck "itself" isn't in the business of representing but is rather something like an *opportunity* for representing. Yet, in providing that opportunity, its sensible features play a crucial role. It is by having the features that it has that it can provide someone possessing the appropriate capacities with the opportunity to see a black horse on a hill. Of course, when looking at the photograph, the person doesn't see the black horse that was photographed. Yet, the fact that a certain such configuration – something that, when considering the photograph like a material object and not a content-bearer, one may qualify as a black speck – should provide the opportunity for representing something as a black horse depends on the particular sensible features of that configuration.

Now back to the question that we raised at the beginning of the section, namely whether "what is represented" by an element in the picture – in Goodman's sense – is established by a relation that is external to any of the features of the given element. One reason why one may object to talking about the relation being external is that there is a story to be told – at least in the case of the photograph – about how the relevant element came about. And that story will have the aforementioned relation, whatever exactly it may be, as its protagonist. That the black speck in the photograph has particular sensible features can be accounted for by a certain story about a set of relations that (presumably) hold between a certain black horse and a certain configuration of ink on a particular piece of photographic paper.

Note, however, that the black speck figures in this story merely as a certain configuration of ink. So while the relation to the horse may explain its particular features, it explains the features of a certain configuration of ink. If a camera were so designed as to *distort* in some particular way what it serves to photograph, there would still be a story to be told about why a certain object actually represents a certain object – "actually represents" here being shorthand for the "what is represented" idea. So in that sense, the relation that establishes "what is represented" by an element in a representation is entirely external to that element. The particular features of the element play no role whatsoever in determining what that element is a representation of (again, "representation" has to be understood here in the sense that it is used in "what is represented"). That kind of relation can obtain between an element and an object irrespectively of the particular features of the element.

Thus, in allowing for such a relation, one conceives representations as hybrid entities, which are composed of two fundamentally different aspects. Dretske (1995: 26) puts this by saying that "facts about the object of representation are *hybrid* facts – part representational, part not". In stating that a certain representation represents a certain object k as having a certain property F, we state two entirely separable things. On the one hand, we state that the representation has the function of providing us with certain information about k, namely information as to whether k has F or what the value of F is. That is what Dretske calls a representational fact, namely a fact about what information a representation is designed to carry. A representational fact is a fact about a representation that concerns its achievement *as* a representation. It is what we glossed before as a take on the representation from an internal viewpoint. But not all facts about representations are representational facts. There is, indeed, an entirely different sort of fact about representations, namely the kind that concerns what particular object a representation is actually about. Indeed, on the view in question, just which object a representation is about is not something that one can determine by looking at the representational facts. So these facts, as to what object is being represented, are of a fundamentally different kind – they are not representational facts.

Thus, on this view, the content of a representation doesn't allow to determine *which* object is being represented. Dretske is particularly lucid about this:

> The speedometer in my car is connected to the axle of my car, not your car. It therefore represents (or misrepresents, as the case may be) the speed of my car, not our car. It is in virtue of this special relation, C, to my car that it can do what other speedometers cannot do – viz., say something (whether truly or falsely) about my car. Other speedometers cannot even say something false about my car. C is the relation such that, when a representational system S is functioning properly, and k stands in C to S, then S will indicate the F of k. If k stands in C to S, then S will indicate the F of k. [...] Changing the way a system is deployed, changing the object that stands in relation C to S, changes what S represents (what objects it represents), but not necessarily what S says (represents) about it. (Dretske 1995: 25)

This leads him to state categorically that a representation doesn't itself allow us to establish which object it represents.

> There is nothing in the content of the representation, nothing the representation says, which makes it about this object rather than that object or no object at all. [...] Since the veridicality of an experience depends on its reference – on what object (if any) it is an experience of – the veridicality of experience is determined, in part by context (C). C makes it

> the case that k is the object S represents as blue. C thereby helps to determine whether the representation (that k is blue) is veridical or not. Nonetheless, the fact that it is k (rather than some other object or no object at all) that stands in relation C to the representation is not what the representation represents. Representations do not (indeed, cannot) represent context. They represent k as being blue, but they do so without representing it to be k that they represent to be blue. (Dretske 1995: 24–25)

Representations can of course be about particular objects, such as, for instance, a particular car, which may be represented on a certain occasion as moving along well above a 90 km/h speed limit. But the relation to the particular object is entirely external to how the object is represented as being. Indeed, the way that it is represented as being doesn't allow to determine just which object is at stake. The speedometer of my car is currently attached to my axle – but it could of course, by unsuspected means, have been attached to quite a different axle so that it would serve to represent the speed of an entirely different car. By taking a step "outside" the representation, we can find out which object it represents as being a certain way. But from within, we have no way of telling which object it turns on.

But, of course, this distinction is a deeply problematic one. Indeed, it involves conceding that representations aren't capable of doing something which, in principle, is their characteristic business. Representations, in the sense that we have been interested in, delimit a certain way for things to be. All the particular situations or states of affairs that make a given representation true – that instance that representation – do so in virtue of the fact that they are an instance of that way for things to be. So all the different situations that make it true have just *that* in common – they are instances of that way for things to be. (One may even consider that representations should *only* be individuated with respect to how they represent things as being. No other features should be considered when determining just what is the same representation. So none of the sensible features with which we give expression to a representation. But we need not deal with that here.) Thus, a singular representation is delimited by the way it takes a particular object to be. The business of such a representation is to establish a connection between a certain question of truth and how a *certain particular* object is. (Is that particular object a certain way that (such) things can be?) The crucial point for our purposes being that the representation just *is* such a connection, *is* a way in which truth can depend on a certain particular object. If representations can't determine which particular object their truth depends on, nothing else can. If facts about representations are indeed hybrid, we can't make truth depend on singularity.

References

Bach, Kent (1987) *Thought and Reference*, Oxford: Clarendon Press.
Dretske, Fred (1995) *Naturalizing the Mind*, Cambridge: MIT Press.
Evans, Gareth (1982) *The Varieties of Reference*, Oxford: Oxford University Press.
Goodman, Nelson (1976) *Languages of Art: An Approach to a Theory of Symbols*, Indianapolis: Hackett.
Kaplan, David (1989) "Demonstratives", in: Joseph Almog, John Perry and Howard Wettstein (eds.): *Themes from Kaplan*, Oxford: Oxford University Press, 481–563.
Kripke, Saul (1980) *Naming and Necessity*, Cambridge: Harvard University Press.
McGinn, Colin (1981) "The Mechanism of Reference", in: *Synthese* 49, 157–186.
Peacocke, Christopher (1975) "Proper Names, Reference, and Rigid Designation", in: Simon Blackburn (ed.): *Meaning, Reference and Necessity*, Cambridge: Cambridge University Press, 109–132.
Recanati, François (1993) *Direct Reference: From Language to Thought*, Oxford: Blackwell.
Travis, Charles (2001) "What Laws of Logic Say", in: James Conant and Ursula Zeglen (eds.): *Hilary Putnam: Pragmatism and Realism*, London: Routledge.
Travis, Charles (2006) *Thought's Footing: A Theme in Wittgenstein's Philosophical Investigations*, Oxford: Oxford University Press.
Travis, Charles (2011) "Truth and Merit", in: Martin Gustafson and Richard Sørli (eds.): *New Essays on the Philosophy of J. L. Austin*, Oxford: Oxford University Press, 175–203.
Wittgenstein, Ludwig (1958) *Philosophical Investigations*, 2nd edition, transl. G. E. M. Anscombe, Oxford: Basil Blackwell. [PI]

Biographical Notes

Avner Baz is Associate Professor of Philosophy at Tufts University. He has written about ethics, aesthetics, perception, judgment, and about the question of philosophical method in the works of Kant, Wittgenstein, Cavell, and John McDowell. He is author of *When Words Are Called For – In Defense of Ordinary Language Philosophy* (Cambridge, MA: Harvard University Press 2012) and *The Crisis of Method in Contemporary Analytic Philosophy* (Oxford: Oxford University Press 2018).

Jocelyn Benoist is Professor of Theory of Knowledge and Contemporary Philosophy at the University of Paris I (Panthéon Sorbonne), Director of Archives Husserl (École Normale Supérieure/CNRS), École Normale Supérieure, France. Amongst his recent books are *Logique du phénomène* (Paris: Editions Hermann 2016) and *L'adresse du réel* (Paris: Vrin 2017).

Juliet Floyd is Professor of Philosophy, Boston University. She is the author of many articles on the history of eighteenth- and twentieth-century philosophy of mathematics, logic, and aesthetics, including many on Wittgenstein, and has co-edited (with Sanford Shieh) *Future Pasts: The Analytic Tradition in Twentieth-Century Philosophy* (Oxford: Oxford University Press 2001) and (with Alisa Bokulich) *Philosophical Explorations of the Legacy of Alan Turing: Turing 100* (Berlin/New York: Springer 2017). Her most recent book, co-authored with Felix Mühlhölzer, *Wittgenstein and the Real Numbers: Annotations to Hardy's A Course of Pure Mathematics* is forthcoming with Springer.

Martin Gustafsson is Professor of Philosophy at Åbo Akademi University since 2010. His central areas of specialization are the philosophy of language and the philosophy of action. His research interests also include the history of analytic philosophy, the philosophy of logic, philosophical methodology, and the philosophy of the human sciences. He has published articles on Anscombe, Austin, Berkeley, Cavell, Davidson, Hacking, Heidegger, McDowell, Quine, Rawls, Sellars, Travis and Wittgenstein. He edited the following books: *Finite but Unbounded: New Approaches in Philosophical Anthropology*, Berlin: De Gruyter 2017 (co-edited with Kevin Cahill and Thomas Schwarz Wentzer) and *The Philosophy of J. L. Austin*, Oxford: Oxford University Press 2011 (co-edited with Richard Sørli).

Matthias Haase is Assistant Professor of Philosophy at the University of Chicago. His research is focused on foundational topics at the intersection of ethics and philosophy of mind. A central historical interest is the tradition of German Idealism, especially the aspects that are tied to Aristotle. He has also written on Wittgenstein and Frege. He is the author of numerous articles, including *The Laws of Thought and the Power of Thinking* (in: Canadian Journal of Philosophy, Suppl. Vol. 35 (2011), 249–297) and *For Oneself and Toward Another: The Puzzle About Recognition* (in: Philosophical Topics 42 (2014), 113–152).

Andrea Kern is Professor of Philosophy at the University of Leipzig. Her interests include epistemology, the philosophy of perception, skepticism as well as anthropological philosophy. She is the author of several articles and editions as well as *Schöne Lust. Eine Theorie der ästhetischen Erfahrung nach Kant* (Frankfurt am Main: Suhrkamp 2000) and *Sources of*

Knowledge: On the Concept of a Rational Capacity for Knowledge (Cambridge, MA: Harvard University Press 2017).

Sandra Laugier is Professor of Philosophy at Université Paris 1 Panthéon-Sorbonne and Senior member of the Institut Universitaire de France. She is the translator of Stanley Cavell's work into French and specializes in Ordinary Language Philosophy (Wittgenstein, Austin, Cavell), American Philosophy, Gender studies, and Ethics of care. She is the author of many publications in French, English, Italian, German, amongst which are *Wittgenstein, les sens de l'usage* (Paris: Vrin 2009); *Wittgenstein, Le mythe de l'inexpressivité* (Paris: Vrin 2010); *Why We Need Ordinary Language Philosophy* (Chicago: University of Chicago Press 2013); *Recommencer la philosophie. Cavell et la philosophie américaine* (Paris: Vrin 2014); *Antidémocratie* (Paris: La Découverte 2017, with Albert Ogien).

Christian Martin is Assistant Professor of Philosophy at LMU Munich. He has written about the philosophy of logic, language and aesthetics. He is author of a monograph on Hegel's "Science of Logic", entitled *Ontologie der Selbstbestimmung* (Tübingen: Mohr Siebeck 2012), as well as various articles on Kant, Schelling, Hegel, Heidegger, Benjamin and Wittgenstein. He is currently finishing a book entitled *Die Einheit des Sinns. Untersuchungen zur Form des Denkens und Sprechens*.

Felix Mühlhölzer has been Professor of Philosophy at the University of Göttingen since 1997. He has published articles on topics in philosophy of science and philosophy of language, and since 2001 has written primarily on later Wittgenstein's philosophy of mathematics. His books include *Braucht die Mathematik eine Grundlegung? Ein Kommentar des Teils III von Wittgensteins Bemerkungen über die Grundlagen der Mathematik* (Frankfurt am Main: Klostermann 2010) and *Wissenschaft* (Stuttgart: Reclam 2011). His most recent book, co-authored with Juliet Floyd, *Wittgenstein and the Real Numbers: Annotations to Hardy's A Course of Pure Mathematics* is forthcoming with Springer.

Charles Travis is Professor of Philosophy Emeritus of King's College London, UK and Professor Afiliado of the Universidade do Porto, Portugal. He works on separating the logical from the psychological, the general from the particular and then, in each case, relating first to second, thus on the relations between perception, thought and language. He is writing a book on Frege.

David Zapero received his PhD from the Sorbonne. He is currently a post-doctoral researcher at the University of Bonn. His research interests are in the philosophy of mind, epistemology, action theory and ethics. His recent publications include *La doctrine kantienne du Faktum de la raison et la justification de la loi morale* (in: Archiv für Geschichte der Philosophie 98 (2016), 169–192); *Liberal Naturalism, Objectivity and the Autonomy of the Mental* (forthcoming in: Inquiry). He is co-editor of a forthcoming volume *Context, Truth and Objectivity: Essays on Radical Contextualism* (London: Routledge 2019).

Index

Anscombe, Elizabeth 12, 14, 21, 74, 182
Aristotle 15, 23, 56, 129f., 310
Armstrong, David 235
Austin, John Langshaw 5f., 64, 254–256, 258, 265–267, 278, 285–292, 300

Bach, Kent 320
Baker, Gordon 1, 232
Baz, Avner 6, 253, 257, 263, 265, 271–273
Benoist, Jocelyn 2, 4, 67, 73, 155
Brandom, Robert 150, 220, 242f.

Cavell, Stanley 6, 64f., 68f., 71, 77f., 83, 85, 256, 267, 272f., 277–281, 283–287, 289–292, 295–301
Conant, James 1, 151

Das, Veena 12, 17, 103, 277f., 298, 300f.
Davidson, Donald 220–222, 224–227, 235
Diamond, Cora 67, 80, 87, 118, 121, 220, 242, 293–295, 298f.
Dretske, Fred 327f.
Dummett, Michael 220f.

Elias, Norbert 75
Emerson, Ralph Waldo 259, 277, 279–285, 290, 297, 300
Evans, Gareth 228, 231, 312, 321

Fara, Michael 234
Floyd, Juliet 2f., 23, 59, 63, 65, 67, 69f., 72–75, 78, 80–85, 87
Foot, Philippa 182
Ford, Anton 144, 185
Foucault, Michel 282
Frege, Gottlob 3f., 11f., 14–21, 23–36, 38–41, 43, 48, 50, 53f., 56, 62, 69, 113, 125f., 145, 168, 227, 230, 258, 311, 314, 319, 321, 325

Garver, Newton 1
Geach, Peter 113, 118
Glock, Hans-Johann 1f.

Godfrey-Smith, Peter 182
Goethe, Johann Wolfgang 161, 179–181, 183f.
Goffman, Erving 287–289, 292
Goldfarb, Warren 175f., 191, 220
Goodman, Nelson 323, 326
Gustafsson, Martin 3, 5, 13, 173, 182

Haase, Matthias 3, 5, 219, 227
Hacker, Peter M. S. 1f., 8, 14, 140, 173f., 232
Haller, Rudolf 1
Hegel, Georg Wilhelm Friedrich 4, 93–95, 97–101, 103, 105, 109
Hertzberg, Lars 6
Hilbert, David 11f., 30, 85
Horwich, Paul 220
Hunter, John 1

Jackson, Frank 234
Jacobs, Jane 186–188

Kant, Immanuel 31, 63, 95, 97, 256–259, 263, 270, 282–284, 296
Kaplan, David 223, 310–312, 315–317
Kenny, Anthony 232
Kern, Andrea 2, 4, 93, 95
Kimhi, Irad 151, 226
Knott, Hugh 173
Koblitz, Neal 70
Köhler, Wolfgang 270
Kripke, Saul 80, 231, 307–312, 314
Kuusela, Oskari 63, 174–178, 191

Laugier, Sandra 3, 6, 64, 70, 78, 277, 285, 293f., 299
Laurence, Benjamin 185
Leibniz, Gottfried Wilhelm 48f., 265
Leslie, David 82
Lewis, David 220f., 235, 265f.

Maddy, Penelope 13, 17
Majetschak, Stefan 2

Malcolm, Norman   1, 85
Martin, Benjamin G. 75
Martin, Christian   1, 2, 4, 87, 144, 149
McDowell, John   94–97, 101, 139, 220, 225, 230, 232 f., 242, 321
McGinn, Colin   308, 322
Merleau-Ponty, Maurice   6, 253, 256, 258 f., 261 f., 264–266, 269 f., 273
Millikan, Ruth Garrett   222
Moltmann, Friederike   246
Monk, Ray   74
Moyal-Sharrock, Danièle   2
Mühlhölzer, Felix   1, 3, 5, 10, 16, 23 f., 74, 85, 87
Mulhall, Stephen   60
Murdoch, Iris   293

Ogien, Albert   294, 299

Pargetter, Robert   234
Peacocke, Christopher   241, 307
Pippin, Robert   94
Prior, Elisabeth   234
Putnam, Hilary   49, 72 f.

Quine, Willard Van Orman   84, 235

Raatzsch, Richard   179
Recanati, François   265, 308, 312–323
Rhees, Rush   72, 174–179
Rowe, M. W.   179
Ryle, Gilbert   234

Savigny, Eike von   1 f., 18 f., 24
Schlick, Moritz   12, 135

Schulte, Joachim   1 f., 14, 24, 140, 173, 179
Sellars, Wilfrid   223, 227–229, 243 f.
Simon, Josef   70
Sluga, Hans   64, 87
Spohn, Wolfgang   196
Stern, David   2, 64
Stroud, Barry   220

Taylor, Charles   295
Tejedor, Chon   2
Thomae, Johannes   23–30, 32 f., 35, 39
Thompson, Michael   99, 182, 224
Thoreau, Henry David   279, 281
Travis, Charles   2 f., 11, 134, 265, 269, 272, 307, 325
Turing, Alan M.   3, 59 f., 72 f., 79–85, 87

von Uexküll, Jakob   62

Waismann, Friedrich   12, 14, 23, 26 f., 29, 31 f., 35, 44, 173, 176, 180–183, 189
Wedelstaedt, Almut Kristine von   24, 73
Wiggins, David   222
Williamson, Timothy   223
Wittgenstein, Ludwig   1–27, 29, 31–33, 35–38, 41, 44 f., 48–51, 53, 55 f., 59–69, 71–80, 82–87, 93–95, 97, 103–109, 114, 118, 121 f., 124, 126–128, 135, 137 f., 140–150, 155–168, 170, 173–188, 190–192, 219–227, 229–233, 235 f., 242, 244, 247, 253–260, 262–269, 271–274, 277–279, 283–286, 292, 294–300, 305–307
Wright, Cripin   220, 241–243
Wright, Georg Henrik von   220, 241–243

www.ingramcontent.com/pod-product-compliance
Lightning Source LLC
Chambersburg PA
CBHW021801220426
43662CB00006B/148